KU-268-625

Frank Lloyd Wright

FROM WITHIN OUTWARD

Frank Lloyd Wright
FROM WITHIN OUTWARD

RICHARD CLEARY

NEIL LEVINE

MINA MAREFAT

BRUCE BROOKS PFEIFFER

JOSEPH M. SIRY

MARGO STIPE

 Guggenheim MUSEUM

Published on the occasion of the exhibition
Frank Lloyd Wright: From Within Outward
Solomon R. Guggenheim Museum, New York
May 15–August 23, 2009
Guggenheim Museum Bilbao
Fall 2009

An exhibition co-organized by the Solomon R. Guggenheim
Foundation and the Frank Lloyd Wright Foundation

The Leadership Committee for *Frank Lloyd Wright: From Within
Outward*, with a founding gift from the Thorton Tomasetti Foundation,
is gratefully acknowledged.

The exhibition *Frank Lloyd Wright: From Within Outward* and its
accompanying catalogue and public programming inaugurate a
year-long celebration in 2009–10 of the 50th Anniversary of the
Solomon R. Guggenheim Museum, New York. For more information,
please visit www.guggenheim.org/50.

THE FIFTIETH
ANNIVERSARY
OF THE
GUGGENHEIM
MUSEUM

LEEDS COLLEGE OF ART + DESIGN
06/09
LIBRARY
724·9
WRI

R 55473

First published in the United States of America in 2009 by
SKIRA RIZZOLI PUBLICATIONS, INC.
300 Park Avenue South, New York, NY 10010
www.rizzoliusa.com

Guggenheim Museum Publications
1071 Fifth Avenue
New York, NY 10128

ISBN: 978-0-8478-3262-0 (hardcover)
ISBN: 978-0-8478-3263-7 (softcover)
LCCN: 2009920656

© 2009 The Solomon R. Guggenheim Foundation, New York, and
the Frank Lloyd Wright Foundation, Scottsdale, Arizona.
All rights reserved.

© 2009 Skira Rizzoli Publications
Essays by Margo Stipe and Bruce Brooks Pfeiffer © 2009 The Frank
Lloyd Wright Foundation, Scottsdale, Arizona. "Wright and
Worshipping Communities" © 2009 Joseph M. Siry; "Frank Lloyd
Wright and the Romance of the Master Builder" © 2009 Richard
Cleary; "Making Community Out of the Grid" © 2009 Neil
Levine; "Wright in Baghdad" © 2009 Mina Marefat.

All Frank Lloyd Wright drawings © 2009 The Frank Lloyd Wright
Foundation, Scottsdale, Arizona.

All rights reserved. No part of this publication may be reproduced,
stored in a retrieval system, or transmitted in any form or by any
means, electronic, mechanical, photocopying, recording, or otherwise,
without prior consent of the publisher.

Design: Tsang Seymour
Editorial: Dung Ngo, Douglas Curran
Production: Maria Pia Gramaglia, Kaija Markoe
Printed by Amilcare Pizzi, Milan

Distributed to the U.S. trade by Random House, New York
2009 2010 2011 2012 2013 / 10 9 8 7 6 5 4 3 2 1

Front and back cover:
Two details of Fair Pavilion for the Marin County Civic Center (project)
San Rafael, California, 1957
© 2009 The Frank Lloyd Wright Foundation
For full caption information, see page 346.

Frontispiece:
Meeting House, First Unitarian Society of Madison,
Shorewood Hills, Wisconsin, 1946–52
Photo by David Heald
Courtesy Solomon R. Guggenheim Foundation

Hardcover edition endsheets:
Hillside Theater #2 curtains (detail),
Taliesin III, Spring Green, Wisconsin, 1952
Photo by Kathleen Chesley

Frank Lloyd Wright in Solomon R. Guggenheim Museum
under construction, New York, ca. 1957
Photo by Sam Falk

CONTENTS

FRANK LLOYD WRIGHT FOUNDATION

PRESIDENT AND C.E.O.
Phil Allsopp, RIBA

TRUSTEES
Daniel F. Marquardt, Chairman

Indira Berndtson
Shawn Rorke-Davis
David Elgin Dodge
Sandra Shane DuBow
Robert H. R. Dryburgh
Karen Ellzey
Don Fairweather
Ronne Hartfield
David Mohney
Gerald Lee Morosco
Frank N. Owings, Jr.
Tony Puttnam
Arnold Roy
Frederick P. Stratton, Jr.
Steven G. Zylstra

THE SOLOMON R. GUGGENHEIM FOUNDATION

HONORARY TRUSTEES IN PERPETUITY
Solomon R. Guggenheim†
Justin K. Thannhauser†
Peggy Guggenheim†

HONORARY CHAIRMAN
Peter Lawson-Johnston

CHAIRMAN
William L. Mack

PRESIDENT
Jennifer Blei Stockman

VICE-PRESIDENTS
Frederick B. Henry
Wendy L-J. McNeil
Edward H. Meyer
Stephen C. Swid
Mark R. Walter

DIRECTOR
Richard Armstrong

TREASURER
Edward H. Meyer

SECRETARY
Edward F. Rover

DIRECTOR EMERITUS
Thomas M. Messer

TRUSTEES
Jon Imanol Azua
Robert Baker
Janna Bullock
John Calicchio
Mary Sharp Cronson
Carl Gustaf Ehrnrooth
David Ganek
Frederick B. Henry
Peter Lawson-Johnston
Peter Lawson-Johnston II
Howard W. Lutnick
William L. Mack
Linda Macklowe
Wendy L-J. McNeil
Edward H. Meyer
Amy Phelan
Vladimir O. Potanin
Stephen M. Ross
Mortimer D. A. Sackler
Denise Saul
James B. Sherwood
Raja W. Sidawi
Jennifer Blei Stockman
Stephen C. Swid
John S. Wadsworth, Jr.
Mark R. Walter
John Wilmerding

HONORARY TRUSTEES
Hannelore Schulhof

EMERITUS TRUSTEES
Robert M. Gardiner
Barbara Jonas
Samuel J. LeFrak†
Seymour Slive

EX OFFICIO TRUSTEES
Tiqui Atencio Demirdjian,
    President, International Director's Council
John Leopoldo Fiorilla,
    Chairman, Executive Committee,
    Peggy Guggenheim Collection Advisory Board

As of January 2009

PREFACE

(preceding pages)
Unity Temple, Oak Park,
Illinois, 1905–08, interior view.
Photo by David Heald
Courtesy Solomon R. Guggenheim Foundation

Fifty years after the opening of the Solomon R. Guggenheim Museum, and fifty years after the death of the great architect who designed it, the Solomon R. Guggenheim Foundation and the Frank Lloyd Wright Foundation have joined forces to present *Frank Lloyd Wright: From Within Outward*. This collaboration comes as an important event for both organizations. Our common and enduring bonds extend beyond the Guggenheim Museum building and our particular interest in architecture to the impact that great design can have on communities and cultures worldwide. Frank Lloyd Wright (1867–1959) was arguably the most influential American architect of the twentieth century. Over the course of a seventy-year career, he developed a concrete language in which exterior form was an integral expression of the spaces within a building. For Wright, form not only followed function, but form and function became one. He believed that walls and roofs could define and differentiate without confining. Therefore, he designed his buildings from within outward. Wright's ambition to have all aspects of a work merge together and interact with each other has been a leitmotif for both the Guggenheim and the Wright foundations. After all, as Wright stated in his 1931 lecture "In the Realm of Ideas," "Why any principle working in the part, if not working in the whole?"

The Frank Lloyd Wright Foundation, based in Scottsdale, Arizona, is a leading global multidisciplinary center for education, scholarship, debate, and research committed to the place of architecture and the arts in enriching the quality and dignity of life. The foundation's mission is to educate and engage diverse audiences through programs that encourage innovative thinking about the relationships between architecture and design and the natural environment. Equally, the foundation hopes to inspire a quest for beauty, balance, and harmony in the creation of buildings and spaces that enrich daily life while also preserving the works, ideas, and innovative spirit of Frank Lloyd Wright for the benefit of this and future generations. Wright established the foundation in 1940 to be the repository of his life's work. It owns and operates Taliesin in Spring Green, Wisconsin, and Taliesin West in Scottsdale (Wright's own homes and studios); the professionally accredited

Frank Lloyd Wright School of Architecture; and the Frank Lloyd Wright Archives, widely regarded as the largest single-artist facility of its kind worldwide. Both Taliesin and Taliesin West are National Historic Properties and are on the United States World Heritage Tentative List. Over the coming years, the Frank Lloyd Wright Foundation will develop a larger platform to promote the positive effects that well-designed spaces can have on shaping culture, a message that it shares with the Guggenheim Foundation and the main reason for our collaboration on this celebratory exhibition.

As part of its mission, the Solomon R. Guggenheim Foundation seeks to promote the understanding and appreciation of art, architecture, and other manifestations of visual culture, primarily of the modern and contemporary periods. Among its most popular exhibitions ever were two highlighting architecture: the 2001 retrospective of the work of Frank Gehry and a retrospective of the work of Zaha Hadid in 2006. These successes have demonstrated the great potential architecture and design can wield in encouraging people to think about culture differently. The connection between design, architecture, and other forms of art—especially in the urban context—provides the museum a rich new area for exploration. To this end, the museum has started working enthusiastically on a broader program in which architecture and design become a means of expression to document, divert, and direct our increasingly urban societies.

To celebrate its fiftieth anniversary in 2009, the Solomon R. Guggenheim Museum recently completed a three-year restoration. In September 2008, Mayor Michael R. Bloomberg presided over the ceremony at which the building was unveiled in sterling condition. That evening, a site-specific projection of illuminated text by acclaimed artist Jenny Holzer, titled *For the Guggenheim*, was premiered as it entered the museum's collection. With the building restored, the museum is ready for a year-long celebration that *Frank Lloyd Wright: From Within Outward* inaugurates. In honor of this special year, the museum is also producing a commemorative video that documents the history of the building, presenting a symposium during the Wright exhibition, and planning a series of special events to welcome the world to See It New as part of the campaign to reacquaint everyone with the treasures within the museum and the treasure that the museum is itself. And for those whose affection and admiration commit them to ensuring the future health of the museum building and collections, the Guggenheim Society has been established for the occasion as we celebrate architecture, art, and innovation, our fiftieth-anniversary themes.

Both the Solomon R. Guggenheim and the Frank Lloyd Wright foundations are grateful to the Thornton Tomasetti Foundation for its founding gift to the exhibition's Leadership Committee. An exhibition as complex as *Frank Lloyd Wright: From Within Outward* would have not been possible without the dedication of a large and passionate curatorial team with representatives from both the Frank Lloyd Wright Foundation and the Solomon R. Guggenheim Foundation. Together they have worked hard to make Wright's work accessible to new generations. We would like to thank Bruce Brooks Pfeiffer, Director of the Frank Lloyd Wright Archives, for his valuable insights and wonderful anecdotes; Margo Stipe, Curator and Registrar of Collections, for her admirable patience and determination; and Oskar Muñoz, Assistant Director of the Frank Lloyd Wright Archives, for his thorough research. At the Solomon R. Guggenheim Museum, we extend our thanks to Thomas Krens, Senior Advisor for International Affairs, who served as curator for the exhibition, and to David van der Leer, Assistant Curator, Architecture and Design; Maria Nicanor, Curatorial Assistant; and Violeta Janeiro, Curatorial Intern, who have enlarged upon the original initiatives for the exhibition, its educational programs, and this catalogue.

Phil Allsopp, RIBA,
President and Chief Executive Officer,
Frank Lloyd Wright Foundation

Richard Armstrong,
Director, Solomon R. Guggenheim Foundation
and Museum

CURATORIAL ACKNOWLEDGMENTS

Darwin D. Martin House, Buffalo, New York,
1902–04, view toward newly rebuilt conservatory.
Photo by David Heald
Courtesy Solomon R. Guggenheim Foundation

This exhibition, its catalogue, and all the educational programs that stem from it are the results of true collaboration, hard work, and profound dedication on the part of many individuals who have graciously devoted their time and passion to the work of Frank Lloyd Wright, all in search of a better and more humane architecture. Without the talented professionals with whom we have had the privilege of working in the past months, the complex task of carrying out this endeavor in such a short time would have never materialized into this book and the exhibition celebrating the fiftieth anniversary of the building of the Solomon R. Guggenheim Museum.

Frank Lloyd Wright: From Within Outward is, above all, the result of a very close collaboration between the Solomon R. Guggenheim Museum and the Frank Lloyd Wright Foundation. For this reason, we would first like to thank Thomas Krens, curator of *Frank Lloyd Wright: From Within Outward* and Senior Advisor for International Affairs, Solomon R. Guggenheim Foundation, and Phil Allsopp, RIBA, President and Chief Executive Officer, Frank Lloyd Wright Foundation, for seeing the importance of bringing together the organizations' joint interests in such fashion. Their initial conversations and willingness to work together were the origin of this project. We are also grateful to Richard Armstrong, Director, Solomon R. Guggenheim Foundation and Museum, and Nancy Spector, Chief Curator, Solomon R. Guggenheim Museum, for having fully supported us in all respects.

We would also like to acknowledge the hard work of Mónica Ramírez-Montagut, former Assistant Curator, Architecture and Design, at the Solomon R. Guggenheim Museum. Ms. Ramírez Montagut worked with the Frank Lloyd Wright Foundation curatorial team to develop a preliminary checklist and initiated discussions with an advisory committee comprised of Wright scholars to define the overall concept and goals for the exhibition. We would like to extend our sincere thanks to these committee members for their valuable contributions: Richard Cleary, David De Long, Neil Levine, Mina Marefat, Nicholas Olsberg, and Joseph M. Siry. In addition, Ms. Marefat lent her great passion for Frank Lloyd Wright's Baghdad projects to the effort, acting as curatorial consultant for this important section of the exhibition.

We owe our foremost gratitude to the lenders to the exhibition for their willingness to share the valuable works in their collections on this important and celebratory occasion. The core of *Frank Lloyd Wright: From Within Outward* comprises more than 200 drawings, photographs, and other original materials provided by the Frank Lloyd Wright Foundation Archives in Scottsdale, Arizona. But loans from several other individuals and institutions proved essential to our forming a

coherent and complete explanation of Wright's work. Special thanks are due to James Gubelmann, Peter Lawson-Johnston, Gilbert and Lila Silverman, and Erving and Joyce Wolf for loans from their collections, as well as to Tracy Meyers, Curator, Heinz Architectural Center, Carnegie Museum of Art, Pittsburgh, and Alexander von Vegesack, Director, Vitra Design Museum, Weil am Rhein, Germany, for arranging loans from their institutions.

Looking for a fresh approach to Wright's work, many new materials were commissioned especially for *Frank Lloyd Wright: From Within Outward*. We are grateful to David Heald, Director of Photographic Services and Chief Photographer, Solomon R. Guggenheim Museum, for his efforts and commitment, as well as to Kristopher McKay, Assistant Photographer; Carin Johnson, Photography Archive Coordinator; and Duncan Ball, Lighting Assistant, for all their work in making original photography for the exhibition and this catalogue. Traveling around the country to shoot various Frank Lloyd Wright sites, Heald was fortunate to have the help and hospitality of numerous individuals who graciously opened the spaces in their care. At Taliesin East, Spring Green, Wisconsin, we thank Tom Waddell, Artifact Collection Manager; Becky Rex, Special Events and Media Coordinator; Keiran Murphy, Historic Research; Jim Erickson, Estate Manager; Cornelia Brierly; Frances Nemtin; and Donna O'Donnell. We equally thank Jim Dennis, owner, and Bill Martinelli at the Herbert Jacobs House, Madison, Wisconsin; Susan Koenig and Donna Bordwell at the Unitarian Meeting House, Shorewood Hills, Wisconsin; Eric Jackson-Forsberg, Curator, at the Darwin D. Martin House, Buffalo, New York; Father James Dokos and Kelly Fuchs at the Annunciation Greek Orthodox Church, Milwaukee, Wisconsin; Colleen E. Cooney at the S. C. Johnson & Son, Inc. Administration Building, Racine, Wisconsin; and David Wilke, Business Manager, and Rev. Alan C. Taylor, Senior Minister at Unity Temple Unitarian Universalist Congregation, Oak Park, Illinois. Additional thanks are due to photographer Robin Hill, whose skilled photographs of the Florida Southern College campus have also been included in the exhibition.

In addition to photography, new models were also commissioned specifically for the exhibition. We appreciate the work of Mikolaj Szoska, Model Coordinator, Solomon R. Guggenheim Museum, in bringing this tremendous effort together. For the newly designed and fabricated models, we were fortunate to work with Michael Kennedy, President, Kennedy Fabrications and Architectural Models, and Situ Studio, both of New York.

To further explain Wright's projects to contemporary audiences, we commissioned 3-D rendering animations. For the realization of this enormous task, we are extremely thankful to Mohsen Mostafavi, Dean, and Allen Sayegh, Lecturer in Architecture, at the Harvard Graduate School of Design and their outstanding team of students, as well as to Bob Corbett at Madison Area Technical College and his dedicated students. Without their generosity and diligence, we would have never been able to achieve this crucial aspect of the exhibition.

Relating the work of Frank Lloyd Wright to contemporary architectural practices was of special importance to us. Therefore, we asked Diller, Scofidio + Renfro to explore the ways in which different Frank Lloyd Wright spaces function throughout the country. We are grateful to Elizabeth Diller and Ricardo Scofidio as well as to Bobby Pietrusko. Their creative take on the interaction between the Guggenheim's spaces and the museumgoer has been executed to great success.

We would also like to acknowledge the key role of Indira Berndtson, Administrator of Historic Studies at the Frank Lloyd Wright Archives, who for many years has developed and expanded the oral history project of the archives. Her participation has been indispensable to the exhibition's innovative audio component.

Conceiving an exhibition of this scope for display on Wright's own Guggenheim ramps could only come with a deep understanding of space and a creative approach to design. We were fortunate to be able to count on an outstanding exhibition design team. At the Guggenheim Museum, our most sincere appreciation goes to Melanie Taylor, Manager of Exhibition Design, and Jarrod Beck, Exhibition Designer, who spearheaded the design efforts from the inception of this project. Our thanks also go to Shradda Aryal, Exhibition Design Coordinator; Jaime Roark, Senior Exhibition Designer; and Caroline Razook, Exhibition Designer. Working alongside the Guggenheim team, we were lucky to have the crucial skills and know-how of Wendy Evans Joseph, FAIA, Partner, and Jonathan Lee, Project Designer, from Wendy Evans Joseph Architecture, New York.

Frank Lloyd Wright's original drawings play a central role in the exhibition. They would not have been available to us without the conservation expertise of T. K. McClintock, Director; Lorraine Bigrigg, Senior Conservator; David Colombo, Conservator; and Deborah La Camera, Conservator, at Studio TKM, Somerville, Massachusetts; as well as that of the Guggenheim Museum's Jeffrey Warda, Associate Conservator for Paper, and Elisabeth Jaff, Senior Preparator for Paper. For their unerringly professional care and handling of these fragile works, we are enormously grateful.

The realization of the exhibition design was made possible thanks to the work of David Bufano, Manager of Art Services and Preparations, and his extraordinary team. We also recognize the hard work of Marcia Fardella, Chief Graphic Designer; Mary Ann Hoag, Lighting Designer; Paul Kuranko, Multimedia Specialist; Barry Hylton, Senior Exhibition Technician; Peter B. Read, Manager of Exhibition Fabrications and Design; and Michael Sarff, Construction Manager.

The logistics of bringing together works in so many different media from diverse locations was gracefully handled by the Guggenheim's Registration Department, particularly by Maria Paula Armelin, Associate Registrar.

From the Exhibition Management Department, we could not have done without the exceptional skills and advice of Jessica Ludwig, Director of Planning and Implementation, New York, together with that of Alison Weaver, Director of Programs and Operations, Affiliates, who have been instrumental in organizing the New York and Bilbao venues of the exhibition. Working closely with them have been Sarah Austrian, General Counsel, and Sara Geelan, Associate General Counsel, at the Solomon R. Guggenheim Museum, and Karyn Osterman, Legal Counsel, and Kristel Nielsen, Paralegal, at the Frank Lloyd Wright Foundation.

The personnel and long-time associates of the Frank Lloyd Wright Foundation provided critical assistance in many respects. We are grateful to O. P. Reed Jr. for his appraisal work with the drawings and Harold Mailand, Director, Textile Conservation Services, Indianapolis, for his valuable suggestions for the transport and display of the Taliesin East curtain. We also thank Jim Erickson, Estate Manager, Taliesin; Dan Vernon, Kevin Dobbs, and Kelly Hannah of the Taliesin Preservation, Inc. crew, as well as Bruce Severson, model maker, for their help and guidance at Taliesin with the crating and packing of the historical models; and Suzette Lucas, Editor of *Frank Lloyd Wright Quarterly*, for her kind editorial advice.

This catalogue would not have been possible without a close collaboration between the Guggenheim Museum's Publications Department and Skira Rizzoli Publications. At the Guggenheim, we are particularly grateful to Elizabeth Levy, Director of Publications; Elizabeth Franzen, Associate Director of Publications, Editorial; Stephen Hoban, Managing Editor; and Domenick Ammirati, Senior Editor. At Skira Rizzoli Publications, the catalogue production was expertly managed by Dung Ngo, Senior Editor, Architecture and Design, and edited by Douglas S. Curran, Editor. The book was beautifully designed by Patrick Seymour, Principal; Laura Howell, Designer; and Andrew Hardy, Designer, at Tsang Seymour, New York.

Central to the catalogue have been the rich, insightful contributions of its authors: Richard Cleary, Neil Levine, Mina Marefat, Bruce Brooks Pfeiffer, Joseph M. Siry, and Margo Stipe. Their essays shed new light on the work of Frank Lloyd Wright and his essential contributions to the understanding of space in its myriad manifestations. Additionally, we have greatly benefited from conversations with and insight from Angela Starita, Project Researcher, who has kindly shared valuable information with us during her research and coordination for the book about the Solomon R. Guggenheim Museum building itself, also published during this fiftieth-anniversary year.

Frank Lloyd Wright: From Within Outward is accompanied by a wide variety of educational programs envisaged by both the Guggenheim's and the Frank Lloyd Wright Foundation's Education staff. We must acknowledge Kim Kanatani, Gail Engelberg Director of Education; Christina Yang, Associate Director of Education, Public Programs; and Sharon Vatsky, Associate Director of Education, School Programs; as well as Shawn Rorke-Davis, Director, Education Outreach, Frank Lloyd Wright Foundation, who lent us her long-time experience with Wright's educational programming.

Additionally, we would like to thank Benjamin Prosky, Director of Special Events, Columbia University, Graduate School of Architecture, Planning and Preservation, for so generously collaborating with us in the planning stages of the exhibition symposium and related lectures.

Moreover, we would like to show our appreciation to the Frank Lloyd Wright School of Architecture's Victor Sidy, AIA, NCARB, Dean, and Aris Georges, Professor of Architecture, for their essential contribution on Taliesin's shelter program, which we feature in an exhibition at the Sackler Center taking place in conjunction with *Frank Lloyd Wright: From Within Outward*. Thank you also to Saskia Jordá, from the Taliesin Artist Residency Program.

For their work and contribution to all development and fundraising efforts, we must extend our gratitude both to the Guggenheim's Development Department staff and to the team at A. L. Brourman Associates, who acted as Fundraising and Public Relations Counsel for the Frank Lloyd Wright Foundation and Taliesin Preservation, Inc. At the Guggenheim, we remain grateful to Adrienne Hines, Executive Director, Major

Gifts; Mary Ann Routledge, Director of Capital Campaign; Helen Warwick, Director of Individual Development; Ben Whine, Associate Director of Individual Development; John Wielk, Executive Director for Corporate and Institutional Development; Stephen Diefenderfer, Special Events Manager; and Lindsay Gabryszak, Development Associate. At A. L. Brourman, we equally thank Audrey Brourman, President; Mark Lynch, Senior Vice President, Fundraising Counsel; Rob DeOrio, Vice President; Mary Gilbert, Senior Public Relations Consultant; and Yvonne Beninati, Senior Fundraising Consultant.

As with any exhibition of this scope, a long list of additional Guggenheim staff members have been crucial in completing this project, among them: Eleanor Goldhar, Deputy Director for External Affairs; Laura Miller, Director of Marketing; Betsy Ennis, Director of Public Affairs; Marc Steglitz, Chief Operating Officer; Karen Meyerhoff, Managing Director for Business Development; Maria Celi, Director of Visitor Services; and Francine Snyder, Director of Library and Archives.

Our exceptional group of interns have devoted their time, enthusiasm, and positive attitudes to the exhibition at all its different stages. In the Curatorial Department, we thank Violeta Janeiro, Cayetana Nicanor, Viola Romoli, and Daisy Wong, and in Exhibition Design, Paul Dallas, Meri Lee Helmer, Hye-Vin Kim, Erik Krautbauer, Ian Mills, and Somya Singh.

We are extremely grateful to all of these individuals for their unconditional support of this project. *Frank Lloyd Wright: From Within Outward* could not have happened without them.

Bruce Brooks Pfeiffer,
Director,
Frank Lloyd Wright Foundation Archives

Margo Stipe,
Curator and Registrar of Collections,
Frank Lloyd Wright Foundation Archives

Oskar Muñoz,
Assistant Director,
Frank Lloyd Wright Foundation Archives

David van der Leer,
Assistant Curator, Architecture and Design,
Solomon R. Guggenheim Museum

Maria Nicanor,
Curatorial Assistant, Architecture and Design,
Solomon R. Guggenheim Museum

FRANK LLOYD WRIGHT: FROM WITHIN OUTWARD PROJECT TEAM

EXHIBITION

GUGGENHEIM MUSEUM

Thomas Krens, curator and Senior Advisor for
    International Affairs, Solomon R. Guggenheim
    Foundation
David van der Leer, Assistant Curator, Architecture
    and Design
Mónica Ramírez-Montagut, former Assistant Curator,
    Architecture and Design
Maria Nicanor, Curatorial Assistant, Architecture
    and Design
Heather Christensen, former Project Associate
Violeta Janeiro, Intern
Cayetana Nicanor, Intern
Viola Romoli, Intern
Daisy Wong, Intern

FRANK LLOYD WRIGHT FOUNDATION

Bruce Brooks Pfeiffer, Director, Frank Lloyd
    Wright Archives
Oskar Muñoz, Assistant Director, Frank Lloyd
    Wright Archives
Margo Stipe, Curator and Registrar of Collections,
    Frank Lloyd Wright Archives

GUGGENHEIM MUSEUM AND ASSOCIATES

ADMINISTRATION

Richard Armstrong, Director, Solomon R.
    Guggenheim Foundation and Museum
Marc Steglitz, Chief Operating Officer
Karen Meyerhoff, Managing Director for
    Business Development
Brendan Connell, Director and Counsel
    for Administration
Boris Keselman, Chief Engineer of Facilities
Lakshmi Mohandas, Project Associate

ART SERVICES AND PREPARATIONS

David Bufano, Chief Preparator
Barry Hylton, Senior Exhibition Technician
Paul Bridge, Exhibition Technician
Derek Deluco, Exhibition Technician
Jeffrey Clemens, Senior Preparator
Elisabeth L. Jaff, Senior Preparator

CONSERVATION

Jeffrey Warda, Associate Conservator, Paper

CONSTRUCTION

Michael Sarff, Exhibition Construction Manager

DEVELOPMENT

Adrienne Hines, Executive Director of Major Gifts
John L. Wielk, Executive Director of Corporate and
    Institutional Development
Stacy Dieter, Director of Corporate Development
Brynn Myers, Director of Institutional Development
Mary Ann Routledge, Director of Capital Campaign
Helen Warwick, Director of Individual Development
Brady Allen, Associate Director of Development
    Operations
Stephen Diefenderfer, Associate Director of
    Museum Events
Bronwyn Keenan, Associate Director of Special Events
Ben Whine, Associate Director of Individual
    Development
Lindsay Gabryszak, Development Associate
Mona Islam, Prospect Research Coordinator

EDUCATION

Kim Kanatani, Gail Engelberg Director of Education
Christina Yang, Associate Director of Education,
    Public Programs
Sharon Vatsky, Associate Director of Education,
    School Programs

EXHIBITION DESIGN
Melanie Taylor, Manager of Exhibition Design, Solomon
    R. Guggenheim Museum
Jarrod Beck, Exhibition Designer, Solomon R.
    Guggenheim Museum
Shradda Aryal, Exhibition Design Coordinator,
    Solomon R. Guggenheim Museum
Jaime Roark, Senior Exhibition Designer, Solomon R.
    Guggenheim Museum
Caroline Razook, Exhibition Designer, Solomon R.
    Guggenheim Museum
Paul Dallas, Intern
Meri Lee Helmer, Intern
Hye-Vin Kim, Intern
Erik Krautbauer, Intern
Ian Mills, Intern
Somya Singh, Intern

Wendy Evans Joseph Architecture
Wendy Evans Joseph, FAIA, Partner
Jonathan Lee, Project Designer

EXHIBITION MANAGEMENT
Jessica Ludwig, Director of Planning and
    Implementation, New York
Alison Weaver, Director of Programs and
    Operations, Affiliates

EXTERNAL AFFAIRS
Eleanor R. Goldhar, Deputy Director for
    External Affairs
Nora Semel, External Affairs Associate

FABRICATION
Peter B. Read, Manager, Exhibition Fabrication
    and Design
Christopher George, Chief Fabricator
Richard Avery, Chief Cabinetmaker
David Johnson, Chief Framemaker
Doug Hollingsworth, Cabinetmaker
Peter Mallo, Cabinetmaker
Ashley Stevenson, Assistant Fabricator

FINANCE
Amy West, Director of Finance
Christina Kallergis, Budget Manager of Program
    and Operations
Sari Sharaby, Senior Financial Analyst
Bennett Lin, Financial Analyst

GRAPHIC DESIGN
Marcia Fardella, Chief Graphic Designer
Concetta Pereira, Production Supervisor
Janice Lee, Senior Graphic Designer
Liana Weinstein, Graphic Designer

LEGAL
Sarah Austrian, General Counsel
Sara Geelan, Associate General Counsel
Dana Wallach, Assistant General Counsel

LIBRARY AND ARCHIVES
Francine Snyder, Manager of Library and Archives
Rebecca Clark, Art Librarian

LIGHTING
Mary Ann Hoag, Lighting Designer

MARKETING
Laura Miller, Director of Marketing

MEDIA AND PUBLIC RELATIONS
Betsy Ennis, Director, Media and Public Relations
Lauren Van Natten, Senior Publicist
Claire Laporte, Media Relations Associate

MULTIMEDIA
Paul Kuranko, Multimedia Specialist

PHOTOGRAPHY
David M. Heald, Director of Photographic Services
    and Chief Photographer
Kim Bush, Manager of Photography and Permissions
Kristopher McKay, Assistant Photographer
Carin Johnson, Photography Archive Coordinator
Duncan Ball, Lighting Assistant

PUBLICATIONS
Elizabeth Levy, Director of Publications
Elizabeth Franzen, Associate Director of
    Publications, Editorial
Melissa Secondino, Associate Director of
    Publications, Production
Stephen Hoban, Managing Editor
Edward Weisberger, former Senior Editor
Domenick Ammirati, Senior Editor
Helena Winston, Associate Editor
Minjee Cho, Associate Production Manager
Angela Starita, Researcher

REGISTRAR
Maria Paula Armelin, Associate Registrar
    for Exhibitions

RETAIL DEVELOPMENT AND PURCHASING
Ed Fuqua, Book Buyer
Katherine Lock, Retail Buyer

RIGHTS AND REPRODUCTIONS
Sharon Dively, Rights and Reproductions Manager and
    Photo Researcher

THEATER AND MEDIA SERVICES
Michael P. Lavin, Director of Theater and
    Media Services
Stephanie Gatton, Assistant Theater Manager
Norman Proctor, Projectionist
Jesse Hulcher, Display Technician

VISITOR SERVICES
Maria Celi, Director of Visitor Services and
    Retail Operations
Trevor Tyrell, Operations Manager of Visitor Services
Felicia Isabella, Coordinator of Visitor Services
Emily Johnson, Group Sales and Box Office Manager

WEB SITE
Jennifer Otten, Web Designer
Kimberly Riback, Associate Web Editor
Veena Rao, Video Production Coordinator

FRANK LLOYD WRIGHT
FOUNDATION AND ASSOCIATES

ADMINISTRATION
Phil Allsopp, RIBA, President and Chief Executive Officer
Craig Barth, Vice President of Finance
Rob Jones, Vice President of Campus Planning,
    Restoration and Development

ART PREPARATION
O. P. Reed Jr.
Tom Waddell, Artifact Collection Manager, Taliesin
Jim Erickson, Estate Manager, Taliesin
Dan Vernon, Taliesin Preservation, Inc.
Kevin Dobbs, Taliesin Preservation, Inc.
Kelly Hannah, Taliesin Preservation, Inc.

CONSERVATION
T. K. McClintock, Director, Studio TKM
Lorraine Bigrigg, Senior Conservator, Studio TKM
David Colombo, Conservator, Studio TKM
Deborah La Camera, Conservator, Studio TKM
Harold Mailand, Director, Textile Conservation Services

EDUCATION AND RESEARCH
Indira Berndtson, Administrator of Historic Studies,
    Frank Lloyd Wright Archives
Shawn Rorke Davis, Director, Education Outreach
Victor E. Sidy, AIA, NCARB, Dean, Frank Lloyd Wright
    School of Architecture
Aris Georges, Professor of Architecture, Frank Lloyd
    Wright School of Architecture
Elizabeth Dawsari, Director, William Wesley
    Peters Library

EXHIBITION MANAGEMENT
Phil Allsopp, RIBA, President and Chief Executive Officer,
    Frank Lloyd Wright Foundation

PUBLICATIONS
Suzette Lucas, Editor, *Frank Lloyd Wright Quarterly*

RETAIL LICENSING AND DEVELOPMENT
Doug Volker, Director of Licensing and
    Product Development
Sherry Dillard, Administrative Assistant

LEGAL
Karyn Osterman, Legal Counsel
Kristel Nielsen, Paralegal

MARKETING, DEVELOPMENT, MEDIA,
AND PUBLIC RELATIONS
A. L. Brourman Associates
Fundraising and Public Relations Counsel,
    Frank Lloyd Wright Foundation and Taliesin
    Preservation, Inc.
Audrey Brourman, President
Mark Lynch, Senior Vice President,
    Fundraising Counsel
Rob DeOrio, Vice President
Yvonne Beninati, Senior Fundraising Consultant
Mary Gilbert, Senior Public Relations Consultant

CATALOGUE

Skira Rizzoli Publications
Karen Hansgen, Associate Publisher
Dung Ngo, Senior Editor
Douglas S. Curran, Editor
Shannon McBeen, Intern

Tsang Seymour
Patrick Seymour, Principal
Andrew Hardy, Designer
Laura Howell, Designer

FOREWORD

Frank Lloyd Wright: From Within Outward is a celebration of architecture and its potential to enrich our lives. It is both a tribute to a great twentieth-century architect who believed beautiful, functional architecture was critical to any vibrant culture and a challenge to the peoples of the twenty-first century to demand more from those who build the places where they live, work, and play so that such a vibrant culture might remain within our grasp.

Frank Lloyd Wright was passionate about the importance of architecture and the arts to one's quality of life and believed that an existence without either was a poor one indeed. He created spaces that, for those who experience them, are a joy to be in. Wright proposed an architecture that was expressive beyond any known at the time and that was accessible to all. During the course of his long career, he developed a new sense of building that focused on form being true to function without sacrificing beauty, neither hindered by nor related to any known styles. Crafted from within outward, his spaces provide refuge and prospect, uniting as one entity a building, its inhabitants, and the natural world. Wright saw his ideas for such transformational space, which respects both the humanity sheltered within it and the natural world without, as the wave of the future. And, as if the new millennium were just around the corner, he was already speaking in his 1927 text "The New World" about his ideas for the twenty-first century.

Unfortunately, the message conveyed by the spaces Wright designed fails to reach the majority of us today. The pivotal influence that architecture and design have on who we are as a society is still often given short shrift, with such "artistic" endeavors being considered expensive niceties rather than necessities. In a twist of logic that qualifies as bizarre, given the inescapable presence of the built environment in our lives, architecture too often has been excluded from the urban-planning table, so that monotonous and mundane building developments rise to shape the experiences of millions of people in the most uninspired fashion. As we wonder why so few of us are surrounded by spaces that we really love, spaces that resonate with who we really are, we believe that Wright's ideas about space, and the amazing diversity of design solutions that developed out of those ideas, can provide valuable lessons for us as we move to address the urgent issues that confront society today. It is our hope that this exhibition and its accompanying catalogue will inspire visitors and readers to think differently about their surroundings. We follow Wright in his steadfast and enthusiastic belief that good architecture has a crucial role in deciding who we are as a society, and we reexamine his vision for a new world based on a desire to improve the built environment so that we can all live healthier, more stimulating, and more creative lives instilled with beauty, harmony, and wonder. In so doing, we seek not merely to honor the glories of the past but to help improve the future.

Phil Allsopp, RIBA,
President and Chief Executive Officer, Frank Lloyd Wright Foundation

Thomas Krens,
Senior Advisor for International Affairs, former Director, Solomon R. Guggenheim Foundation

Taliesin III, Spring Green, Wisconsin, 1925–59, living room interior.
Photo by David Heald
Courtesy Solomon R. Guggenheim Foundation

Frank Lloyd Wright: From Within Outward

MARGO STIPE

Looking back upon this enormous deposit to man's credit, and keeping in mind that just as man was in his own time and place so was his building in its time and place, we must remember that architecture is not these buildings in themselves but far greater. We must believe architecture to be the living spirit that made buildings what they were. It is a spirit by and for man, a spirit of time and place. And we must perceive architecture, if we are to understand it at all, to be a spirit of the spirit of man that will live as long as man lives. It begins always at the beginning. It continues to bestrew the years with forms destined to change and to be strange to men yet to come.
—Frank Lloyd Wright, "Some Aspects of the Past and Present in Architecture,"
from Architecture and Modern Life *(1937), reprinted in* The Essential Frank Lloyd Wright:
Critical Writings on Architecture, *p. 284*

Hillside Theater #2, Taliesin III, Spring Green,
Wisconsin, 1952, interior of theater with curtain.
Photo by David Heald
Courtesy Solomon R. Guggenheim Foundation

Of all the arts, architecture may be the least understood and the most underappreciated by mainstream America. We take buildings for granted not only because they have always been there but also because frequently there is little to take notice of. So-called starchitects get a lot of press for their most recent museums and apartment towers, but on Main Street the architect-designed building is rare, and charming historic districts remain the exception rather than the rule. Too often developers work with designers to create functional buildings that are bereft of interest and aesthetic appeal.

Frank Lloyd Wright: From Within Outward is an exhibition about the importance of the built environment and its impact on the quality of our lives. Wright holds a very special place in twentieth-century architecture for his amazing inventiveness and the incredible diversity of his designs, both built and unbuilt. His work is also celebrated for its awe-inspiring beauty and tranquility. Whether private home, workplace, religious edifice, or cultural attraction, Wright sought to unite human beings, buildings, and nature in physical and spiritual harmony. To realize materially such a union, Wright created environments of simplicity and repose through carefully composed plans and elevations based on consistent, geometric grammars, weaving the materials into structures that would complement and intensify both the beauty of the site and the physical, emotional, and social experience of the space. Those who live or work in Wright buildings know firsthand this magic of Wright's transformational space, how it has been created to be constantly in touch with the changing manifestations of the natural world. By reuniting the interior of the human shelter with the natural environment outside, new experiences and patterns are created, the human spirit is awakened, and everyday life enriched.

With the planet in crisis and sustainability at the top of almost everyone's agenda, there has never been a more crucial time for reflection about how we live and what the consequences of the choices we make now will have on future generations. Specific to the purposes of this exhibition is recognition of the need to look critically at the built environment around us and ask what we can do to make it not only more sustainable environmentally but also more nourishing to the human spirit. At this critical turning point as we look for a direction forward, it seems appropriate to also look back at the work of an architect who took as his mission the spiritual reawakening through architecture of the American citizen to the dynamic and imaginative promise of the democracy our country was founded upon. Wright's goal was nothing less than the reinvention of the built environment in order to promote our development as individuals, enhance and enrich the social rituals and patterns of our lives, and encourage meaningful reengagement with the world around us, all of which are particularly timely and worthy of our attention today.

Frank Lloyd Wright: From Within Outward presents this work not as a retrospective or as examples of designs to be imitated or copied but rather as a collection of principles and innovative ideas that, creatively embraced, may still be found to offer solutions to the challenges of the twenty-first century. It is hoped that in addition to the message of the exhibition itself—that creative and inspiring architecture is worth demanding—its venue, the Solomon R. Guggenheim Museum, will reinforce and underscore the power creative and challenging architecture can exert on the human psyche.

Frank Lloyd Wright (1867–1959) was very much a man of his time. Born just two years after the end of the American Civil War, he was witness to the extraordinary changes that swept the world from the leisurely pace of the nineteenth-century horse and carriage to the remarkable speed of the twentieth-century satellite-launching rocket. But unlike many of his contemporaries who accepted such changes with reluctance, Wright welcomed and embraced the social and technological changes made possible by the Industrial Revolution and enthusiastically initiated his own architectural revolution.

Wright was born in rural Wisconsin and spent much of his youth among his mother's family, the remarkable Lloyd-Jones clan, in the Wisconsin valley where they had settled and where Wright himself would later build his own home, Taliesin. Farmers, teachers, and preachers, they were dedicated Unitarians well versed in the writings of Ralph Waldo Emerson (1803–1882) and the transcendentalists, which would also inform much of Wright's strong belief in American democracy and the deep spirituality of the natural world. Both gave him faith in the underlying order of the world as we experience it and constant inspiration for his architecture.

Wright always claimed it was his mother's choice that he became an architect, but his own determination led him to leave the University of Wisconsin after only two terms and set out for Chicago in 1887 in search of work in an architectural office. Talent, luck, connections, and timing found him in the office of the prestigious firm of Adler & Sullivan, where he remained as chief of design for six years before opening his own office in 1893.

By the turn of the twentieth century, Frank Lloyd Wright had started a revolution in residential design. In an effort to redefine American architecture, he set aside the imported models that nineteenth-century architects had embraced and created what became known as the Prairie Style. Searching for a design solution that addressed the needs of the contemporary family, he lowered overall heights, eliminated attics and basements where he could, and introduced free-flowing interior spaces, walls of art glass, and a central, substantial hearth around which the family could gather. "Freedom of floor space and elimination of useless heights worked a miracle in the new dwelling place. A sense of appropriate freedom had changed its whole aspect. The dwelling became more fit for human habitation . . . and more natural to its site. An entirely new sense of space values in architecture began to come home."[1]

By the second decade of the twentieth century, Wright's elevated Prairie House designs gave way to buildings nestled more snugly to the ground, exemplified by his own Taliesin begun in 1911. The simplicity of his earlier work also gave way to the greater ornamentation seen in Chicago's Midway Gardens (1913–14) and Tokyo's Imperial Hotel (1912–22)—dazzling urban entertainment and social centers, both tragically lost through demolition—that gave Wright the rare opportunity to synthesize all the arts within one building. Returning from Japan in 1922, the next dozen years were personally and professionally challenging as well as financially catastrophic. But while only a handful of projects went into construction—the four California textile block houses of 1923–24 (Millard, Storer, Freeman, and Ennis)—this period was one of great design innovation for Wright, who combined innovative experimentation with new technologies and untried geometries. (Among the unbuilt commissions was the 1924 Gordon Strong Automobile Objective and Planetarium for Sugarloaf Mountain, Maryland, his first spiral design and a project that demonstrated his firm belief in the permanent place of the automobile in American life.)

During the early 1930s, in the depths of the Great Depression, with work still scarce, Wright with his wife,

Olgivanna, founded a school of architecture, the Taliesin Fellowship. He also began his campaign for decentralization with his scheme for Broadacre City, first unveiled in Rockefeller Center in 1935. Almost simultaneously, he received two of his most important commissions: the breathtaking house for Edgar Kaufmann, Fallingwater (1934–37), in bucolic Pennsylvania; and the streamlined and light-flooded S. C. Johnson & Son, Inc. (Johnson Wax) Administration Building (1936–39) for Racine, Wisconsin.

In the 1940s and 1950s Wright concentrated on the development of a building system for the moderate-cost middle-class residence. Calling the system Usonian—first realized in the 1937 house for the Herbert Jacobs family (Madison, Wisconsin)—Wright used nonrectilinear shapes including the circle, triangle, and ellipsis to create dozens of Usonian houses that were constructed around the country. During this time, Wright also designed large public projects like Crystal City (1940) for Washington, D.C., the two Pittsburgh Point Civic Center commissions (1947), and the Plan for Greater Baghdad (1957), all of which remained unrealized but demonstrate the breadth of his urban vision. Wright died just months before the completion of the most challenging and trying commission of his career, the Solomon R. Guggenheim Museum, a project sixteen years in the making, which we celebrate here.

Over the seventy-two years of his career, Wright created designs for residences, shops, hotels, religious structures, skyscrapers, bridges, and museums as well as furniture, art glass, and carpets. From the beginning to the end of his career, his message remained the same: for architecture to have any significance it must be appropriate to "time, place, and man." He argued that only "organic" architecture—that which develops from within outward through integral relation of parts to whole and which is functional in relation to humankind—will have that significance.

In 1957, at age ninety, in a television interview Wright told Mike Wallace that if he had another fifteen years he could change the nation. With missionary zeal, for decades, Wright had preached his philosophy of an organic architecture as the basis for a revitalized democratic society. He was sure, given more time, he would reach the masses and convert them to his cause. He did not live long enough to see the nation accept his vision, but his buildings and ideas for a better life for all Americans continue to influence new generations of architects and enthusiasts because of their humanity, respect for and connection to the natural world, and incredible beauty.

Almost exactly one hundred years ago, Wright wrote: "That individuality in a building was possible for each home-maker, or desirable, seemed at that time to rise to the dignity of an idea. Even cultured men and women care so little for the spiritual integrity of their environment; except in rare cases they are not touched, they simply do not care for the matter so long as their dwellings are fashionable or as good as those of their neighbors and keep them dry and warm. A structure has no more meaning to them aesthetically than has the stable to the horse. And this came to me in the early years as a definite discouragement."[2]

That same practice persists today fueled by the limited catalogue of standardized designs developers offer to home buyers conditioned to expect no more. Opposed to this meager, but materially expedient, offering—which Wright called the work of plan-factories—he promoted architecture as portraiture and believed that the architect had the responsibility to create a design that supports, encourages, and reflects the individuality of the client, not the whim of fashion or the idiosyncrasies of the architect. He wanted to create "biographies and poems . . . appealing to the center of the human soul . . . [characterizing] in a building those who are to live in it."[3]

Wright stated repeatedly in his writings that architecture's chief role was as "background or framework for the human life within [its] walls and a foil for the nature efflorescence without."[4] Properly designed, this "background" would provide inspiring surroundings for all activities, whether for family, work, or religious or social gatherings. Though working against the tide, Wright was remarkably successful as demonstrated by Unity Temple (Oak Park,

Illinois, 1905-08), Taliesin (Spring Green, Wisconsin, 1911-59), the Herbert Jacobs House #1 (Madison, Wisconsin, 1936-37), and the S. C. Johnson & Son, Inc. Administration Building and Research Tower (Racine, Wisconsin, 1936-39 and 1943-50), all featured in the exhibition. Within each of these, and many more, there is an intensely poetic power and repose worthy of more formally sacred spaces that move the experience of them to the plane of the transcendental.

While building is about foundations, walls, and roofs, ultimately architecture should be about the space those elements shape and how people experience that space. Among the most compelling achievements of Wright's architecture was his radical reworking of space. With the structural changes in the Prairie Houses Wright opened up to continuous space the boxes within boxes in which people were housed, "to animate the building as if it were a continuous spatial discourse rather than a series of separate words."[5]

Reference is often made to an "oriental" quality that characterizes much of his architecture, and even Wright began to see his space in Asian terms after an encounter with the Taoist void in *The Book of Tea:* "The reality of a room . . . was to be found in the vacant space enclosed by the roof and walls, not in the roof and walls themselves."[6] Or, as Wright has paraphrased it, "The reality of the building does not consist in the roof and walls, but in the space within, to be lived in."[7] I believe Wright misunderstood the Eastern concept of the void but in doing so only underestimated what he had, in fact, achieved. If Wright's space was not Eastern, it also was not particularly Western. Architect Isozaki Arata addresses the variance in an essay on Wrightian space, where he writes: "Any attempt to discuss Wright's space in terms of its multifarious historical and cultural antecedents is doomed to failure, for their vestiges, exemplified by Wright's reworking of Lao-tzu's fundamental principle, are rephrased and irretrievably buried in every aspect of his work. In order to understand Frank Lloyd Wright there seems very little need to examine the numerous currents of twentieth century architecture or the development of the concept of space since the Renaissance. . . . The incomparably individual process of Wright's work is the unprejudiced incorporation of the legacy of every civilization, of Whitman and Lao-tzu, of the Aztec and Momoyama Japanese. . . . Here is space to which no civilization can lay claim."[8]

Wright space engages the observant immediately. Approaches are always carefully designed and choreographed. One moves toward an entrance as one would move through a Japanese garden, the eye caught by something only just revealed by the twisting paths of movement, the changing perspectives, and the angles of repose. Interior space is equally disarming: rarely is proportional harmony so sensitively crafted. Relying on human scale and a predetermined unit system as the defining measures for placement of every feature and detail, the buildings exhibit the eloquence of a symphony.

Among Wright's greatest spaces are his own homes, Taliesin in Spring Green, Wisconsin, and Taliesin West (1937–59) in Scottsdale, Arizona, where the architect, ever alive to new opportunities, constantly experimented with new ideas, technologies, and materials. "Taliesin" is a Welsh word meaning "shining brow" and in the first instance makes reference to Wright's siting of the original house on the brow of a hill in his native Wisconsin. But Taliesin was also the name of "a Welsh poet, a druid bard who sang to Wales the glories of the Fine Arts,"[9] and the appropriateness of this name can hardly be lost on any visitors to Wright's homes, where buildings and landscapes, furniture and fine art all combine to create spaces of great beauty and islands of serenity amid the architectural mediocrity that largely dominates the American landscape.

Both at Taliesin and Taliesin West, the buildings and the gardens, orchards, and fields all contribute to the total composition, fitting as smoothly into the natural terrain as if they had grown there. Wright said of Taliesin: "Taliesin was to be an abstract combination of stone and wood as they naturally met in the aspect of the hills around about. And the lines of the hills were the lines of the roofs, the slopes of the hills their slopes, the plastered surfaces of the light wood-walls, set back into shade beneath broad eaves, were like the flat stretches of sand in the river below and the same in color, for that is where the material . . . came from."[10] At Taliesin West, the sun-loving desert masonry construction, inspired by the natural masonry of the area, seems as if it were excavated from the surrounding environment. "Sun-acceptance in building means that dotted-lines and wall surfaces eagerly take the light and play with it and break it up and render it harmless or drink it in until sunlight blends the building into place with the creation around it."[11] What Wright once said of Japanese architecture applies equally to his Taliesins: "[The] buildings, like the rocks and trees, grew in their places. [The] gardens were idealized patterns of their landscapes. They were native shrines, in themselves a form of worship for their native land."[12]

Wright was deeply spiritual and passionately in love with life here on earth, which he saw as the materialization of spirit. He called Nature, which he often chose to spell with a capital N, his church and said it was all of the body of God we would ever see. He wrote: "Man takes a positive hand in creation whenever he puts a building on the earth beneath the sun. If he has a birthright at all, it must consist in this: that he, too, is no less a feature of the landscape than the rocks, trees, bears or bees of that nature to which he owes his being."[13] To Wright, architecture was not just about the physical building; it also embraced the human lives lived within and the natural landscape. For Wright, housing the human spirit in worthy fashion demands the deepest involvement of nature, from the form itself to the choice of materials used to realize the structure, to its placement on the site, and to the method of construction used so that it would grow as easily and be shaped to harmonize with its surroundings in much the same organic fashion as a tree. The result was a recomposition of the natural materials of the area into a structure that would complement and intensify the beauty of the site as well as provide poetry and comfort for the soul.

Wright believed architecture is life and therefore buildings are entities like living organisms. Bruno Zevi captured it well when he wrote:

> In defining Wright's architecture as organic, we mean essentially two things: first that his building are entities like human organisms, and secondly that they are functional in relation to man. . . . In the human organism there is an intrinsic correspondence between internal constitution and outward appearance. . . . When functionalism stripped buildings bare, . . . people began to see that unity in architecture means the unity of interior spaces, from whence springs the unity of volume in a house conceived in terms of walls enclosing this space and its continuation in the decorative treatment of the surfaces of the walls. A Wright house is an organism in that its fundamental and substantive theme is space, the voluminal enclosure is the projection of this space, and the decorative patterns, the choice of materials and ornamentation, are designed to give value and accent to the spatial concept. No one but a maniac with hallucinations could in one lifetime have created the Prairie houses, Falling Water [sic] and the Museum of Non-Objective Painting, if these were considered from the exterior as plastic phenomena. Instead, they are the results of a method of spatial creation applied to diverse themes under different conditions. In the light of this spatial interpretation, Wright's architecture, seemingly so manifold and arbitrary, is more coherent than that of any of the functionalists who betray the real problems of architecture with a coherence that is entirely formal and extraneous. The vitality of Wright's structure, the power of his buildings, his unbelievable technical daring, the permanent fecundity of his genius are explicable in the light of this conception of a building as a living reality, growing and organic.[14]

The challenges of the twenty-first century mandate that human beings must change the way we live here on Earth and in the process offer new opportunities for invention and creativity in many fields. But as science and industry charge forward to meet the needs of the future, the health of the planet in all of its ecological diversity must top the list of criteria that need to be met. It is also critical that the well-being of the human spirit be reintroduced into the equation, and what better way to address that than by improving the buildings we inhabit? Wright wrote: "Whether people are conscious of it or not, they actually derive countenance and sustenance from the 'atmosphere' of the things they live in or with. They are rooted in them just as a plant is in the soil in which it is planted."[15] Surrounded by mediocrity, we have forgotten the healing and restorative power of beauty and comfort. It is time to recognize the necessity of beauty and comfort, long viewed as luxuries, to our spiritual health. Instead of the one-size-fits-all approach of developers, it means carefully considered designs that focus on the quality of space, not the quantity, and the actual patterns of the lives lived in that space whether individual residence or apartment or place of work, worship, or leisure. Such spaces would enrich our lives and encourage us to develop individually our best abilities and participate more fully in the life of the communities of which we are a part. This is the message of Wright's architecture. It remains as relevant today as it was one hundred years ago. We simply need to heed the call and rise to the occasion.

The essays that follow in this publication look at how Wright approached the larger social context of the built environment by addressing community needs while still ensuring and protecting the privacy of the individual and family. They developed from long discussions about Wright's relevance to the present. All enlighten us to the prophetic nature of Wright's work and the continuing significance of his ideas, if not necessarily the forms with which he expressed them. Joseph M. Siry looks at Wright's communal buildings for worship and drama and how they are designed to bring their audiences into the experience rather than leave them as spectators; Neil Levine considers the importance of the Prairie House within the broader concept of community planning; Richard Cleary concentrates on the community of builders Wright engaged to get his buildings built with their vision intact; and Mina Marefat writes about the "architect's quest for redefining the meaning of buildings and reshaping the cityscape to embody a joyous spirit and a sustainable style of life through his designs for greater Baghdad."[16] Bruce Brooks Pfeiffer delves more fully into some of the projects featured in the exhibition in the brief essays that appear in the plates section.

This collection of essays expands still further our understanding of the breadth of Wright's vision and the ways in which he sought to implement it. The buildings themselves celebrate that vision's realization into spaces of often enormous transformational power that will continue to speak to those who have the heart and mind to listen.

NOTES

1. Frank Lloyd Wright, *An Autobiography* (San Francisco: Pomegranate, 2005), p. 165.
2. Wright, "In the Cause of Architecture," *Architectural Record*, 1908. Reprinted in Bruce Brooks Pfeiffer, ed., *The Essential Frank Lloyd Wright: Critical Writings on Architecture* (Princeton and Oxford: Princeton University Press, 2008), p. 36.
3. Wright, "Architect, Architecture and the Client," 1896. Reprinted in Pfeiffer, ed., *Frank Lloyd Wright: Collected Writings, Vol. 1* (New York: Rizzoli, 1992), p. 29.
4. Wright, "In the Cause of Architecture," p. 46.
5. Bruno Zevi, "Frank Lloyd Wright and the Conquest of Space," *Magazine of Art*, May 1950, p. 188.
6. Okakura Kakuzo, *The Book of Tea* (Rutland, VT; Tokyo: Charles E. Tuttle, 1956), p. 45.
7. As seen in a wall carving in the Pavilion at Taliesin West.
8. Arata Isozaki, *Frank Lloyd Wright: Johnson and Son, Administration Building,* Global Architecture I (Tokyo: A.D.A EDITA, 1970), p. 2.
9. Wright, *An Autobiography*, p. 167.
10. Ibid., p. 171.
11. Wright, "To Arizona," *Arizona Highways,* 1940. Reprinted in Pfeiffer, ed., *Collected Writings, Vol. 4* (New York: Rizzoli, 1994), p. 36.
12. Wright, "The Print and the Renaissance," 1917. Reprinted in Pfeiffer, ed., *Collected Writings, Vol. 1*, p. 152.
13. Wright, *Architecture and Modern Life* (1937). Reprinted in *The Essential Frank Lloyd Wright*, p. 277.
14. Zevi, pp. 189–90.
15. Wright, *The Natural House* (1954). Reprinted in Pfeiffer, ed., *Frank Lloyd Wright: Collected Writings, Vol. 5* (New York: Rizzoli, 1995), p. 112.
16. Mina Marefat, "Wright's Baghdad: Ziggurats and Green Visions," in *City of Mirages: Baghdad, From Wright to Venturi,* edited by Pedro Azara (Barcelona: Department de Composició Arquitectònica, 2008), p. 150.

Wright and Worshipping Communities

HIS ARCHITECTURE AS THE SOCIAL SPACE OF RELIGIONS

JOSEPH M. SIRY

Why not, then, build a temple, not to GOD in that way—more sentimental than sense—
but build a temple to man, appropriate to his uses as a meeting place, in which to study man himself
for his God's sake? A modern meeting-house and good-time place.
Build a beautiful ROOM proportioned to this purpose. Make it beautiful in this simple sense.
A natural building for natural Man.
    —Frank Lloyd Wright, on Unity Temple, in An Autobiography *(1932)[1]*

Beth Sholom Synagogue, Elkins Park,
Pennsylvania, 1953–59, northeast view into
main upper sanctuary (detail of Figure 19).
Photo © Balthazar Korab

Among the many types of social spaces that Frank Lloyd Wright imagined and built in his long career, the auditorium for worship was central to his life's achievement. The best-known among such buildings include Unity Temple in Oak Park, Illinois (1905–08), and Beth Sholom Synagogue in Elkins Park, Pennsylvania (1953–59), yet these major works were part of a long series of built and unbuilt projects for religious structures, as well as theaters that Wright conceived as temple-like rooms for the presentation of drama. Although created for varied individual and institutional clients, and in different settings, Wright's religious auditoriums share a common concern for mutual visibility and audibility to enhance the communal nature of worship. He was also concerned with the symbolic or figurative character of each of these projects, which were not only to be functionally optimal for meeting but also iconographically legible as representations of religion or sacredness whose form he specifically shaped for the clients' particular denominational cultures. In both pragmatic and symbolic terms, Wright's social spaces for worship were decisive for defining their communities both to themselves and to external audiences near and far.

WRIGHT'S FORMATION AND UNITY TEMPLE

Wright's engagement with rooms for worship was rooted in his childhood experience of the church buildings where his father, the Reverend William Cary Wright, both preached and played the organ. In his recollections of those years, Frank Lloyd Wright wrote of being powerfully moved by the music, but he made no comment on the church auditoriums or exteriors. The earliest works of religious architecture with which Wright was involved were the Unity Chapel (1885–86), for his extended maternal Lloyd Jones family and their neighbors in their valley south of Spring Green, Wisconsin, and his uncle Rev. Jenkin Lloyd Jones's All Souls Church (1885–86) in the Oakwood district on Chicago's South Side. The architect for both was Joseph Lyman Silsbee, Wright's first architectural employer, although Wright was evidently involved in the design and interior construction of Unity Chapel. Wright was a member of his uncle's church after his arrival in Chicago, while the country chapel would later serve as the setting for services for his Taliesin Fellowship. The yard was Wright's first place of burial, as it was the burial site for members of his mother's family.[2]

While these early church buildings were important places in Wright's personal story, they were small, intentionally residential in scale, and distinctly Unitarian in their simple, non-ecclesiastical meeting rooms and exterior forms. Yet Wright soon encountered a far more elaborate style of interior architecture for auditoriums when he apprenticed with architects Dankmar Adler and Louis Sullivan in their Chicago firm of Adler & Sullivan from 1887 to 1893. Known nationally for their outstandingly successful Auditorium Building in Chicago (1886–90), these architects

Figure 1
Adler & Sullivan, Kehilath Anshe Ma'ariv, southeast corner,
3301 Indiana Avenue and Thirty-third Street, Chicago, Illinois,
1889–91, as Pilgrim Baptist Church, interior, looking east;
largely destroyed by fire in 2006.
Photo © Cervin Robinson, 2008

Figure 2
Frank Lloyd Wright and Dwight Heald Perkins,
Abraham Lincoln Center (project), Chicago, Illinois,
1903, interior perspective of auditorium looking north,
rendered by Burch Burdette Long.
The Frank Lloyd Wright Foundation
FLLW FDN # 0010.001

developed a distinct style of theater interiors that integrated excellent circulation, acoustics, visibility, and highly original schemes of coloration and ornament. Wright's development during this decisive phase of his training also included work on the series of synagogues that the firm designed for Chicago congregations, among the most important of which was a new building for Adler's own synagogue, Kehilath Anshe Ma'ariv (1889–91) (fig. 1). Its main auditorium was arguably Wright's first involvement with religious architecture on a supraresidential scale. Functionally, its most distinctive attribute was its acoustic excellence, said to have been developed by Adler with the memory in mind of the voice of his own father, Rabbi Liebman Adler, who had served the congregation for decades in earlier facilities. This quality was enhanced in part by the room's wood-vaulted ceiling, which towered above the main floor and balconies on either side and to the rear. The tall broad span overhead encompassed and newly defined the Reform congregation to itself as the oldest Jewish community in Chicago, newly housed in a style of architecture that Louis Sullivan described as modern, and without precedent in its ornamental program.[3]

Wright combined his knowledge of Unitarian spaces for religious gathering and Adler and Sullivan's approach to auditoriums in his first commission for a major public hall, the project that became the Abraham Lincoln Center in Chicago (1897–1905), as Lloyd Jones's successor institution to the neighboring All Souls Church. His preliminary designs for its auditorium include an interior sectional perspective showing rising tiers of seats around three sides of both the main level and upper balcony, facing the frontal platform and podium (fig. 2). Although Wright had left the project before its completion and dedication in April 1905, his extensive studies for the center's major room directly influenced his design for the new Unitarian Universalist church in Oak Park, Unity Temple, on which Wright began work in the summer of that year.[4] Intended to be unlike long-naved basilican churches, Unity Temple had a cubic auditorium with galleries on three sides facing a frontal pulpit. Wright's first church was primarily an expression of the auditorium as a space of collective worship (fig. 3). While only 35 feet wide between balcony fronts, Unity Temple's auditorium seats 450 in pews on the main central floor, and lower and upper balconies around three sides, all within intimate range of the frontal central pulpit and the organ screen behind. Clerestory windows on all four sides and a coffered ceiling with art-glass lights in each bay create an amply lit worship room like a meetinghouse, where all see and hear each other while focused on the pulpit.

Figure 3
Unity Temple, Oak Park, Illinois,
1905–08, interior looking south.
Photo by David Heald
Courtesy Solomon R. Guggenheim Foundation

In presenting Wright's design to Oak Park, where medievally styled churches of other Protestant denominations were the norm, Unity Temple's minister noted that "without tower or spire it expresses the spirit of the ideal. By its form it expresses the thought, inherent in the liberal faith, that God should not be sought in the sky but on earth among the children of men."[5] In the spirit of Unitarian appreciation for world religions, Unity Temple's concrete exterior alluded to temple forms in antiquity, including Japanese and Mayan works likely known to Wright, to embody the ideal of a transcendent religious unity then advocated in liberal circles (fig. 4). As its minister wrote, "Informed by the same spirit which characterized the ancient temples, this structure typifies the thought 'while religions are many, religion is one'. . . . The past and the present forms of religion are thus brought together in a spirit of unity. The temple form is especially fitted to a liberal church whose faith is that all religions are of God, are the attempts of man to feel after and find him 'in whom we live and move and have our being.'"[6] As he would do in later religious structures, Wright here created a symbolic form that was to represent its faith.

In each work, he chose a distinct geometric figure for the building's basic form to characterize the religious life therein. In Unity Temple, this figure is the square and the cube, whose 1:1:1 ratio of dimensions signified unity. Wright's emphasis on characterizing his congregational clients corresponded to the older theoretical ideal taught at the École des Beaux-Arts, that architectural forms should convey an institution's or an individual's character.[7] In 1896 Wright had written in general of the architect's role: "the opportunity to characterize men and women in enduring building material for their betterment and the edification of their kind is really one of the world's fine opportunities." For an institution as for an individual, the architect "may reveal [the client], he may interpret the better side of him that appeals to his imagination and give him something to grow to."[8]

THE MODERN THEATER AND THE DEMOCRATIC CHURCH BUILDING
At the same time that Wright designed Unity Temple, he was supporting a local initiative favoring theater of elevated cultural character in his suburb of Oak Park. In Wright's view, echoing an idea voiced through the 1800s, theater had a cultural function like religion, and the ideal theater would have the character of a temple. This ideal inspired his first client for a theater, Aline Barnsdall, who supported her own alternative theater company in Chicago and who commissioned Wright to design an ideal theater for her estate at Olive Hill in Los Angeles. From early 1915 to about 1920, Wright made several versions of this project and, although none were built, they all shared a key common

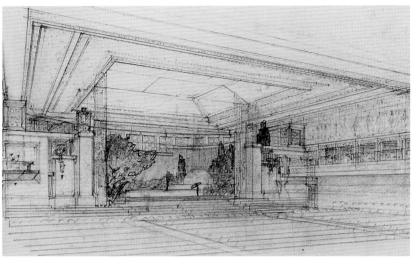

Figure 4
Unity Temple, Oak Park, Illinois, 1905–08,
viewed from west.
The Frank Lloyd Wright Foundation
FLLW FDN # 0611.0011

Figure 5
Olive Hill Theater Complex for Aline Barnsdall (project),
Los Angeles, California, interior perspective,
looking toward stage, ca. 1918.
The Frank Lloyd Wright Foundation
FLLW FDN # 2005.064

theme: to unite stage and audience in one architectural space that would reinforce the cultural ideal of theater as a communal and spiritual experience. This aim was central to European modernist theater, which Barnsdall knew first-hand. Wright, while he may have known of European avant-garde theater, is recorded as having denied the value of such precedent. Rather he praised ancient Greek theaters and traditional Japanese theater, whose intimate spaces for actors and audience he knew well from his years in Tokyo, where he designed a small theater that was built in his Imperial Hotel (1912–22). His perspective of this Barnsdall Theater's projected interior, likely dating from 1918, shows the audience and stage in one room, with no framing proscenium separating these realms (fig. 5). A central ceiling vault spans over audience and stage, and a diaphanous curtain is drawn aside to left and right, accentuating their spatial unity. Piers upholding incense burners flank the curtains, but space flows around them. The continuous orna-mental frieze on the sides, in front of and behind the stage, similarly abolishes a proscenium-like divide. This ideal interior recalls Unity Temple as a unified space of social gathering. Wright reportedly said to Barnsdall: "A theater is architecture, just as a house or a church is. I have improved the forms of churches and houses and office buildings, and if left alone I will give you the finest theater in the world."[9]

Wright's theater for Barnsdall was never built, yet its basic premise as a temple for culturally elevated drama underlay his later solutions for the ideal theater, including unbuilt projects for Woodstock, New York (1931–32), and Hartford, Connecticut (1948–49), and his built Kalita Humphreys Theater for the Dallas Theater Center (1955–59) (fig. 6). In these designs, he developed a plan for seating based on what he called the reflex angle, meaning groups of seats arranged at 30-degree angles around a frontal stage projecting out into the audience. One interviewer noted that Wright described the proscenium as a "door between the audience and the play," and that Wright "would tear down that door and the wall and," as Wright said, "unify the audience and the show." He "would give the audience, by means of seating, acoustical and ceiling arrangements, a sense not only of identity with the play, but with each other," creating what Wright called "a sense of being in an audience."[10] As Wright's apprentice W. Kelly Oliver wrote, the Dallas Theater Center was "to create the same feeling of intimacy that is found in [the] small Taliesin Theaters," which Wright built for his own Taliesin Fellowship from the 1930s to the 1950s. According to Oliver:

[Being] only twelve rows in depth, the Dallas auditorium flows into the stage with only a small line as demarca-tion. Human scale is not forgotten. A solitary figure on the bare stage is not dwarfed by a monumental prosce-nium but rather finds himself in scale with the low-hanging balconies above the side stages and the arched openings at either side. Both seats and stage seem to wrap around each other . . . walls and ceilings pass from auditorium to stage . . . space is created that has constant movement. The actor is no longer forced to project himself in the Theater Center but finds himself a part of this moving space. And, for the first time in the history of theater becomes *of* this space rather than *in* it.[11]

This last claim resonates with a long-standing modernist emphasis on integration of actors and spectators in theater. The spatial reinforcement of the audience's sense of its own collectivity was central to Wright's later religious

Figure 6
Kalita Humphreys Theater, Dallas Theater Center,
1955–59, interior, looking northwest across
auditorium and stage.
The Frank Lloyd Wright Foundation
FLLW FDN # 5515.0018

Figure 7
Annie M. Pfeiffer Chapel, Florida Southern College,
Lakeland, 1938–41, interior, looking north.
The Frank Lloyd Wright Foundation
FLLW FDN # 3816.0080

Figure 8
Annie M. Pfeiffer Chapel, Florida Southern College,
Lakeland, 1938–41, interior, looking southwest,
showing flat ceiling skylights inside west structural columns
and cantilevers supporting lantern walls with central
skylight as rebuilt after 1944 hurricane, and after
remodeling of pulpit and seating, completed 1967.
The Frank Lloyd Wright Foundation
FLLW FDN # 3816.0073

Figure 9
Community Christian Church, Kansas City, Missouri,
1939–42, view from west. The Bonfils Chapel and
entrance at the lower right were added in 1944 and the
steel cross sculpture at left was added in 1976.
Photo © 2000 Robert D. Stout
Courtesy of Community Christian Church,
Kansas City, Missouri

Figure 10
Meeting House, First Unitarian Society of Madison,
Shorewood Hills, Wisconsin, 1946–52.
Photograph © Balthazar Korab

architecture. In his view, his ideal theater form had a quasi-sacred function that distinguished it from commercial play-houses. When the director of the Dallas Theater Center, Paul Baker, asked Wright about space for scenery at stage level, Baker recalled: "He did not want space offstage right and left, and he told me—and this is very important—'I do not want my temple filled up with old dirty scenery stage left and right.' He felt that if we had ramps going down [to a storage space below stage level] and very little offstage area that we would keep the temple clean and beautiful and there would be no place to put scenery and junk of that kind."[12] In his list of concerns about Wright's early plans, Baker also noted that the lobby was too small for the playhouse, specifying that "the theater undoubtedly will need space where coffee can be prepared for the audiences and space for dispensing machines of various kinds." Wright shot back with a biblical allusion: "Paul! Do you really visualize the cheapening effect of a food and drink bar at the very threshold of the temple? It would reduce the atmosphere of the whole edifice to the level of a hot-dog stand? All that milling for drinks, etc., just where you enter the edifice will make the theater like a hot-dog stand in the portico of a church."[13]

Wright used a variant of the reflex-angle plan that he developed for theaters in most of his later religious auditoriums, such as the Annie M. Pfeiffer Chapel for Florida Southern College in Lakeland (1938–41) and the Community Christian Church in Kansas City, Missouri (1939–42). The first of these, built for President Ludd Spivey as both the auditorium and chapel for a liberal Methodist college, had a spatially compact plan of reflex angles on a main floor and balcony above, where "seating is so arranged that no one in the audience is more than fifty feet away from the rostrum and everyone has a direct view of the speaker."[14] Nearly a thousand chairs were required to hold the entire student body, set into a room focused on the original pulpit's V-shaped prow projecting into the space's center (fig. 7). As one observer wrote of the interior, "it seems that the visitor has been transported to the stage of an ancient theater similar to that built by the Greeks many years ago."[15] Over the room's center, Wright set a towering lantern as a crown through which abundant, constantly changing natural light passes into the space (fig. 8). This tower's engineering recalls Unity Temple's, for "most of the weight of the building is carried on four large, hollow piers adjacent to each of the four entrances," with balconies and roofs cantilevered from the columns on a network of reinforced concrete beams.[16] For Wright, the cantilever conveyed an ideology: "It is just like the democratic principle that we subscribe to; that is why I have always referred to this as the architecture of democracy: the freedom of the individual becomes the motive for society and government."[17]

The democratic ideal was central to the Reverend Burris Jenkins's Community Church in Kansas City, which had broken with the regional branch of the liberal Disciples of Christ to adopt an open membership policy (fig. 9). Jenkins sought to receive "members from all other denominations" on the basis of "an entire equality," so that his church "became in reality a community church, undistinguished by any sectarian name, practice or spirit."[18] This policy helped to make his Community Church, which styled itself as "everybody's church," the largest Protestant congregation in Kansas City, with 4,200 members.[19] When its building burned in 1939, Wright was asked to design a new auditorium that could function as a theater or a cinema as well as a sanctuary, since the church, aspiring to be "the social center for the masses," hosted dramatic and musical performances and screened popular films.[20] His design thus incorporated the reflex-angle seating that he had developed for theaters. As Wright recounted in his autobiography in 1943, the novelty of the building's light steel and gunite construction as he originally designed it was not accepted by Kansas City building officials. Yet, as dedicated in 1942, the Community Church, with its exterior cantilevered balconies, did read as strikingly modernistic and nonsectarian, without overtly religious symbols, since Jenkins and his congregation intended it to be "the church of the future."[21]

Figure 11
Meeting House, First Unitarian Society of Madison,
Shorewood Hills, Wisconsin, 1946–52, interior,
looking northwest toward pulpit and choir loft.
Photograph © Balthazar Korab

Conveying a democratic social ideal through geometry and structure was central to the architecture of Wright's church building for the First Unitarian Society of Madison (1946–52). Conceived as a "country church," in the tradition of Unity Chapel, this building was a relocation of its congregation to a then-rural site looking across fields to Lake Mendota, with the building's triangular prow projecting north from the saddle of its hill (fig. 10). In its semirural simplicity, the church is a rough stone–walled edifice with light wood trusses and some cantilevered steel supporting the soaring roof. As the minister had written to Wright: "We conceive the core to be one large room which will be usable for all the functions of a parish calling for a large assembly room. That is this one room will be adaptable for worship, lectures, forums, recreation, dinners, movies, recitals, dramatics."[22] They wanted "a building without its major auditorium limited to a special purpose, such as a worship service. The main room should be a multiple-purpose room like the modern living room, and that is just what it will be, the living room of the parish."[23] Wright shaped a concise triangular room whose seating could be variably arranged in front of its stone pulpit below the organ and choir loft (fig. 11). As he wrote in 1946: "Cannot religion be brought into a human scale? Can it not be humanized and natural?" Asking what would make a church "tolerable in the life of a genuine democracy," he proposed that it be simple: "A pleasant well-proportioned room in human scale with a big fireplace and a plain table for flowers and the Book; —the sky pilot on the floor with his flock—the whole business bright with sun and a wide prospect."[24] The result was social space that embodied Wright's ideal of democratic character in modern church architecture.

THE STEEL CATHEDRAL AND BETH SHOLOM
One important line of inquiry in Wright's designs for worship was the unbuilt Steel Cathedral of 1926 for New York City and its adaptation in his realized Beth Sholom Synagogue of 1953–59, in Elkins Park, north of Philadelphia (fig. 12). For these, Wright worked with two clients, the Reverend William Norman Guthrie of the Church of St. Mark's-in-the-Bouwerie and Rabbi Mortimer J. Cohen. Both were supremely well informed about religious architecture, and both were concerned to create buildings that would embody their visions of modern, democratic worship. Guthrie, who had known Wright since 1908 when he had lectured in Oak Park, Illinois, and admired Wright's Unity Temple there, brought to his work with Wright a lifelong familiarity with European cathedrals and a deep knowledge of

Figure 12
Beth Sholom Synagogue, Elkins Park,
Pennsylvania, 1953–59, view northeast
from Old York Road.
Photograph by author

non-Western faiths, combined with a desire to create an American worship hall that would house rituals of a universal religion for the diverse groups in New York City. His ideas were an alternative to the Cathedral Church of St. John the Divine, whose fundraising and building in the 1920s were led by the city's Episcopal bishop, who disapproved of Guthrie's practices. Guthrie set forth his ideas in at least two texts, one an Easter sermon of 1925 on "A Modernist View of a Cathedral" and a lecture also of that spring entitled "Two Cathedrals: One Historic, One Prophetic."[25]

Guthrie's sketches conveyed his basic ideas to Wright. Unlike St. John the Divine, with its long nave meant to accommodate religious processions, Guthrie envisioned "a vertical Cathedral more in keeping with the best we build today in this alarming City."[26] Instead of the nave, Guthrie imagined that "the many chapels that surround the apse [of St. John the Divine], might offer us a Gothic Cathedral completely so surrounded, and that all these chapels might be used as denominational sanctuaries."[27] Among his sketches accompanying this text, Guthrie drew the plan and section of a polygonal edifice with thirteen sides, one of which would be a grand portico and the other twelve would be chapels for rotating use by different religions around the central "holy tower" (figs. 13, 14). Guthrie described a lofty steel and stained-glass central space as combining the vast interior dome of Florence Cathedral with the outward monumentality of an Egyptian pyramid, both of which he knew firsthand. At its center would be neither pulpit nor altar, but a deeply sunken orchestra pit, with multiple organs intoning responsively out of view. Atop the pit, covered by a raised circular drumlike platform, would be a vast translucent bowl full of clear water, ever bubbling and fresh, from which leaping geysers meeting in the center would maintain a crystal dome. Above that water bowl would be another smaller one of wrought metal containing dancing flames of fire, below yet a third colossal bowl containing burning incense. Guthrie believed that all city dwellers should have access to the more spectacular scenes in nature, so he imagined that down from the various heights of the great enclosed hall would "dart living light of every conceivable mixture of hues," like the aurora borealis or northern lights.[28] Around the tower, Guthrie wrote, "ascends a spiral footway for dancers and huge processional movements, up, up, and up, beyond the reach of the pursuing eye, or pouring down to us out of the invisible."[29] He thought that such a space, if realized, would stimulate New Yorkers to renounce sinful activities of all kinds, so as to reshape the whole city's moral well-being.

Wright's drawings for what he labeled the "Steel Cathedral" project are undated, but were likely made in late 1927 to illustrate Guthrie's text, which Wright possessed (figs. 15, 16). The drawings show Wright's transformation of Guthrie's idea into a hexagonal building composed of two overlapping equilateral triangles set on an enormous raised platform. Between three sets of entrances were six hexagonal chapels. The cathedral's central triangular floor space would step down to "the fountain of illuminations," that is, a hexagonally framed pool within which was the focal "altar of the elements." Overhead is a structural triangle that Wright labeled as "main sloping supporting girders" A, B, and C aligned with the entrances. At their bases these girders had a spread of 2,100+ feet or 0.4 miles, which would

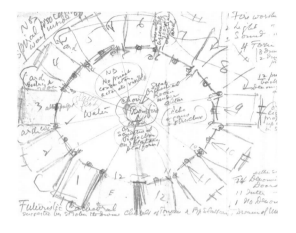

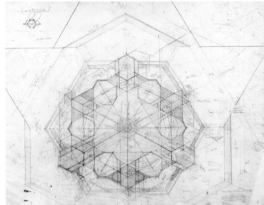

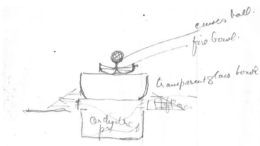

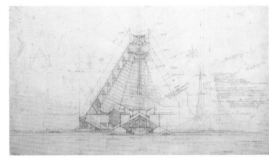

also be the structure's height. This section keyed to Wright's plan shows that the structure would have dwarfed the Eiffel Tower and the Great Pyramid at Cheops, even as it assimilated ideas from both. The steel-and-glass canopy would have spiral ramps from bottom to top, with crowning gardens. As Guthrie envisioned 600-foot spires rising from his twelve chapels, so Wright depicted spires around the cathedral's tripod, and an enormous one atop its apex from which would soar light shafts at night.

Wright's drawings convey an enthusiasm for this fantastic project. He wrote to Guthrie: "And we might build it before we died—Who knows?. . . It is too great a scheme to be dropped or lost."[30] Clearly the Steel Cathedral, whose plans were unpublished in Wright's lifetime, was one source for his later design for Beth Sholom, whose leadership may never have known of its origins in Wright's project for Guthrie. Founded in north Philadelphia in late 1918, and named House of Peace in thanks for the armistice ending World War I, Beth Sholom was a Conservative Jewish congregation that chose as its first rabbi Mortimer J. Cohen, who had admired Wright's work since at least 1917, after he had studied at the City College of New York. After his start at Beth Sholom in 1920, Cohen and his wife traveled to Europe and Palestine in 1927, and he collected images of Mount Sinai. After World War II, like many American Jewish urban congregations, Beth Sholom decided to follow its membership's move to the suburbs, where it purchased a site on Old York Road in Elkins Park, north of Philadelphia, building a school and social center there in 1952. Cohen urged his congregation to relocate their synagogue there, and developed his ideas into a design consisting of his own sketches and an explanatory text that he shared with his friend, sculptor Boris Blai, who urged that they be sent to Wright, with whose work at Florida Southern College Blai had been familiar as a teacher there.[31]

Soon after he contacted Wright in late 1953, Cohen sent Wright his sketches for a synagogue that would represent "the American spirit wedded to the ancient spirit of Israel." Like the Steel Cathedral, Beth Sholom was to be simultaneously futuristic and archaic. Cohen was also seeking a monument of national importance from the country's greatest living architect, whom he compared to Michelangelo at St. Peter's or Wren at St. Paul's. And he wanted it to represent Philadelphia, as the beacon of American liberties. Following Dr. Joseph Hertz, who edited the first English-language commentary on the Torah (the first five books of the Hebrew Bible, beginning with Genesis), Cohen focused on the idea of the Tabernacle as a "wandering Mt. Sinai," the site where Yahweh had given Moses the Ten Commandments, as the foundation of Judaism. In this spirit Cohen sent to Wright, with his initial instructions in late 1953, images of Mount Sinai, showing the craggy summit in the desert, views of ancient and medieval European

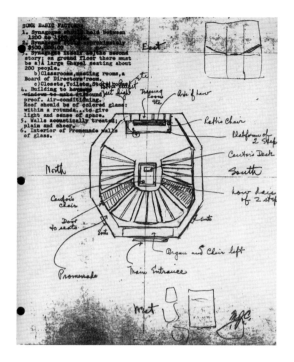

Figure 17
Rabbi Mortimer Cohen, sketch plan for Beth
Sholom Synagogue accompanying letter to
Frank Lloyd Wright, 16 November 1953.
Beth Sholom Archives, Elkins Park, Pennsylvania

Figure 18
Beth Sholom Synagogue, Elkins Park, Pennsylvania,
1953–59, interior perspective, study for original drawing,
pencil on paper, 1 March 1954.
The Frank Lloyd Wright Foundation
FLLW FDN # 5313.021

synagogue interiors, and reconstructions of Solomon's Temple. Cohen also sent Wright "a very rough sketch of [Beth Sholom's] interior."[32] Cohen's plan shows not a basilican nave, but an octagonally focused space with the rabbi at the bimah, or reading desk, set democratically at the congregation's center, as in medieval synagogues (fig. 17).

In Wright's original design of March 1954, Cohen's octagon had become an irregular hexagon with the ark (the repository for the scrolls of the Torah) and the bimah at the eastern end of the floor of seating sloping down to them. Perhaps the most revealing drawing is a sectional perspective that shows the worship room as a great tetrahedral glass pyramid, accessed via ramps from the main entrance below, so that in rising up to the level of the ark containing the Torah scrolls, worshippers would recall Moses's ascent up Mount Sinai to receive the Law, as divinity's revelation to Israel (fig. 18). The drawing shows rays of light emitted from the ark, as the center of spiritual energy. The synagogue was conceived as a symbolic form, much like the Steel Cathedral. As Wright said to Cohen as the building neared completion, "You provided me with the ideas and I tried to put them into architectural form," much as Guthrie's ideas had inspired Wright's project for the Steel Cathedral thirty years before.[33] While rooted in Jewish belief, Wright's synagogue was also to have broader significance, as a crystalline or diamond-like symbol of the ancient revelation of divine law (fig. 19). This biblical law's future import, was, in Cohen's view, universal, just as Guthrie saw the Steel Cathedral as a setting for a universal religion. As Cohen wrote, "[T]he Jewish religion reflects not only its internal perplexities but is part of the world struggle for meaning and purpose and worth."[34] Such ideas echoed Wright's own early formation in a liberal Unitarian tradition, with its emphasis on comparative appreciation of all the world's religions. This likely provided a frame of reference for his work with both Guthrie and Cohen, for whom Wright transcended conventions of religious architecture to imagine unique forms. Both projects grew from clerical visions that had bridged from sectarian to universal principles.

In terms of chronology and symbolism, among Wright's works, the closest comparison to Beth Sholom is the Annunciation Greek Orthodox Church in Wauwatosa, Wisconsin, which selected Wright in November 1955 (fig. 20). Working drawings were completed before he died in April 1959, and the church was completed in 1961. As Wright said referring to Pfeiffer Chapel, Beth Sholom, and Annunciation, "All forms of religion have a basic desire to function in harmony with their beliefs and I try to help them—to materialize their ideas in something beautiful for all humanity. It's the architect's job."[35] The plans that Wright developed showed a circular building inscribed in a motif like a Greek cross with four structural piers upholding the bowl-like sanctuary. The whole was crowned by a low dome as a single shell of reinforced concrete. Its shape was akin to that of the church of Hagia Sophia in Istanbul, which Annunciation's building committee had asked Wright to consider as a central point of reference for its religious heritage. The reference functioned in a way analogous to presenting Beth Sholom as a moving Mount Sinai, instantly

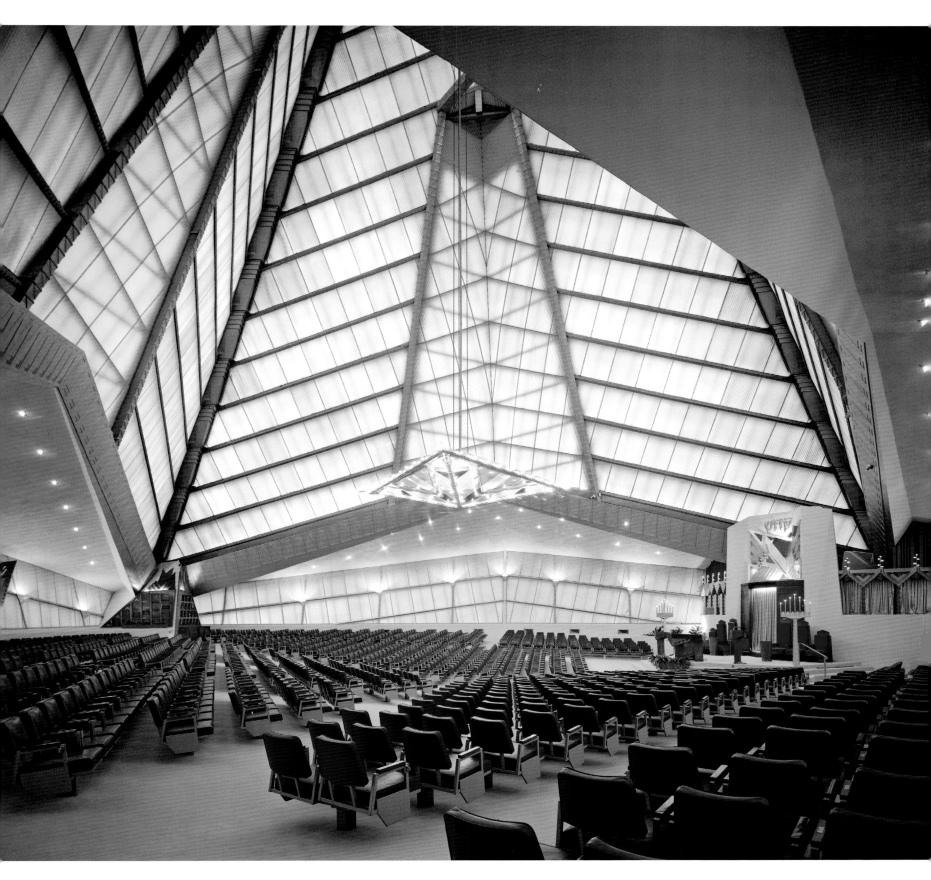

Figure 19
Beth Sholom Synagogue, Elkins Park, Pennsylvania, 1953–59,
view northeast into main upper sanctuary showing colored-glass
light basket (center) and frontal platform with ark (right).
Photograph © Balthazar Korab

Figure 20
Annunciation Greek Orthodox Church,
Wauwatosa, Wisconsin, 1956–61, exterior view.
Photo by David Heald
Courtesy Solomon R. Guggenheim Foundation

conveying strong associations specific to those who identified with a tradition. Inside, circular rows of pews on the main floor and balcony seat a total of eight hundred people (fig. 21). The chairman of the building committee favored the seating plan's communal image and the dome: "This looked to me like the dome was the church, and yet it was utilitarian at the same time. When you hear of seating a thousand people in a church with no pillars to obstruct your vision and nobody sitting more than sixty feet from the sacristy, this impressed me a lot. This is what *ekklesia* means in Greek, you know: you are part of the group."[36] As in his earlier rooms for worship, Wright here created a space for the whole community to see and know itself.

Wright's approach to the sacred auditorium reveals aspects of his art that distinguished it within the history of modern architecture. Like others in the modernist movement, his interior halls were structurally innovative and expressive in their use of the steel or steel-reinforced concrete skeleton, often featuring accentuated cantilevers as a signature motif. Long spans enabled by steel created the sense of interior wholeness in his auditoriums, whose spatial volumes were uninterrupted by columns so as to achieve an ideal of unity. Yet apart from these modernist conventions, each of Wright's sacred spaces had a form that signified its spiritual aims. Although interiors like those of Beth Sholom and Annunciation Greek Orthodox Church contained explicit religious symbols in their furnishings, his others as a rule did not. Rather, in each, the form of the space itself conveyed sacredness.

In all of these works, Wright was concerned generally with the question of modernity in architecture just as his clerical clients confronted the question of what would appropriately be modern religious life. To an extent, the issue of modernity in religion transcended denominational specificity, just as architectural modernity was a problem that went beyond particular building types or their settings. Yet for both religion and architecture, appropriate modern expression depended in part on how the present defines itself with respect to tradition and to place. In his religious works, Wright sought to create solutions that were specifically expressive of the faiths that his buildings housed, in each case choosing a distinct geometric figure as a form that would define space and structure, as he did with the spiral in the Solomon R. Guggenheim Museum, which he also thought of as a temple. As he wrote in 1958: "There seems to be something in the human mind that requires a special particularizing of reverence. That is why we have different religions—each seeking its own relationship with the divine. And it's why we seek different styles in church architecture."[37] Each of his solutions engaged with this question of the right relation of style to ideology. Because of this aim, Wright's biography as a religious architect captures what made his work unique among modernists.

Figure 21
Annunciation Greek Orthodox Church,
Wauwatosa, Wisconsin, 1956–61,
interior as built, looking northeast.
The Frank Lloyd Wright Foundation
FLLW FDN # 5611.0053

NOTES

1. Frank Lloyd Wright, *An Autobiography* (1932), in Bruce Brooks Pfeiffer, ed., *Frank Lloyd Wright: Collected Writings, Vol. 2: 1930–1932* (New York: Rizzoli, 1992), p. 212. This essay draws on my book in progress, *Beth Sholom: Frank Lloyd Wright and Modern Religious Architecture*. Overviews of Wright's religious architecture include Jonathan Lipman, "Consecrated Space: The Public Buildings of Frank Lloyd Wright," in Robert McCarter, ed., *Frank Lloyd Wright: A Primer on Architectural Principles* (New York: Princeton Architectural Press, 1991), pp. 193–217; Richard Joncas, "III: Buildings for Worship," in David G. De Long, ed., *Frank Lloyd Wright and the Living City* (Milan: Vitra Design Museum and Skira Editore, 1998), pp. 100–13; and the film *Sacred Spaces: The Houses of Worship Designed by Frank Lloyd Wright* (Reel Shop Productions, 2005).

2. Joseph M. Siry, *Unity Temple: Frank Lloyd Wright and Architecture for Liberal Religion* (New York: Cambridge University Press, 1996), pp. 13–24.

3. On Adler and Sullivan's building for Kehilath Anshe Ma'ariv, see Bernhard Felsenthal and Herman Eliassof, *History of Kehilath Anshe Maarabh* (Chicago, 1897), pp. 56–57; Hyman L. Meites, ed., *History of the Jews of Chicago* (Chicago: Jewish Historical Society of Illinois, 1924), p. 171; Hugh Morrison, *Louis Sullivan: Prophet of Modern Architecture* (New York: Norton, 1935), pp. 124–25; Morris Gutstein, *A Priceless Heritage: The Epic Growth of Nineteenth Century Chicago Jewry* (New York: Bloch, 1953), pp. 78–80; Lauren Weingarden Rader, "Synagogue Architecture in Illinois," in *Faith and Form* (Chicago: Spertus College Press, 1976), pp. 40–43; George A. Lane, *Chicago Churches and Synagogues* (Chicago: Loyola University Press, 1981), pp. 64–65; Sarah Nazimova, "The Evolution of a Congregation's Identity: Adler & Sullivan's Kehilath Anshe Ma'ariv Synagogue" (honors thesis, history of art, Wesleyan University, 1986); Robert C. Twombly, *Louis Sullivan: His Life and Work* (New York: Viking/Penguin, 1986), pp. 248–49; Charles E. Gregersen, *Dankmar Adler: His Theaters and Auditoriums* (Athens, OH: Swallow Press/Ohio University Press, 1990), pp. 74–75; and David Van Zanten, *Sullivan's City: The Meaning of Ornament for Louis Sullivan* (New York: W. W. Norton, 1999), pp. 47–48. Sarah C. Mollman, ed., *Louis Sullivan in the Art Institute of Chicago: The Illustrated Catalogue of Collections* (New York: Garland, 1989), p. 49, noted seating plans by John Baptiste Fischer. Speaking of his work as a designer with Adler & Sullivan, Wright later recalled, "Anshe Maariv is still there in Chicago on South Michigan Avenue to attest the folly of the experiments I made in violent changes of scale in actual building construction as I had seen lieber-meister practice it in ornament with startling success." Wright, *Genius and the Mobocracy* (1949), in Bruce Brooks Pfeiffer, ed., *Frank Lloyd Wright: Collected Writings, Vol. 4: 1939–1949* (New York: Rizzoli, 1994), p. 362. In 1920 the building was sold to its present owners, the Pilgrim Baptist Church, among the most musically renowned African American congregations in Chicago. K.A.M. Pilgrim Baptist was largely destroyed by fire in January 2006. Outer limestone and brick walls still stand. See Howard Reich, "History Burns with Church," *Chicago Tribune*, 8 January 2006, sec. 4, pp. 1, 6.

4. Siry, *Unity Temple*, pp. 32–50; and Siry, "The Abraham Lincoln Center in Chicago," *Journal of the Society of Architectural Historians* (hereafter JSAH) 50 (September 1991): 235–65.

5. Rev. Rodney F. Johonnot, *The New Edifice of Unity Church* (Oak Park, IL: Unity Church, 1906), p. 18.

6. Johonnot, *New Edifice of Unity Church*, pp. 15–16. Johonnot's closing quoted St. Paul's letter to the Athenians in the Areopagus, as recorded in Acts 17:24–28.

7. Donald D. Egbert, *The Beaux-Arts Tradition in French Architecture* (Princeton: Princeton University Press, 1980), pp. 122–24.

8. Wright, "Architect, Architecture, and the Client" (1896), in Bruce Brooks Pfeiffer, ed., *Frank Lloyd Wright: Collected Writings, Vol. 1: 1894–1930* (New York: Rizzoli, 1992), pp. 29–30.

9. Norman Bel Geddes, *Miracle in the Evening*, ed. William Kelley (Garden City, NY: Doubleday, 1960), pp. 161–64. Bel Geddes (p. 164) reported that Wright said: "Aline, the true theater is an architectural structure. The simpler the stage is kept, the greater will be the things done upon it. The classic Greek stages were without equipment for lighting and scenery." Allegedly Wright said (p. 156): "The theater in Europe died in Athens in 500 b.c....The New York theater managers are a lot of carnival people who are accepted by the public because no one has come along with anything better. The theater in Japan offers much greater variety." On Wright's designs for Barnsdall's theaters, see Kathryn Smith, *Frank Lloyd Wright, Hollyhock House, and Olive Hill: Buildings and Projects for Aline Barnsdall* (New York: Rizzoli, 1992); and Alice Friedman, "No Ordinary House: Frank Lloyd Wright, Aline Barnsdall, and Hollyhock House," in *Women and the Making of the Modern House: A Social and Architectural History* (New York: Abrams, 1998), pp. 32–63. Wright's studies for Barnsdall were the basis for his later designs. When he first talked with director Paul Baker about the Dallas Theater Center in 1955, Baker recalled that Wright "said he would be glad to build a building for us but...we would have to use the plans he had drawn up in 1915" for Barnsdall. "If we wanted to use those plans, then he'd be glad to do it." Oral Memoirs of Paul and Kitty Baker, 25 July 1990, Baker Interview, no. 3, p. 47 (Waco, TX: Baylor University Institute of Oral History, Texas Collection).

10. Wright, quoted in Eugene Lewis, "Theaters' 'Picture' Stage Obsolete, Architect Says," *Dallas Times Herald*, 9 August 1955. Wright's New Theatre as presented for Hartford "combines the old simplicity of the Greek and Elizabethan theatre with a new brilliance possible only in the machine age." *The New Theatre* (Hartford, CT: New Theatre Corporation, 1949), n.p. It was said of Wright's unbuilt Hartford plan: "The hexagonal shape of the Wright theater will be unfamiliar to those accustomed to the squeezed rectangles of Broadway. It is not, however, as the exhibit catalogue states—'a clean break with all past traditions.' An audience of Shakespeare's time would find the protruding stage and the semicircle of seats very similar to the plan of its own playhouses. In fact, it is an idea that, like so many others, goes back to the Greeks." "Wright's Hartford Theater Shown in a New York City Museum Exhibit," *Architectural Forum* 90, no. 5 (May 1949): 163.

11. W. Kelly Oliver, "The Wright Taliesin Theaters," in Leonard E. B. Andrews, ed., *Dallas Theater Center* (Dallas, 1960), n.p.

12. Baker, interview with Joyce Cory, summer 1966, quoted in Cory, *The Dallas Theater Center: An Idea That Was Big Enough* (Dallas: Dallas Theater Center, 1980), p. 43.

13. Wright to Paul Baker, 29 January 1958. Dallas Theater Center Archives, box 169, folder 6. Dallas Public Library. Wright's remarks recalled Jesus's turning the money changers out of the Temple in Jerusalem. See Matthew 21:12–13 and John 1:13–16.

14. "Southern to Open Chapel," *Tampa Sunday Tribune*, 9 March 1941, pt. 3, p. 7, quoted in Siry, "Frank Lloyd Wright's Annie M. Pfeiffer Chapel for Florida Southern College: Modernist Theology and Regional Architecture," *JSAH* 63, no. 4 (December 2004): 509.

15. "Chapel Is Like Old Theater," *Southern*, 20 April 1940, p. 8, quoted in Siry, "Pfeiffer Chapel," p. 516.

16. William S. Chambers, Jr., "Innovations in College Chapel Architecture," *Architectural Concrete* 8 (1942): 17, quoted in Siry, "Pfeiffer Chapel," p. 522.

17. Wright, talk to Taliesin Fellowship, published as "A New Sense of Space," in Olgivanna Lloyd Wright, *Frank Lloyd Wright: His Life, His Work, His Words* (New York: Horizon Press, 1966), pp. 155, 158–59, quoted in Siry, "Pfeiffer Chapel," p. 525.

18. Burris Jenkins, quoted in "Linwood Community Church Excluded from Cooperative Circle of Other Christian Churches," *Kansas City Post*, 2 January 1930. On the Community Church, see Wright, *Autobiography* (1943), in Pfeiffer, ed., *Frank Lloyd Wright: Collected Writings, Vol. 4: 1939–1949* (New York: Rizzoli, 1994), pp. 187–90; and Siry, *Beth Sholom: Frank Lloyd Wright and Modern Religious Architecture*, in progress.

19. Jenkins, *Where My Caravan Has Rested* (Chicago and New York: Willett, Clark, 1939), p. 214, cited in Sue Darrett, Fran Rollins, and Betty Kinser, *Community Christian Church: A Centennial History, 1890–1990* (Kansas City, MO: Community Christian Church, 1990), p. 21.

20. Jenkins, "The Community Church," *Christian Community* 2, no. 9 (March 21, 1936), p. 9.

21. Rev. Joseph Cleveland, "The Church of the Future," in *Program of Dedication: Community Church, Kansas City, Missouri* (1942). Disciples of Christ Historical Society, Nashville, TN.

22. Rev. Kenneth Patton to Wright, 22 April 1946. Frank Lloyd Wright Archives (hereafter FLWA), fiche id. no. U48E01. On Wright's church building for the First Unitarian Society of Madison, see Mary Jane Hamilton, "The Unitarian Meeting House," in Paul Sprague, ed., *Frank Lloyd Wright and Madison: Eight Decades of Architectural and Social Interaction* (Madison: Elvehjem Museum of Art, 1990), pp. 179–88; republished with modifications as *The Meeting House: Heritage and Vision* (Madison, WI: Friends of the Meeting House, 1991).

23. Patton, "The Church of Tomorrow," *Christian Register* 126, no. 6 (June 1947), p. 241.

24. Wright, "Starched Churches" [review of John R. Scotford's *The Church Beautiful: A Practical Discussion of Church Architecture* (Boston: Pilgrim Press, 1945), *Christian Register* 125, no. 8 (August 1946), p. 362], in Bruce Brooks Pfeiffer, ed., *Frank Lloyd Wright: Collected Writings, Vol. 4: 1939–1949* (New York: Rizzoli, 1994), p. 298.

25. Guthrie's sermon, "A Modernist View of a Cathedral," was reported in "Super-Cathedral, 1,500 Feet High, Seating 25,000, Is Urged by Dr. Guthrie," *San Francisco Examiner*, 13 April 1925, p. 1. The handwritten notes for this sermon are in the Guthrie Papers, Harvard Andover Theological Library (hereafter HATL). It was noted in "Religious Services," *San Francisco Examiner*, 11 April 1925, p. 16. It may have been based on or anticipated his sermon, "Two Cathedrals: One Historic, Another Prophetic," typescript, in Guthrie Papers, HATL. On the Steel Cathedral, see Henry-Russell Hitchcock, *In the Nature of Materials: The Buildings of Frank Lloyd Wright 1887–1941* (1942; New York: Da Capo Press, 1975), p. 82; Arthur C. Drexler, *The Drawings of Frank Lloyd Wright* (New York: Horizon Press, for The Museum of Modern Art, 1962), plates 114, 273, p. 301; Herbert Muschamp, *Man about Town; Frank Lloyd Wright in New York City* (Cambridge: M.I.T. Press, 1983), pp. 47–58; Yukio Futagawa and Bruce Brooks Pfeiffer, eds., *Frank Lloyd Wright, Volume 10: Preliminary Studies 1917–1932* (Tokyo: A.D.A. Edita, 1984), pp. 132–33; Futagawa and Pfeiffer, ed., *Frank Lloyd Wright, Volume 5: Monograph, 1924–1936* (Tokyo: A.D.A. Edita, 1990), pp. 36–37; Robert Stern, Gregory Gilmartin, Thomas Mellins, *New York 1930: Architecture and Urbanism between the Two World Wars* (New York: Rizzoli, 1987), pp. 167–69; Richard Joncas, "'Pure Form': The Origins and Development of Frank Lloyd Wright's Non-Rectilinear Geometry" (Ph.D. diss., Stanford University, 1992), pp. 258–67; Anthony Alofsin, *Frank Lloyd Wright: The Lost Years: A Study in Influence* (Chicago: University of Chicago Press, 1993), pp. 298–301; Alofsin, "Frank Lloyd Wright and Modernism," in Terence Riley, ed., *Frank Lloyd Wright, Architect* (New York: The Museum of Modern Art, 1994), p. 40; Richard Joncas, "III: Buildings for Worship," in David G. De Long, ed., *Frank Lloyd Wright and the Living City* (Milan: Vitra Design Museum and Skira Editore, 1998), pp. 56, 102–04; George L. Hersey, *Architecture and Geometry in the Age of the Baroque* (Chicago: University of Chicago Press, 2000), pp. 205–09; and Otto Antonia Graf, "Enspacement: The Main Sequence from 4 to 6; Analysis of Wright's Steel Cathedral Project," in Robert McCarter, ed., *On and By Frank Lloyd Wright: A Primer of Architectural Principles* (London: Phaidon, 2005), pp. 144–69.

26. Guthrie, "Two Cathedrals," p. 16.

27. Ibid., p. 17.

28. Ibid., p. 27.

29. Ibid., pp. 25–26.

30. Wright to Guthrie, 9 November 1928. FLWA, fiche id. no. A004A06.

31. On Beth Sholom, see Patricia Talbot Davis, *Together They Built a Mountain* (Lititz, PA: Sutter House, 1974). Earlier Rabbi Cohen had authored a guide: *Beth Sholom Synagogue: A Description and Interpretation* (Elkins Park, PA: Beth Sholom Synagogue, 1959). See also *Beth Sholom Synagogue: Gold Anniversary, 1919–1969* (Elkins Park, PA, Beth Sholom Synagogue, 1969); Brendan Gill, *Many Masks: A Life of Frank Lloyd Wright* (New York, Putnam, 1987), pp. 461–73; and George M. Goodwin, "Wright's Beth Sholom Synagogue," *American Jewish History* 86: 3 (September 1998): 325–49.

32. Cohen to Wright, 16 November 1953. FLWA, fiche id. no. B170B06.

33. Wright, quoted in "New World Synagogues," *Time* 73, no. 9 (2 March 1959), p. 54.

34. Cohen, "Of Religious Interpretation of Life" [review of Eugene Kohn's *Religion and Humanity* (New York: Reconstructionist Press, 1953)], in *Jewish Exponent* 124 (21 May 1954), p. 49.

35. Wright, "Is It Good-By to Gothic?" *Together* (May 1958), in Bruce Brooks Pfeiffer, ed., *Frank Lloyd Wright: Collected Writings, Vol. 5: 1949–1959* (New York: Rizzoli, 1995), p. 229. See John Gurda, *New World Odyssey: Annunciation Greek Orthodox Church and Frank Lloyd Wright* (Milwaukee: Milwaukee Hellenic Community, 1986).

36. Stanley Stacy, quoted in Gurda, *New World Odyssey*, p. 76.

37. Wright, "Is It Good-By to Gothic?" (1958), in Pfeiffer, ed., *Wright: Collected Writings, Vol. 5*, p. 229.

Frank Lloyd Wright and the Romance of the Master Builder

RICHARD CLEARY

Apprentice Alfred Bush nailing redwood fascia
boards on a roof at Taliesin West, early 1940s.
Below him is a wall of "desert rubble stone"
consisting of rubble set in concrete (detail of Figure 12).
Photo © 2009 Pedro E. Guerrero

As Darwin Martin and his family were moving into their unfinished house in Buffalo, New York, in November 1905, Frank Lloyd Wright acknowledged lapsed deadlines and confessed, "I am getting discouraged but will make some desperate efforts this coming year to build up a coterie of capable, honest workmen, or manufacturers, who don't want to get rich quick and who love fine work for its own sake"[1] (fig. 1). The remark was to some degree a self-serving measure intended to distract Martin from Wright's own role in the delays, but it also was a heartfelt expression of an enduring concern: controlling the translation of his vision into a tangible work of architecture. This problem is familiar to designers as well as anyone who has remodeled a kitchen, and while it can be regarded as an inescapable challenge of architectural practice, Wright charged the pragmatic task of obtaining quality materials and workmanship with romantic notions of work and the art of building.

Some architects seeking to minimize the gap between design and construction limit the scope of their practices to a scale requiring minimal dependence on intermediaries. Legendary in this respect was Carlo Scarpa, who in the mid-twentieth century worked exclusively in the Italian Veneto, where he created meticulously detailed buildings with a group of dedicated craftsmen. Wright, however, sought to chart a course that would allow him to simultaneously develop a national practice, experiment with innovative construction processes, and enjoy strong relationships with master builders. These intentions were not readily compatible, and over the course of his seventy-two-year career he experimented with the organization of his practice in his efforts to reconcile them. At times, as in his experience with Martin and Martin's contractor, Oscar S. Lang, he did find those "who love fine work for its own sake," but in other instances his expectations of that love exceeded what others could give.

Wright regarded an individual's work ethic to be a fundamental dimension of character and asserted this notion as a theme of his *Autobiography,* published in 1932 (revised 1943). In the opening pages he wrote of his maternal grandfather, Richard Lloyd Jones, teaching his children "to add tired to tired and add it again" as they established their homestead in the Helena Valley near Spring Green, Wisconsin.[2] This essential ethic of farm life was reinforced by Wright's Protestant religious formation and transformed into an aesthetic principle through his exposure to the writings of John Ruskin. "The truth, decision, and temperance, which we reverently regard as honorable conditions of the spiritual being," Ruskin declared in *The Seven Lamps of Architecture*, "have a representative or derivative influence over the works of the hand, the movements of the frame, and the action of the intellect."[3]

As a youth working alongside his extended family in the "valley of the God-Almighty Joneses," to use Maginel Wright Barney's phrase, Wright encountered a Welsh stonemason who might have stepped from the pages of Ruskin.[4] From the late 1870s, "twinkling-eyed, bewhiskered" David Timothy was responsible for much of the stonework of the buildings erected by the family in the valley, including their chapel (1885–86), on which Wright worked, and Hillside Home School (1887, 1901–03), which he designed[5] (figs. 2, 3). Timothy's death in 1909 brought Wright's uncle, the distinguished Unitarian minister Jenkin Lloyd Jones, from Chicago to officiate at the funeral. In his eulogy, he hailed "[t]he humble stone mason, . . . who allowed no stone, however humble, to remain out of plumb, or any line uncorrected by his experienced eye; the modest craftsman, who in humblest garb, the work-a-day clothes of a laborer, walked in and out among you here, a sage and a saint; a man who, though skilled as a workman, was more loved and noted for the clearness of his mind and the kindness of his heart."[6]

Nearly fifty years later, Wright continued to honor Timothy, "the old Welsh stonemason," for teaching him the technique of "dry wall footings" (shallow foundations resting on a bed of gravel prepared to drain water and thus

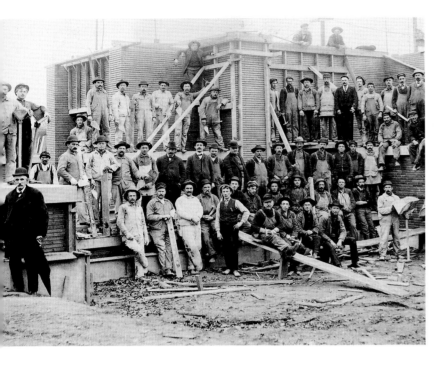

Figure 1
Darwin D. Martin House, Buffalo, New York, 1902–04,
construction crew, ca. 1904.
Courtesy University Archives,
State University of New York at Buffalo

Figure 2
Hillside Home School, Spring Green, Wisconsin, 1901–03.
Detail of pier at entrance, masonry by David Timothy. At the
corners of this pier and of the exterior walls, the otherwise
roughly dressed stone is finished with a smooth face, creating
a sharp edge that casts a crisp shadow in the sunlight.
Photo by author

Figure 3
Hillside Home School, Spring Green, Wisconsin, 1901–03.
Entrance, masonry by David Timothy.
Photo by author

prevent movement during freeze and thaw cycles) that he employed on a variety of buildings throughout his career.[7]

When the nineteen-year-old Wright left Wisconsin for Chicago in 1887 to begin his career in architecture, he worked briefly in the office of Joseph Lyman Silsbee, who had designed the family chapel, before moving on to the firm of Adler & Sullivan, where he remained for nearly six years as Louis Sullivan's assistant before starting his own practice in 1893. At Adler & Sullivan, in particular, Wright encountered a form of architectural practice unlike the intimate, artisanal culture of the Helena Valley.[8] The complexity of the firm's commercial and civic buildings and the rapid pace of construction required a hierarchal and increasingly specialized organization of architects, consulting engineers, and contractors. In realizing the Auditorium Building, the Chicago project under way when Wright arrived, the point man for coordinating the web of contractors (there was no general contractor) was Dankmar Adler's assistant, Paul Mueller. Three years older than Wright, Mueller had immigrated to Chicago from Germany in 1881 with some technical education in engineering and had worked with a variety of firms involved with the design and erection of steel structures before joining Adler & Sullivan about 1886.[9]

Mueller and Wright quickly developed a friendship and confidence in each other's professional abilities that continued beyond their years at Adler & Sullivan. While Wright's residential commissions did not require the specialized skills of Mueller on staff, Wright turned to him as the general contractor or project manager for his more complex commissions, beginning with the Larkin Company Administration Building in Buffalo (1902–06) and including Unity Temple in the Chicago suburb of Oak Park (1905–08), Midway Gardens in Chicago (1913–14), and the Imperial Hotel in Tokyo (1912–22). Wright valued Mueller's instinctive ability to grasp his intentions and find ways of realizing them within the constraints of contemporary building practice and celebrated Mueller's contributions in his account of Unity Temple in the *Autobiography*: "Now Paul Mueller comes to the rescue, reads the scheme like easy print. Will build it for only a little over their appropriation—and does it [fig. 4]. He takes it easily along for nearly a year but he does it. Doesn't lose much on it in the end. [Wright's rosy recollection overlooked Mueller's bankruptcy after the building's completion.] It is exciting to him to rescue ideas, to participate in creation. And together we overcame difficulty after difficulty in the field, where an architect's education is never finished."[10] Following Mueller's death in 1934, Wright sought to forge similar relationships with others, notably William Wesley Peters, who exercised his architecture and engineering skills within the Taliesin Fellowship, and engineer Mendel Glickman and contractor Ben Wiltscheck, who, like Mueller, served as outside consultants.[11]

Wright's studio in the Chicago suburb of Oak Park had an ambience markedly different from that of the Adler & Sullivan office in the tower of the Auditorium Building. The studio's physical arrangement as an extension of his home embodied ideals of the Arts and Crafts movement regarding total design and the blurring of the boundaries between

Figure 4
Unity Temple, Oak Park, Illinois, 1905–08. Construction photo, 1907. As a cost-saving measure, Wright and Paul Mueller planned the design of the building to minimize the quantity and variety of the formwork for the concrete walls, which can be expensive to fabricate. This view shows how the forms were reset as the construction progressed upward.
The Frank Lloyd Wright Foundation
FLLW FDN # 0611.0054

Figure 5
Frank Lloyd Wright Studio, Oak Park, Illinois, 1897. Chair and vases by Wright, sculpture by Richard Bock.
The Frank Lloyd Wright Foundation
FLLW FDN # 9506.0015

personal life and work (fig. 5). The occasional presence of other artists such as the sculptor Richard W. Bock may be seen as a step toward achieving another Arts and Crafts ideal—that of the seamless interactions among designers, craftsmen, and manufacturers, which Wright had affirmed in his 1901 lecture, "The Art and Craft of the Machine." Although the setting was unusual, the studio's organizational structure in the first years of the twentieth century would have been familiar to clients and contractors.[12] Wright had surrounded himself with skilled and inventive associates. Among them were Walter Burley Griffin, who managed the office, and Marion Mahony, both of whom had professional degrees in architecture, and William Drummond, who, like Griffin, was a registered architect. A number of other men and women were employed as draftsmen. In principle, the studio was well staffed to handle design development and construction supervision for multiple commissions, but Wright compromised this promise by his casual regard of deadlines and inconsistency in delegating responsibility. The result inspired William Martin to remark to his brother, Darwin, in 1904, "Certainly if Wright's *plans* [italics original] appear to be 'queer,' his business methods are more so."[13] A year later, Darwin admonished Wright, "Be punctual. Though the heavens fall be punctual. Delays of months running into years are killing."[14]

Wright needed capable assistants to practice on the scale to which he aspired yet relinquished control reluctantly and was suspicious of his employees' loyalties when they took independent action. By the time Griffin left the firm in 1906 to strike out on his own, Wright had come to think of his practice less in terms of a principal and associates than as a master and apprentices. In 1908, he wrote of the studio as "our little university" populated by young people, "in every case almost wholly unformed . . . patiently nursed for years in the atmosphere of the work itself."[15] At the time, the statement was more aspiration than fact, but it was a vision that he would maintain and eventually realize with the creation of the Taliesin Fellowship in 1932.

In the fall of 1909, Wright closed the studio, abandoned his family, and departed for Europe with Mamah Borthwick Cheney and no clear plans for the future. When he returned a year later, he struggled to rebuild his practice. His decision to anchor his life on ancestral land in the Helena Valley, Wisconsin, while developing a client base in Chicago required two offices, one in the city and the other within his new home, Taliesin. His staff varied according to the work at hand and sometimes was no more than a single assistant. A few of his draftsmen had worked in the Oak Park studio, but he mostly looked beyond "the old guard" in an effort to start fresh rather than resume what he had put aside.[16]

Wright's efforts to explore different ways of working emerge clearly in two projects of the 1910s, Taliesin and the American System-Built Houses. At Taliesin, Wright returned to the world of the artisan and surrounded himself with a community of dedicated workers—the spiritual descendents of David Timothy (fig. 6). Recounting the experience in

Figure 6
Taliesin I, Spring Green, Wisconsin, 1911,
construction crew, ca. 1911.
Special Collections Dept., J. Willard Marriott Library,
University of Utah

Figure 7
Taliesin I, Spring Green, Wisconsin, 1911,
workroom, ca. 1911. The view of the fireplace and
built-in shelving captures the character of the carpentry
and stone masonry throughout Taliesin I.
Special Collections Dept., J. Willard Marriott Library,
University of Utah

Figure 8
American System-Built House, Model C-3, 1915–17,
ground-floor plan.
The Frank Lloyd Wright Foundation
FLLW FDN # 1082.001

the *Autobiography*, he recalled them by name: Ben Davis, "the creative cusser"; William Weston, "a carpenter such as architects like to stand and watch work"; and Billie Little, who had built houses for him in Oak Park. Wright particularly singled out the stonemasons, Father Larson ("the old Norse"), Dad Signola, and Philip Volk: "Country masons laid all the stone with the stone quarry for a pattern and the architect for a teacher. The masons learned to lay the wall in the long, thin, flat ledges natural to the quarry, natural edges out. As often as they would lay a stone they would stand back to judge the effect. They were soon as interested as sculptors fashioning a statue; indeed, one might imagine they were sculptors as they stepped back, head cocked to one side, to get the general effect."[17] The relatively slow pace of work and Wright's familiarity with his workforce allowed him to improvise, and the buildings of Taliesin, in their original form and as we know them today, reflect an intricate history of design changes and the labor of many hands.[18] The resolution of details and the quality of the workmanship range from rough to elegant, but the overall concept governing the choice of materials and their use absorbs accidental and deliberate variation into the whole (fig. 7).

As Taliesin took its initial shape, burned in the tragic fire of 1914, and was rebuilt, Wright also devoted attention to a project that aimed to eliminate improvisation and restrict the builder's role to the strict execution of instructions that could be followed without close supervision by the architect. The American System-Built Houses were a venture in partnership with Arthur L. Richards, a Milwaukee, Wisconsin, real estate developer, who had been a client of Wright's since 1911. Its gestation appears to have been longer than its two-year formal existence from 1915 to 1917, but during this brief period Wright produced designs for approximately three dozen residences.[19]

The premise of the American System-Built Houses was to offer middle-class home buyers the opportunity to build customized homes with guarantees of price and quality. Working with a licensed dealer/contractor, the customer would select a base scheme and adapt it by choosing among a set of modular variations that allowed flexibility in plan, orientation, and roof configurations (fig. 8). Building components, including precut lumber, doors, and windows would be sent to the jobsite from a mill and warehouse in Milwaukee. The business plan had much in common with other mail-order-house enterprises of the time, including the well-known Modern Homes of Sears, Roebuck and Co., but an important difference is the modularity of Wright's system (for which he planned 138 types), which offered a degree of customization unmatched by the competition.

The American System-Built Houses were an opportunity for Wright to reach a large audience throughout the Midwest (if not the nation) without locking his practice into the time-consuming management of small, individual commissions. They also allowed him to control the quality of building materials at the point of supply and the quality of craftsmanship through standardized production of components at the mill and construction in the field by certified builders. With this system Wright placed his faith in a process of production rather than in the individual judgment of a master builder.

Despite a much-publicized launch, Wright abruptly broke off his partnership with Richards in 1917. It is difficult to say if the company would have survived had he continued, but if he did abandon this venture prematurely, he did not relinquish his efforts to develop new approaches to house building. Prefabrication would continue to intrigue him, and in 1954 after other unrealized efforts over the years, he joined forces with a young Wisconsin builder named Marshall Erdman to offer a family of house designs that were to be built using precut and prefabricated components.[20]

The concrete block houses Wright built in and around Los Angeles, California, in the 1920s were another

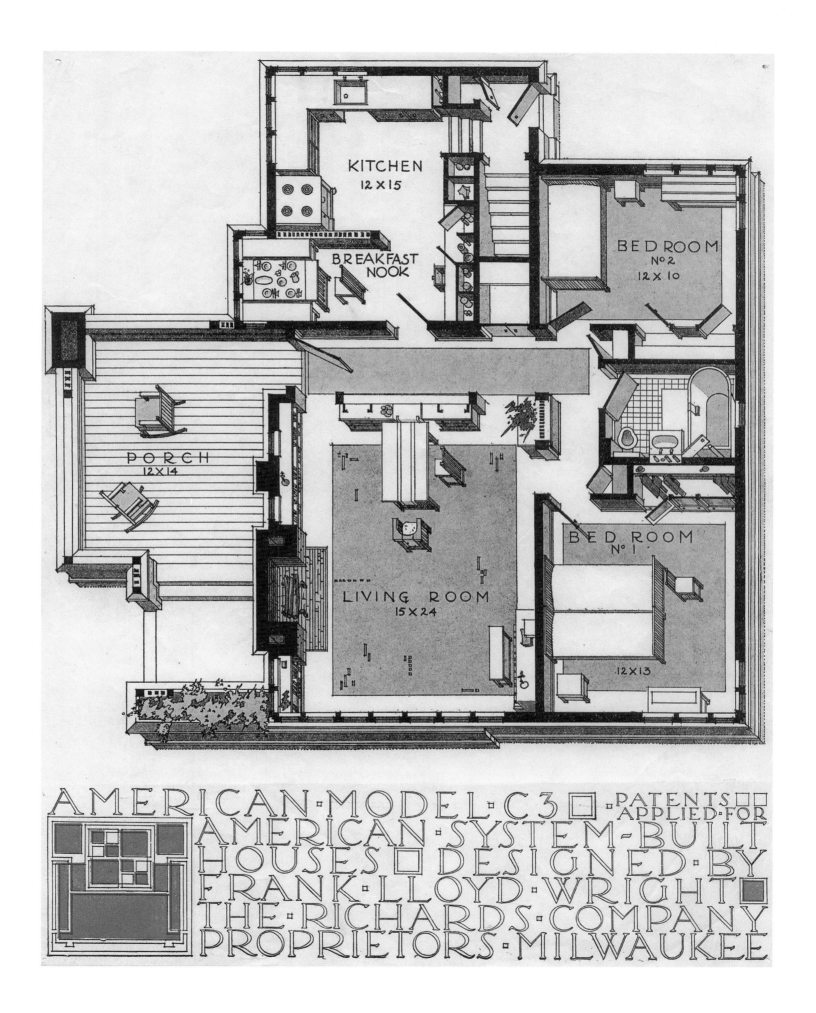

KITCHEN
12 X 15

BREAKFAST
NOOK

BED ROOM
Nº 2
12 X 10

PORCH
12 X 14

LIVING ROOM
15 X 24

BED ROOM
Nº 1
12 X 13

AMERICAN·MODEL·C3□·PATENTS□□
APPLIED·FOR
AMERICAN·SYSTEM-BUILT
HOUSES□·DESIGNED·BY
FRANK·LLOYD·WRIGHT□
THE·RICHARDS·COMPANY
PROPRIETORS·MILWAUKEE

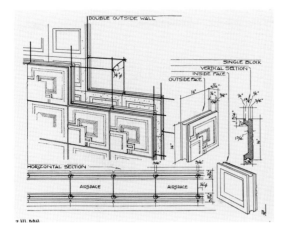

Figure 9
Textile Block Construction, 1921. Wright's "textile block" system of
construction, so named because of the way he perceived the
concrete blocks and steel reinforcement as being woven together.
The Frank Lloyd Wright Foundation
FLLW FDN # 2111.004

Figure 10
John Storer House, Hollywood, California, 1923. Construction photo
dated 13 May 1924. Wright built four concrete-block houses in the
Los Angeles area. All were under construction in 1924. This view of
the Storer House shows the stacks of concrete blocks, fabricated
on-site, awaiting assembly.
Frank Lloyd Wright Foundation
FLLW FDN # 2304.0010

Figure 11
Frank Lloyd Wright at Taliesin with apprentices Lee Kawahara
and Peter Mathews, ca. 1949. At Taliesin and Taliesin West, Wright
was able to minimize the gap between design and construction by
communicating his intentions directly to his corps of apprentices
attuned to his principles.
Photo by Lois Davidson Gottlieb

radical departure from normative building practice. Unlike the layered construction of the American System-Built Houses, which had a conventional wood frame clad with exterior and interior finish materials, their patterned concrete blocks served as both structure and finish (fig. 9).[21] Wright's descriptions of his "textile block" system are vivid, and there is a romantic dimension to the work of assembling the house with blocks formed from aggregate excavated from the site and woven into walls with bars of steel reinforcement. But the diagrams belie the system's complexity. The construction of the Samuel and Harriet Freeman House, for instance, required seventy-six block types and nearly 10,000 blocks manufactured on-site with hand tools (for a similar example, see fig. 10). Myriad details had to be resolved in their positioning, reinforcement, and weather sealing.[22]

As prototypes rather than a mature system, the California houses demanded Wright's close attention in the production of construction documents and construction, but marital, financial, and professional challenges distracted him. In contrast to the business plan for the American System-Built Houses which prescribed a carefully controlled path from standardized design through centralized distribution of materials to construction by designated builders, the management of the concrete block houses was improvised. Robert Sweeney's account of their history notes how Wright's indecision about anchoring his practice in Los Angeles or Taliesin complicated the design process of these unique commissions by limiting his ability to meet with clients and spreading the preparation of working drawings between southern California and the Midwest. In addition, the logic of the textile block system, perfectly clear in Wright's own mind, was not readily embraced by local contractors. Wright sought to nurture expertise by encouraging the contractor of the Alice Millard House (La Miniatura), a Pasadena builder named A. C. Parlee, to undertake subsequent commissions, but the relationship ended badly with finger-pointing and lawsuits.[23] Wright's son, Lloyd, a landscape architect and architect who had preceded him in California, bore the brunt of mediating his father's vision and the circumstances of the jobsite. He even served as the contractor for the John Storer and Freeman houses, but the task was far from easy. Besides the inherent tensions of being Wright's son and trying to develop his own practice, Lloyd had limited authority for exercising his judgment and was subject to second-guessing by his father.

Reflecting on the experience in 1927, Wright acknowledged, "None of the advantages which the system was designed to have were had in the construction of these models. We had no organization," but the problems had not diminished his confidence.[24] He continued to refine the system and in the 1950s applied it to modest houses intended for young families. "Here then," he wrote in 1954, "within moderate means for the free man of our democracy, with some intelligence and by his own energy, comes a natural house designed in accordance with the principles of

Figure 12
Apprentice Alfred Bush nailing redwood fascia
boards on a roof at Taliesin West, early 1940s.
Photo © 2009 Pedro E. Guerrero

Figure 13
Masons splitting sandstone boulders into building
stone for the construction of Kentuck Knob,
(I. N. Hagan House), Chalk Hill, Pennsylvania, 1953.
Photo by I. N. Hagan

organic architecture."[25] In Wright's mind the textile block system allowed a GI and his family to realize the romantic ideal of the self-sufficient farmer-builder and to build for themselves a fully modern house. With the role of contractors reduced to providing specialized skills, the family became the willing hands of the architect, whose aesthetic intentions were embedded in the system of construction. Wright did not limit his encouragement of client-builders to home owners. For the first buildings of Florida Southern College (begun 1938), students using the textile block system did much of the work, and the congregation of the Unitarian Meeting House (1945–51) in Shorewood Hills, a suburb of Madison, Wisconsin, assisted contractor Marshall Erdman by providing labor on designated workdays.[26]

The formation of the Taliesin Fellowship in 1932 realized the "little university" of young people that Wright had described twenty-four years earlier (fig. 11). The apprentices' education included the hard manual farm labor he had experienced in his youth as well as the ongoing construction of Taliesin, where they absorbed the lessons and work ethic of country builders, such as the mason Charlie Curtis, who instructed his charges, "Boys, get the feel of the rock in your hands or it 'taint no use."[27] In 1938, the Fellowship added the construction of Taliesin West near Scottsdale, Arizona, to its program of work (fig. 12). Like their Wisconsin counterparts, the buildings of Taliesin West tell the story of their making through the variations evident in the distinctive masonry of "desert rubble stone," as Wright called it, and the rough-sawn timber framing.

Wright intended the apprentices' work at Taliesin and Taliesin West as training for future assignments as his representative on jobsites. The ambition was straightforward, but he approached it in a number of different ways in his residential commissions.[28] When dispatched as clerks of the works, the apprentices typically received a stipend from Wright and room and board from the clients. In the absence of a general contractor, they assisted the clients in the selection and coordination of subcontractors as well as monitored the quality of work. During the Fellowship's early years, they had little collective experience to draw on and faced steep learning curves. Such was the case of Edgar Tafel and Bob Mosher, both of whom were in their mid-twenties when Wright sent them to oversee the construction of Fallingwater, cantilevered over a mountain stream in western Pennsylvania. Their hard work and absolute loyalty to his principles offset their inexperience.

Among the critical tasks of supervision at Fallingwater and other commissions utilizing stone masonry was coaching the masons in Wright's preferred style of setting stone. His insistence on laying it in accordance with its natural bedding could be specified in construction documents, but the character-giving selection and placement of individual stones in rhythmic courses required firsthand communication. As in the construction of Taliesin, Wright wanted the masons to feel their work with the pride of "sculptors fashioning a statue" and exercise their own creativity within the general patterns of his architectural scheme. The importance of this lesson was such that the only direct supervision in the construction of Kentuck Knob (I. N. Hagan House, 1953–56) was when apprentice Allen (Davy) Davison approved the use of sandstone boulders as a source for building stone (they were split into pieces that could be

Figure 14
Master mason Jess Wilson and assistants laying the inner
face of the cavity wall in the master bedroom of Kentuck Knob
(I. N. Hagan House), Chalk Hill, Pennsylvania, 1955. The red
tidewater cypress framing would contain the windows and
support the roof.
Photo by I. N. Hagan

coursed) and watched over the masons' first efforts to erect a wall (figs. 13, 14).[29]

The Usonian houses Wright designed from the mid-1930s to the end of his life included innovative constructional systems, such as thinly layered wood walls with exterior and interior finishes that could be prefabricated in a shop (rarely done) or built on-site, and unusual, spatially exciting geometries. The unconventional requirements made it difficult to estimate costs, especially labor, and many contractors shied away from clients approaching with a set of Wright's drawings in hand. Anxious to demonstrate the feasibility of his schemes, he went to great lengths to help clients realize them. For the John C. Pew House in Shorewood Hills, Wisconsin (1938–39), he designated apprentice (and son-in-law) William Wesley Peters, who had an independent income, as general contractor. In an interview nearly fifty years later, Peters described how he and another apprentice, Cary Caraway, did their best to meet the Pews' $6,700 budget (equivalent to about $100,000 in today's dollars) by using recycled materials, employing a small crew, and doing much of the work themselves. Despite such efforts, he recalled losing approximately $1,100 on the commission.[30]

Paul R. and Jean S. Hanna acted as their own general contractor for the construction of their house in Palo Alto, California (1935–37).[31] They enlisted the aid of cabinetmaker and builder Harold Turner, who advised them on hiring and the coordination of trades. Seeking to develop a corps of contractors familiar with the design of Usonian houses, Wright invited Turner to Taliesin for immersion in the spirit and practices of the Fellowship. The construction of the house required ongoing and sometimes trying communication between Palo Alto and Taliesin, but all parties emerged from the process with ample goodwill. Turner, as Wright had hoped, went on to serve as adviser or contractor for over a half-dozen other Usonian houses.[32]

Wright celebrated the success of the Taliesin Fellowship and his progress in bringing builders like Harold Turner into the fold in the second edition of the *Autobiography*. "But the time when we can thus build our own buildings, milling our own materials," he acknowledged, "is not yet."[33] Until that moment arrived, he understood he had to assuage contractors' fears that they would lose their shirts on his buildings. This was the subtext of the confident gaze of builder Jim De Reus looking out from the pages of the February 1959 issue of *House & Home* magazine, a publication for home builders analogous to today's *Fine Homebuilding* (fig. 15).[34] Having built two Wright houses in Oskaloosa, Iowa, De Reus assured his fellow contractors that he hadn't lost money on the commissions. He observed that while his crew had to devote extra time when handling materials that doubled as structure and finish, the attention to detail invigorated them. He concluded, "I think every one of us is a better workman today because of this house."[35] De Reus was a not a country builder like "twinkling-eyed, bewhiskered," David Timothy. He was a modern businessman with a payroll to meet and clients demanding homes with the latest improvements. But the old Welsh mason would have appreciated the spirit of his words, as did Wright, who died four months after their publication.

Today, most of the memories of those who had a hand in realizing Wright's buildings must be recounted by others, and many of their stories have been lost. Yet his architecture allows us to glimpse traces of their hands in the rhythm of masonry, the joinery of woodwork, and the detail of screwheads in common alignment. All speak to Wright's lifelong belief in the dignity of labor as an expression of human intention.

Figure 15
Contractor Jim De Reus and crew in front of the Carroll Alsop House,
Oskaloosa, Iowa, 1947. In the caption, De Reus states, "The crew and
I are proud of this Frank Lloyd Wright house. Here we are on the gravel
court leading up to the entrance. That's me in front. Behind me, from
left to right: three masons, tender, concrete finisher, driver, apprentice,
and three carpenters."
Photo by Hedrich-Blessing
Chicago History Museum

NOTES

1. Frank Lloyd Wright to Darwin D. Martin, 21 November 1905. Quoted in Jack Quinan, *Frank Lloyd Wright's Martin House: Architecture as Portraiture* (Princeton, NJ: Princeton Architectural Press, 2004), p. 144.

2. Frank Lloyd Wright, *An Autobiography* (New York: Duell, Sloan and Pierce, 1943), p. 7.

3. John Ruskin, *The Seven Lamps of Architecture* (1849; New York: Noonday Press, 1961), p. 12.

4. Maginel Wright Barney, *The Valley of the God-Almighty Joneses* (New York: Appleton-Century, 1965).

5. Wright, *Autobiography*, 388.

6. Frances Nemtin, *Web of Life* (Nemtin, 2001), pp. 4–5.

7. Frank Lloyd Wright, *The Natural House* (1954; New York: New American Library, 1970), p. 141.

8. Before his move to Chicago, Wright had gained some experience in an office environment when he worked as a draftsman in Madison for the engineer Alan Conover during his brief time as a student at the University of Wisconsin. Mary Jane Hamilton with Anne E. Biebel and John O. Holzheuter, "Frank Lloyd Wright's Madison Networks," in Paul E. Sprague, ed., *Frank Lloyd Wright and Madison: Eight Decades of Artistic and Social Interaction* (Madison: Elvehjem Museum of Art, University of Wisconsin, 1990), p. 2.

9. For a perceptive study of Mueller and his working relationship with Wright, see Andrew Saint, *Architect and Engineer: A Study in Sibling Rivalry* (New Haven, CT: Yale University Press, 2007), pp. 249–57.

10. Wright, *Autobiography*, p. 159.

11. Saint, *Architect and Engineer*, p. 257. Peters, whom Wright referred to as his "right bower," played a central role in the realization of buildings Wright designed from the 1930s to the end of his life. Over the same span, Mendel Glickman advised Wright on specific engineering issues. Ben Wiltscheck was the contractor for the Johnson Wax buildings, Wingspread, and the Community Church in Kansas City, Missouri. Wright's account of his relationship with Wiltscheck echoes his description of the relationship he had had with Mueller, "There was real cooperation, confidence in each other's ability all around, and all the time." Wright, *Autobiography*, p. 470.

12. Paul Kruty traces the evolution of Wright's organization of the studio in "At Work in the Oak Park Studio," *Arris: Journal of the Southeast Chapter of the Society of Architectural Historians* 14 (2003): 17–31.

13. William Martin to Darwin D. Martin, 20 May 1904, quoted in Quinan, *Martin House*, p. 88.

14. Darwin D. Martin to Frank Lloyd Wright, 26 December 1905, quoted in Quinan, *Martin House,* pp. 150–51.

15. Frank Lloyd Wright, "In the Cause of Architecture" (1908; reprinted in *Frank Lloyd Wright: Collected Writings, Vol. 1: 1894–1930*, Bruce Brooks Pfeiffer, ed. (New York: Rizzoli and the Frank Lloyd Wright Foundation, 1992), p. 98.

16. Anthony Alofsin examines Wright's efforts to rebuild his practice in *Frank Lloyd Wright—The Lost Years, 1910–1922: A Study of Influence* (Chicago: University of Chicago Press, 1993), pp. 67–72. He quotes Wright's letter to Taylor Woolley of 22 April 1911, mentioning the "old guard," p. 68. In addition, see Paul Kruty, *Frank Lloyd Wright and Midway Gardens* (Urbana: University of Illinois Press, 1998), pp. 19–21.

17. Wright, *Autobiography*, p. 171.

18. I thank Carol Johnson and Keiran Murphy of Taliesin Preservation, Inc. for sharing their knowledge of Taliesin's construction history.

19. For the American System-Built Houses, see Kenneth Martin Kao, "Frank Lloyd Wright: Experiments in the Art of Building," *Modulus* 22 (1993): 79–90.

20. For Wright's collaboration with Marshall Erdman, see Paul E. Sprague, "The Marshall Erdman Prefabricated Buildings," in Sprague, ed., *Frank Lloyd Wright and Madison*, pp. 151–67.

21. See Robert Sweeney, *Wright in Hollywood: Visions of a New Architecture* (Cambridge, MA: MIT Press, 1994).

22. A fine-grain history of the Freeman House is forthcoming from Jeffrey Chusid.

23. Wright to A. N. Rebori, 15 September 1927, quoted in Sweeney, *Wright in Hollywood*, p. 118.

24. Sweeney, *Wright in Hollywood*, p. 118.

25. Wright, *Natural House*, p. 208. He called these houses "Usonian Automatics."

26. See Joseph M. Siry, "Frank Lloyd Wright's Annie M. Pfeiffer Chapel for Florida Southern College: Modernist Theology and Regional Architecture," *Journal of the Society of Architectural Historians* 63, no. 4 (December 2004): 505–06, 515–16; Mary Jane Hamilton, "The Unitarian Meeting House," in Sprague, ed., *Frank Lloyd Wright and Madison*, pp. 181–82.

27. Nemtin, *Web of Life*, p. 21.

28. John Sergeant, *Frank Lloyd Wright's Usonian Houses: The Case for an Organic Architecture* (New York: Whitney Library of Design, 1976), pp. 121ff.

29. Bernadine Hagan, *Kentuck Knob: Frank Lloyd Wright's House for I. N. and Bernadine Hagan* (Pittsburgh, PA: Local History Co., 2005), pp. 17–18, 22.

30. William Wesley Peters interviewed by Greg Williams, 29 November 1989, Frank Lloyd Wright Archives. Peters also served as general contractor for the Theodore Baird House in Amherst, Massachusetts.

31. Paul R. and Jean S. Hanna, *Frank Lloyd Wright's Hanna House: The Clients' Report*, 2nd ed. (Carbondale, IL: Southern Illinois University Press, 1987).

32. Following his experience with the Hannas, Turner had responsibility for the construction of the Rebhuhn, Suntop, Winkler-Goetsch, Christie, Affleck, and Wall houses.

33. Wright, *Autobiography*, p. 450.

34. "Builder Jim De Reus Tells You: 'What We Learned from Frank Lloyd Wright,'" *House & Home*, 15, no. 2 (February 1959): 126–33.

35. De Reus, *House & Home*, 126.

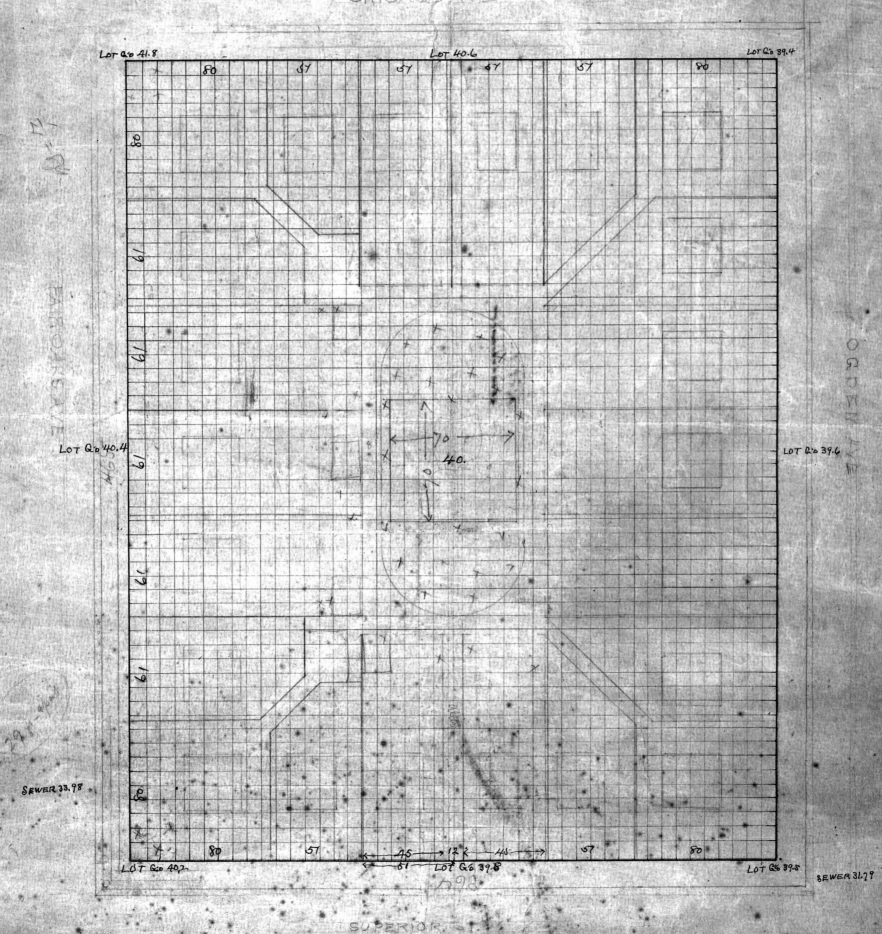

SEWER 31.04

EST. G'd 42·7

EST. G'd 40.

SEWER 30.23

CHICAGO AVE

LOT G'd 41.8   LOT 40.6   LOT G'd 39.4

80   57   57   57   57   80

80

61

61

LOT G'd 40.4   61   70   40.   LOT G'd 39.6

61

61

SEWER 33.98

80

80   57   45   12   45   57   80
LOT G'd 40.2   61   LOT G'd 39.8   LOT G'd 39.5

SEWER 36.79

SUPERIOR ST

Making Community Out of the Grid

WRIGHT'S QUADRUPLE BLOCK PLAN AND THE ORIGIN OF THE PRAIRIE HOUSE

NEIL LEVINE

Roberts Block (project),
Ridgeland (later annexed by Oak Park), Illinois, 1896.
The Frank Lloyd Wright Foundation
FLLW FDN # 9705.006

Frank Lloyd Wright has generally been thought of primarily as an architect of the single-family suburban house whose interest in planning for the greater community only dates from his proposal of the 1930s for the decentralized, automobile-based Broadacre City. This essay challenges that point of view. It treats what is arguably Wright's most important contribution to the history of early modern architecture, the revolutionary Prairie House he developed between the turn-of-the-twentieth century and the beginning of World War I. It shows that the idea of the Prairie House did not originate in a self-reflexive formal investigation of the domestic type but began with an investigation of a larger social concept for community planning consistent with the egalitarian framework of the American gridiron that defines the Chicago landscape. Finally, it argues that the architect's ideas for the social aspects of community planning did not start with Broadacre City but go back to his earliest work.

At the source of the problem lie two common misconceptions, namely, that (1) the house Wright designed for the Willits family in 1902 and completed the following year in Highland Park, a suburb north of Chicago, was the architect's first Prairie House (figs. 1, 2) and (2) whatever site planning may have been involved in this and other similar houses owed its aesthetic to the Picturesque tradition exemplified in late nineteenth-century America by Frederick Law Olmsted and, in particular, his design with Calvert Vaux for the relatively nearby suburb of Riverside (1868–69; fig. 3).[1] It is true that the Willits House typifies the Prairie House—with its emphatic horizontal lines, overhanging eaves, interpenetrating forms, central chimney mass, and, especially, its pinwheeling plan that provides a new type of dynamic interior space appearing to flow uninterruptedly from the inside out—and thus echoes the extensiveness of the Midwestern prairie. More to the point, the pivoting, centralized focus of the plan is ordinarily read as an index of the autonomous character of the design as well as the process whereby it came into being. Freestanding, independent, the center and source of its own spatial energies, the Willits House appears to have been developed from formal imperatives rooted solely in the design of the individual house itself.

Historians have pointed to a series of earlier designs by the architect to locate the seeds of this development and thus reinforce the sense of an autonomous, internal formal evolution of the domestic type. Usually this genealogy begins with the house the architect designed for himself in 1889 and completed the following year in Oak Park, the suburb west of Chicago where Wright eventually established his office (figs. 4, 5). The Frank Lloyd Wright Home and Studio, as it is now called, predicts certain aspects of the Willits House in its deployment of a central fireplace core to act as a fulcrum for the spaces that may be said to pivot around it and open to the outdoors. More important, the freewheeling, somewhat rustic and casual character of this design substantiates the second common misconception of Wright's early suburban architecture, which is its dependence on the aesthetic of the Picturesque. While this may represent an accurate reading of the pre–Prairie Style houses, it certainly is not true of the mature Prairie House nor of the site planning such later houses involved.

Riverside, which is just three miles southwest of Oak Park, would have shown Wright exactly how the Picturesque aesthetic affected not just the design of individual houses but how such houses were to be grouped together to form an ensemble (fig. 3). The suburb was planned with winding streets, broad expanses of lawn, and open green spaces to create an image of a rural landscape made domestic. Instead of lining up side by side in regimented rows and facing one another directly across orthogonally laid-out streets, the single-family houses follow a more seemingly naturalis-

Figure 1
Willits House, Highland Park, Illinois, 1902–03,
exterior (before March 1908).
Photo by Henry Fuermann
Private Collection

Figure 2
Willits House, ground-floor plan (redrawn ca. 1940).
Published in Henry-Russell Hitchcock, *In the Nature of Materials:
The Buildings of Frank Lloyd Wright, 1887–1941*, 1942

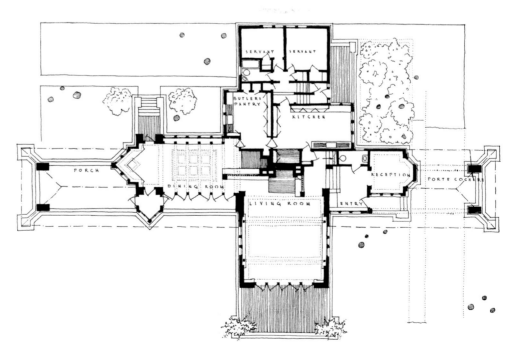

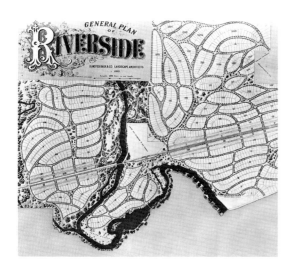

Figure 3
Frederick Law Olmsted and Calvert Vaux,
Riverside, Illinois, 1868–69, master plan.
Courtesy of the National Park Service,
Frederick Law Olmsted National Historic Site

Figure 4
Frank Lloyd Wright House, Oak Park, Illinois, 1889–90,
exterior (before 1896).
Private Collection

Figure 5
Frank Lloyd Wright House, Oak Park, Illinois, 1889–90,
ground-floor plan (as of 1890).
Published in Henry-Russell Hitchcock, *In the Nature of Materials:
The Buildings of Frank Lloyd Wright, 1887–1941*, 1942

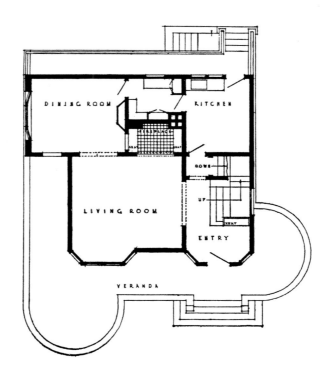

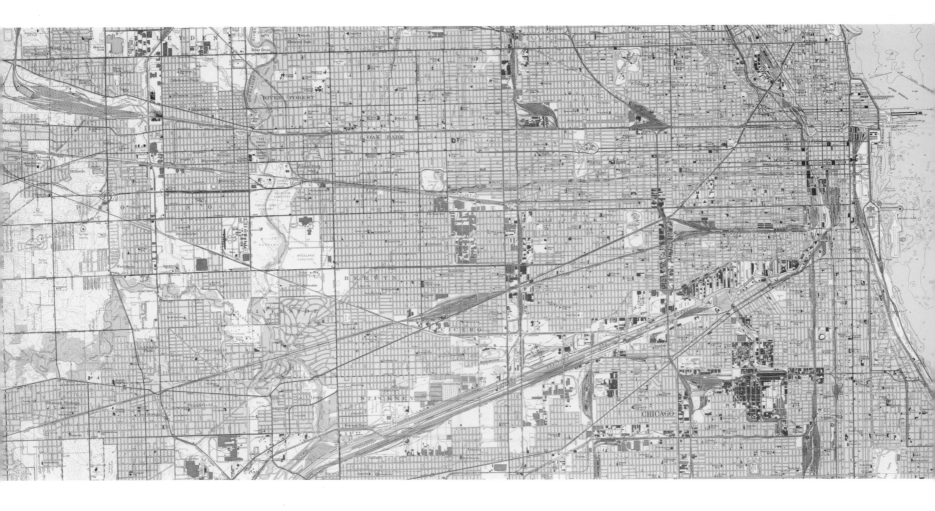

Figure 6
Chicago Loop and Western Suburbs. Map of Chicago and Vicinity,
Ill.-Ind., Sheet No. 2 of 3 (Chicago Loop), 1953, detail. Riverside is in
lower-left-hand corner.
United States Department of the Interior Geological Survey.
Map Collection, Pusey Library, Harvard University

tic pattern, allowing for multiple and varying vistas as well as for a critical degree of isolation and self-containment.
For Olmsted, this "naturalism" and distinctiveness represented an escape from the hard and cold commercialism of
the urban core, which was characterized in his view, and most particularly in the case of Chicago, by a relentless,
monotonous, and mechanical grid. In contrast to "the ordinary directness of line in town-streets, with its resultant
regularity of plan, . . . suggest[ing] eagerness to press forward, without looking to the right or the left," Olmsted,
in his "Preliminary Report upon the Proposed Suburban Village at Riverside" recommended "the general adoption,
in the design of your roads, of gracefully-curved lines, generous spaces, and the absence of sharp corners, the idea
being to suggest and imply leisure, contemplativeness and happy tranquility." Moreover, "[t]he general plan of such
a suburb," he continued, should "be not only informal, but . . . positively picturesque, and when contrasted with
the constantly repeated right angles, straight lines, and flat surfaces which characterize our large modern towns,
thoroughly refreshing."[2]

For all its importance in the history of American architecture and planning, Riverside remained an anomaly in
the suburban development of Chicago and, most significantly for us, a cipher for Wright. Completely at odds with the
metropolitan grid that extends out from the Loop to the north, south, and west, the Riverside experiment was never
replicated within the inner ring of suburbs and remains to this day entirely uncharacteristic of the area and its prairie
environment (fig. 6). Laid out on a grid in 1830, Chicago followed the orthogonal pattern imposed on the western
territories of the new United States by the rectangular land survey system instituted between 1785 and 1796. The
accurate surveying and evenhanded distribution of land mandated by the survey have been interpreted as a fundamental basis for the democratic institutions of citizenship and community self-government, creating an environment
of transparency and egalitarianism that the urban historian André Corboz has gone so far as to characterize as
"utopian."[3] As the Chicago suburbs expanded into the surrounding prairie in the late nineteenth century, the
Enlightenment grid governed their formation. Wright fully understood the value and significance of the grid in

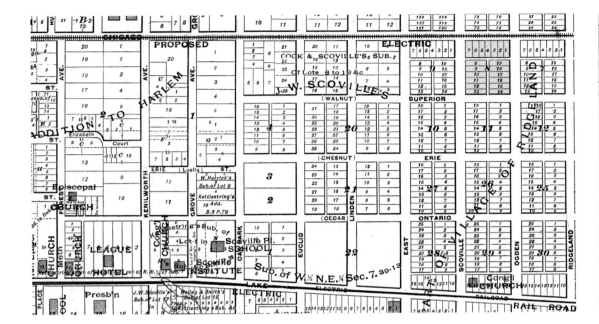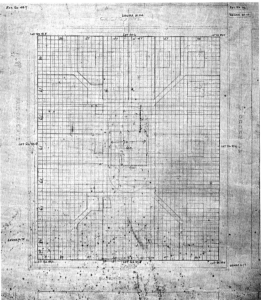

Figure 7
Plat map showing Ridgeland (later annexed by Oak Park),
Illinois, 1894. Roberts block indicated in yellow.

Figure 8
Roberts Block (project),
Ridgeland (later annexed by Oak Park), Illinois, 1896.
The Frank Lloyd Wright Foundation
FLLW FDN # 9705.006

building community. Despite the fact that he eventually designed two houses for Riverside, he never took its plan as a model. Indeed, he rejected it in favor of the very "right angles, straight lines, and flat surfaces" Olmsted saw as so uninspiring and uninteresting.

FIRST ROBERTS MASTER PLAN, 1896

Wright's earliest effort at providing a residential architecture suitable to the individual needs and community aspirations of his suburban clients precedes his design of the Prairie House by a few years and sets the stage for its creation out of the conditions established by the grid. In 1896 the architect's friend, neighbor, and fellow Unitarian Charles E. Roberts commissioned of Wright a development plan for an entire block, seven blocks to the east of Wright's own Oak Park house (fig. 7).[4] The little-known site plan, preserved in the Wright Archives, is quite startling (fig. 8). It provides a unique insight into how the architect approached the problem of group design at this very early stage in his career—as well as the germ of the idea for the first Prairie House.[5]

In what is the earliest known use by the architect of graph paper, the lot lines and building footprints are lightly sketched in pencil over a grid drawn in red ink to indicate the 8-foot squares and in black to indicate the outside border of the property lines.[6] Wright commonly employed a "unit system of design" by the early 1900s, but the underlying grid was rarely revealed.[7] Nor did it have the same function as in the Roberts block master plan. In the later examples, the module was based on the width of the casement window and was an internal device for creating a consistent and integrated structural/proportional system. Rather than serving as an abstract compositional tool to control the design and ultimately the construction of an individual building, the grid in the Roberts master plan materially defines the terrain of a community of houses. It echoes the preexisting grid that governs the system of subdivision of the suburb as a whole and thus makes it clear that Wright conceived the Roberts project in terms of the larger social network of the metropolitan area.

The innovative aspect of Wright's master plan lies in the way it manipulates the grid to provide both a community focus as well as a more lucrative investment potential for the developer. Instead of the nineteen building lots shown platted on the 1894 map, Wright's plan offered twenty-two. Moreover, whereas all the lots in the existing plat were equal in width and oriented toward Chicago Avenue, which resulted in a T-shaped alley system, Wright's project is arranged in a more evenhanded manner around a central community space. How novel this was may be understood by recalling that English Garden City ideas of the same sort did not make their appearance until the middle of the following decade.[8] The central garden court in the Roberts plan is a little over 100 feet wide by 200 feet long. Delineated as an oval, it forms a generous public space at the same time as it provides access to stables and/or garden sheds. The characteristic and often-maligned alley is reduced to a narrow passage leading into the court from Superior Street on the south.

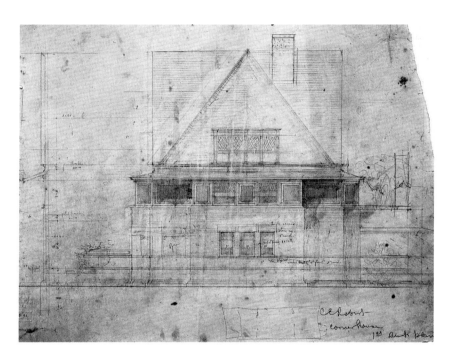

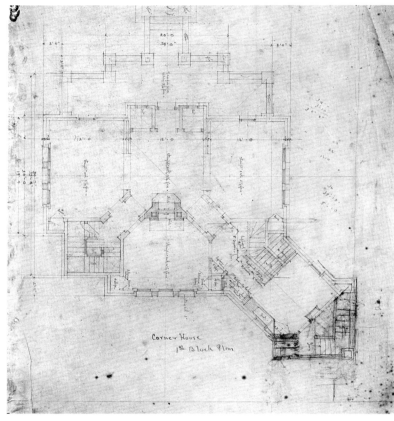

Figure 9
Roberts Block (project), Ridgeland (later annexed by Oak Park),
Illinois, 1896, Corner House, elevation.
The Frank Lloyd Wright Foundation
FLLW FDN # 9705.001

Figure 10
Roberts Block (project), Ridgeland (later annexed by Oak Park),
Illinois, 1896, Corner House, ground floor plan.
The Frank Lloyd Wright Foundation
FLLW FDN # 9705.002

The actual house designs for the Roberts development are not particularly noteworthy. There are drawings for six of them, and all are extremely modest in size.[9] Only the four corner houses have any intrinsic interest, and that has to do with the special emphasis placed on the corners of the site by the master plan (figs. 9, 10). The square corner houses elaborate on the design of Wright's own (corner) house (fig. 4). The Roberts corner houses are the most ample of the twenty-two proposed as well as the most spatially complicated in plan. In addition to features like a full-width porch and two-sided central fireplace, they have angled kitchens and service stairs that link them by means of diagonal pathways to the central oval. The explicit connection to the center from the corners is, indeed, what gives the master plan its special interest—and relevance to Wright's work to come.

The community space of the oval is defined in its center by a square, 70 feet to a side, which echoes the square corner lots. The master plan can thus be read, first, as breaking down the city grid into the smaller square units of the graph paper on which it is drawn and, then, building up from those units a modular organization that privileges the corners and equates them with the center. Wright clearly was intrigued by the larger pattern that could be visualized from this and soon began thinking about how to resubdivide the rectangular grid of the city into an ideal, square

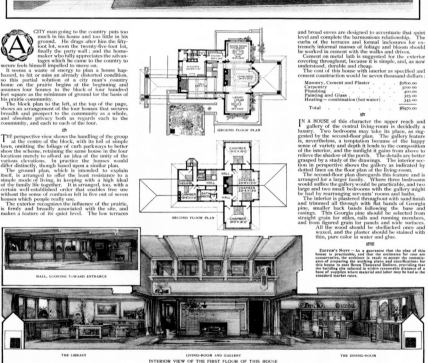

Figure 11
"A Home in a Prairie Town,"
Ladies' Home Journal, February 1901.

scheme where only corner lots exist and the center becomes the point of communal tangency. The type plan he called the "quadruple block plan" done for the *Ladies' Home Journal* four years later represents the first outcome of this thinking. It also marks the first appearance of the Prairie House.

THE QUADRUPLE BLOCK PLAN AND *LADIES' HOME JOURNAL*, "A HOME IN A PRAIRIE TOWN," 1900–01

Wright saw an opportunity to develop the potential of the Roberts block plan when he was asked by the *Ladies' Home Journal* to contribute to the "New Series of Model Suburban Houses which Can be Built at Moderate Cost" the magazine was planning to publish beginning with its October 1900 issue. Of the fourteen contributions that appeared between then and January 1902, Wright's "A Home in a Prairie Town," published in February 1901, was the only one to expand the commission beyond the scope of a single house into a design for a group of houses forming a community (fig. 11). Aside from a second design Wright contributed to the July 1901 issue, it was also the only

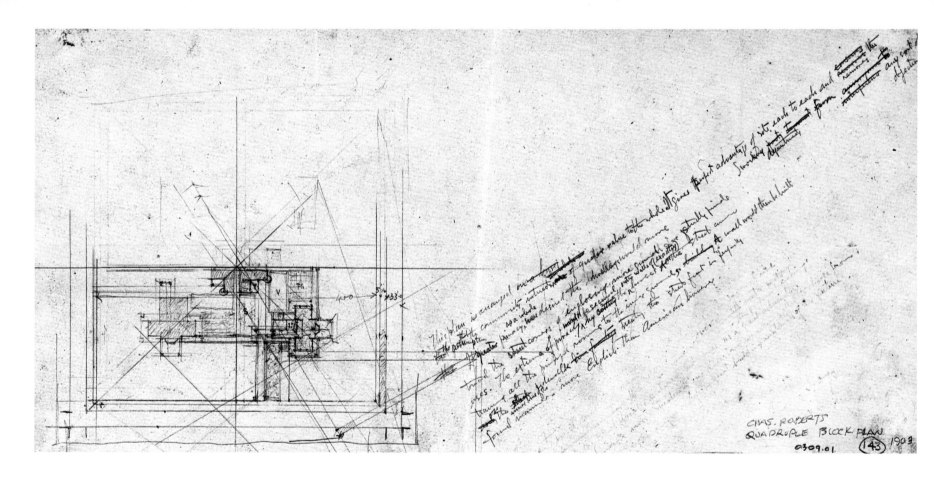

CHAS. ROBERTS
QUADRUPLE BLOCK PLAN
0309.01 (143) 1903

Figure 12
"A Home in a Prairie Town,"
Ladies' Home Journal, February 1901,
detail of quadruple block plan and perspective.

Figure 13
Roberts Quadruple Block Plan (project),
1900, sketch plan.
The Frank Lloyd Wright Foundation
FLLW FDN # 0309.001

one explicitly to rely on and instrumentalize the grid in its conception.[10]

Despite the priority usually accorded the Willits House, the "Home in a Prairie Town" has often been viewed as the architect's initial outline of the Prairie House, manifesting all the characteristic features of extended horizontal lines, interpenetrating volumes, a focal freestanding fireplace, and an intimate connection with the suburban Chicago site.[11] But all that takes on greater significance when one realizes that Wright did not think of or present the house as an autonomous object. Set in a box at the top of the page, above the title and main body of the article, are the plan and perspective of four identical houses forming what Wright called here for the first time—and clearly labeled—the "quadruple block plan" (fig. 12).[12]

Wright's text reinforces the primary aspect of the group design and the fundamental importance of community vis-à-vis the individual. It begins with a discussion of the overall scheme as a pretext and justification for the design of the four separate houses. After noting in the first sentence how "a city man going to the country puts too much in his house and too little in his ground," the second paragraph begins by stating that "it seems a waste of energy to plan a house haphazard, to hit or miss an already distorted condition." Wright then makes his key point, which is that "this *partial* solution of a city man's home on the prairie begins at the beginning and assumes four houses to the block of four hundred feet square as the minimum of ground for the basis of his prairie community." He goes on to explain that "the block plan . . . at the top of the page . . . shows an arrangement of the four houses that secures breadth and prospect to the community as a whole and absolute privacy both as regards each to the community and each to each of the four."[13]

The preliminary sketch plan for the house grouping (fig. 13) manifestly illustrates the pinwheeling concept underlying the design and offers compelling evidence that Wright arrived at this rotational concept at least two years before the Willits commission and, most important, as a direct consequence of considering the design of the single house in terms of the overall framework of the grid.[14] The drawing (often misdated to 1903 owing to Wright's own later annotation in the lower right-hand corner) allows us to see clearly the degree to which the cross-axial composition of each house, and the rotational pinwheeling that relates each to the others, are congruent with and fundamentally derived from the orthogonal framework of the square block.

The generous 4-acre site was initially quartered to create four 1-acre corner lots, each having two 200-foot frontages. Each house is centered on a point equidistant from the sidewalks and interior property lines. The sidewalks thus establish a crucial datum concentric with the surrounding streets and integral to the coherence of the four separate residences. The cross-axial disposition of the intersecting wings of each house restates this outer boundary as a broadly defined interior square. As can be more fully seen in the published perspective of the group, this internal block-within-a-block is demarcated by low parapet walls that extend from the outer reentrant angles of the wings of one house to those of the next. And at the very center of this heavily treed compound is a final square, divided into pinwheeling quadrants forming stables reached by driveways that parallel the four houses' entrance walks. The pinwheeling of the houses ensures each one an exclusive street entrance as well as privacy in its exposure to the central garden.

On an abstract level, the quadruple block plan is all about framing and quartering, center and periphery, nucleus and edge. If we focus on the resultant pinwheeling, the plan reads, as might be expected, from the inside out. But when we focus on the underlying and predominant quartering and framing, we are forced to read the plan from the periphery to the center, which is precisely how Wright pictured it in the perspective. There, the purpose and meaning of the project become clear. Each concentric square denotes a degree of movement inward from the public to the private/communal. The sidewalks frame an expanse of lawn that foregrounds the group of houses whose shared walls in turn frame an inner compound fully visible only to the inhabitants. In providing a sense of shared community through the creation of a common rear garden, the inner court's dense foliage also helps to screen one neighbor from the next while masking the back-to-back stables.[15]

There is no evidence of Picturesque planning here. The street plat is not only fully acknowledged; it is reified in the enclosed central garden. The individual house and the community plan are dependent on one another, and both in turn, or rather from the beginning, were dependent on the metropolitan grid and its reinstantiation in the design process. The Prairie House took its cross-axial, elongated, and space-defining form from its origin in this larger social project.

ADAPTATION OF THE QUADRUPLE BLOCK PLAN TO THE ROBERTS BLOCK, 1903
Five months after the publication of "A Home in a Prairie Town," a project by Wright to construct a "colony" or "community" in Oak Park consisting of two blocks of four houses each based on the quadruple block plan was announced in both Chicago and Oak Park newspapers.[16] Little else is known about this venture, or whether Charles Roberts was behind it. In any case, Roberts gave Wright the go-ahead two years later, to redesign the block for which he had done the 1896 master plan. Adapting the quadruple block plan to the site in 1903, Wright labeled the design a "Community

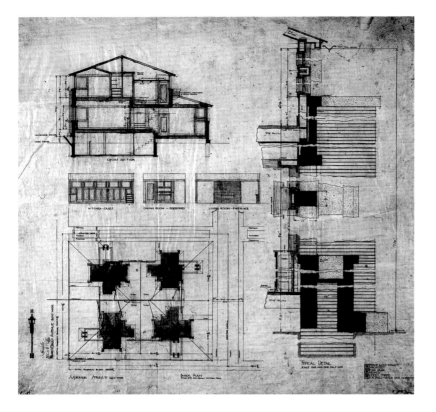

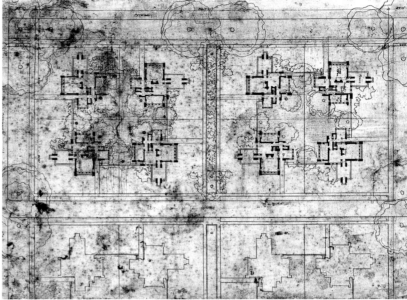

Figure 14
Roberts Block (project), "C. E. Roberts Community Project
for Twenty-Four Dwellings", Oak Park, Illinois, 1903,
partial block plan, sections, interior elevations, and structural details.
The Frank Lloyd Wright Foundation
FLLW FDN # 0309.013

Figure 15
Roberts Block (project), Oak Park, Illinois, 1903,
half-block plan, redrawn and idealized, ca. 1903.
FLLW FDN # 0309.020

Project" (fig. 14). No doubt sensing a determination on his client's part to see the project through this time, Wright produced a set of presentation drawings done in ink on backed linen detailed down to a thirty-second of an inch.[17]

By the time Roberts asked Wright for this revised master plan, development in Oak Park was rapidly moving east, and Chicago Avenue was becoming a crucial artery. Street paving, sidewalks, and streetlights for the area were all voted in 1902–03. (It is interesting to note that the north orientation device in the lower left-hand corner of figure 14 looks distinctly like an early streetlamp.) No doubt in response to the pressure for development, Wright exploited the quadruple block plan concept to increase the number of houses on Roberts's property from the twenty-two he had earlier proposed to twenty-four (in fact, four more than were eventually built after 1906 when Roberts sold off his holdings).

A partial plan of four houses was included on one of the presentation drawings, while a slightly later, idealized plan of the upper, or northern, half of the block shows twelve of the twenty-four houses (figs. 14, 15).[18] In comparison with the *Ladies' Home Journal* design, each individual house lot was reduced from nearly an acre to a little more than a sixth of an acre, and the stables in the center of the earlier group were eliminated. Moreover, since the houses themselves were larger on average, as well as more numerous, than those in the 1896 plan, the greater ratio of built to open space made it necessary to consider in detail the relationship between public and private/communal space and the means of access from one to the other.

The individual houses, all identical and to be built of brick, represent Wright's most advanced thinking to date in terms of the disaggregation and abstraction of architectural elements (fig. 16). They predict, in this regard, the Martin House and Larkin Building in Buffalo, both of which were completed by 1906 based on designs worked out in 1904.[19] But more than simply updating the form of the standardized Prairie House unit, Wright was mainly concerned with how the grouped houses would relate to one another in such a tight situation and, especially, how pedestrian and vehicular circulation would work. The pinwheeling was meant to take care of privacy issues and sight lines.

To give each group of four houses a sense of interconnectedness and seclusion from the public way while at the same time maintaining a continuity with the metropolitan grid, the level of the interior gardens, defined by the parapet wall connecting each of the four houses to the others, was depressed below grade. (This can be seen in the upper left and lower right elevations.) And to provide for circulation, Wright broke the block down into six miniblocks separated from one another either by pedestrian ways called "esplanades" or by vehicular passages called "courts." Instead of a single multipurpose alley, there was now a finer mesh of different types of passageways offering both greater openness as well as a sense of scale more attuned to the size of the residential units themselves.

The finished presentation drawings, as noted, show only one of the six groups of four houses (fig. 14). The house lots are oblong with the longer dimension paralleling the shorter side of the block. A 36-foot-wide "court" bisects the block in a north-south direction, while two 18-foot-wide "esplanades" planted with flower beds intersect the "court" at

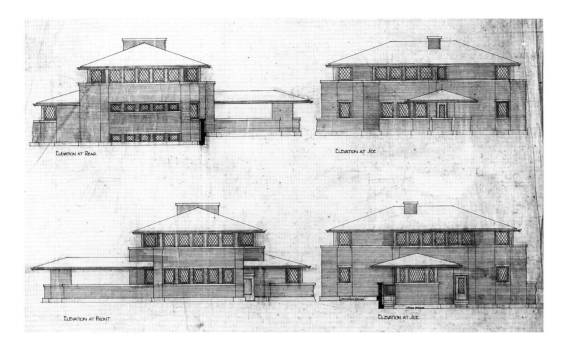

Figure 16 (top left)
Roberts Block (project), Oak Park, Illinois, 1903.
The Frank Lloyd Wright Foundation
FLLW FDN # 0309.012

Figure 17 (top right)
Roberts Block (project), Oak Park, Illinois, as built out in
1906–10. Aerial photograph, 2003: Chicago Avenue at top;
Elmwood (formerly Ogden) Street on right; Superior Street on
bottom; and Scoville (formerly Fair Oaks) Avenue on left.
Courtesy of Oak Park Village

Figure 18 (bottom)
Roberts Block (project), Oak Park, Illinois, 1903,
sketch perspective.
The Frank Lloyd Wright Foundation
FLLW FDN # 0309.018

third points of the block.[20] Because of the radically unconventional character of the design, it is not easy to form a picture of how the community would have been experienced or even what it actually might have looked like. One of the perspectives Wright drew for his client enables us to do so, especially when we compare it with an aerial photograph of the block as built out after Roberts disposed of it (figs. 17, 18).

The existing houses, constructed mainly between 1906 and 1910, are extremely close together (some no more than 12 feet apart) and exclusively oriented to the street. They turn their backs on one another and their sides to one another as well as to the two main cross streets. The unidimensional, linear pattern of facades explicitly denies the bidimensional character of the street grid. And the leftover spaces behind the houses, made up of deep yards butting up against an alley, reinforce the uniform aspect of the street condition as a facade. Wright's quadruple block plan, by contrast, activates the entire space of the block in full recognition of the two-dimensional qualities of the grid in plan as well as its three-dimensional qualities as a latticework in space (figs. 15, 18). It is nonhierarchical, evenly textured, and dynamic in its overall organization. Houses, gardens, and streets are interwoven in a pattern that moves through a graduated sequence of scales from the public to the private/communal, allowing the one to interpenetrate the other and to define the idea of "community" in dialectical terms—as a grouping of interconnected houses and as a subdivision of the underlying grid.

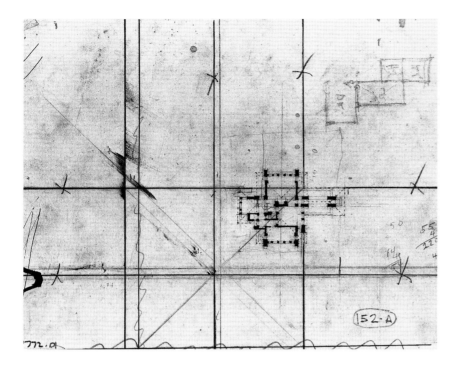

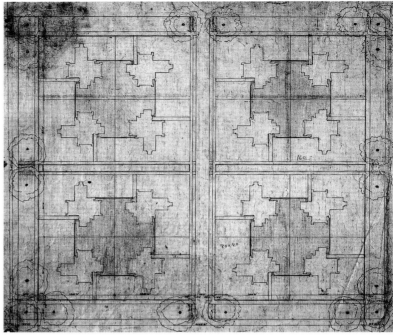

Figure 19
Expanded Roberts Block (project),
Oak Park, Illinois, 1903, house template
for different-size blocks.
The Frank Lloyd Wright Foundation
FLLW FDN # 0019.009

Figure 20
Expanded Roberts Block (project),
Oak Park, Illinois, 1903, plan for sixteen
houses on 435-foot-long block.
The Frank Lloyd Wright Foundation
FLLW FDN # 0309.002

WRIGHT'S PROLIFERATION OF THE QUADRUPLE BLOCK PLAN

Roberts called a halt to the second iteration of the project either late in 1903 or early the following year. Whether the result of a further commission from his client or his own obsession with the resubdivision of the grid based on the quadruple block plan, Wright continued to work on the idea and developed multiple versions of the Roberts design for different-size blocks and varying numbers of houses. The idealized half-block plan illustrated in figure 15 was part of this sequence. No doubt unhappy with the oblong shape of the house lots as originally proposed, Wright had his office draft a plan of twelve houses with the lots squared up as much as possible and rotated 90 degrees.[21] In so doing, the "esplanade" became the north-south passage reserved exclusively for pedestrians, and the two east-west "courts" became private streets. Placing the narrower circulation path on the north-south axis and limiting it to pedestrian movement served to distinguish it from the typically divisive central alley and thus give the block as a whole a greater sense of coherence. By contrast, the wider "courts" cutting through from east to west and providing access for vehicles and pedestrians worked to break down the scale of the block and ensure a greater degree of porousness within and without.[22]

There are nine other surviving plans directly related to the idealized 1903 Roberts project.[23] The entire group of drawings was done by the same hand (or hands), on exactly the same kind of backed linen, and with the same inks and watercolors as were utilized for the commissioned design. More important, all the drawings made use of a small house plan template as a means to standardize the design process (fig. 19).[24] And despite the variation in the length of the blocks studied, all were approximately the same width as the one Roberts owned.[25]

One of the plans is for a 435-foot-long block containing sixteen houses in four groups (fig. 20); two are for a thirty-two-house development on a block 685 feet long; and four are also for a thirty-two-house development but on a 750-foot-long block. In the most finished drawing of the last group, the house lots are nearly square and the courts run in the short direction, as they do in the idealized Roberts half-block plan (fig. 21). The houses at one end are rendered at ground-floor level, whereas those at the other are drawn at roof level. Only the latter have garages or stables. In order to provide access to two of the houses, the pedestrian esplanade dividing the block down its length was interrupted and replaced by a narrow mews. The standardization of the house type remained absolute, however, as no porte cocheres were added to these eight structures.

The standardization of the Prairie House design in these plans for the proliferation of the Roberts block project and the house unit's replication by means of a template make it abundantly clear that Wright was more interested in questions of spatial relationships at the larger scale of the community than he was in those of the individual house per se.[26]

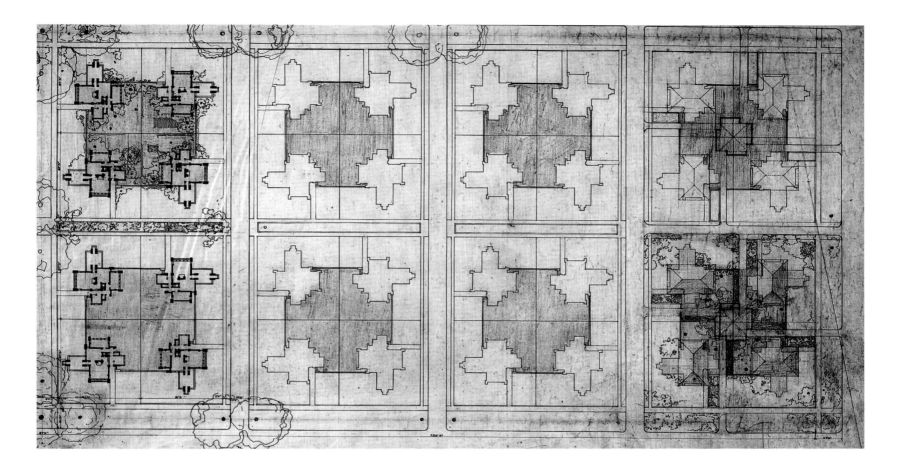

Figure 21
Expanded Roberts Block (project),
Oak Park, Illinois, 1903, plan for thirty-two
houses on 750-foot-long block.
The Frank Lloyd Wright Foundation
FLLW FDN # 0309.003

As in the "Home in a Prairie Town," the grouping of houses essentially preceded the design of the house itself. That is not to say that the development of the Prairie House type was an insignificant factor for him. But it must always be borne in mind that the quadruple block plan served as the matrix for these formal developments from the beginning and that its geometry, as a sign of community, became for the architect the generative framework for the ideal resub-division of the metropolitan Chicago grid. And although Wright never got the chance to build any community like those described, each of his characteristic Prairie Houses bears some trace of its origins in the concept of the quadruple block plan.

ACKNOWLEDGMENTS

This essay is indebted to Bruce Brooks Pfeiffer, Oskar Muñoz, and Margo Stipe of the Frank Lloyd Wright Archives for their unstinting willingness to allow me access to drawings and other primary materials. I am especially thankful to Pfeiffer for taking the time to look at many of the drawings with me and to offer his invaluable insights. I am also grateful to William Jerousek, Michael Koperniak, Frank Lipo, Sandra Sokol, John Thorpe, and Fred Zinke for their help on material specifically related to Oak Park. The text grew out of a talk first delivered at the symposium "Paris-Chicago circa 1850–1900: Parallels Morphological and Conceptual" held in Chicago and Oak Park in September 2000. Many of my ideas owe much to discussions with David Van Zanten, the organizer of the symposium. Expanded, the text forms the first part of a book, tentatively entitled The Urbanism of Frank Lloyd Wright, which I am in the process of completing.

NOTES

1. I intentionally use the word "common" to qualify the word "misconception" regarding the Willits House as the first Prairie House. The matter is more complicated. The Willits House has fundamentally been seen as the "first" (a) because it was built and (b) because it was generally thought to have been begun in 1901 and not 1902. Henry-Russell Hitchcock, in his *In the Nature of Materials: The Buildings of Frank Lloyd Wright, 1887-1941* (1942; rpr., New York: Da Capo Press, 1975), pp. 33-34, pointed to the project for "A Home in a Prairie Town," discussed later in this essay, as the "first Prairie house." Wright, several years earlier than Hitchcock, referred to the 1893-94 Winslow House in River Forest, Illinois, as "the first 'prairie house'" in his "Recollections: United States, 1893-1920," *Architects' Journal* 84 (16 July 1936): 78 and (30 July 1936): 142. For the place of the Bradley and Thomas houses in this chronology, see note 12 below.

2. Olmsted, Vaux & Co., "Preliminary Report upon the Proposed Suburban Village at Riverside, near Chicago, by Olmsted, Vaux & Co. Landscape Architects," 1 September 1868, in *The Papers of Frederick Law Olmsted*, ed. David Schuyler and Jane Turner Censer, vol. 6, *The Years of Olmsted, Vaux & Company, 1865-1874* (Baltimore and London: Johns Hopkins University Press, 1992), pp. 280, 286-87.

3. André Corboz, "Les Dimensions culturelles de la grille territoriale américaine," in *Le Territoire comme palimpseste et autres essais*, ed. Sébastien Marot (Besançon, France: Editions de l'Imprimeur, 2001), pp. 172-84. Other recent interpretations of the grid countering the earlier idea of its barrenness, monotony, and dullness include Andro Linklater, *Measuring America: How an Untamed Wilderness Shaped the United States and Fulfilled the Promise of Democracy* (New York: Walker, 2002); and Dell Upton, *Another City: Urban Life and Urban Spaces in the New American Republic* (New Haven and London: Yale University Press, 2008), esp. pp. 113-79.

4. The block, which was in the Village of Ridgeland until that was annexed by Oak Park in 1902, is bounded by Chicago Avenue on the north, Fair Oaks (later renamed Scoville) on the west, Superior on the south, and Ogden (later renamed Elmwood) on the east. The dimensions, indicated as 465 by 364 feet, refer to the outside property lines and exclude everything from the sidewalk to the street curb. Roberts began acquiring the block in 1889 and completed the package by 1895, the year streetcar service to downtown was initiated on Chicago Avenue. Recorder of Deeds Office, Cook County, Chicago, IL. I thank Heidi Galles for providing me with this information. Wright's house is on the corner of Chicago and Forest avenues (see fig. 7).

5. Though an extreme case, this drawing is typical of many of those discussed in this essay in being either previously unpublished or almost unknown. In addition, many of the drawings in the Wright Archives were, in the past, misdated and/or misidentified, therefore causing confusion in the rather scarce scholarly literature on the subject. Aside from my own "*The Quadruple Block Plan*: l'obsession de Frank Lloyd Wright pour la grille/The Quadruple Block Plan and Frank Lloyd Wright's Obsession with the Grid," *EaV: La revue de l'école nationale supérieure d'architecture de Versailles/Versailles Architecture School Journal* 11 (2005/2006): 64-68, there has only been passing reference to this project in the literature, and that only since the 1980s and often marked by errors.

6. It is unclear whether the idea of using gridded paper was Wright's. The lot and sewer numbers in ink are not in his hand, but all the pencil indications, including the house footprints, street names, internal passageways, and dimensions of the central area are by the architect or one of his staff.

7. The drawings for the two Gerts summer cottages in Whitehall, Michigan (1902), where the grid lines are also red, are an exception. The grid lines in the plans of the Martin House, Buffalo (1902-06), Unity Temple, Oak Park (1905-08), and the Coonley House, Riverside (1906-09) in the January 1928 *Architectural Record* were added for the publication. An often quoted letter of 1904 from Charles E. White, Jr., one of the draftsmen in Wright's studio (and Charles E. Roberts's son-in-law), notes that "all. . .[Wright's] plans are composed of units grouped in a symmetrical and systematic way," adding that this use of the "unit system" was, in his view, "Wright's greatest contribution to Architecture." Charles E. White, Jr., to Walter Willcox, 13 May 1904, in "Letters, 1903-1906, by Charles E. White, Jr. from the Studio of Frank Lloyd Wright," ed. Nancy K. Morris Smith, *Journal of Architectural Education* 25 (Fall 1971): 105. White began working for Wright in 1904.

8. One is tempted to think of the design as a transformation into suburban terms of the typical Anglo-American urban square of the eighteenth and early nineteenth centuries.

9. The six house designs were meant to serve as models. Of the six, three are labeled on the drawings as "House 1," "House 2," and "House 4," and one as a "Corner House." Numbers 1 and 2 are dated 16 January and 20 January 1896, respectively. Although none of the other drawings are dated, there is no reason to think that they are much later. There is no evidence to support the dating by the Frank Lloyd Wright Archives of the Corner House and master plan to 1897, nor for the assumption that they are for a different project.

10. Wright was the only architect represented by two designs. His "A Small House with 'Lots of Room in It'" appeared in the July 1901 issue of the magazine. Among the other contributors were Ralph Adams Cram, Wilson Eyre, Elmer Grey, Milton Medary, and Bruce Price.

11. The word "town" typically referred at the time to a suburban rather than rural community. As pointed out in note 1 above, it was Henry-Russell Hitchcock, in his *In the Nature of Materials*, who originally referred to the "Home in a Prairie Town" as the prototype for the Prairie House. However, it is unclear whether the drawings for the "Home in a Prairie Town" precede or follow the Bradley and Hickox houses in Kankakee, Illinois, both of which were designed in June 1900 and represent the first built manifestations of the concept. The Thomas House in Oak Park, which was built in 1901, is a close adaptation of the main facade of "A Home in a Prairie Town." The tight site did not allow for the full use of the plan.

12. The most relevant secondary sources for this and other projects based on the quadruple block plan are the following: David P. Handlin, *The American Home: Architecture and Society, 1815-1915* (Boston and Toronto: Little, Brown, 1979), pp. 141-66, 158-66; Gwendolyn Wright, *Moralism and the Model Home: Domestic Architecture and Cultural Conflict in Chicago, 1873-1913* (Chicago and London: University of Chicago Press, 1980), pp. 132-49, 280-94; D. P. Handlin, "The Context of the Modern City," *Harvard Architecture Review* 2 (Spring 1981): 76-89; G. Wright, "Architectural Practice and Social Vision in Wright's Early Designs," in *The Nature of Frank Lloyd Wright*, ed. Carol R. Bolon, Robert S. Nelson, and Linda Seidel (Chicago and London: University of Chicago Press, 1988), pp. 98-124; Donald Leslie Johnson, "Origin of the Neighbourhood Unit," *Planning Perspectives* 17 (2002): 227-45; and D. L. Johnson, "Frank Lloyd Wright's Community Planning," *Journal of Planning History* 3 (February 2004): 12-19.

13. Frank Lloyd Wright, "A Home in a Prairie Town," *Ladies' Home Journal*, February 1901, p. 17.

14. The plan for Wright's second *Ladies' Home Journal* design, "A Small House with 'Lots of Room in It,'" developed the pinwheel idea adumbrated in "A Home in a Prairie Town" into the precise form it later took in the Willits House.

15. It appears that there were no fences dividing one backyard from another, although it is impossible to say this for sure.

16. "New Idea for Suburbs. Plan of Frank Lloyd Wright," *Chicago Evening Post*, 12 July 1901, p. 8; reprinted in *Oak Park Reporter*, 18 July 1901, p. 4.

17. Although the drawings are not dated, there is no reason to doubt the 1903 date generally given for the project. It may well have carried over into 1904. A letter from Charles White to Walter Willcox, undated though thought to be from 1904, in Smith, "Letters," p. 107, states that "Father Roberts" now "is think-

ing of going ahead with the Wright scheme of twenty [*sic*] houses on his block."

18. For the idealized half plan, see note 22 below. That plan was incorrectly published by Wright as being for the 1900–1901 "Home in a Prairie Town" in his *Ausgefürhte Bauten und Entwürfe von Frank Lloyd Wright* (Berlin: Ernst Wasmuth, 1910[–11]). In part as a result of this, its exact place in the chronology of quadruple block plan iterations has been confused in the scholarship on the subject.

19. The plan of the Martin House is literally that of "A Home in a Prairie Town," disaggregated and abstracted according to the design evolution reflected in the 1903 Roberts houses.

20. While the dimensions for the four-house grouping are correct, the overall ones for the Superior Street and Scoville Avenue frontages are reversed. In addition, the latter was initially indicated by its former name, Fair Oaks.

21. This had the effect of increasing the length of the block (to the inside of the sidewalks) from 465 to 558 feet.

22. At the very same time, the office produced an alternate version of the plan for the southern half of the block showing a very different configuration of buildings and public ways (FLW0309.019; formerly FLW0019.004). In this plan, for which Walter Burley Griffin, one of Wright's draftsmen at the time, was probably mainly responsible, the houses no longer pinwheel, nor are they centered on their lots. Instead, they are combined into pairs and brought up to the sidewalks along the east-west streets and "courts." Rather than forming self-contained compounds in the middle of each block, the groups of four form unities across the space of the private streets. Low walls linking the rear verandas of the houses run in a north-south direction to create long internal gardens that continue across the "courts" through sidewalk cuts and bedded plantings. An even more expansive lawn runs north-south down the center of the block, cut off from public access both on the south and the north by a second low wall that appears to continue around the perimeter of the entire block. Each house has a walkway entrance as well as what appears to be a driveway shared with its neighbor, which leads one to suspect that this alternate plan may have been an exercise to see how garages or stables could be accommodated on the site. Four back-to-back structures would easily fit into the walled spaces defined by the two pairs of neighboring houses, while the gardens protected by the outer walls could have served as recreation areas. There has been a certain degree of confusion on the issue of Griffin's role in Wright's suburban planning. Donald Leslie Johnson, *The Architecture of Walter Burley Griffin* (Melbourne and Sydney: Macmillan Company of Australia, 1977), p. 41, claimed that "the initial developmental work on the Quadruple Block Plans of Wright was

given to Griffin," even though Griffin only joined Wright's staff in June 1901, four months after the project was published. Following that line of thought, Charles E. Aguar and Berdeana Aguar, *Wrightscapes: Frank Lloyd Wright's Landscape Designs* (New York: McGraw-Hill, 2002), pp. 55–58, attributed *both* versions of the Roberts 1903 block design to Griffin based on a selective reading of the notes Grant Carpenter Manson took in 1940 while interviewing Marion Mahony Griffin, Walter's wife and a former Wright employee as well. What Manson actually recorded was the following: "Griffin at once showed a flair for town-planning, which incited F.L.W.'s jealous emulation—that the so-called 'Quadruple Block Plan' of F.L.W.'s was the result—but very bad, she thinks—entirely the wrong approach—the houses should not be placed toward the interior, but rather toward the exterior, of the block—and no alleys or driveways." Grant Carpenter Manson, "Records of F. L. Wright," Oak Park Library, Oak Park, IL, Card 2 recto. Writing twenty-five years earlier, Marion Mahony Griffin, "Democratic Architecture—II. Its Development, Its Principles and Its Ideals," *Building* 14 (12 August 1914): 91, stated that Wright's "first [*sic*] typical group plan" had the four houses grouped "primarily in the centres of blocks, leaving the whole of the yards to the street frontage, giving no privacy and necessitating long drives and walks for access to the houses." Seeing the impracticalities of this, Walter Burley Griffin "led to a reversal of the four house scheme, building on the corners instead of the centre of the block." I am grateful to Cammie McAtee for providing me with a transcription of Manson's interview.

23. Since only three of these, including the one described in the note above, follow the alternate Griffin scheme of organization, it can be assumed that Wright much preferred the quadruple block plan type. One of the nine is a drawing (FLW0309.006) that, instead of illustrating a composition of quadruple block plans, shows a series of street-facing conventional houses on one side of the block and a series of Wright-type houses on the other. While the purpose of this drawing has generally been interpreted as showing the superiority of the Wright-type houses to the conventional ones, I would argue that it was probably done to make the point that the actual design of the houses was insignificant as compared to the resubdivision produced by the quadruple block plan.

24. Interestingly, the template was preserved by Wright and, though never previously published, is in the Wright Archives.

25. The difference was 367 as opposed to 364 feet.

26. The template continued to be used as late as 1912–13 when, in response to a request from the City Club of Chicago's civic secretary, George Hooker, Wright produced a design for a thirty-two-block residential neighborhood based on the quadruple

block plan. Though expressly not part of the competition for the design of a Model Quarter Section organized by the club, Wright's project was exhibited in the spring of 1913 along with the other entries and published in the book documenting the competition: Alfred B[eaver] Yeomans, ed. *City Residential Land Development: Studies in Planning. Competitive Plans for Subdividing a Typical Quarter Section of Land in the Outskirts of Chicago*, Publications of the City Club of Chicago (Chicago: University of Chicago Press, December 1916), pp. 96–102.

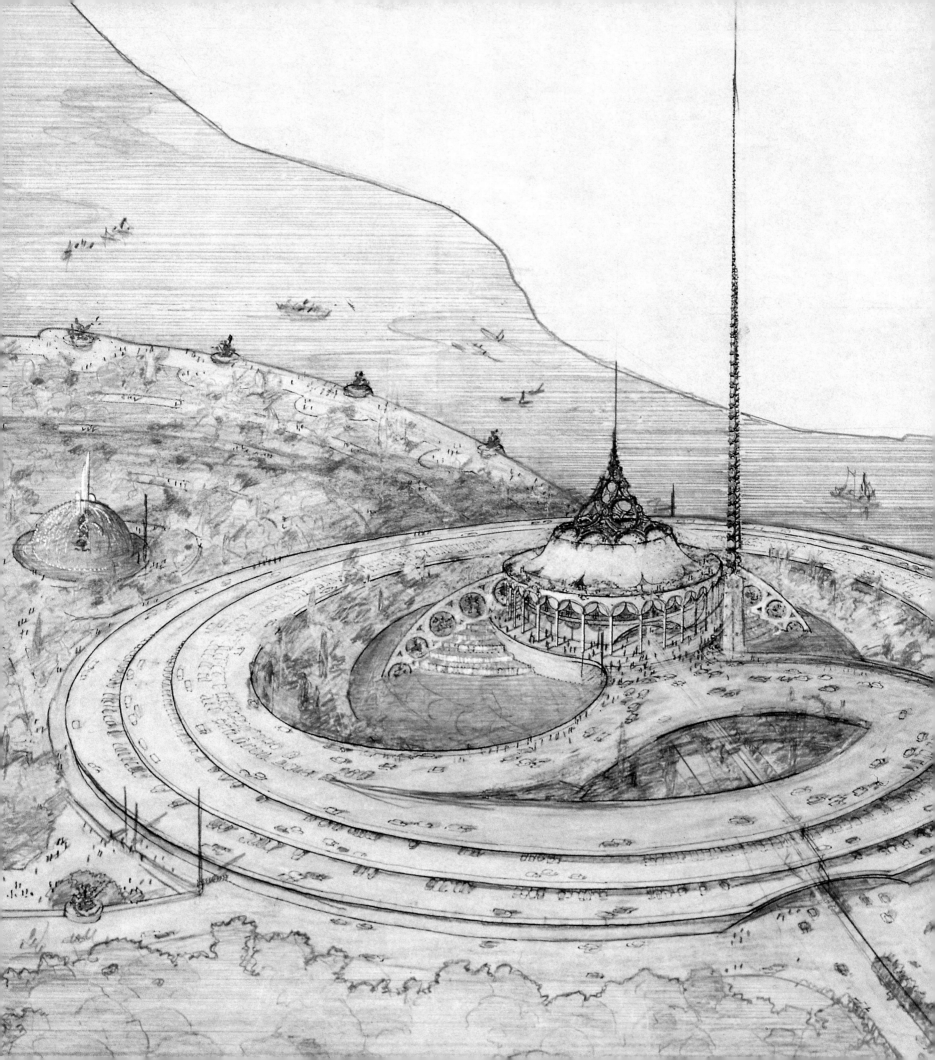

Wright in Baghdad

URBAN LIFE MORE BEAUTIFUL

MINA MAREFAT

Crescent Opera, Civic Auditorium, Garden
of Eden, Plan for Greater Baghdad (project),
Baghdad, Iraq, 1957, aerial view (detail of Figure 3),
32 1/4 x 54 1/8 inches (81.9 x 137.5 cm).
The Frank Lloyd Wright Foundation
FLLW FDN # 5733.007

In 1958, at age ninety-one, Frank Lloyd Wright publicly presented his drawings for a consummate urban center in Baghdad, Iraq. The plan for an island in the Tigris, a "Greater Baghdad Cultural Center" called Edena after the Garden of Eden, included a commissioned opera house he translated into a civic auditorium;[1] a planetarium; a landscaped park with pools, fountains, and waterfalls; buildings for ancient sculpture and contemporary art; a bazaar; a botanical garden and zoological park; a monument to the eighth-century caliph Haroun al-Rashid (Hārūn ar-Rashīd); a processional boulevard and butterfly bridge lined with merchant kiosks; a casino; an amphitheater; a heliport; radio and television towers; and a circular university campus across the river, all related in a constellation of spirals and ziggurats (fig. 1).[2] Other drawings showed a commissioned post and telegraph building for downtown Baghdad.[3]

Hardly a year after a preparatory trip to Baghdad,[4] Wright produced almost a hundred drawings, many of them 3 to 6 feet in each dimension, most rendered in color, the majority bearing evidence of his hand.[5] More eloquently than anything the voluble architect proffered about the philosophy, intentions, and achievements of his design,[6] the Baghdad drawings articulate Wright's sense of what a multivalent urban space could be. Beheld together, at full size, these drawings intimate a mature urban plan that promised to be as coherent and pathmaking as Fallingwater (1934–37) had been for domestic architecture.[7] Just as he had opened out the compartmentalized interior to reconfigure the house, the increasingly open, multifunctional plans Wright evolved in the years from Broadacre City (1930–35, unbuilt) through Crystal City (1940, unbuilt) explored progressively unconventional scenarios for harmonious urban living. Wright's culminating work in Baghdad elaborated his ideal of the spirit (that sense of interior he traced to the philosophy of Lao-Tzu)[8] in space (a continuous flow), liberating human imagination, action, and interaction.

In the Edena design is the signature of this evolved sense of urban sociability: barriers removed, forms intermingling. The corollary, of course, is continuity, the flow bringing things and people together. Over more than sixty years, Wright had embraced architectural, philosophical, and literary traditions from Asia.[9] Many influences absorbed early became part of his way of thinking about space and about the city. When he integrated the ziggurat throughout the Baghdad plan, for instance, it was as a long-pondered form addressing many challenges he had been working out since Sugarloaf in the 1920s.[10] Vincent Scully astutely characterized Wright as a "synthesizer of traditions that go deep,"[11] but, in a sense, a form such as the ziggurat synthesized Wright, animating his imagination for so long that it evolved into a unique idiom for the permeability of conventional boundaries—between West and East, past and present, the familiar and the novel, interior and exterior, and, most clearly in Baghdad and the Solomon R. Guggenheim Museum, boundaries between spaces and between persons. Wright's practice of urban design for a deep experience of community hinged on the permeability of boundaries, on a destabilizing enactment of new and multiple relations between things.

The drawings in their totality have emergent, surprising qualities. It is as if Wright intuitively grasped what Walter Benjamin called the dialectical image, in which "what has been comes together in a flash with the now to form a constellation."[12] This image is a juxtaposition, or partial superimposition, of things categorically removed from each other—past and present, West and East, familiar and novel. Dialectical images exist in tension, arresting and often disturbing, almost as a double vision. The quintessential home of the dialectical image is, of course, the modern city.[13]

For a man of Wright's sensibility, the dialectical image is not theory applied but an intuitive, affecting presence. The Baghdad drawings offer elements large and small that resonate with a visionary past recuperated into a visionary future, Eastern sensibility yoked to Western technology, cultural aims realized through practical economies of construction. Benjamin intended the dialectical image to violently disrupt modern perceptions and alter consciousness. Wright, also an avid critic of modernity, intuitively created dialectical images that suggested surprising possibilities for harmony against the disruptions of modern urbanity. While Wright engaged many ideas explored in earlier projects,

Figure 1
Plan for Greater Baghdad (project),
Baghdad, Iraq, 1957, aerial view,
34 15/16 x 52 inches (88.7 x 132.1 cm).
The Frank Lloyd Wright Foundation
FLLW FDN # 5733.008

This original rendering in colored pencil and ink on tracing vellum was
signed by Frank Lloyd Wright and dated 20 June 1957. Wright also
sent to the government of Iraq a large hand-colored photomural of this
drawing. His dedication of the design for the island in the Tigris he
called Edena paid homage to ancient sites of human civilization.
Connecting this uninhabited island (once called Pig Island) to both
shores with monumental boulevards and butterfly bridges, he created
a tourist resort island long before such visions became popular.
Although his notes on the ambitious plan exude confidence, Wright
later said, "I sort of came in on the tail end of things, so what impression
I can make now, I do not know—but I am going to try" (Taliesin
Fellowship talk, 23 June 1957, transcript, pp. 6–7).

Figure 2
Plan for Greater Baghdad (project),
Baghdad, Iraq, 1957, conceptual sketch,
36 x 71 inches (91.4 x 180.3 cm).
The Frank Lloyd Wright Foundation
FLLW FDN # 5733.037

This drawing, colored pencil on tracing vellum, confirms what many
interviewed witnesses, including John Rattenbury and Alvin Louis
Wiehle, stressed: Wright was hands-on when it came to the Baghdad
project. In fact, William Wesley Peters contemporaneously docu-
mented Wright's level of involvement: "[O]n this single sheet [Wright
himself] sketched the Opera House and Auditorium, the parking ziggurat, the Casino, the Museum, the Art Gallery, the river bridge, the
university, library, Merchant's Kiosks, Statue of Haroun Al Rashid, and a
number of smaller sketches meant as directions to his subordinates"
(Peters, video interview, 14 February 1991, Taliesin West, transcript, p. 3).

Figure 3
Crescent Opera, Civic Auditorium, Garden
of Eden, Plan for Greater Baghdad (project),
Baghdad, Iraq, 1957, aerial view,
32 1/4 x 54 1/8 inches (81.9 x 137.5 cm).
The Frank Lloyd Wright Foundation
FLLW FDN # 5733.007

This presentation drawing in colored pencil and ink on tracing vellum
was signed by Frank Lloyd Wright and dated 20 June 1957. The sepia
print of this drawing was rendered, colored, and sent to Baghdad. This
principal building commissioned to Wright by Iraq's Development
Board became the centerpiece of his vision for a cultural center he
called the Plan for Greater Baghdad. He designed the Opera with
iconography and landscaping to reinforce the symbolic, cultural significance of Islamic and pre-Islamic heritage and mythology associated
with Mesopotamia as the cradle of civilization. The dome and spire are
reminiscent of a mosque, an association Wright developed further by
orienting to Mecca the boulevard leading to it. Twin statues of Adam
and Eve under a water dome of fountains were the chief focal points of
the circular public garden of Edena planted as a lush citrus orchard.
The park perimeter featured statues of man, woman, and child of various races and cultures, underlining the historical associations of the
garden with the cradle of civilization.

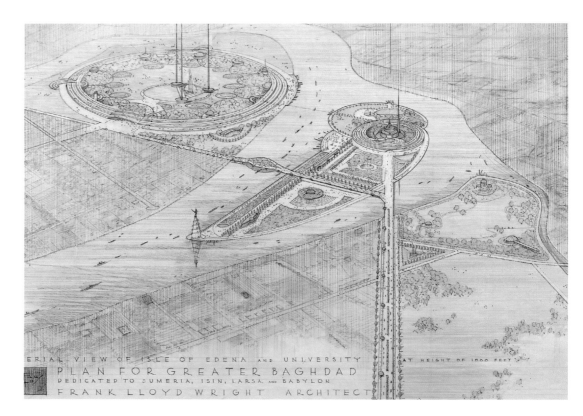

there is no prior model for Baghdad. As a panoply of dialectical images, it retains a quality of the unexpected that has led some critics to see a "phantasmagoria" both "gratuitous" and "improbable."[14]

The drawings spiral us through the Isle of Edena, looking up and down, ahead and behind, at large and minute features as befits the multiple perspectives and planes in play in the urban plan. We can follow out major themes of Wright's architecture in general and his urban vision in specific. The first invites a focus on the universal and the partic-ular as they occur in the spatial geometries of Edena and the historical and cultural inflections of its structures and landscapes. The second turns attention to the urban social life the drawings suggest.

THE SYMBOLIC CITY

At every level, Edena is structured around the interplay of the universal and the particular. The two modes interani-mate: the detail is constant reminder of the whole.[15] In Edena, Wright looked to harmoniously modulate the particular phases of the universal through geometry[16]—the universal at the abstract level—for an architecture built on natural meanings and harmonies. The circular geometry of Baghdad is a conscious culmination of a Wrightian spatial sym-bolism of wholeness and harmony beyond the scale of individual buildings.[17] As important, Wright knew that Baghdad's original plan was circular.[18]

Late in Wright's career, curvilinear geometry becomes more dimensional and complex as the exuberant prolif-eration of circles large and small combines with arcs, crescents, ziggurats, and spires. Edena's interlocking circles appear at different scales and on different planes; arcs, crescents, spirals co-occur in a complex dynamic. The prelim-inary aerial perspective drawings (fig. 2) suggest an encompassing, intricate geometry of structured intersecting curves, a shell-like configuration crafted into the island.[19] Circles and the visible and invisible triangulations between them create the regulating lines defining the Baghdad Cultural Center and the university campus as a single whole.[20] Letting landscape and the "rhythmic structure in Nature"[21] guide the sizes and relationships of circles,[22] Wright begins with the largest circle of the university incorporating a multiplicity of circular buildings around the campus perimeter. The spiral tightens into a pair of interlocking circles for the Opera House and the Garden of Eden park with large round Adam and Eve fountains (fig. 3). The circles-within-circles pattern repeats in the perimeter garden statues, representing cultures of the world. The tip of the island culminates in the smallest circle, the base of the monument to Haroun al-Rashid. The invisible triangles between these principal circles mediate connections between public places

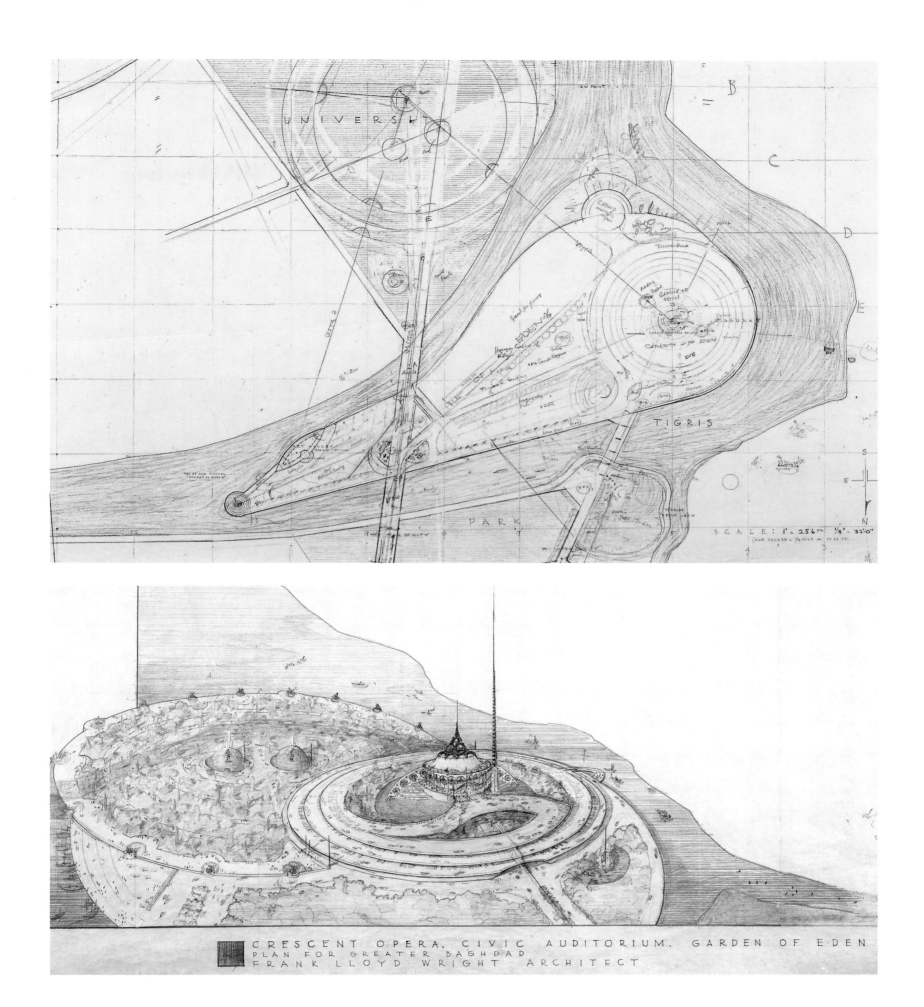

CRESCENT OPERA, CIVIC AUDITORIUM. GARDEN OF EDEN
PLAN FOR GREATER BAGHDAD
FRANK LLOYD WRIGHT ARCHITECT

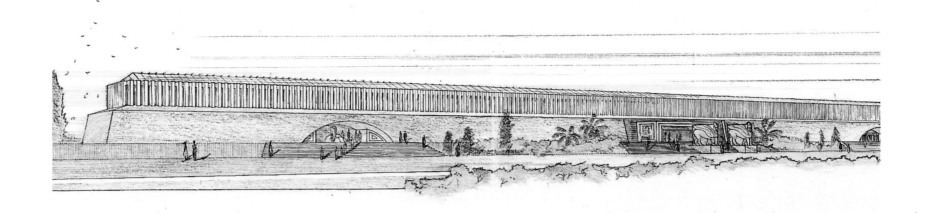

TUDY FOR MUSEUM
R GREATER BAGHDAD
UMERIA, ISIN, LARSA AND BABYLON
OYD WRIGHT ARCHITECT

Figure 4
Sculpture Museum, Plan for Greater Baghdad (project),
Baghdad, Iraq, 1957, perspective,
19 ½ x 6 ¼ inches (49.5 x 15.9 cm).
The Frank Lloyd Wright Foundation
FLLW FDN # 5748.004

Impressed by a visit to the Baghdad museum where he saw the rich collection of Sumerian artifacts, Wright decided that the civic center required a museum that both echoed and featured ancient sculpture of the region. In his assessment, "you needn't start with Greek civilization now … go back to the Sumerian, and we'll see what we can do with the go-back, coming forward." Thus positioning history not as a dead past but a living heritage informing the present and future, he also adjudged it in this case to be "more exquisite, more beautiful" with "more of the feeling of the poetic principle in it than ever existed before" (Taliesin Fellowship talk, 16 June 1957). The linear, 640-foot building has deep arches that suggest both a bridge and the arches of ancient viaducts. Its circular fountains and Assyrian lions flanking the monumental entrance arch anticipate the approach to the Mesopotamian galleries of the renovated Louvre.

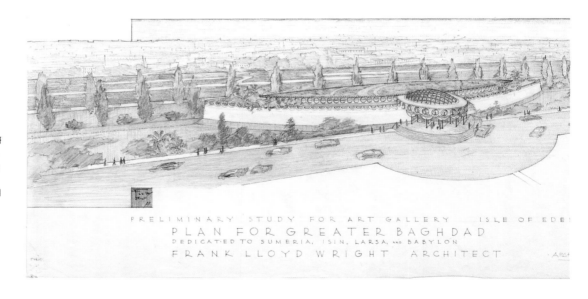

PRELIMINARY STUDY FOR ART GALLERY   ISLE OF EDE
PLAN FOR GREATER BAGHDAD
DEDICATED TO SUMERIA, ISIN, LARSA, AND BABYLON
FRANK LLOYD WRIGHT ARCHITECT

Figure 5
Art Gallery, Plan for Greater Baghdad (project),
Baghdad, Iraq, 1957, aerial view,
20 x 48 inches (50.8 x 121.9 cm).
The Frank Lloyd Wright Foundation
FLLW FDN # 5749.005

Colored pencil on tracing vellum signed by Wright and dated 30 June 1957. The colored print was sent to the Iraqi government. A gallery for contemporary art was one of two museums Wright included in the cultural center. A handwritten note on the drawing underlines the term "archeseum," suggesting that he may have conceived this building as a specialized museum dedicated to the art of architecture. Engaged for many years with the design of the Guggenheim Museum, Wright was keen to send his ideas to Iraq's king, hoping that they would win royal approval. Never one to discard an unbuilt concept, Wright later offered an almost identical design for the Arizona State University art museum.

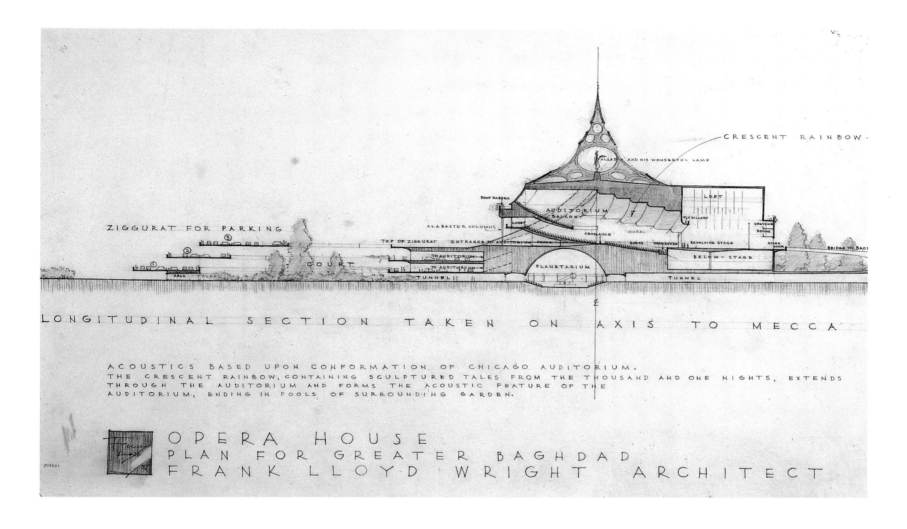

LONGITUDINAL SECTION TAKEN ON AXIS TO MECCA

ACOUSTICS BASED UPON CONFORMATION OF CHICAGO AUDITORIUM.
THE CRESCENT RAINBOW, CONTAINING SCULPTURED TALES FROM THE THOUSAND AND ONE NIGHTS, EXTENDS
THROUGH THE AUDITORIUM AND FORMS THE ACOUSTIC FEATURE OF THE
AUDITORIUM, ENDING IN POOLS OF SURROUNDING GARDEN.

OPERA HOUSE
PLAN FOR GREATER BAGHDAD
FRANK LLOYD WRIGHT ARCHITECT

Figure 6
Opera House, Plan for Greater Baghdad (project),
Baghdad, Iraq, 1957, longitudinal section taken on
axis of Mecca, 18 13/16 x 43 11/16 inches (47.8 x 111 cm).
The Frank Lloyd Wright Foundation
FLLW FDN # 5733.031

This presentation drawing, colored pencil on vellum, shows the opera house/civic auditorium rising above three layers of ziggurat parking. The planetarium below the auditorium is accessible directly from the adjacent garden. Citing Adler & Sullivan's Chicago auditorium as the model, the most perfectly acoustic building of its kind, Wright creates a signature crescent rainbow acoustical ceiling. "This poetic extension of the acoustic principles as a feature of the crescent also divides the opera from the civic auditorium and thus cupped over the proscenium to carry sound as hands would be cupped over the mouth" (FLLW, Preface, "Crescent Opera," p. 2). At the top of the open dome a golden statue of Aladdin and his lamp represents human imagination. Confidently assuring his clients that the sculpture could be made by local artists and craftsmen, some of whom he had encountered personally in Baghdad, Wright addressed social concerns and provided for "general social uplift needed to enliven the old crafts and arts of the kiln."

and determine locations of bridges and streets, including the main boulevard oriented toward Mecca.[23]

Following a dictum he laid down for Broadacre City—"the landscape becomes architecture just as architecture becomes a kind of landscape"[24] with the emphasis on diversity in unity—Wright brings the circular flows through individual plan elements as well, sometimes moderated by subtle contrasts.[25] A museum for ancient sculpture and a contemporary art gallery lie along the processional route between the civic auditorium and the Haroun al-Rashid monument; a dialectical duo, a museum yin and yang of past and present, playing out around circles and squares. The low, expansive arches of the linear, 640-foot archaeological museum (fig. 4) emphasize its bridgelike appearance, which is modulated by two circular fountains on either side of a main entrance marked by gigantic winged statues of Assyrian lions. The art gallery's distinctive lozenge shape, a form created by the intersection of two circles, gently contrasts with the archaeological museum's vertical curvature. In several sketches it almost appears as a sailboat floating on the Tigris. Inside, the major gallery repeats the lozenge under a central vaulted ceiling raised to allow for a ring of windows and skylights, encircled by the lower minor galleries with rooftop exhibition space. Over the raised circular entrance canopy a translucent dome mirrors a circular pool and fountain below (fig. 5).

The Opera House is the heart, a decentered non-Euclidean heart, of a multiplicity of spaces. Its parti is the elaborate concentric circles of the ziggurat parking below and, above, offset circles tapering to an almost dome-shaped building intersected by a large horseshoe crescent (fig. 7). The center of these circles intersects a principal axis oriented toward Mecca. The revolving circular stage introduces another dimension, motion, as do cascading fountains on either side of the rainbow crescent flowing into the main circular pool. The low arch of the entrance through a lozenge-shaped courtyard also carries the curvilinear geometry into the third dimension. Another series of arches beginning at the proscenium moves the crescent theme through the inside and out the top of the building, where the largest circle encloses the metalwork statue of Aladdin (fig. 6).[26] Aladdin represented imagination, and imagination,

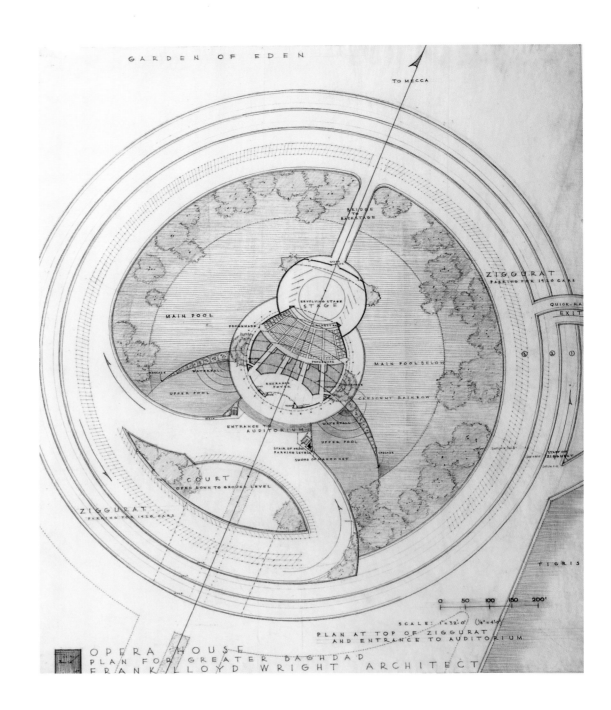

Figure 7
Crescent Opera House, Plan for Greater
Baghdad (project), Baghdad, Iraq, 1957, plan
at top of ziggurat and entrance to auditorium,
42 x 35 ⅝ inches (106.7 x 90.5 cm).
The Frank Lloyd Wright Foundation
FLLW FDN # 5733.028

Presentation drawing of colored pencil on tracing vellum, signed
and dated 1957. Wright conceptually expanded the opera house commission into a multipurpose center for "civic demonstrations, such as
political meetings, conventions, or grand concerts" (FLLW, Preface,
"Crescent Opera"). Thus, flexible seating, what he calls "continental
seating," overlooks a movable revolving stage. The circular geometry
Wright employs at every scale in the civic center is evident here. A
circular pool surrounds the main building intersected by the crescent
arch from which fountains cascade toward the entrance driveway.
On the ground, an oval lozenge-shaped forecourt marks the
main entrance.

Wright believed, "conceives *fabric* of the whole."[27] The statue of Aladdin is integral to the essence of Wright's defini-
tion of design: "We will find all the magic of ancient times magnified. . . . Aladdin's lamp was a symbol merely for
Imagination. Let us take this lamp inside, in the Architect's world."[28]

Wright in Baghdad refines the familiar Euclidean geometry through "reintegration of all units into one fabric."[29]
His virtuosity conjures the more complex geometry of nature itself, the rhythmic repetition of the same form (with
variations) from the smallest elements to the largest, what we might recognize today as fractal geometry.[30]
Championing nature in the recursive use of one shape to create larger and more complex shapes, Wright intuitively
worked out a kind of fractal landscape.[31] The circles, spheres, and ziggurats in each of the buildings cascade into a
congruent whole. This speaks directly to his attempt at a harmonious unity pervading all realms—natural, spiritual,
social.[32] While Wright's geometric competence has been long recognized,[33] his fractal apprehension seems to have
developed over time. Its comprehensive application to city forms breaks new ground.

Within this symbolic geometry of universal harmony, Wright locates the particularities of place, culture, and history. In a typical expression of the particular as both individual and universal, Wright told an Iraqi audience to value
"the priceless heritage of your own ancient intelligence" and "[p]reserve your own spiritual integrity according to the
best of the great oriental philosophies, the spirit which has inspired both East and West."[34] The tales of *A Thousand
and One Nights* were central to Wright's understanding of the spirit of Baghdad and southwestern Asia. As he said, "I

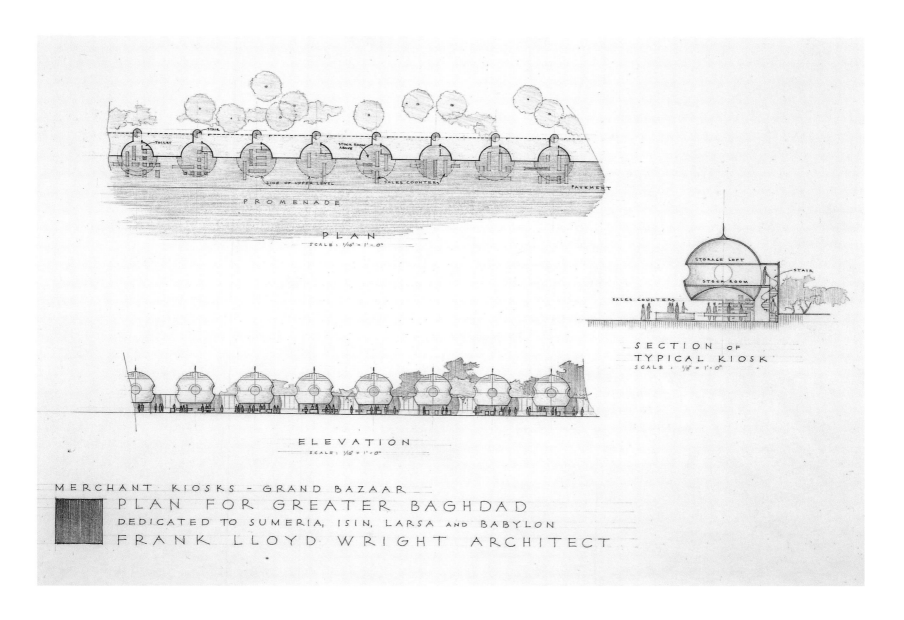

Figure 8
Merchant Kiosks, Plan for Greater
Baghdad (project), Baghdad, Iraq, 1957,
plan, section, and elevation,
23 7/8 x 36 inches (60.6 x 91.4 cm).
The Frank Lloyd Wright Foundation
FLLW FDN # 5750.003

The merchant kiosk is the module for both the grand bazaar at the center of the island and the processional boulevard. Wright's design simultaneously honors the merchant tradition of the Middle East and recognizes the necessity of commercial activity to make the cultural center economically viable. "The scheme creates new merchant interests with fresh opportunity and dignity" (Frank Lloyd Wright, speech to the Iraqi Society of Architects and Engineers, Saadun, May 1957).

believe I knew as a boy every tale of *The Arabian* or *A Thousand and One Nights*—knew them by heart. Even now I read them as when a boy."[35] In this past—distant in time, present throughout his own life—he saw material for Iraq's chance to reinvent itself on its own terms. Arguably, Wright missed some of the realities of a modernizing 1950s Baghdad insofar as he viewed it through the screen of the fabulous. There are tinges of cultural imperialism, too, in his selection of a particular past. Yet Wright's understanding was not wholly enmeshed in Orientalism or popular tales. His Baghdad also registered still-vital building traditions. He had a well-established interest in cultures east of the Mediterranean and was attentive to other aesthetic and architectural traditions as a student of Mesopotamian and Persian building and decorative arts.[36] He wrote, "The evolution from the Sumerian architecture of great ramps, terraces and roadways to the more delicately ornamented arched and domed architecture of the Persians has created a lasting wealth of architectural ideas."[37] As he reimagined the narrative spirit of Haroun al-Rashid's eighth-century Baghdad—a spirit alive in his own life and work—Wright encoded in buildable form associations with Mesopotamia as the birthplace of civilized life and the source of compelling symbols, narratives, and persons, any and all of which could be materials for imagining a unique modern identity.[38]

Particularities of narrative and building traditions are everywhere in Edena. Emblematic are the bazaar's merchant kiosks, Wright's interpretation of the *hojreh*, the shop found in most bazaars in the Arab world. He seems to understand and improve the multipurpose *hojreh* module, designing spherical kiosks to maximize space within, offer upper-level areas for stock and storage, and provide flexibly sized merchandise counters (fig. 8). The circular windows acknowledge the round light sources, oculi, placed in the domes over the paths of traditional souks and bazaars.[39] In the bazaar, Wright echoes but does not mimic past forms still vital in the present.[40] Likewise, he recruits technology to shore up the uninhabited island from frequent floods and uses the structurally purposeful, curved terraces to suggest the legendary Hanging Gardens of Babylon. Symbolic materials from the past thus come together with both local building and decorative traditions and tightly specified modern construction techniques.[41]

Wright used Islamic, biblical, and *A Thousand and One Nights* characters and references throughout Edena, particularly in the Opera House, where he set Aladdin with his lamp at the center of the crenellated exterior canopy.[42] The lamp especially exemplifies Wright's full-circle play with universality and particularity: it transfigures the specific meanings of a story from southwestern Asia into the transcultural value of imagination, "our human divinity," as Wright had it.[43] There is no better instance of the Wrightian dialectical image, however, than the ziggurat. Here the universal and the particular appear "in a flash," coexistent in the harmonious and fluid spiral, Wright's sign of process. The spiraling ziggurat form so evident on Edena—"For Baghdad I suggest this basic principle; the continuous flow of the ancient Ziggurat"[44]—is a most tangible metaphor for the progressive, increasingly inclusive trajectory of his practical alternatives to the violent, alienating, isolating realities of modernity. It is at once a thoroughly modern solution to the tyrannical automobile—ingest it!—and an ancient way to blend architecture and landscape. "This pride we take in organic architecture is just as natural, would be absolutely natural, to the Sumerians. . . . Didn't they do the ziggurat? What's more organic than the ziggurat?"[45] This is the provocation to see two things at once—the universal and particular merged to embody the spiritual and physical unity people need, humanity and nature, past and future, landscape and built environment joined. East and West figure yet again. Wright explicitly counters Rudyard Kipling: "Speaking of the East and West, [Kipling] said, 'These twain shall never meet.' Now if they ever do meet it will be on this philosophical basis of interior strength and this recognition of the human spirit as the true basis of all civilized life."[46]

In Edena's ziggurats, East and West also meet through Wright's personal history of imaginative and aesthetic engagement, his own openness to the influence of non-Western forms.[47] He models enriching cultural interchange. It is not possible—or important—to determine whether he saw the ziggurat as a local form with universal applicability or as an abstract universal form with local expressions. As both at once, the spiral was an incitement to all to share in the more expansive experiences a Wrightian doubled perspective could offer. These circular, spiraling, universal and particular relations display the habits of vision bred by the dialectical aesthetics of permeable harmonies with which Wright saturated urban space: "Any building is the by-product of eternal living force, a spiritual force taking forms in time and place appropriate to man . . . a record to be interpreted—no letter to be imitated. . . . We must believe architecture to be the living spirit that made buildings what they were. It is a spirit by and for man, a spirit of time and place. . . . It continues to bestrew the years with forms destined to change and to be strange to men yet to come."[48]

THE EXPERIENTIAL CITY

What do the drawings tell us about Greater Baghdad as a social space? They certainly communicate Wright's understanding of a city whose significance he grasped on many levels. First, Baghdad was the lively setting of the marvelous *A Thousand and One Nights*, which had inspired him since childhood. Second, it was one of the world's oldest cities, a place he recognized as the seat of civilization connecting its people to the ancient roots of humankind and to a future made possible by oil wealth. Wright was well aware of the import of building in Baghdad at this time, continuing an ambitious program that had already made vast infrastructural improvements. Wright, like his client, was aware that these buildings would represent the symbolic center of a modern Iraqi identity in the Cold War years. As a centering device, the city's integrated space could also engender identity and connect people to roots and thus to potentialities.[49] Last, Baghdad was a golden opportunity for what was likely to be Wright's final urban statement.

These registers overlap to give the Edena plan a larger-than-life feeling. Yet it was designed in a time when "form follows function" was an article of urban design faith. The drawings display a sense of urban function considerably more expansive than that of most architects of the time. The city is to Wright the combined forces of the mundane and the sublime. The sublime is the resonant natural and human geometry and poetry of the city, the memories made and held in a place of human encounter. The mundane encompasses the necessities without which the city could not function— the automobile for mobility, infrastructure against floods and other natural processes, economics. Commerce was an engine necessary to the city sublime, although Wright's commercial city was inflected by both the disavowed recent past of Western materialism[50] and the honored merchant tradition. In cities throughout the Islamic world, the principal commercial zone of the bazaar is generally in close proximity to the mosque.[51] Wright is thus quite on target in centrally locating a bazaar, "the marketplace, a perpetual fair" where people come "to buy, sell and learn . . . in beauty."[52]

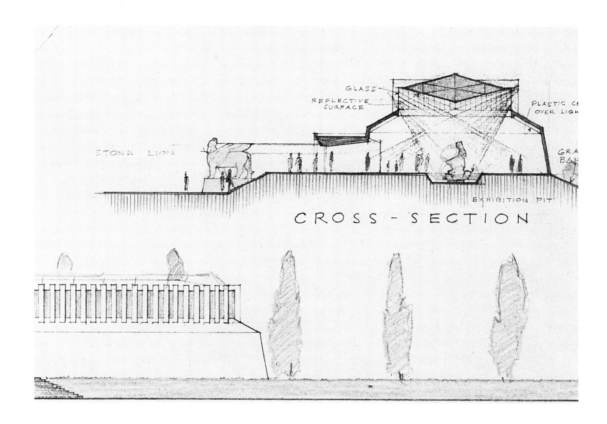

CROSS - SECTION

Figure 9
Sculpture Museum, Plan for Greater
Baghdad (project), Baghdad, Iraq, 1957,
plan, elevation, and section (detail),
18 1/16 x 55 1/8 inches (45.9 x 140 cm).
The Frank Lloyd Wright Foundation
FLLW FDN # 5748.003

Lighting was key to Wright's design of both the museum of ancient
sculpture and the contemporary art gallery. His experience at the
Guggenheim certainly led to insights such as an indirectly lit sunken
exhibition space that permits intimate viewing of the object. Bringing in
natural light reflected by the ceiling prevents direct exposure, an innovation that has become commonplace.

Once again, Wright gestures to more than a received past translated into present value. His plan consciously links mercantile activity, citizenship, and tourism: "[T]he general scheme creates new merchant interests with fresh opportunity and dignity. A new convenience and lively interest for tourists."[53] This loaded comment focalizes a striking dimension of Wright's urban design: the culminating and anticipatory disclosure of the city as a cultural destination and, precisely, a place of pleasure. The Baghdad city center emerges as a late point in the architect's quest to redefine the meaning of buildings and to reshape the cityscape to embody not only a sustainable style of life but also a joyous experience.

In Crystal City, for instance, Wright enfolded a gleaming, glass-spired city within the city of Washington, D.C. Although he repeated only the parking ziggurat from Crystal City, its concepts of mixed uses and the city as delight inflect Baghdad as well.[54] When Wright called Crystal City "this new 'Arabian Nights Entertainment,'" he signaled his deep appreciation for how the Baghdad of stories revealed the potential for amazement and delight in urban space, the city as quasi-magical character traversing time. Remarkably, Wright was able to see that a significant city function is precisely to be the stage of human action and story making. It is a place of expectation, where vibrant encounters create a dynamic social world. Wright's delightful city does not belong to an imagined past. His sustained engagement with Baghdad reminds us that the Baghdad of *A Thousand and One Nights* was a real city inspiring stories and elaborate fantasies that to this day remain part of widely shared, if differently and endlessly interpreted, narratives known around the world. Alone among the famed architects invited to Baghdad, Wright seemed capable of recognizing that a fabled, many-faceted city still existed in the collective imaginations and memories of both East and West. Tales revealing the multilayered delights and memorable spaces that made up the character of Baghdad continued to influence his mature perspectives on urban space in general and the intermingled exciting, entertaining, and edifying—sometimes dialectically constellated—potentialities reverberating through this late work in urban design.

Those potentialities are also visible in the fine points of Edena museum design. For instance, in an elegant section elevation and detail Wright contemplates how to display an object (a rather large one) for proper viewing. The approach is astute and simple. He lowers the object into what he calls "an exhibition pit" to bring the audience a bit closer, to a slightly higher line of vision. He brings natural light from above filtered through a clerestory window and a reflective ceiling prism, enhanced by adjacent indirect lights beneath the "plastic ceiling" (fig. 9).[55] In the management of light and object Wright structures a new relationship between people and object, presaging late twentieth-

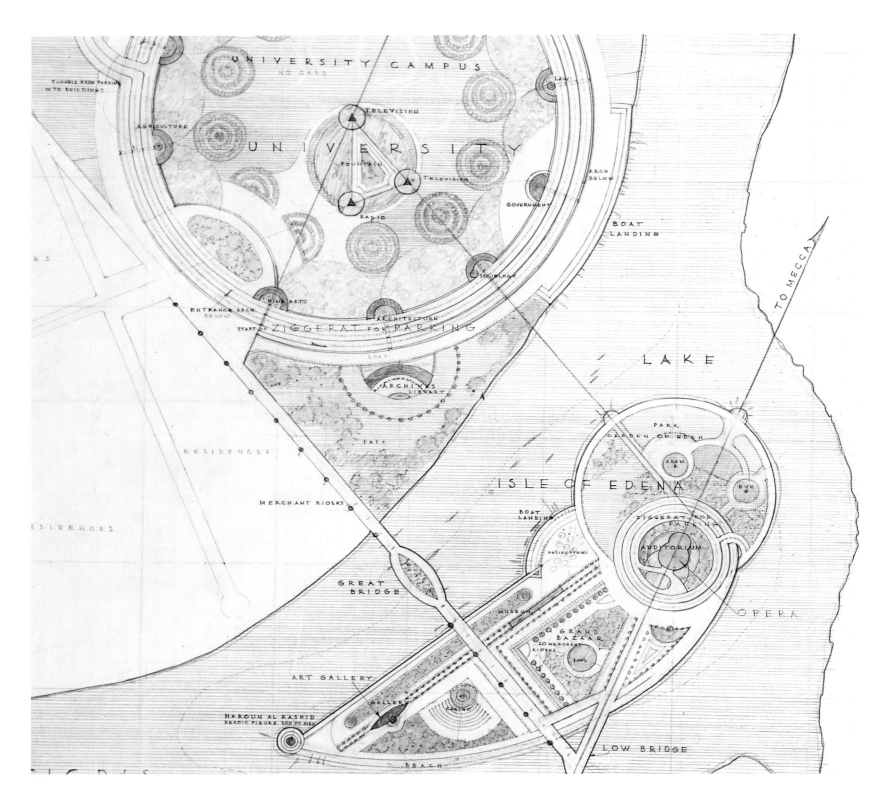

century exhibition design. While specific to the large sculptures Wright had seen in Baghdad, his solution is also general and transformative. His reinvention of ways to see three-dimensional objects is certainly influenced by ten years contemplating the Solomon R. Guggenheim Museum, then under construction.[56]

On a larger scale, the potential for pleasure, for "a life varied and interesting,"[57] is arrayed throughout the fluid geography of the Baghdad Cultural Center, its interleaved historical and real fantasies, each presenting a considered set of vantage points and vistas.[58] In Broadacre, Wright's city center aimed for a kind of holy sociability, a "great concourse or meeting place, where all groups gather to worship by way of the elements: fire, music, water and pageantry. In this way they grow toward unity."[59] Baghdad's ziggurat parking ensures a walking city center and campus for the intimate enjoyment of civic space. The promenade from the Opera House[60] to the Haroun al-Rashid monument is

Figure 10
Plan of Isle of Edena and University,
Plan for Greater Baghdad (project),
Baghdad, Iraq, 1957, site plan (detail),
66 x 36 inches (167.6 x 91.4 cm).
The Frank Lloyd Wright Foundation
FLLW FDN # 5733.033

This presentation drawing, colored pencil on tracing vellum, signed by
Frank Lloyd Wright and dated 20 June 1957, is a version of Wright's own
handmade comprehensive sketch using the signature hard line colored
pencil drawing style he adopted for his office. The location of each of the
elements of the master plan for Baghdad's civic recreation center is
carefully delineated and marked on the drawing. Asked why he had
changed the island into a manmade shape, Wright explained: "I think
this is one of the privileges of architecture—if the man made shape is
architecturally fit to the job.... So why not make the whole thing seem
like a gracious, beautiful building? In the water it would look like a
tremendous ship. With the buildings that connected with it, it would all
look like an architectural circumstance and the Island becomes a building"
(Taliesin Fellowship talk, 23 June 1957).

Figure 11
Monument to Haroun al-Rashid,
Plan for Greater Baghdad (project),
Baghdad, Iraq, 1957, view,
52 5/8 x 28 5/8 inches (133.7 x 72.7 cm).
The Frank Lloyd Wright Foundation
FLLW FDN # 5751.004

The ziggurat-shaped monument to the medieval ruler of Baghdad in its
heroic and golden age was Wright's homage to his favorite childhood
stories' hero of Baghdad in its glory days. Wright mistakenly thought
that Haroun was the founder of Baghdad. The ziggurat form was ancient but also Islamic and its particular shape here is inspired by the
minaret Wright would have seen at Samarra, just a few miles outside of
Baghdad as it was one of the principal tourist destinations. The monumental statue is positioned at the strategic tip of the Island where it
stands as an iconic beacon not unlike the Statue of Liberty. In the
preparatory free hand sketches Wright wrote by hand the name of
Haroun al-Rashid.

HAROUN AL RASHID
FRANK LLOYD WRIGHT ARCHITECT

both edifying and pleasurable. On one side is the grand bazaar with its colorful kiosks near a circular pool and garden
reminiscent of the caravanserai, a festive daily fair. On the other, the archaeological museum with its Assyrian winged
lions flanking large fountains beckons to Sumeria. Its counterpoint, the contemporary Iraqi art gallery, also offers
views of the Tigris from its rooftops. Crossing the butterfly bridge to it (also the main route to Wright's University
campus), one stops at the casino or its outdoor amphitheater. On this route, Wright arrays edification and indulgence,
counterpoising the shops and casino to the museums and the peacefulness of lush landscapes and beaches. Parks,
promenades, gathering places, crossing paths, fountains, and waterfalls interweave throughout as spaces of enjoyment and human encounter, the city center as a place of delight and fantasy. These layers of landscape, built and
natural, entice visitors to explore and wander civic space as a continuous flow (fig. 10).[61]

The spiraling monument to Haroun al-Rashid (fig. 11), just beyond the art gallery, brings to mind not only eighth-
century Baghdad but also the sculpted steps of Persepolis and the beaconlike attitude and position of the Statue of
Liberty, conflating a number of possible places and pasts but rising also toward a welcoming future.[62] Wright certainly
recalls the city of Haroun, not as a literal page from *A Thousand and One Nights* nor an anachronistic, Colonial
Williamsburg–style re-creation but as the constellated, richly associative possibilities of a delightful past variously
inflecting today and tomorrow, a dialectically fascinating space most "varied and interesting" undergirded by the fluid
geometry of wholeness and harmony.

Today, the element of fantasy in urban projects is implicit and, often enough, expected. That was not the case in
1950s Baghdad, where a Western-educated elite supervising a very successful modernization program embraced
projects in the mainstream of International Style.[63] At that time and in that place, Wright's anticipation of an urban
sensibility we might cautiously call postmodern looked antimodern, improbable, perhaps unserious.[64] The substantive
nature of Wright's urban perspective, however, is most boldly underlined by the Central Post and Telegraph Building,
where he created something both older and newer than modernism. It is, perhaps, the quintessential dialectical image.

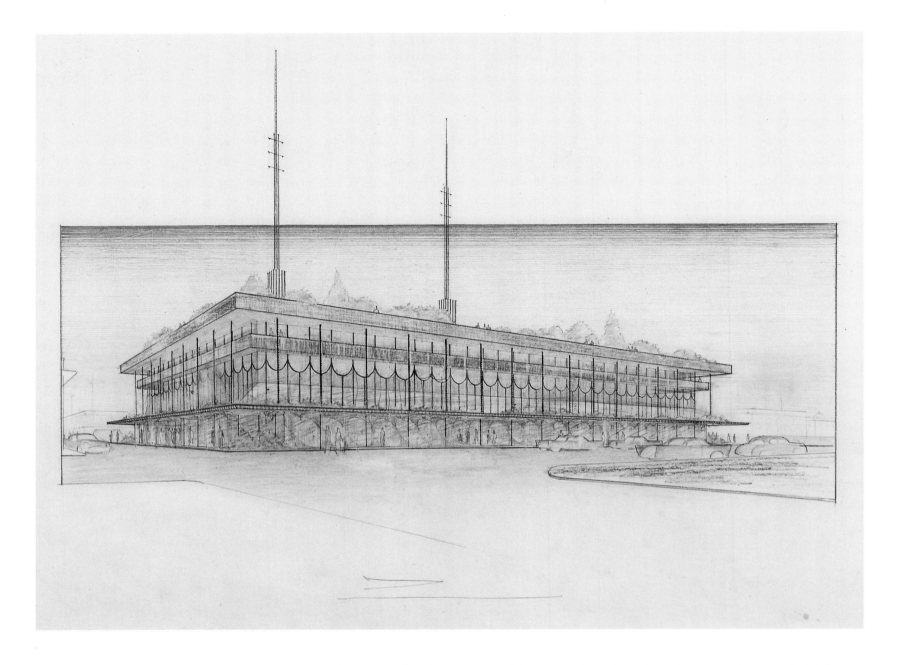

Figure 12
Central Post and Telegraph Building (project),
Baghdad, Iraq, 1957, perspective,
28 ½ x 36 ⅜ inches (72.4 x 92.4 cm).
The Frank Lloyd Wright Foundation
FLLW FDN # 5734.007

The young King Faisal invited Wright to design Baghdad's Central Post and Telegraph headquarters when the architect visited Baghdad in 1957. While the functional, orthogonal building contrasts sharply with the circular geometries of the cultural center and the university, its simplicity understates the ecological and technological innovation of this building, nicely detailed in his drawings. Located in a busy section of the city on Baghdad's famous Rashid Street, the design weds practical, elegant, pre-modern Middle Eastern climatic solutions, classic forms, and modern amenities into a remarkable model of sustainable building. It features a roof insulated with a deep layer of earth planted with greenery, a sheltering trellis above, and a glass facade designed to avoid exposure to direct sun as another trellis forms a green mesh frame over the sidewalk on every side. Each elevation shows an overhead arbor carrying greenery. Inside, a sunken courtyard, visible from the street, embraces pools, fountains, and more greenery, as vital to heat mitigation as the roof and exterior designs.

While its rectangular scheme is not out of place among the modernist boxes then rising in downtown Baghdad, it is, as he says, an internally lit "jewel box" that brilliantly weds practical, elegant, premodern Middle Eastern climatic solutions, classic forms, and modern amenities into a model of sustainable building, a remarkable green design that would be enthusiastically embraced today (figs. 12, 13).[65]

Expressed in the magical, expansive relations of spiral, arc, and circle, Frank Lloyd Wright's Baghdad Cultural Center spills out as cascading spaces interwoven to express the sense of mobility, the importance of vistas and horizons present and past, the ambivalent pleasures of human exchange and commerce. In Baghdad, Wright achieves protean intersections of practicality and fantasy, past and future, universality and locality, all within his long-standing, passionate engagement with creating the geometry of a humane architecture enabling "happiness and a life more beautiful and safe," as he put the ideal to his Iraqi audience.[66] Had Wright's Baghdad designs been built, their multilayered geometry and meanings might well have worked dialectically, as Benjamin hoped, to disrupt settled perceptions and subtly alter consciousness.

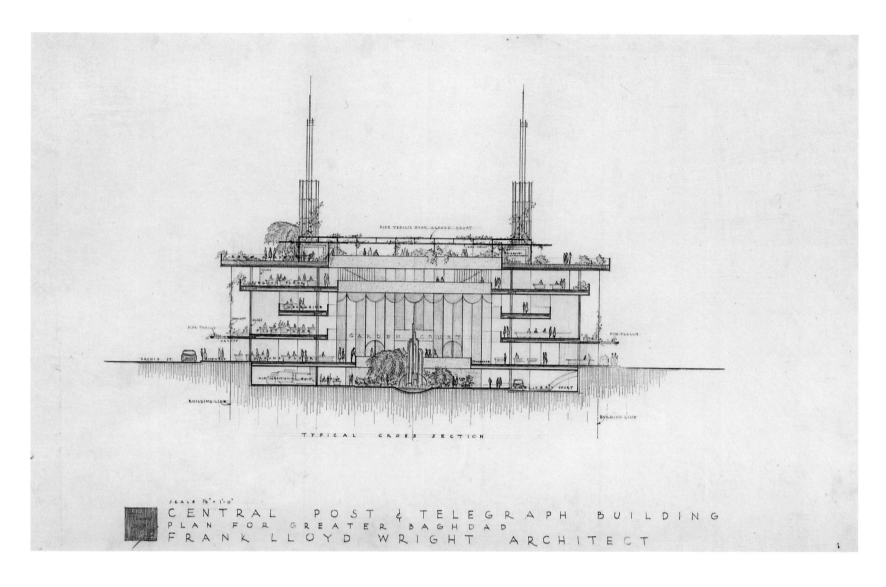

Figure 13
Central Post and Telegraph Building (project),
Baghdad, Iraq, 1957, section,
28 ^{15}/$_{16}$ x 47 ^{5}/$_{16}$ inches (73.5 x 120.2 cm).
The Frank Lloyd Wright Foundation
FLLW FDN # 5734.015

The presentation rendering using color pencil on tracing vellum, designed by Wright and dated 21 July 1957, was among a second set of development drawings sent to Baghdad in printed form. The section drawing shows how Wright ingeniously conceived a dialectical play between traditional regional architecture and technological innovation. The sunken internal courtyard with fountains is reminiscent of Persian domestic architecture. A covered roof of green vines stretched over cables creates a cooling microclimate. The inventive hollow tubing system, or Lally columns, enable warm air to escape and cool air to recirculate through the building. Although he provided for air-conditioning, Wright's strategy was to reduce the need through passive or organic means. The insulated green roof, the courtyard, and the fountain creates evaporative cooling, an "organic air conditioning system" influenced by Wright's observation of local wind towers.

Clearly, in 1958 Frank Lloyd Wright commanded a provocative urban vocabulary with a decidedly nonmodern inflection. Including imagination in the functions of the city, he opened out a harmonious geometry into multiplied dialectical structures and imagery. In his last years, he suggestively wrote about a "new time/space."[67] The engaging mystery of Baghdad is finally, perhaps, its architectural rejection of linear time and space in favor of the fruitful, dialectical juxtaposition of moments retrospective and anticipatory, local and universal, a remarkably evocative "framework of reality" in which new urban experiences remain ever open: "Architecture is the triumph of Human Imagination over materials, methods, and men, to put man into possession of his own Earth." As Wright elaborated, "It is at least the geometric pattern of things, of life, of the human and social world. It is at best that magic framework of reality that we sometimes touch upon when we use the word 'order'" (fig. 14).[68]

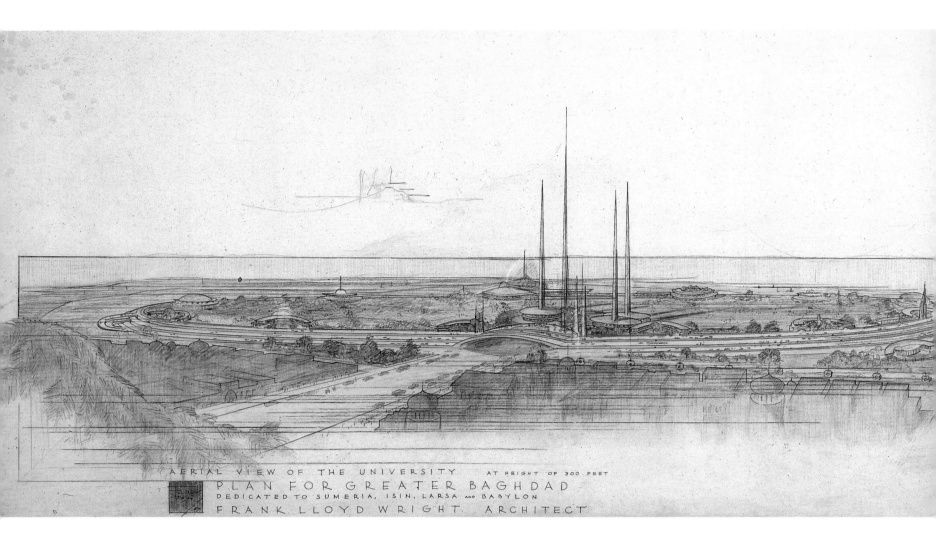

AERIAL VIEW OF THE UNIVERSITY   AT HEIGHT OF 300 FEET
PLAN FOR GREATER BAGHDAD
DEDICATED TO SUMERIA, ISIN, LARSA AND BABYLON
FRANK LLOYD WRIGHT . ARCHITECT

Figure 14
Baghdad University, Plan for Greater
Baghdad (project), Baghdad, Iraq, 1957,
aerial view, 30 x 65 inches (76.2 x 165.1 cm).
The Frank Lloyd Wright Foundation
FLLW FDN # 5759. 005

This original drawing is rendered in colored pencil and ink. Signed by Wright on 20 June 1957, this "drawing has a great deal of Mr. Wright's personal work on it," according to William Wesley Peters in his memorandum and drawing list of the Baghdad Project made on November 18, 1963. Wright designed a university campus knowing full well that Walter Gropius already had the commission. In all likelihood he hoped his impressive and comprehensive design would win the approval of the king, who had already given him permission to use his private island for the Opera. Wright explained how the design differed from his earlier campus design for Florida Southern University: "Baghdad University is one designed all at the same time, and on a different plan entirely because the traffic problem has grown and grown and grown until even in Baghdad today there is no use in attempting to build buildings until you have disposed of the car. Now the old ziggurat gives you an opportunity to suck them all in, hide them from sight . . . the car disappears, and the ziggurat is a good basis for the architecture. . . . Well, now that gives you a campus entirely free of cars and convenient to every building on the campus so that the buildings all face the campus with their backs to the ziggurat, . . . So, this Baghdad problem is much more modern than Florida Southern" (Taliesin Fellowship talk, 25 August 1957).

NOTES

1. Wright was invited to design an opera house by Iraq's Development Board, then pursuing the second phase of a successful infrastructural and architectural improvement program funded by oil revenues the new nation had negotiated with the United Kingdom. In 1957, the board commissioned four other Baghdad projects to architects from the West: Walter Gropius, Baghdad University; Le Corbusier, a sports complex; Gio Ponti, Development Board headquarters building; and Alvar Aalto, a museum. The story of Wright in the context of this unique Baghdad architectural venture is the subject of a book manuscript I am now finalizing. Discussions of the Baghdad projects include Mina Marefat, "Wright's Baghdad," in Anthony Alofsin, ed., *Frank Lloyd Wright, Europe and Beyond* (Berkeley: University of California Press, 1999), pp. 184–263; Mina Marefat, "Bauhaus in Baghdad: Walter Gropius' Master Project for Baghdad University," *Docomomo* (Docomomo International), no. 35 (September 2006): 78–86; Mina Marefat, "1950s Baghdad Modern and International," *TAARII Newsletter* (The American Academic Research Institute in Iraq), no. 2–2 (Fall 2007): 1–7; Mina Marefat, "Architecture Baghdad: Les Dessins de Frank Lloyd Wright," *Beaux Arts Magazine*, no. 233 (October 2003): 68–73; Bruce Brooks Pfeiffer, "Frank Lloyd Wright and Baghdad," *Frank Lloyd Wright Quarterly (The Frank Lloyd Wright Foundation)* 15, no. 1 (Winter 2004): 4–17; Neil Levine, *The Architecture of Frank Lloyd Wright* (Princeton, NJ: Princeton University Press, 1996), pp. 383–404; Joseph M. Siry, "Wright's Baghdad Opera House and Gammage Auditorium: In Search of Regional Modernity," *Art Bulletin* (CAA) 87, no. 2 (June 2005): 265–311.

2. The exhibition, attended by some six hundred guests at the Iraqi Consulate in New York City, marked the twenty-third birthday of Iraq's King Faisal. Olgivanna Wright described the reporters and photographers surrounding her celebrity husband. Olgivanna L. Wright, *Our House* (New York: Horizon Press, 1959), p. 214. Many of the drawings also appeared in a Wright-coordinated article, "Frank Lloyd Wright Designs for Baghdad," *Architectural Forum* 108, no. 5 (May 1958): 89–101. Barely two weeks later, *Time* (19 May 1958), p. 80, featured the Baghdad project in glowing terms under the title "New Lights for Aladdin." The *New York Times* also reported on the exhibition (3 May 1958).

3. Wright produced detailed working drawings for this building, commissioned to him during his 1957 Baghdad visit. The announcement of the project was made during Wright's Baghdad visit, when he was photographed with the minister of development. "Mr. Lloyd Wright in Baghdad," *Iraq Times*, 29 May 1957, p. 3.

4. This was Wright's first visit to southwestern Asia; he traveled with his wife, Olgivanna, and his son-in-law, William Wesley Peters. He also traveled to Egypt, where he was received by the family of his apprentice Kamal Amin. Wright was the first of the commissioned architects to go to Iraq. Le Corbusier and Gropius, commissioned earlier, did not go until the fall of 1957.

5. Wright supplemented the master plan print of the London firm Minoprio & Spencely & Macfarlane Architects and Town Planning Consultants, which he used as a base map with aerial photographs and applied planimetric techniques to enlarge the area of the island site and its adjacent peninsula.

6. Wright's commentary includes a preface to and notes accompanying his submitted drawings, Baghdad Plan Notes [2401.379M], hereafter cited as FLLW, *Preface*; "Designs for Baghdad," 89–101–likely ghosted by Wright with a collaborating writer; and a talk to the Iraq Society of Engineers at Saadun in late May 1957, where he laid out his philosophy [2401.378]; hereafter cited as Saadun. I emphasize these sources because they shed light on the ways he expressed his continuing passions, intentions, and arguments in the period when he worked on Baghdad. Although Wright was uncertain about the reception his plan would get, he felt that his economical, imaginative, and expedient solution would be readily accepted if he carefully outlined his intent.

7. For an excellent discussion of Fallingwater, see Richard Cleary's *Merchant Prince and Master Builder: Edgar Kaufmann and Frank Lloyd Wright* (Pittsburgh: Heinz Architectural Center, Carnegie Museum of Art, 1999).

8. "Lao-Tzu declared the reality of a building did not consist in the walls and roof but in the space within to be lived in," Wright told his Baghdad audience. Saadun, p. 5. For much of his life, Wright expounded his interpretation of the Chinese philosopher with appreciation for "that sense of within unfolding, by interior content to achieve genuine expression as individuality." Reprinted in Bruce Brooks Pfeiffer, ed., *Frank Lloyd Wright Collected Writings, Vol. 2* (New York: Rizzoli, 1994), p. 88. Hereafter, this series will be cited as FLLW v.1–5. Wright professed to have an instinctive understanding of this concept, described his discovery as accidental in his Royal Institute of British Architects (RIBA) lectures in 1939. FLLW v.2, p. 299. What is interesting is that the sense of interior (*baten* or *andaroun*) as spatial concept is integral to the understanding of Persian and Islamic architecture as well. For a discussion of this, see Mina Marefat, "Fractured Globalization: A Case Study of Tehran," in Elliott Morss, ed., *New Global History and the City* (Newton, MA: New Global History Press, 2004), pp. 137–74.

9. Anthony Alofsin's "Wright, Influence and the World at Large" and Margo Stipe's "Wright and Japan" and my own essay on Wright's Baghdad in Alofsin's edited volume, *Frank Lloyd Wright, Europe and Beyond* (Berkeley: University of California Press, 1999) address this topic.

10. His unbuilt project for the Gordon Strong Automobile Objective and Planetarium, Sugarloaf Mountain, in Maryland (1924), remains an intriguing proposed pleasure park for cars. As De Long notes, it was Wright's first serious exploration of circular geometries to shape architectural space. David G. De Long, ed., *Designs for an American Landscape 1922–1933*, exh. cat. (New York: Abrams, 1996); this catalogue for the 1996–97 exhibition organized by the Library of Congress and the Canadian Centre for Architecture and the Frank Lloyd Wright Foundation, curated by David G. De Long, presented drawings of unbuilt projects. Among them was Sugarloaf, a highly detailed project incorporating many visionary concepts further developed in later projects. See also Mark Reinberger, "The Sugarloaf Mountain Project and Frank Lloyd Wright's Vision of a New World," *The Journal of the Society of Architectural Historians* 43, no. 1 (March 1984): 38–52.

11. Vincent Scully, *Frank Lloyd Wright* (New York: Braziller, 1960), pp. 30–31.

12. Walter Benjamin, *The Arcades Project*, trans. Howard Eiland and Kevin McLaughlin (Cambridge, MA: Belknap Press, 1999), p. 463 [N3,1]. Benjamin used the dialectical image primarily to characterize the relationship between past and present.

13. Much more can be said about the resonance of the dialectical image with Wrightian themes and practices. One of the most interesting is its association with the romantic, heroic figure of the flaneur, the walker in the city who seeks out and uses shocking images to remake the present. Wright, of course, was not merely a walker in the city but an active shaper and certainly one who, in his more grandiose moments, saw himself as heroic. For more on the dialectical image, see Walter Benjamin, "Theses on the Philosophy of History," in *Illuminations* (New York: Schocken Books, 1968), ed. Hannah Arendt, trans. Harry Zohn, pp. 253–64; Rolf Tiedemann, "Dialectics at a Standstill: Approaches to the *Passagen-Werk*," in *On Walter Benjamin: Critical Essays and Recollections*, ed. Gary Smith (Cambridge, MA: MIT Press, 1991), pp. 185–209.

14. Manfredo Tafuri and Francesco Dal Co, *Modern Architecture*, vol. 2 (New York: Rizzoli, 1986), p. 328.

15. Wright wrote: "Imagination conceives the 'fabric' of the whole. The 'unit' is absorbed as agreeable texture in the pattern of the whole." "In the Cause of Architecture IV. Fabrication and Imagination," *Architectural Record* (1927), reprinted in FLLW vol. 1, p. 243. "The design of the new city," he said of Broadacre City, "sees not value in the part except as the part is harmoniously related to the whole." FLLW v.4, p. 56.

16. As Wright noted in a Taliesin talk, "America and Ancient Sumer," "[O]nly an idea, so far as we have any ability to discern the truth, never dies. This phase of it'll appear there and that phase of it'll appear here, but it goes on." In Bruce Brooks Pfeiffer, *Frank Lloyd Wright: His Living Voice* (Fresno, CA: California State University Press, 1987), transcript of Frank Lloyd Wright talk, 28 December 1958.

17. Vincent Scully noted that from the late 1940s, "[m]any projects by Wright then explored the curve, its continuities, and its engulfments," which he had long associated with infinity and eternal continuity. Scully added, "Water itself, enclosed by the circle, played an archetypal part in many of these designs [including] the Arabian Night's dream of mountains, water, and shimmering surfaces which Wright so gustily imagined for Baghdad." Scully, *Frank Lloyd Wright*, pp. 30–31.

18. "It is worth noting that the original city of Baghdad, built by Haroun al-Rashid was circular and walled when the ziggurat of earth and masonry was a 'natural,'" wrote Wright, in the statement accompanying his Baghdad drawings. FLLW 2401.379M. Like many Westerners, Wright mistakenly associated the city's founding with Haroun al-Rashid (Hārūn ar-Rashīd), whose reign (786–809) was immortalized in *A Thousand and One Nights*. Wright owned multiple copies and editions. The round city of Baghdad was founded in 762 by Abū Ja 'far al-Mansūr, the second Abassid caliph; by the time of Haroun al-Rashid, the fifth caliph, the city was one of Islam's major cultural centers.

19. In the Baghdad work, Wright adhered to some key planning principles he had outlined for Broadacre City, most especially those relating to landscape. As he wrote, the "fundamental Broadacre principle is that all features of this city of the future arise out of the 'lay of the land'—in both character and topography." FLLW v.4, p. 60.

20. Wright wrote: "Geometry is the grammar, so to speak, of form . . . [C]ertain geometric forms have come to symbolize for us and potently to suggest certain human ideas, moods, and sentiments . . . the circle, infinity; the triangle, structural unity; the spire, aspiration; the spiral, organic progress; the square integrity." FLLW v. 1, p. 117.

21. Wright saw Nature, capitalized, as his greatest inspiration. FLLW v.5, p. 159. His interpretation of nature is also key to understanding the concern with part and whole that informs his urban design even more strongly than his architecture. As Nicholas Olsberg has noted, Wright referred to Nature as "inner rightness or universal harmony" and the "ruling principle." See "Introduction" in David G. De Long, ed., *Designs for an American Landscape 1922-1932* (New York: Abrams, 1996), pp. 10–12.

22. "In any organic architecture, the ground itself predetermines all features, climate modifies her, available means limits their function, shapes them." FLLW v.4, p. 48.

23. Both copies of the Minoprio, Spencely and Macfarlane plan show hatch marks, notations, and colored-pencil markings, clues about the design methodology Wright employed to inscribe circles upon the city. The orientation of religious buildings toward Mecca was obligatory; so orienting the principal access to the island on the Tigris is an unusual choice, but it underlines his desire to elevate the Baghdad Cultural Center.

24. FLLW v.4, p. 54.

25. FLLW v.4, p. 48.

26. For an intelligent, detailed reading of the circular geometry, see Joseph M. Siry, "Wright's Baghdad Opera House and Gammage Auditorium: In Search of Regional Modernity," *Art Bulletin* (CAA) 87, no. 2 (June 2005): 265–311.

27. FLLW, "In the Cause of Architecture IV: Fabrication and Imagination," *Architectural Record* (October 1927), reprinted FLLW v.1, p. 243.

28. Ibid. p. 241.

29. FLLW v.4, p. 49.

30. Fractal geometry was first formalized in the late 1970s and early 1980s through the work of Benoit Mandelbrot. See Benoit Mandelbrot, *The Fractal Geometry of Nature* (New York: W. H. Freeman and Company, 1982).

31. The architectural expression he intended was organic, "plastic" and "much more abstract than usual"—what he had earlier characterized as "the harmonious architectural reintegration of all units into one fabric." FLLW v.4, p. 49.

32. "The city of the future," which Wright envisioned as early as Broadacre City, required "a quality of thought and a kind of thinking on the part of the citizen that organic architecture, alone at the present time represents or seems to understand." FLLW v.4, p. 58. For more on Wright's ideas about organic architecture, see Edgar Kaufman Jr., "Frank Lloyd Wright: Plasticity, Continuity, and Ornament," *Journal of the Society of Architectural Historians* 37 (March 1978), and David G. De Long, ed., *Frank Lloyd Wright: Designs for an American Landscape, 1922-1932* (New York: Abrams, 1996), which includes good discussions of the topic by De Long, Nicholas Olsberg, and Anne Spirn. While Wright attends to the subject throughout his writings, a later book, *A Testament* (New York: Horizon Press, 1957), offers insight into the roots of his organic philosophy.

33. Wright himself often emphasized the impact of the Froebel kindergarten blocks with which his mother had first initiated him into the world of geometry: "[W]ith the Froebel 'gifts' then actually as a child I began to be an architect." FLLW v.5, p. 183. "Mother learned that children should not be allowed to draw from casual appearances of Nature until they had first mastered the basic forms lying hidden behind appearances. Cosmic, geometric elements were what should first be made visible to the child-mind." FLLW v.5, p. 159.

34. Wright, Saadun, pp. 6–7. "Buildings are only the natural expression of the experience gained from a life as lived—features of a *people*. There is no real culture possible in this world without architecture in this sense as its basis. There is no nation that can have a culture of its own without an architecture of its own." Ibid., pp. 8–9.

35. Wright, Saadun, p. 1. These tales, many set in Baghdad, were immensely popular during Wright's youth and early career, inspiring symphonies, ballets, musicals, and films. During the same period, archaeological excavations were avidly publicized in stories purveying impressionistic ideas of the region's exotic life. Wright lived in the Chicago area when it was the principal city for the display of artifacts excavated in Iran. For an excellent detailed analysis of the period, see Magnus Bernhardsson, *Reclaiming a Plundered Past: Archaeology and Nation Building in Modern Iraq* (Austin: University of Texas Press, 2005).

36. Wright collected Persian tiles and had great insight into Persian architecture. For a discussion, see Marefat, "Wright's Baghdad," pp. 184–213, 237–63. He sometimes conflated Persia with the whole of historical Mesopotamia, as he tended to conflate Baghdad with Babylon, sometimes to the consternation of Iraqi clients and audiences.

37. Frank Lloyd Wright and Iovanna Lloyd Wright, *Architecture: Man in Possession of His Earth* (Garden City, NY: Doubleday, 1962). The Sumerians, Wright noted in his Saadun speech, originated much that the derivative Greeks did later: "The Sumerians really did invent civilization and I now see the Greeks didn't have so very far to go with it as I thought." Wright, Saadun, p. 5.

38. Wright defined architecture as "the mother art of civilization," relating it to both nature and culture: "human environment may now be conceived and executed according to nature: the nature of Time, Place and Man: native as was always natural to cultures wherever life in the past was strongest, richest and best." FLLW v.5, p. 187.

39. Wright had visited the souks of Baghdad and Cairo during his 1957 trip.

40. Wright was well aware of the distinction between mimicry and interpretation, of "not imitating anything, not trying to reproduce it as it was either . . . surely a mistake." Wright, Saadun, p. 18. Elsewhere, he noted "a record to be interpreted—no letter to be imitated." Frank Lloyd Wright, "Designs for Baghdad," p. 102.

41. "The main structure is of ferro concrete—simple and native materials by native crafts employing the enameled faience of the ancient East and on sculpture and cast beaten metal." FLLW, *Preface*, "Crescent Opera," p. 5. He goes on to encourage em-

ploying native artists and craftsmen throughout construction: "[T]here is nothing difficult or expensive to construct in this opus if sculpture by native artists is available and local crafts stimulated." Wright also considered practical matters, estimating that "a structure such as this could be built in America ... for about $35.00 per square foot" excluding the sculptures and the al-Rashid ziggurat. His total estimated cost was $3.5 million.

42. FLLW, *Preface*, "Crescent Opera," p. 3.

43. FLLW, *Disappearing City.* Reprinted in FFLW v.1, p. 93.

44. Wright, FLLW, *Preface*, p. 5.

45. FLLW, "America and Ancient Sumer," 28 December 1958; transcript in Bruce Brooks Pfeiffer 1987.

46. Wright, *Saadun*, p. 8. Wright's mention of "interior strength" imputes to the universal a quality of interiority. To his Iraqi audience he implored, "You have in Architecture the life of the spirit as *reality* rather than things that go to make up the frame—what we call walls and roofs—materialism." Ibid., pp. 6–7. This is echoed in his sometime injunction to apprentices to design from the inside out, the way he opened the interior as the basis for domestic design, the way the Opera House interior continues outward through its facade and roof into other features of the island.

47. As Joseph Siry has observed, "In Iraq, as for Japan, he proposed an architecture that was technically and functionally modern but that was not alien to place, understood as both natural and human history." See Siry 2005, p. 272.

48. Wright, "Designs for Baghdad," p. 102.

49. "Ideal architecture," Wright had emphasized, is "organic expression of organic social life." FLLW v.4, p. 71.

50. For instance, "I am sorry to see that the West is coming here chiefly by way of its materialism; by way of commercialism instead of by way of the wisdom it should already have gained from Western experience. We are all too well aware now in our nation—the U.S.A.—that we have not taken the right precautions in this connection." Wright, Saadun, p. 4.

51. The orientation toward Mecca is another repeating theme throughout the cultural center, as are mosquelike echoes, from the roof of the Opera House and the shape of the kiosks to an early University mosque design, later erased. In dome and spire, the sacred reverberates through Edena. Wright's plan notes even suggested that the Opera House would be as inspiring "as any religious edifice." On similarities between the Opera House and mosque forms, see Marefat 1999, pp. 200–201, and Siry 2005, pp. 280–81.

52. FLLW v.4, p. 56.

53. FLLW 2401.378.EE, p. 8.

54. As early as 1913, for instance, Wright had planned Midway Gardens in Chicago, an imaginative beer-garden restaurant and entertainment destination that revealed his playful use of sculpture and form in a space of pleasure in the city. Wright's intent: "Light, color, music, movement—a gay place.... imagination ... myself Aladdin.... I believed in magic." His method: "The straight line, square, triangle, and the circle were set to work in this developing sense of abstraction by now my habit, to characterize the architecture, painting, and sculpture of the Midway Gardens." *An Autobiography*, reprinted in FLLW v.2. pp. 230, 234. Further, he thought, "it awakened a sense of mystery and romance to them all to which each responded." Wright's Chicago pleasure palace was unfortunately demolished in October 1929. Ibid., p. 237.

55. FLLW, notes on the drawing 5748.003.

56. This detail invites us to revisit the criticism that Wright's museum designs did not pay attention to the works on display. Critics were instantly polarized in their reaction to the Solomon R. Guggenheim Museum. "A war between architecture and painting, in which both come out badly maimed," declared John Canaday on page one of the *New York Times*; "the most beautiful building in America," retorted Emily Genauer in the *New York Herald Tribune*. "A building that should be put in a museum to show how mad the 20th Century is," editorialized the *New York Daily Mirror*. "Mr. Wright's greatest building, New York's greatest building," said architect Philip Johnson, "one of the greatest rooms of the 20th century." "Frank has really done it," snapped one artist. "He has made painting absolutely unimportant." *Time*, November 1959. Wright helped redefine the restricted notion of painting display prevalent before the Guggenheim. For a good assessment of controversies surrounding the Guggenheim, see Neil Levine, *The Architecture of Frank Lloyd Wright* (Princeton, NJ: Princeton University Press, 1996), pp. 299–363.

57. FLLW v.4, p. 48; As he had proposed in Broadacre, a place suited to "nature culture," the "fresh and vitally humanized landscape." FLLW v.4, p. 56.

58. "We want the electric spark of popular curiosity and surprise to come to life again, along the highways and byways and over every acre of land ... architectural beauty related to natural beauty." FLLW v.2, p. 77.

59. FLLW v.4, p. 55.

60. It is important that Wright designed this structure flexibly as both Opera House and Civic Auditorium, a multipurpose home to not only "high" culture but also political performances and community gatherings.

61. In Baghdad, Wright was finally able to do what he had prescribed, "[t]o gratify what is natural and desirable in the get-together instinct of the community." He had marked out both "natural places of beauty—in our mountains, seasides, prairies, and forests" and "recreation grounds" including "the planetarium, the racetrack, the great concert hall, the various units of national theater, museums, art galleries." FLLW, "Modern Architecture, Being the Kahn Lectures." Reprinted in FLLW v.2, p. 76.

62. Along the processional steps at Persepolis, sculpted figures appear to pay tribute to Darius the Great. Wright clearly saw multiple meanings. He described the Opera House in a way that could apply to the monument and many other aspects of Edena: "peculiarly splendid, significant throughout of Arabic history and may become a gratifying apex for meeting place of the Cultures of the East and West." FLLW 2401.378.HH, p. 4.

63. Most notably, Walter Gropius's influential Baghdad University, as well as Le Corbusier's sports complex and Gio Ponti's Development Board headquarters building, all of which were constructed.

64. I use "postmodern" advisedly but somewhat idiosyncratically simply to signal dimensions of Wright's vision that were genuinely ahead of the time. I do not mean to conflate his approach with the sometimes shallow lifting of features from various eras and styles more typical of the architectural postmodernism of the 1980s.

65. Among the reasons that none of Wright's Baghdad designs were built were a violent coup and two subsequent changes of government and the accompanying political storms. However, Wright's delivery of (and failure to follow up personally on) designs clearly outside the high modernist style his clients expected had to be a strong contributing factor.

66. Wright, Saadun, p. 10.

67. Wright pioneered in recognizing the transformative impact of mobility—automobile and airplane—on the city. He saw that "space scale has changed throughout" and that movement would be a planning norm as "space can be reckoned by time rather than by feet and inches." FLLW v.4, p. 52. "It is significant that not only have *space* values entirely changed to *time* values now ready to form new standards of movement-measurement, but a new sense of spacing based on speed is here ... and the horizon keeps widening." FLLW v.5, p. 284.

68. Frank Lloyd Wright, "The Logic of Contemporary Architecture as an Expression of This Age," *Architectural Form*, May 1930. Frank Lloyd Wright and Baker Brownell, *Architecture and Modern Life* (New York: Harper and Brothers, 1937). Both sources appear in FLLW: v.1, p. 340, and v.3, p. 214.

Plates

What follows is a selection of imagery intended to represent some of the projects featured in the exhibition *Frank Lloyd Wright: From Within Outward*, which opened at the Solomon R. Guggenheim Museum in New York on May 15, 2009, of which this volume is the catalogue. The imagery is organized chronologically and especially focuses on nine projects. The texts for eight of these projects have been written by Bruce Brooks Pfeiffer, while the ninth one, the scheme for Baghdad, is introduced by Mina Marefat.

A NOTE ABOUT THE HIGHLIGHTED PROJECTS BY BRUCE BROOKS PFEIFFER

Out of Frank Lloyd Wright's enormous oeuvre, consisting of several hundred designs for buildings constructed as well as projects for those that were not, nine have been selected to represent his solutions for buildings that address the need for a gathering of people into a particular architectural space.

These include a space of worship, Unity Temple; spaces for cultural events, the Solomon R. Guggenheim Museum and the projects for Baghdad; a space for the touring public to view a scenic attraction, the Gordon Strong Automobile Objective and Planetarium; a space for work, the Johnson Administration Building; a space for a hotel, apartments, shops, and a theater, the Crystal City; and a space for commercial, cultural, and social gathering, the Pittsburgh Point Park Civic Center.

These are all rather large projects and buildings that represent Wright's solutions on a likewise large scale. We would be remiss, however, to overlook the American home. Residential work represents by far the majority of commissions that Wright received during a career that spanned over seven decades. In his own words, "The house of moderate cost is not only America's major architectural problem but the problem most difficult for her major architects." [1] In order to represent this concern, this problem that Wright solved with great success in his designs for the Usonian Houses, the Herbert Jacobs House has been included in this group of highlighted designs. Here the gathering of people is relatively confined to the American family, and Wright's design honors and glorifies that unit— the family—with a home of moderate cost.

Finally, we highlight Taliesin, Frank Lloyd Wright's home in Wisconsin. Built in 1911, it was destroyed by fire in 1914. The rebuilt home, Taliesin II, was destroyed by another fire, in 1925, and rebuilt as Taliesin III. In the beginning, Taliesin was a space for Wright, family members, a few draftsmen, and workers on the farm. Later, all that changed, and it became a space for community and education, and as such it remains to this day.

NOTES

1. Frank Lloyd Wright, *Architectural Forum,* 1938. Reprinted in Bruce Brooks Pfeiffer, ed., *The Essential Frank Lloyd Wright: Critical Writings on Architecture* (Princeton and Oxford: Princeton University Press, 2008), p. 309.

Highlighted Projects

Arizona State Capital, "Oasis" (project)
Phoenix, Arizona, 1957
Perspective (detail)
Color pencil and sepia ink on paper
35 x 45 5/8 inches (89.5 x 115.9 cm)
The Frank Lloyd Wright Foundation
FLLW FDN # 5732.002

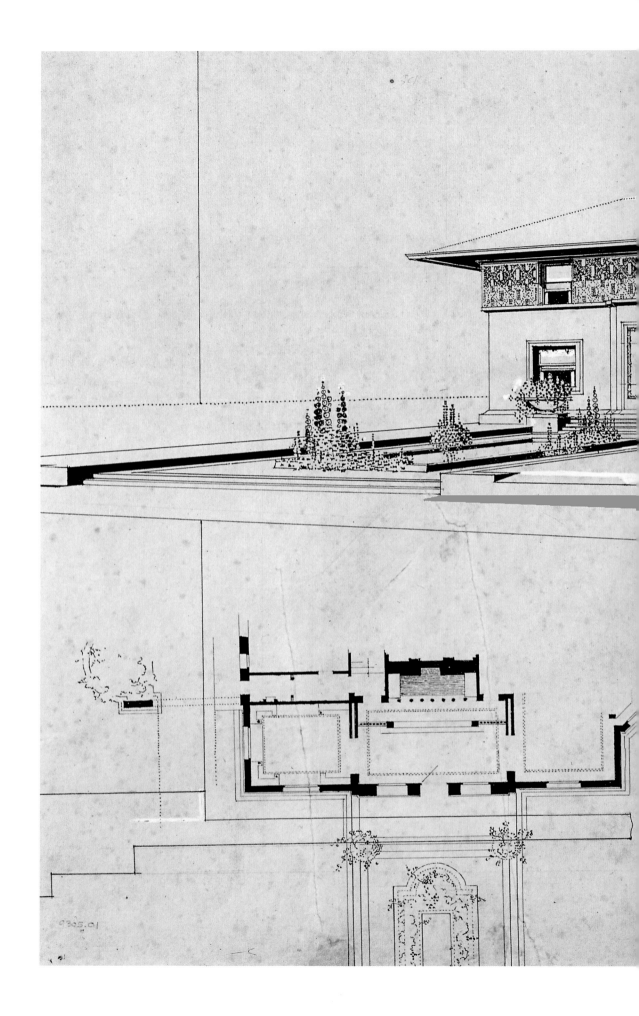

William H. Winslow House
River Forest, Illinois, 1893–94
Perspective
Ink on paper
16 ¼ x 23 ⅛ inches (41.3 x 58.7 cm)
The Frank Lloyd Wright Foundation
FLLW FDN # 9305.001

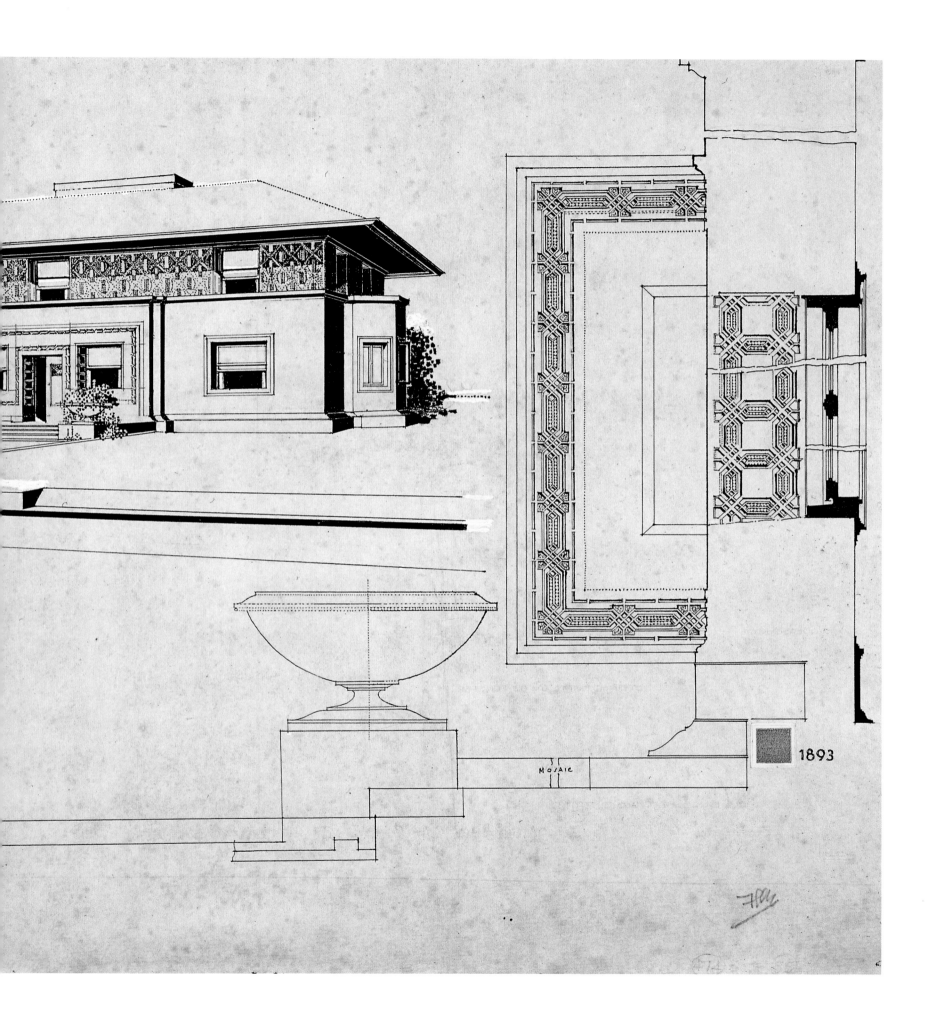

MOSAIC

1893

Frank Lloyd Wright Oak Park Studio
Oak Park, Illinois, 1897
Perspective
Graphite pencil and sepia ink on paper
6 x 19 ½ inches (15.2 x 49.8 cm)
The Frank Lloyd Wright Foundation
FLLW FDN # 9506.001

Ward W. Willits House
Highland Park, Illinois, 1902–03
Perspective
Ink and watercolor on paper
8 1/2 x 32 inches (21.6 x 81.3 cm)
Private collection
FLLW FDN # 0208.001

Larkin Company Administration Building (demolished)
Buffalo, New York, 1902–06
Perspective
Graphite pencil on paper
23 ⅝ x 12 ⅝ inches (60 x 32.1 cm)
The Frank Lloyd Wright Foundation
FLLW FDN # 0403.001

Larkin Company Administration Building (demolished)
Buffalo, New York, 1902–06
Partial plan and perspective
Sepia ink on paper
34 ⅜ x 21 ⅛ inches (87.3 x 53.7 cm)
The Frank Lloyd Wright Foundation
FLLW FDN # 0403.002

1903

Larkin Company Administration Building (demolished)
Buffalo, New York, 1902–06
Interior court view
The Frank Lloyd Wright Foundation
FLLW FDN # 0403.0046

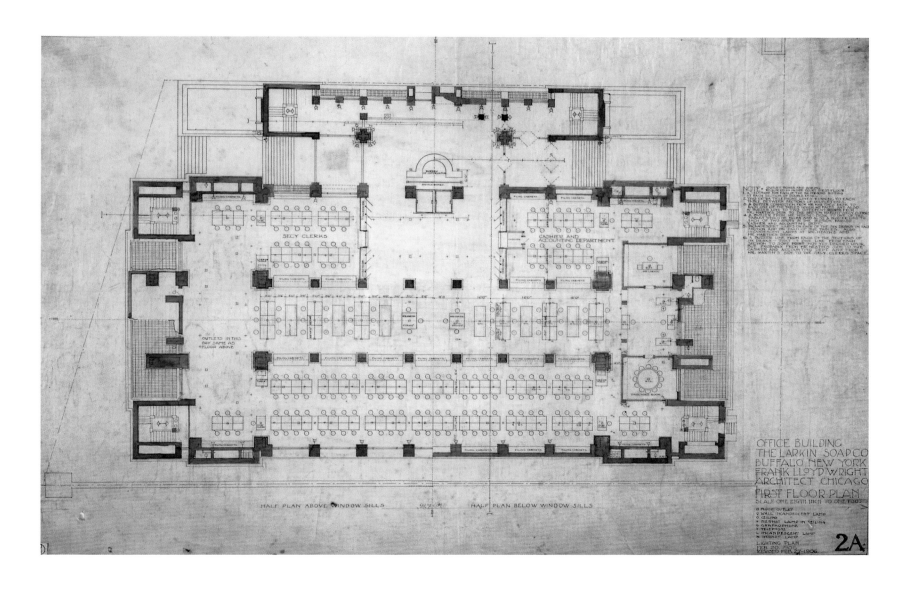

Larkin Company Administration Building (demolished)
Buffalo, New York, 1902–06
First floor plan
Ink on tracing cloth
24 3/8 x 36 7/8 inches (61.9 x 93.7 cm)
The Frank Lloyd Wright Foundation
FLLW FDN # 0403.065

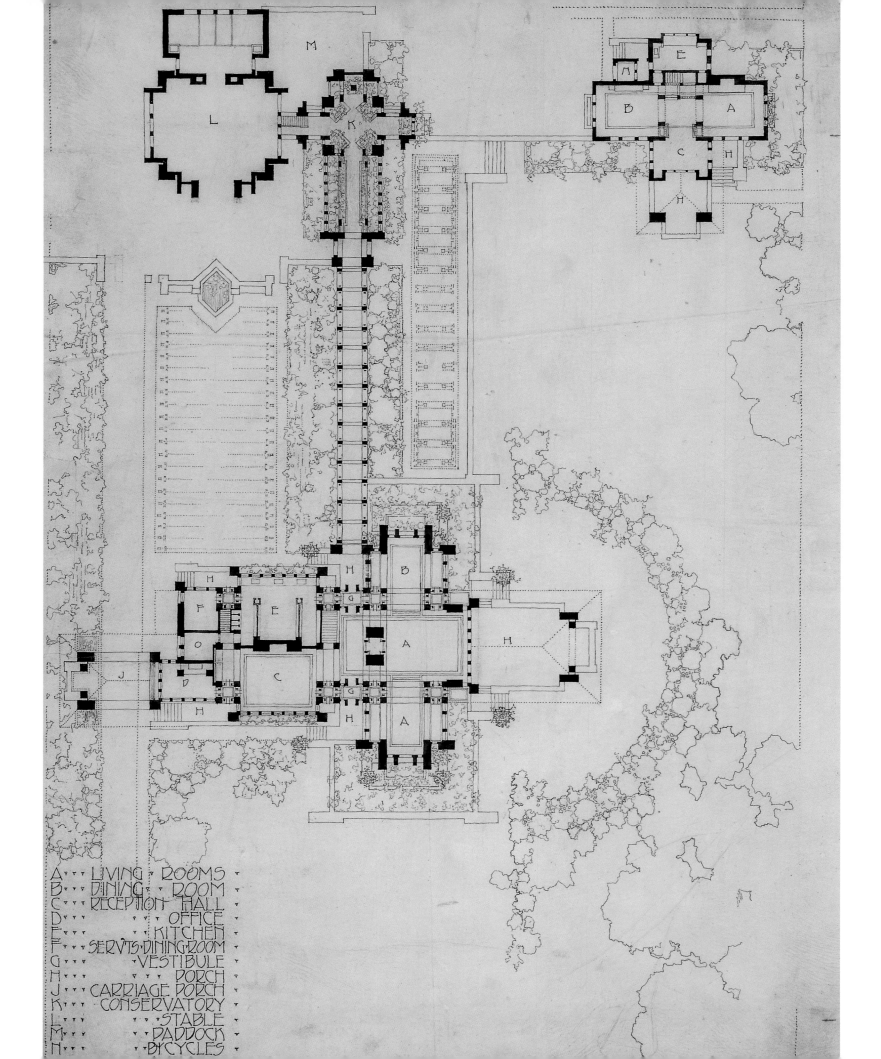

A···LIVING·ROOMS·
B···DINING·ROOM·
C···RECEPTION·HALL·
D·············OFFICE·
E·············KITCHEN·
F···SERV'TS·DINING·ROOM·
G·············VESTIBULE·
H·············PORCH·
J···CARRIAGE·PORCH·
K···CONSERVATORY·
L·············STABLE·
M·············PADDOCK·
N·············BICYCLES·

Darwin D. Martin House
Buffalo, New York, 1902-04
Plan
Ink on paper
21 ³/₄ x 15 ¹/₂ inches (55.2 x 39.4 cm)
The Frank Lloyd Wright Foundation
FLLW FDN # 0405.002

Darwin D. Martin House
Buffalo, New York. 1902-04
Perspective
Graphite pencil and color pencil on paper
18 x 36 inches (45.7 x 91.4 cm)
The Frank Lloyd Wright Foundation
FLLW FDN # 0405.027

UNITY TEMPLE

Unity Temple
Oak Park, Illinois, 1905–08
Exterior
The Frank Lloyd Wright Foundation
FLLW FDN # 0611.0010

Unity Temple (opposite)
Oak Park, Illinois, 1905–08
Studies for columns
Graphite pencil on paper
21 x 16 inches (53.3 x 40.6 cm)
The Frank Lloyd Wright Foundation
FLLW FDN # 0611.008

Unity Temple (following pages)
Oak Park, Illinois, 1905–08
Perspective
Ink and watercolor on art paper
11 ½ x 25 inches (29.2 x 63.5 cm)
The Frank Lloyd Wright Foundation
FLLW FDN # 0611.003

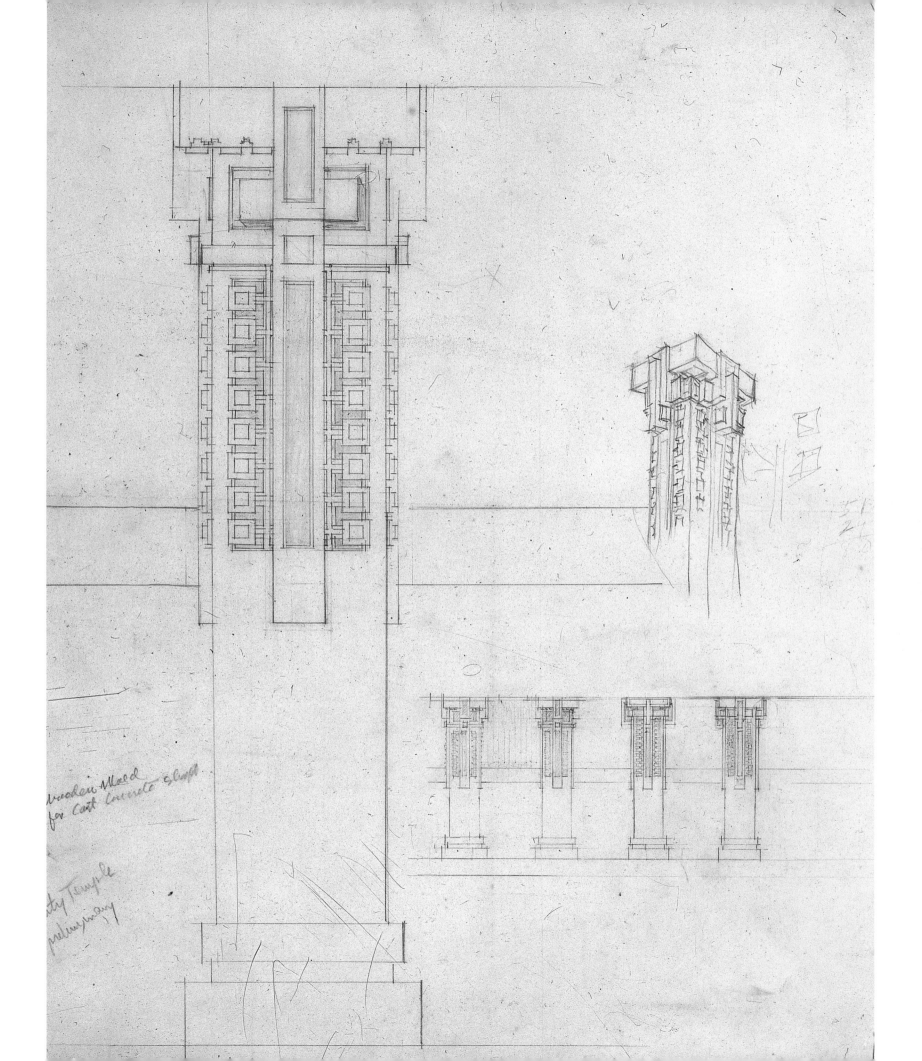

Wooden Mold
for Cast Concrete Shaft

...ity Temple
preliminary

In the drawing, the inscription on the building reads:

FOR THE WORSHIP OF GOD
AND THE SERVICE OF MAN

UNITY TEMPLE

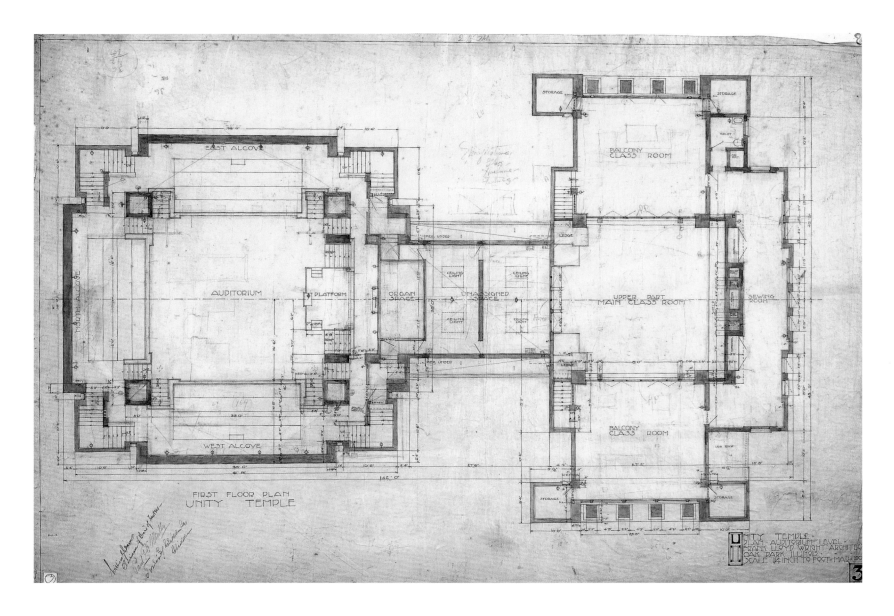

FIRST FLOOR PLAN
UNITY TEMPLE

Unity Temple
Oak Park, Illinois, 1905–08
Plan for auditorium level
Ink on tracing cloth
28 ¾ x 42 ¼ inches (73 x 107.3 cm)
The Frank Lloyd Wright Foundation
FLLW FDN # 0611.012

A NEW CHURCH FOR USONIA

When Unity Church, Oak Park, Illinois, burned to the ground on the night of 4 June 1905, a building committee was immediately established and charged with the task of selecting an architect for the new building. Charles E. Roberts was a member of that committee, as well as being a client and friend of Frank Lloyd Wright's. Roberts was quite a remarkable man in his own right, an inventor among other attributes, and he strongly urged the committee to settle on Wright as their architect. Wright later recollected, "Committee decisions are seldom above mediocre unless the committee is dominated by some strong individual. In this case the committee was so run by Charles E. Roberts—inventor. He was the strong man in this instance or Unity Temple would never have been built."[1] When meeting with the committee, Wright explained that rather than a church of traditional design, in the typical Colonial style with a tall steeple pointing to heaven, "Why not, then, build a temple, not to God in that way—more sentimental than sense—but build a temple to man, appropriate to his uses as a meeting place, in which to study man himself for his God's sake? A modern meeting house and a good-time place."[2]

Wright also described the pastor, Reverend Rodney F. Johonnot, as "[a] liberal. His liberality was thus challenged, his reason was piqued and the curiosity of all was aroused. What would such a building look like? They said they could imagine no such thing. 'That's what you came to me for,' I ventured. 'I can imagine it and I will help you to create it.' ... The first idea was to keep a noble room for worship in mind, and let that

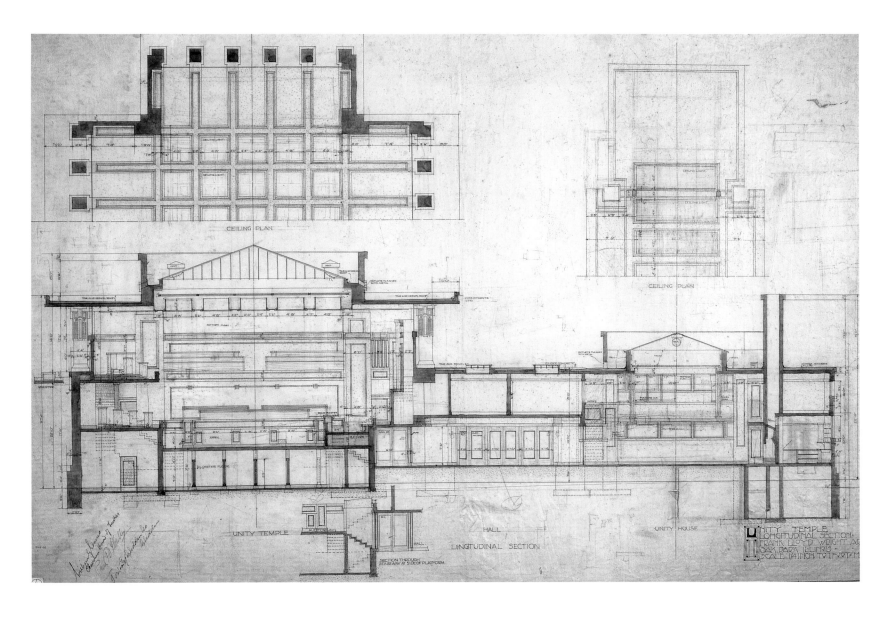

Unity Temple
Oak Park, Illinois, 1905-08
Longitudinal section and ceiling plan
Ink on tracing cloth
28 ¾ x 42 ⅝ inches (73 x 108.3 cm)
The Frank Lloyd Wright Foundation
FLLW FDN # 0611.016

sense of the great room shape the whole edifice. Let the room inside be the architecture outside."[3]

Wright being a Unitarian himself,[4] his mother the daughter of a crusading Unitarian minister, realized that Unity was the ultimate belief in the Unitarian faith—the unity of all things. For Wright, the square seemed the perfect symbol for Unity—equal on all sides—to express this faith in architectural form.

As Wright started work on this new commission, a budget of $45,000 (equivalent to about $1,095,000 in today's dollars) was set to construct a church that would house a congregation of four hundred members. The site selected for the new building was on the corner of Lake Street and Kenilworth Avenue, Oak Park. Lake Street was the lesser in length, and its location prompted Wright to consider a structure wherein the

entrance would be on the Kenilworth Avenue side. This, of course, abnegated the conventional front door of the church, which would most likely have been on Lake Street, a main thoroughfare in the town. His plan, therefore, took into account two considerations for the church—Unity Temple and Unity House, with Unity Temple reserved for worship, while Unity House was the secular section, containing Sunday school classrooms and other ample spaces for the church's social functions. The temple is square, Unity House, rectangular. Dividing the two is an entrance foyer wherein a turn in one direction gains Unity Temple, in the other direction, Unity House.

In consideration of the somewhat limited budget, Wright chose concrete—as the cheapest material in the architectural world—to accomplish this design.

UNITY TEMPLE

Unity Temple
Oak Park, Illinois, 1905–08
Interior
The Frank Lloyd Wright Foundation
FLLW FDN # 0611.0007

Furthermore, in connection with the symbol of the square, by designing the main temple wherein the four sides were equal, he was saving in the making of the formwork into which the reinforced concrete would be poured.

Considering how to enter or leave the temple, Wright devised an ingenious plan wherein the congregation, entering at the north side of the auditorium, can either mount a few steps, or enter a "cloister" that runs along both the west and east sides of the building. From this cloister there is a view looking into the auditorium, but the cloister being on a lower level, members of the congregation, should they come into the building after

service has begun, are barely noticeable. From the cloister steps proceed to the main floor of the auditorium, while staircases on the north side mount to alcoves and balconies on the east, west, and north sides. The pastor's platform is situated within full view of the entire congregation. Behind that platform is the organ console, the organ's mechanical space being directly behind and partially over the entrance foyer below. When the service is over, the members of the congregation exit forward toward the foyer and pass by the pastor, rather than turning their backs on him. This seemed, to Wright, a more human and congenial way to end the service and leave the building.

Unity Temple
Oak Park, Illinois, 1905–08
Exterior
The Frank Lloyd Wright Foundation
FLLW FDN # 0611.0011

Four large columns support the cantilevered concrete slab roof over the auditorium. The columns also carry the ducts for heating. The slab, thus cantilevered, is not supported by the exterior walls of the room. The walls became what Wright termed as "screen features." They rise high above to shield the congregation from the noise of the streetcars and traffic outside on Lake Street. Where the "screens" meet the slab roof, there are stained-glass windows. The slab itself is pierced throughout for overhead stained-glass skylights. The amber and yellow windows bring a sense of a sunny day into the church even during cloudy or rainy weather.

On one interior perspective, Wright later inscribed, "Sense of Space to be lived in the REALITY of the bldg. The big room coming through—the outside coming in."[5] And on yet another interior perspective, he inscribed, "The unlimited overhead. Interior space enclosed by screen-features only. Idea later used in Johnson bldg Racine, Wis."[6]

This sense of the walls becoming nonsupporting screens in Unity Temple marks a most important achievement in Wright's development—beginning with the Hillside Home School living room, Spring Green, Wisconsin, and followed by the Larkin Company

Administration Building, in Buffalo. But what he was attempting in those two buildings finally came to fruition in Unity Temple. Speaking of the Larkin Building, he said, "There began the thing that I was trying to do . . . and I followed that up with Unity Temple where there were no walls of any kind, only features; and the features were screens grouped about interior space. The thing that came to me by instinct in the Larkin Building began to come consciously in the Unity Temple. When I finished Unity Temple, I had it. I was conscious of the idea. I knew I had the beginning of a great thing, a great truth in architecture. And now architecture could be free."[7]

NOTES
1. Frank Lloyd Wright, *An Autobiography* (San Francisco: Pomegranate, 2005), pp. 152–53.
2. Ibid., p. 154.
3. Ibid.
4. Several of Wright's clients at this time were either Unitarians or Christian Scientists, both denominations being typically American.
5. Frank Lloyd Wright, FLLW FDN # 0611.002.
6. Frank Lloyd Wright, FLLW FDN # 0611.009.
7. Frank Lloyd Wright to the Taliesin Fellowship, 13 August 1952. Transcript 1014.044, pp. 16–17.

E. E. Boynton House
Rochester, New York, 1907–08
Perspective
Graphite pencil and color pencil on paper
11 1/4 x 33 3/4 inches (28.6 x 85.7 cm)
The Frank Lloyd Wright Foundation
FLLW FDN # 0801.001

Mrs. Thomas Gale House
Oak Park, Illinois, 1909
Perspective
Ink, watercolor, white gouache, and collage on paper
12 ³/₄ x 16 ¹/₈ inches (32.4 x 41 cm)
The Frank Lloyd Wright Foundation
FLLW FDN # 0905.001

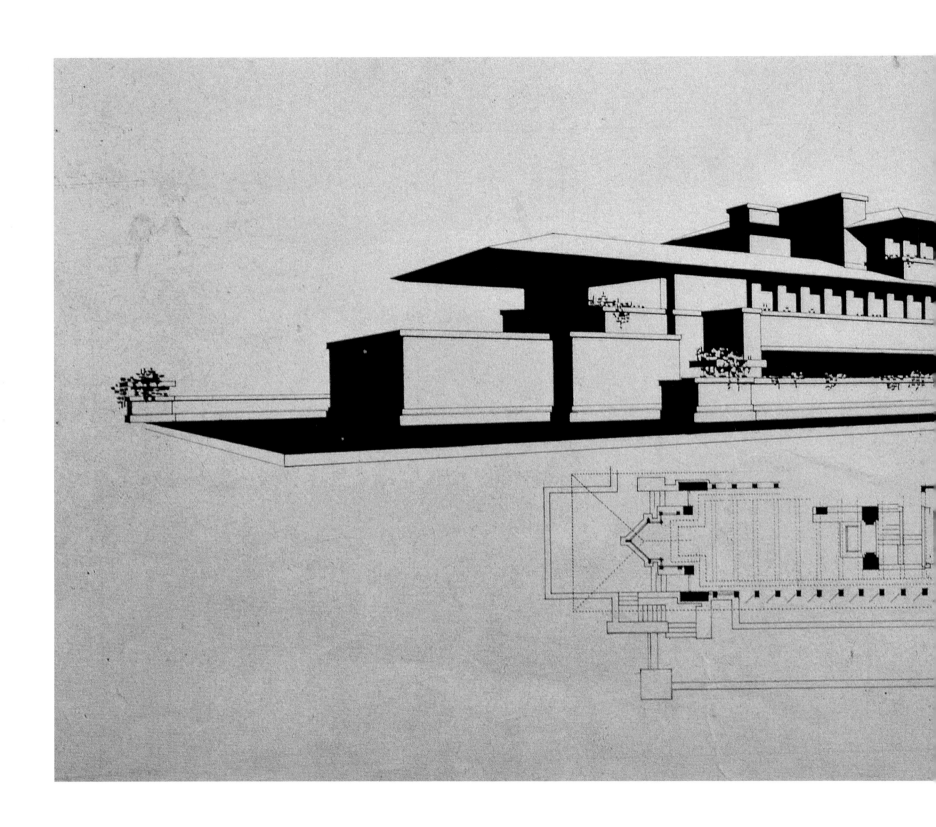

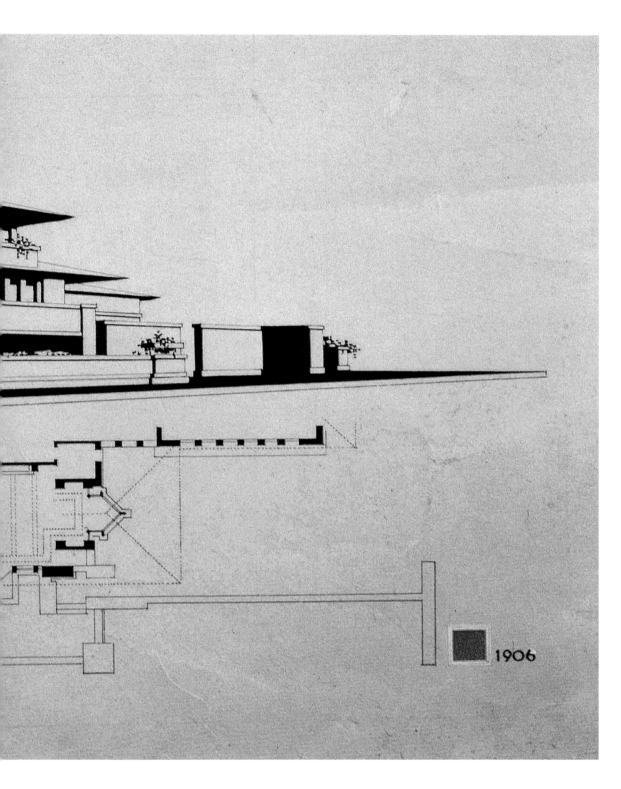

1906

Frederick C. Robie House
Chicago, Illinois, 1908-10
Plan and perspective
Sepia ink on art paper
22 x 35 inches (55.9 x 88.9 cm)
Private collection
FLLW FDN # 0908.003

TALIESIN

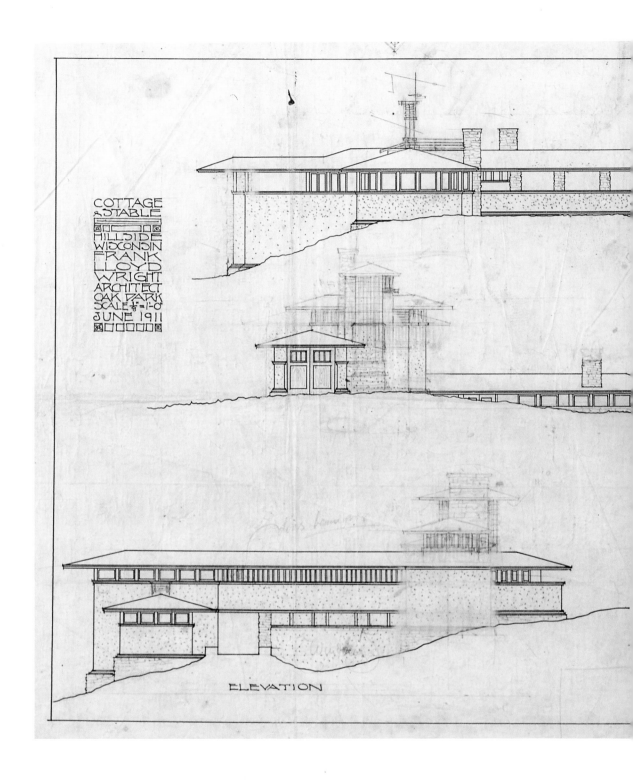

COTTAGE
& STABLE
HILLSIDE
WISCONSIN
FRANK
LLOYD
WRIGHT
ARCHITECT
OAK PARK
SCALE ⅛"=1'-0"
JUNE 1911

ELEVATION

Taliesin I
Spring Green, Wisconsin, 1911
Elevations
Ink on tracing cloth
24 x 40 inches (61 x 101.6 cm)
The Frank Lloyd Wright Foundation
FLLW FDN # 1104.004

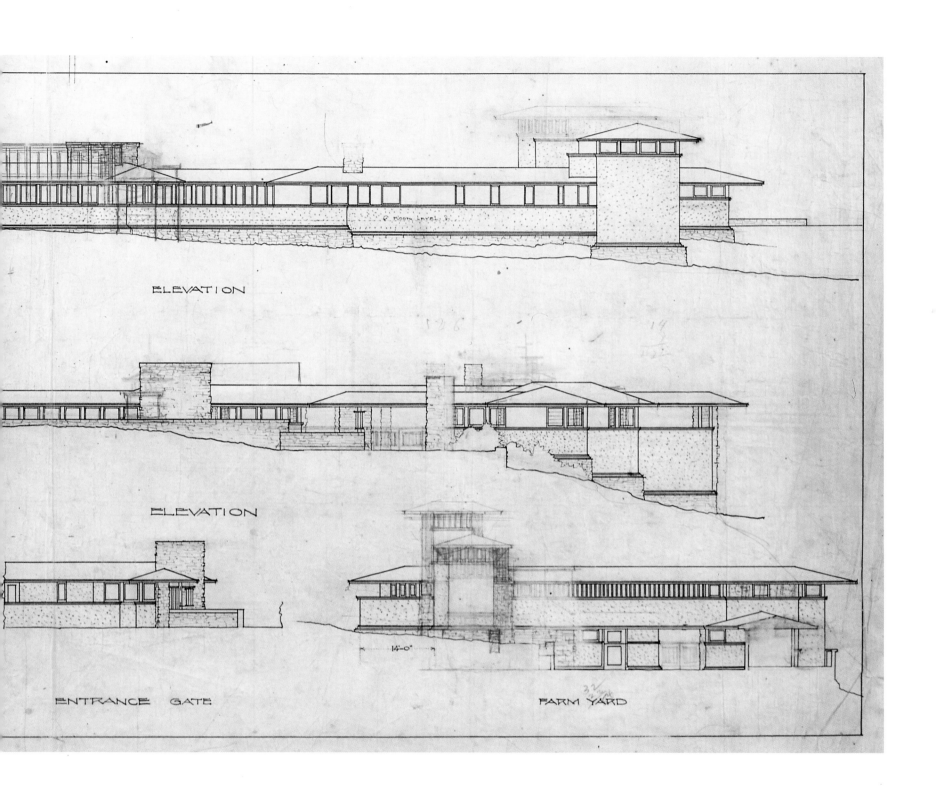

ELEVATION

ELEVATION

ENTRANCE GATE

14'-0"

FARM YARD

TALIESIN

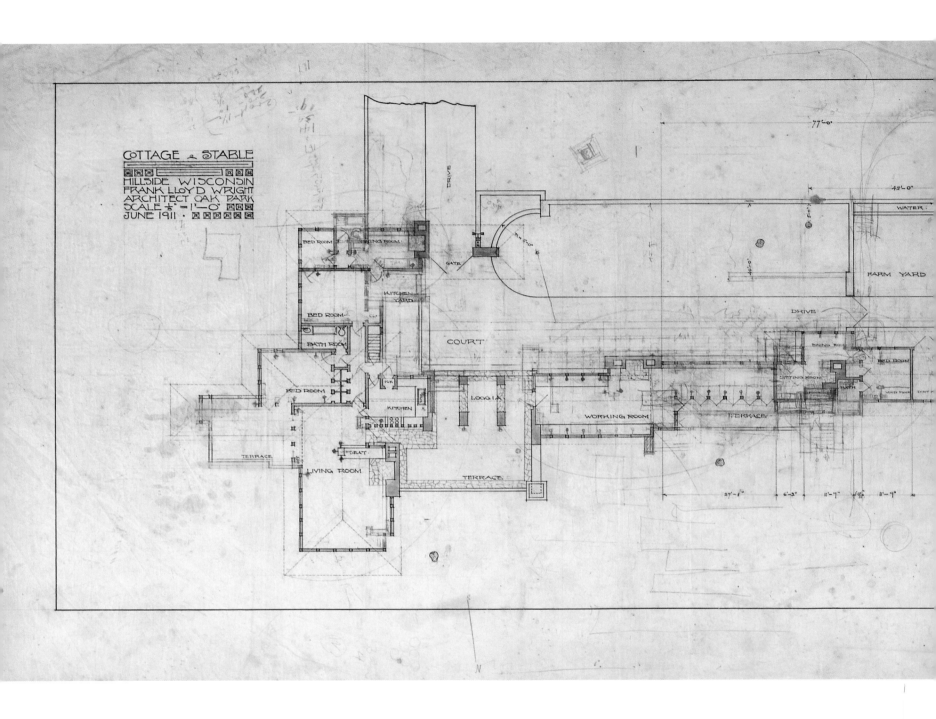

Taliesin I
Spring Green, Wisconsin, 1911
Plan
Graphite pencil, ink, and ink wash on tracing cloth
21 ¼ x 39 ¾ inches (54 x 101 cm)
The Frank Lloyd Wright Foundation
FLLW FDN # 1104.003

FRANK LLOYD WRIGHT'S TALIESIN:
HIS MOST CHERISHED BUILDING
In 1911 Frank Lloyd Wright built his home Taliesin on
the brow of a Wisconsin hill in the valley settled by his
maternal Welsh grandfather, Richard Lloyd Jones. Up
to that time Wright had lived in the Chicago suburb of
Oak Park where, in 1889, he had built a house for his
growing family. In 1897, four years after he had opened
his architectural practice in Chicago, to his house he
added a studio, which provided a reception office,

library, drafting room, and private office. This Oak Park
Studio he himself referred to as the Oak Park work-
shop. Here he and his draftsmen carried on their work,
while at the same time he maintained, for the convenience of his clients, an office in downtown Chicago.

By 1909, however, Wright had admittedly grown
weary of his work. "This absorbing, consuming phase
of my experience as an architect ended about 1909.
I had almost reached my fortieth year. Weary, I was
losing grip on my work and even my interest in it. . . .

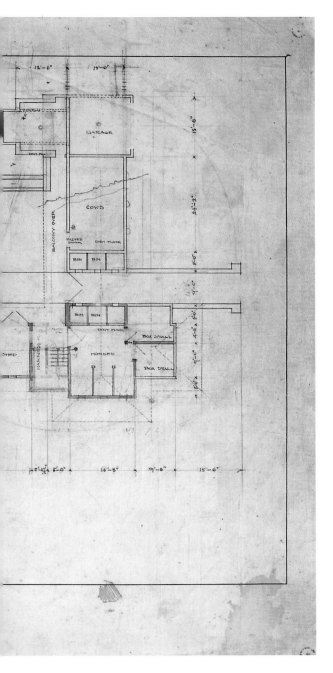

Everything, personal or otherwise, bore heavily down upon me. Domesticity most of all."[1]

He had fallen in love with Mamah Borthwick Cheney, wife of his client Edwin Cheney. At this time, 1909, he received a proposal from the German publisher Ernst Wasmuth inviting him to prepare drawings for a monograph of his work. Taking Mamah along with him, deserting his wife and six children but providing for them as best he could for the time he would be away, they sailed for Germany and arrived in Berlin on 7 November. By 24 November, he had signed a contract with Wasmuth for the publication of a two-volume monograph. In 1910 Mamah went to Sweden to meet the feminist Ellen Key and eventually settled in Leipzig to teach languages. Wright, meanwhile, had gone on to Florence and established a residence for himself in the hill town of Fiesole. He arranged for his son Lloyd and draftsman Taylor Woolley to join him in order to prepare the drawings for the monograph. Mamah soon left Germany and arrived at Fiesole. By the autumn, drawings for the monograph were complete, and sent to Berlin. Ongoing issues with the publication, however, kept Wright and Mamah from a final return to the States until spring of 1911.

Life for him in Oak Park was still a closed road, and accordingly he took temporary residence in an apartment in Chicago. The question loomed as to where he would eventually live and work. It seemed most logical to him to return to the valley of his ancestors in Wisconsin, a place well known and very dear to his heart, a place of his boyhood summers, and where he had later built several buildings. "Work, life and love I transferred to the beloved ancestral Valley wherein my mother foreseeing the plight I would be in had bought the low hill on which Taliesin now stands and offered it to me now as a refuge."[2]

As noted, this was the valley to which his maternal grandfather, Jones, had come from Wales. A Unitarian minister, his impassioned preaching brought upon him the accusation of heresy, and he therefore gathered his family and left Wales, heading for Wisconsin, where

another family member had earlier established himself. After a grueling sea voyage and trying to set down roots in other Wisconsin locations, he finally chose this valley bordering the Wisconsin River. Out of a dense wilderness, he carved farmlands and meadows, built homes and barns. His sons grew to become farmers and ministers, his daughters, educators. The Lloyd Jones clan was deeply steeped in the transcendental thought of the time, especially the writings of Ralph Waldo Emerson and the English poets, foremost among them William Blake. Wright spent his boyhood summers on the farm of his Uncle James. It was a hard and painful experience for the boy, living the life of a farmer, and as the family motto went, "Adding tired to tired and then adding it all over again." Yet this rigorous life on the farm instilled in Wright an abiding love and faith in the agrarian way of life, while at the same time he was steeped in the transcendentalism of his mother, aunts, and uncles. This would prove to be a constant and strong fiber in his life, from which he would endlessly draw strength and inspiration.

Some of Wright's earliest architectural work took place in the Jones Valley, known to him in his boyhood years. In 1886 Joseph Lyman Silsbee designed a chapel, Unity Chapel, for the Lloyd Jones family, set in the family graveyard with a forest of pine trees planted on one side of the property for family picnics. The young Wright was responsible for the dropped ceiling of repetitive square wood panels. In later life he claimed it as his first work in architecture. At the same time, his aunts, Jane and Ellen Lloyd Jones had established the Hillside Home School. It was a home school for boys and girls ages five to eighteen, with a curriculum far in advance for its time. Wright, when he had just arrived in Chicago in the spring of 1887, designed for his aunts the Home Building, a shingle-style three-story structure. Ten years later, the aunts asked Wright to design a windmill for the reservoir on a hill above the school buildings and visible all around the valley. Wright named the tower Romeo and Juliet and always referred to it as his first "engineering-architecture." The windmill stood

TALIESIN

Taliesin I
Spring Green, Wisconsin, 1911
Exterior of living room
The Frank Lloyd Wright Foundation
FLLW FDN # 1104.0004

Taliesin I
Spring Green, Wisconsin, 1911
Views of living room
The Frank Lloyd Wright Foundation
FLLW FDN # 1104.0060

Taliesin I
Spring Green, Wisconsin, 1911
View of exterior court over roofs
The Frank Lloyd Wright Foundation
FLLW FDN # 1104.0005

on a high hill. Romeo, the lozenge-shaped element that protruded out of the plan, acted as a storm prow toward the southeast (from where the prevalent storms usually came), and carried the pump rod for the well along with the support for the windmill wheel. Juliet, the octagon element of the plan, was supported by iron rods anchored in the stone, bolted to the uprights, and floored every ten feet. At the top of Juliet there is an observation platform, reached by an outside iron ladder secured to the tower. Thus interlocked together, if Juliet fell, Romeo would fall likewise. But the tower weathered storm after storm for almost a century. When the iron supports finally gave way, the tower was demolished and then rebuilt and stands, proudly, today.

In 1902 the aunts Jane and Ellen requested a new school building, since they had outgrown the Home Building. The one stipulation they required of their nephew was that the building be made of stone and oak. This was in consideration of their Welsh Druid background, wherein stone and oak trees were sacred. Wright complied as they had wished with a structure that contained a large assembly room, additional classrooms, a gymnasium, a woodworking shop, and two galleries, the Dana Gallery, funded by Wright's client Susan Lawrence Dana, and the Roberts Gallery, likewise funded by another Wright client, Charles E. Roberts, the man responsible for Wright's getting the job to design Unity Temple. This building, with modifications and

additions, served as the home of the Taliesin Fellowship, a school for architects founded by Wright and his wife Olgivanna in 1932 and prospering today as the Frank Lloyd Wright School of Architecture.

When Wright acquired the school and all its property, he tried over and over again to modify the scale of the 1887 three-story shingle Home Building, which stood adjacent to the Hillside Home School building of 1902. (Finally exasperated with the problem, he demolished the Home Building in 1950.)

Now, in 1911, he returned to Jones Valley. In his biography, he writes:

Taliesin was the name of a Welsh poet, a druid-bard who sang to Wales the glories of fine art. Many legends cling to that beloved reverend name in Wales. . . . Since all my relatives had Welsh names for their places, why not Taliesin for mine? Literally the Welsh word means "shining brow."

This hill on which Taliesin now stands as "brow" was one of my favorite places when as a boy looking for pasque flowers I went there in March sun while snow still streaked the hillsides. When you are on the low hill-crown you are out in mid-air as though swinging in a plane, the Valley and two others dropping away from you leaving the tree-tops standing below all about you.

TALIESIN

Taliesin II
Spring Green, Wisconsin, 1914
Aerial perspective
Ink on paper
16 x 19 inches (40.6 x 48.3 cm)
The Frank Lloyd Wright Foundation
FLLW FDN # 1403.002

·SECTION THROUGH COURT LOOKING EAST·

·SECTION THROUGH COURT LOOKING WEST·

·SECTION THROUGH REAR COURT LOOKING NORTH·

·SECTION THROUGH FORE COURT LOOKING SOUTH·

Taliesin II
Spring Green, Wisconsin, 1914
Four elevations
Ink on tracing cloth
30 5/8 x 43 5/8 inches (77.8 x 110.8 cm)
The Frank Lloyd Wright Foundation
FLLW FDN # 1403.013

And "Romeo and Juliet" still stood in plain view over to the southeast. The Hillside Home School was just over the ridge. As a boy I had learned to know the ground-plan of the region in every line and feature. For me now its elevation is the modeling of the hills, the weaving and the fabric that clings to them, the look of it all in tender green or covered with snow or in full glow of summer that bursts into glorious blaze of autumn. I still feel myself as much a part of it as the trees and birds and bees are, and the red barns. Or as the animals are, for that matter....[3]

It was unthinkable to me, at least unbearable, that any house should be put *on* that beloved hill. I knew well that no house should ever be *on* a hill or *on* anything. It should be *of*

the hill. Hill and house should live together each the happier for the other. It was still a very young faith that undertook to build that house. It was the same faith, though, that plants twigs for orchards, vineslips for vineyards, and small whips to become beneficent shade trees. And I planted them all about.[4]

Wright's description of the gardens and farmlands around the house are perhaps the most rhapsodic of all his writings. He was engaged totally in the life of the farm, the produce, the animals, the romance of the harvest, and the storing of the produce in the root cellar. It is as if he had returned to that childhood life that was, then, so strenuous and difficult for him, but now "[a]ll these items of livelihood came back—improved from boyhood. And so

Taliesin II
Spring Green, Wisconsin, 1914
View from Midway Hill
The Frank Lloyd Wright Foundation
FLLW FDN # 1403.0044

began a 'shining brow' for the hill, the hill rising unbroken above it to crown the exuberance of a life in all these rural riches."[5]

In the nearby hills were stone quarries from which cartloads of yellow sand limestone were drawn by horses up the hill to form courts, walls, pavements, and massive stone fireplaces with great stone chimneys. Sand from the banks of the Wisconsin River was brought up the hill, and the color of the sand became the color of the plastered walls. The roofs are sheathed in cedar shingles left to weather a silver-gray. Rooflines reiterated the hills and valleys, the roofs spreading wide and generously over the plaster walls beneath or the bands of glass windows.

In his autobiography, Wright wrote of his purpose: "Taliesin was to be the recreation ground for my children and their children perhaps for many generations more. This modest human programme in turns of rural Wisconsin arranged itself around the hilltop in a series of four varied courts leading one into the other, the courts all together forming a sort of drive along the hillside flanked by low buildings on one side and by flower gardens against the stone walls that retained the hill crown on the other."[6]

Without doubt, Taliesin was the most personal and the most cherished building that Frank Lloyd Wright ever designed. "When I am away from it, like some rubber band stretched out but ready to snap back immediately the pull is relaxed or released, I get back to it happy to be there again."[7]

That happiness was brutally shattered on 15 August 1914. While Wright was away in Chicago working on the finishing touches of Midway Gardens, a desperate telephone call came to him informing him that a servant at Taliesin had run amok, setting fire to the living quarters. As the occupants ran out, the man had slain seven persons, including Mamah and her two children, who were visiting her; a draftsman, Emil Brodelle; the young son of William Weston; the gardener, David Lindblom; and a faithful workman, Thomas Brunker. Wright took the train from Chicago accompanied by Edwin Cheney, father of the children, and Wright's son John, who was working with him on the Midway Gardens. They arrived at dusk to find the living quarters

TALIESIN

Taliesin II
Spring Green, Wisconsin, 1914
Exterior from garden
The Frank Lloyd Wright Foundation
FLLW FDN # 1403.0028

Taliesin II
Spring Green, Wisconsin, 1914
Interior view of living room
The Frank Lloyd Wright Foundation
FLLW FDN # 1403.0041

Taliesin III
Spring Green, Wisconsin, 1925–59
Living room fireplace
The Frank Lloyd Wright Foundation
FLLW FDN # 2501.0010

of Taliesin still smoldering from the fire and seven bodies laid out on the courtyard. The working part of the building remained, saved by William Weston.

In his autobiography, Wright recalled, "In the little bedroom back of the undestroyed studio I remained in what was left of Taliesin I. . . . The gaping black hole left by the fire in the beautiful hillside was empty, a charred and ugly scar upon my own life. . . . I got no relief in any faith nor yet any in hope, except repulsion, I could feel now only in terms of rebuilding. As days passed into nights I was numb to all but the automatic steps towards rebuilding the home that was destroyed by hateful forces. . . . Steadily, stone by stone, board by board, Taliesin II began to rise from the ashes of Taliesin I."[8]

Late in 1915, Taliesin II stood in place of the first

Taliesin, "a more reposeful and a fine one."[9] Relief in the form of new work arrived with the commission to design the new Imperial Hotel in Tokyo. After making some initial sketches at Taliesin, and showing them to Aisaku Hayashi, the general manager of the hotel, who had come to Taliesin to offer the job to Wright, an official invitation arrived from Tokyo informing Wright to come at once to Japan.

Following the tragedy of 1914, Wright received a letter from a person who claimed she had undergone a similar tragedy and would like to meet him. Miriam Noel, after an appointment had been arranged, came to his office in Chicago. He found her brilliant, sophisticated, and "had evidently been very beautiful and was so distinguished by beauty still. A violet pallor. . . . Mass

TALIESIN

Taliesin III
Spring Green, Wisconsin, 1925–59
View from below
The Frank Lloyd Wright Foundation
FLLW FDN # 2501.0186

of dark red-brown hair. Clear-seeing eyes with a green light in them. Carriage erect and conscious—figure still youthful. . . . A trace of illness seemed to cling to her in the continuous but perceptible shaking of her head."[10]

Miriam accompanied him on his several trips to Japan, where he was overseeing the design and construction of the hotel, but their life there was filled with tension, threats, and sudden outbursts on her part. Upon their return to Taliesin in 1922, Wright was finally granted a divorce from his first wife, Catherine, and thinking marriage might improve their relationship, Wright and Miriam married in 1923. The marriage, however, proved ill-fated. "With marriage she seemed to lose what interest she had in life at Taliesin and become more than ever restless and vindictive. Finally, under circumstances altogether baffling—she left 'to live a life of her own.' To oppose her now in the slightest degree meant violence. I did not really wish to oppose her. . . . So the final arrangements for a divorce were made

by Judge James Hill while I stayed on at Taliesin."[11]

On 20 April 1925, Taliesin II suffered a fate similar to that of Taliesin I—a fire that once again destroyed the living quarters. "When about a year I had finally separated from Miriam, one evening at twilight as the lightning of an approaching storm was playing and the wind was rising, I came down from the evening meal in the little detached dining room on the hill-top to the dwelling in the court below to find smoke pouring from my bedroom. Again—there it was—Fire!"[12]

Within twenty minutes the living quarters of Taliesin were gone, and gone with them were cases and cases of Asian art that Wright had acquired during his sojourn in Japan. Fortunately, this time, there was no loss of life. He could easily rebuild Taliesin, but he grieved over the loss of those art objects: "Images whose souls belonged and could now return to the souls that made them—the precious works of art that were destroyed. I had not protected them. Yes . . . a poor

Taliesin III
Spring Green, Wisconsin, 1925-59
Hydro House
The Frank Lloyd Wright Foundation
FLLW FDN # 2501.2185

trustee for posterity, I. But they should live on in me, was the thought with which I consoled myself."[13]

By this time, Olgivanna Lazovich Hinzenberg was living with Wright at Taliesin. Born in Cetinje, Montenegro, she was educated in czarist Russia. At the age of nineteen, she married Volodia Hinzenberg, a Russian architect several years her senior. They had a child, Svetlana. In 1919 she met the Greek Armenian philosopher G. I. Gurdjieff while she was living in Tiflis (Tbilisi), Georgia, and she was immediately drawn to his presence.

"He had a beautifully closely shaven head and classic features, with a fine nose and strong jaws; his eyes were dark and luminous. It was a noble face, with the traditional oriental black moustache which seemed natural on his face. His expression was of profound strength and great compassion. He was part Greek and part Armenian."[14]

Following that first meeting, and several others, she decided to become one of his pupils. With him and his

group, she traveled to Istanbul, Dresden, Paris, and eventually Fontainebleau-Avon where he established his school in the Château de Prieuré. By 1924, he told Olgivanna that he had taught her all he could and that she should resume her life. She had separated from her husband, who had migrated to Chicago. Gurdjieff advised her to go there and try to rebuild their marriage, mainly for the sake of their child, Svetlana. It was thus on 30 November 1924 that she and Wright accidentally met during a performance of the Russian ballerina Tamara Karsavina, whom Olgivanna had earlier seen perform in Moscow. Olgivanna hurried to the theater so as not to miss the first curtain. What happened next she relates in her autobiography:

I found at the box office that there was only one ticket left which someone had just turned in. It was in a box with others. Trying to find my way to the box, down a long, dimly lit corridor, I saw, some

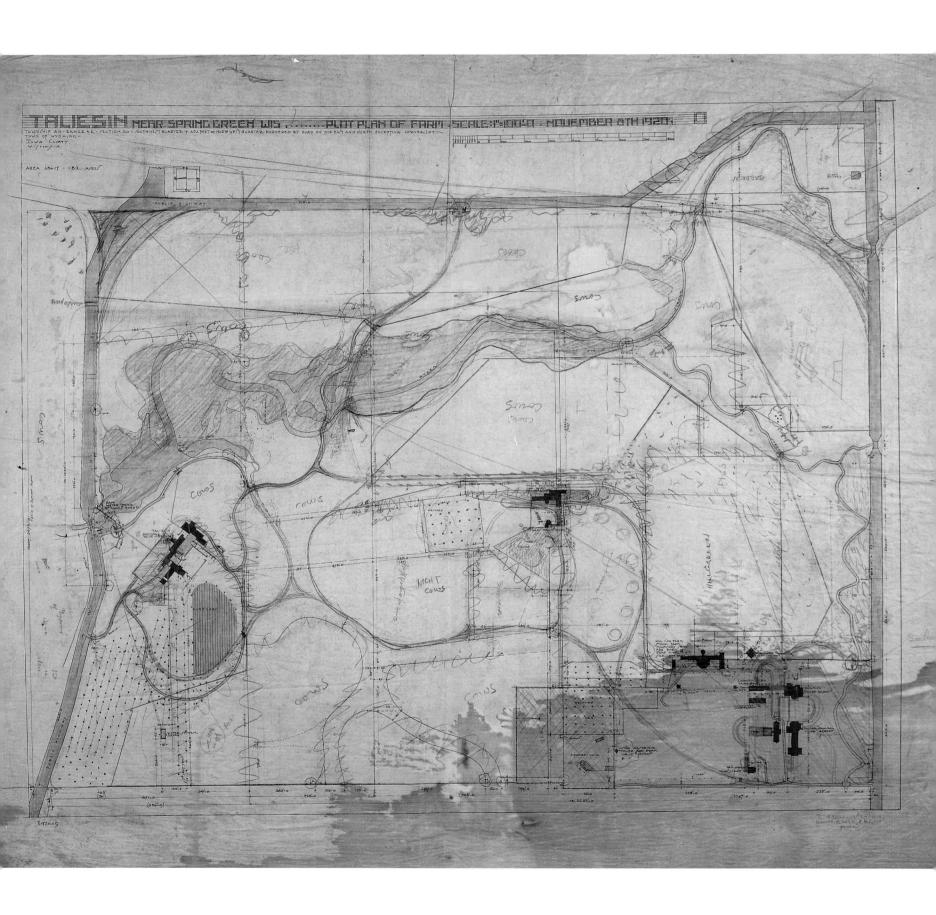

Taliesin Farmlands
Spring Green, Wisconsin, 1920–59
Site plan
Color pencil and ink on tracing cloth
35 x 42 inches (88.9 x 106.7 cm)
The Frank Lloyd Wright Foundation
FLLW FDN # 3420.005

Taliesin III
Spring Green, Wisconsin, 1925–59
Aerial view
The Frank Lloyd Wright Foundation
FLLW FDN # 2501.1355

distance ahead of me in a crowd of people, a strikingly handsome, noble head with a crown of wavy grey hair. The image of a Georgian poet whose portrait I had stopped to look at every day on my way to school in Tiflis floated in and out of my mind. And now suddenly this head, all but hidden in a sea of strangers held a great fascination for me. But then I lost sight of the face and also lost my way to the box. A young usher escorted me towards it and when I sat down in the chair he indicated, the curtain had already gone up. My chair was by the side of the man I had glimpsed in the crowd. My heart beat fast; I dared not look at him again. What I saw on the stage dissolved into that world when I was fourteen, into the theater in Tiflis, into the street with the portrait in the window which I saw daily on

my way to school. Suspended somewhere between two worlds, I heard a voice next to me say directly to me, "Don't you think that these dancers and the dances are dead?" I nodded my head quickly, looking at him again to make my two worlds harmonize. He made a broad gesture with his hand toward the audience. "It is all right," he said, "The dancers are dead and so is the audience; they are well matched." And he smiled, looking at me with unconcealed admiration. I knew then that this was to be.[15]

When she had taken her seat in the box next to Wright, he later recorded that:

I secretly observed her aristocratic bearing, no hat, her dark hair parted in the middle and smoothed over her ears, a light small shawl over her shoulders, little or no makeup, very simply dressed. French, I thought—very French . . . and yet perhaps Russian? Whatever her nationality I instantly liked her looks and wondered who she was and where from. And why. Losing all interest in the stage. Although I can perfectly see Karsavina poised on one toe as she stood when the gentle stranger entered the box and my life.[16]

Shortly after their first meeting, while walking together in the street in Chicago, Wright invited her to come to Taliesin. "I promise you one thing," he said gaily, "from now on you won't be seen for the dust."[17]

"'Oh yes, I will come,' she replied, 'because I want to meet life with you. . . .' With ebullient gaiety he took my arm and we walked quickly in the brisk air of twilight. We walked like that all our life together."[18]

Although living together at Taliesin II, they were both waiting for divorces; he from Miriam Noel, and she from Volodia Hinzenberg. She also pleaded for custody of Volodia's and her child, Svetlana. It was that evening in April when Taliesin II was consumed by fire that she told Wright that she was going to have his child. Their daughter, Iovanna, was born the following December. Her name derived from Iovan, Olgivanna's father, and Anna, Wright's mother.

Taliesin III was thus built over the ashes of Taliesin II, a larger home in all aspects. It was a home for Wright and his new family. The living room was enlarged with a higher ceiling over the dining area. The former loggia, which was mainly a small area between two rooms, was expanded to a much larger space, reaching up two stories with a balcony. Above the bedroom area at the end of the building Wright added a second story with bedrooms for the two girls. This led into the balcony over the loggia and down a corridor to an opening over the living room.

Taliesin, as he wrote about it originally, was planned for his children and their children for generations to come. However, Taliesin III did not see that vision materialize, but something else took place instead. When, in 1932, Wright and Olgivanna opened their private home to found a school for architectural students, the private family soon expanded into an "extended family" composed of young men and women of the newly founded Taliesin Fellowship.

That extended family persists to this day as the Frank Lloyd Wright School of Architecture. As the beauty and tranquility of the building nourished and inspired people within it since 1911, so, too, does it continue to generate that same atmosphere as it becomes a haven for anyone in search of finer values, in whatever phase of work and study, even beyond the art of architecture and into the quest for a richer and truer meaning of life in all its aspects—environmental, personal, and spiritual.

NOTES

1. Frank Lloyd Wright, *Frank Lloyd Wright: An Autobiography* (San Francisco: Pomegranate, 2005), pp. 162–63.
2. Ibid., p. 167.
3. Ibid.
4. Ibid., pp. 168–69.
5. Ibid., p. 170.
6. Ibid., p. 171.
7. Ibid., p. 368.
8. Ibid., pp. 188–89.
9. Ibid., p. 190.
10. Ibid., p. 210.
11. Ibid., p. 260.
12. Ibid., p. 261.
13. Ibid., p. 262.
14. Olgivanna Lloyd Wright, *Autobiography* (unpublished), chap. 4, p. 10.
15. Ibid., chap. 11, pp. 2, 3.
16. Frank Lloyd Wright, *An Autobiography*, p. 509.
17. Olgivanna Lloyd Wright, *Autobiography*, chap. 11, p. 19.
18. Ibid.

Taliesin III
Spring Green, Wisconsin, 1925–59
Exterior view
Photo by David Heald
Courtesy Solomon R. Guggenheim Foundation

TALIESIN

Hillside Theater #2, Taliesin III
Spring Green, Wisconsin, 1952
Interior view with curtain
Photo by Allen Lape Davison
The Frank Lloyd Wright Foundation
FLLW FDN # 5213.0115

Midway Gardens (demolished)
Chicago, Illinois, 1913–14
Aerial perspective
Graphite pencil, color pencil, and ink on tracing cloth
16 ⅛ x 40 ⅛ inches (41 x 101.9 cm)
The Frank Lloyd Wright Foundation
FLLW FDN # 1401.007

Midway Gardens (demolished)
Chicago, Illinois, 1913–14
View of Summer Garden
The Frank Lloyd Wright Foundation
FLLW FDN # 1401.0032

Midway Gardens (demolished)
Chicago, Illinois, 1913–14
Interior furniture
Pencil and ink on paper
16 ⅛ x 20 inches (41 x 50.8 cm)
The Frank Lloyd Wright Foundation
FLLW FDN # 1401.020

Midway Gardens (demolished)
Chicago, Illinois, 1913–14
Interior
The Frank Lloyd Wright Foundation
FLLW FDN # 1401.0039

Cinema for San Diego (project)
San Diego, California, 1915
Perspective
Ink and watercolor on art paper
19 x 14 ³/₄ inches (48.3 x 37.5 cm)
The Frank Lloyd Wright Foundation
FLLW FDN # 0517.002

1897

FRANK LLOYD WRIGHT ARCHITECT 1897 San Diego 190

American Ready-Cut System Houses, "Model C-3"
Milwaukee, Wisconsin, 1915–17
Perspective
Lithograph
19 x 12 inches (48.3 x 30.5 cm)
The Frank Lloyd Wright Foundation
FLLW FDN # 1506.117

American Ready-Cut System Houses, "Model C-3"
Milwaukee, Wisconsin, 1915–17
Isometric plan
Ink on paper
19 x 15 inches (48.3 x 38.1 cm)
The Frank Lloyd Wright Foundation
FLLW FDN # 1506.137

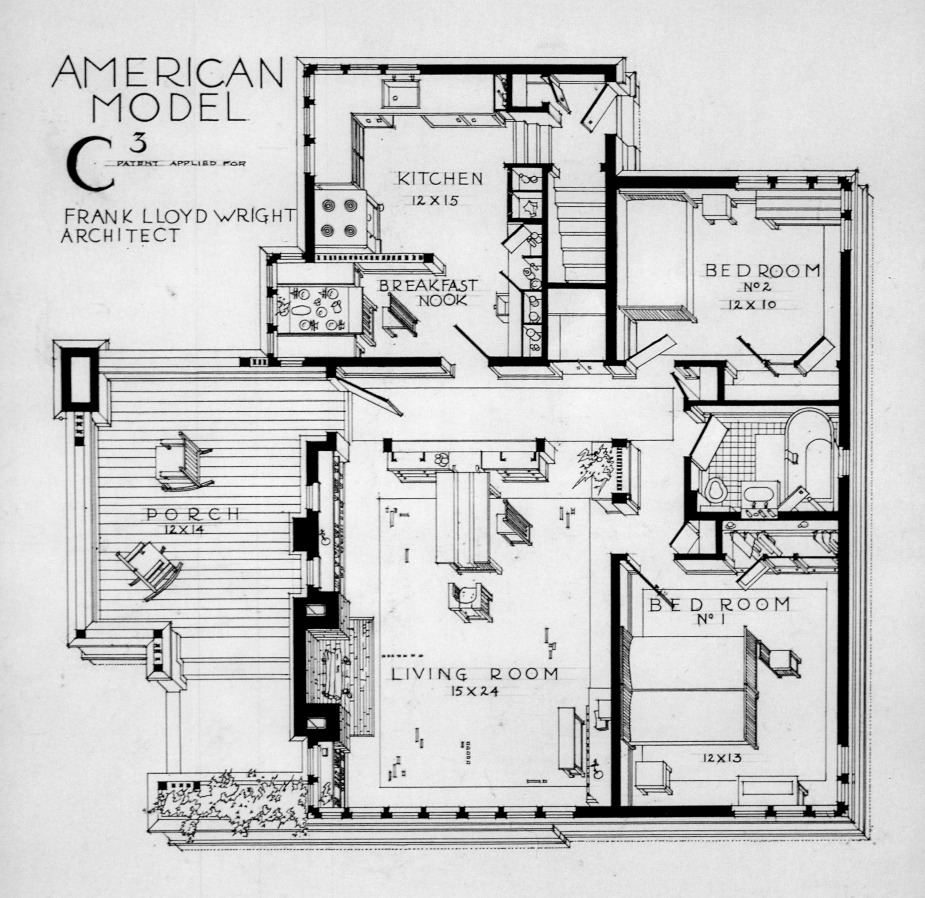

AMERICAN
MODEL
C³
PATENT APPLIED FOR

FRANK LLOYD WRIGHT
ARCHITECT

KITCHEN
12 X 15

BREAKFAST
NOOK

BED ROOM
N°2
12 X 10

PORCH
12 X 14

BED ROOM
N° I

LIVING ROOM
15 X 24

12 X 13

(preceding pages)
Imperial Hotel (Scheme #2, demolished)
Tokyo, Japan, 1912–22
Aerial perspective
Graphite pencil and color pencil on tracing paper
12 x 24 inches (30.5 x 61 cm)
The Frank Lloyd Wright Foundation
FLLW FDN # 1509.017

Imperial Hotel (Scheme #2, demolished)
Tokyo, Japan, 1912–22
Interior perspective
Graphite pencil on paper
18 7/8 x 18 1/8 inches (47.9 x 46 cm)
The Frank Lloyd Wright Foundation
FLLW FDN # 1509.020

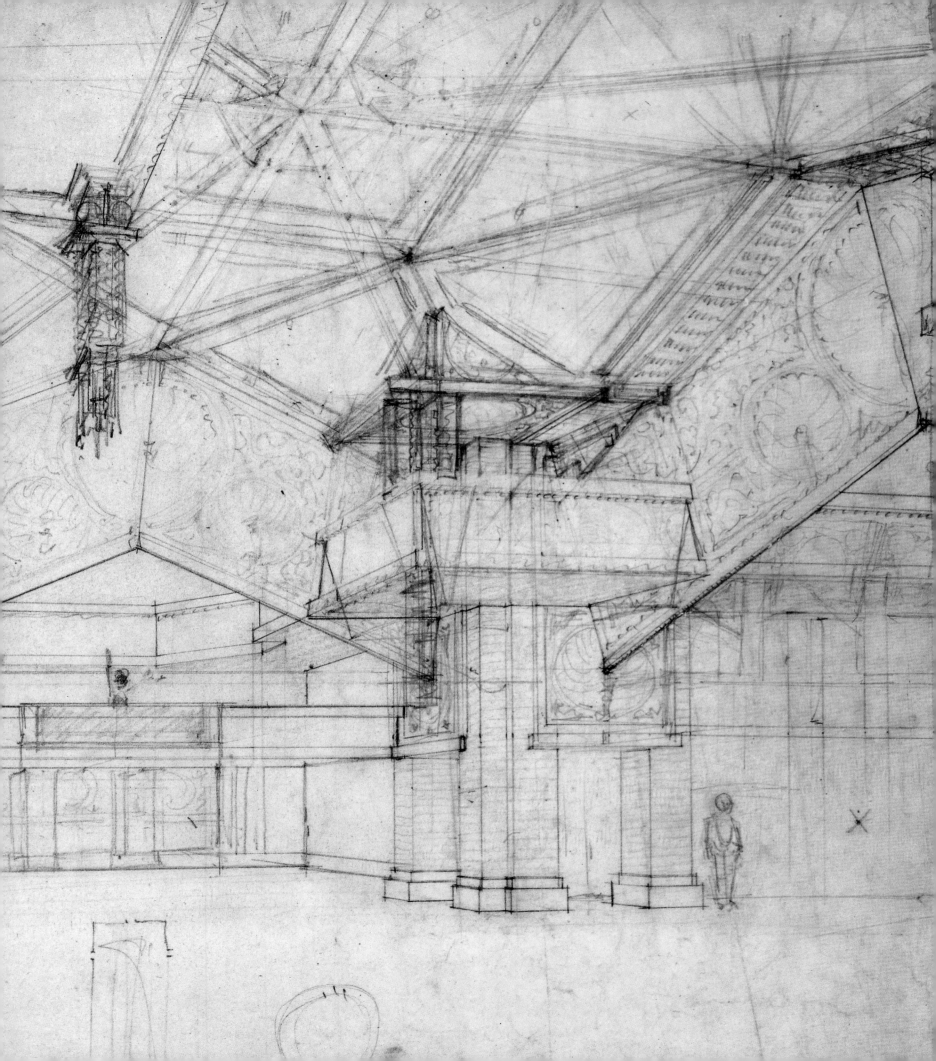

Imperial Hotel (Scheme #2, demolished)
Tokyo, Japan, 1912–22
Exterior Tea Garden
The Frank Lloyd Wright Foundation
FLLW FDN # 1509.0054

Imperial Hotel (Scheme #2, demolished)
Tokyo, Japan, 1912–22
Peacock Room Banquet Hall
The Frank Lloyd Wright Foundation
FLLW FDN # 1509.0268

Aline Barnsdall House, "Hollyhock House"
Los Angeles, California, 1916–21
Perspective
Photographic print
10 $\frac{5}{8}$ x 30 $\frac{3}{8}$ inches (27 x 77.2 cm)
The Frank Lloyd Wright Foundation
FLLW FDN # 1705.061

Aline Barnsdall House, "Hollyhock House"
Los Angeles, California, 1916–21
View into courtyard
The Frank Lloyd Wright Foundation
FLLW FDN # 1705.0090

Aline Barnsdall House, "Hollyhock House"
Los Angeles, California, 1916–21
Living room
Photo by Michael Freeman

Olive Hill Theater Complex for Aline Barnsdall (project)
Los Angeles, California, 1918
Perspective
Graphite pencil and color pencil on paper
6 ¹⁄₂ x 22 ³⁄₄ inches (16.5 x 57.8 cm)
The Frank Lloyd Wright Foundation
FLLW FDN # 2005.003

Alma Bersoldi   (Club luma)

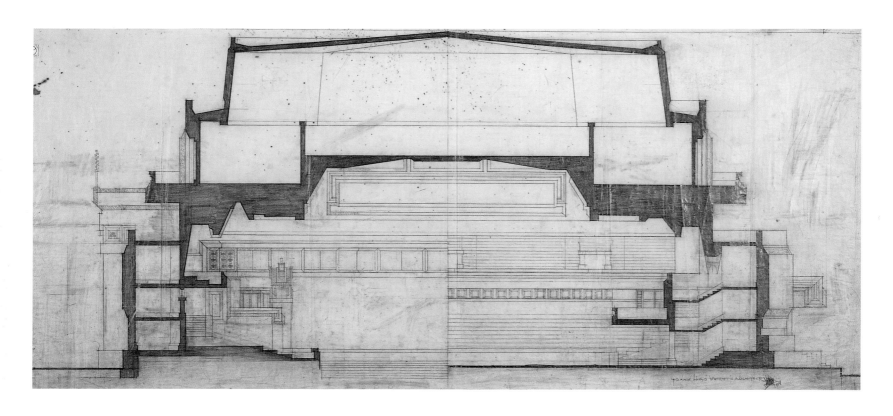

Olive Hill Theater Complex for Aline Barnsdall (project)
Los Angeles, California, 1918
Cross section
Graphite pencil and ink wash on tracing cloth
21 x 45 inches (53.3 x 114.3 cm)
The Frank Lloyd Wright Foundation
FLLW FDN # 2005.007

Olive Hill Theater Complex for Aline Barnsdall (project)
Los Angeles, California, 1918
Model
The Frank Lloyd Wright Foundation
FLLW FDN # 2005.0011

Doheny Ranch Resort (project)
Beverly Hills, California, 1923
Perspective
Graphite pencil and color pencil on paper
17 x 22 ½ inches (43.2 x 57.2 cm)
The Frank Lloyd Wright Foundation
FLLW FDN #2104.006

Doheny Ranch Resort (project)
Beverly Hills, California, 1923
Perspective
Graphite pencil on paper
24 x 40 inches (61 x 101.6 cm)
The Frank Lloyd Wright Foundation
FLLW FDN # 2104.025

Lake Tahoe Summer Colony (project)
Lake Tahoe, California, 1922–24
Perspective
Graphite pencil and color pencil on paper
21 3/4 x 15 inches (55.2 x 38.1 cm)
The Frank Lloyd Wright Foundation
FLLW FDN # 2205.001

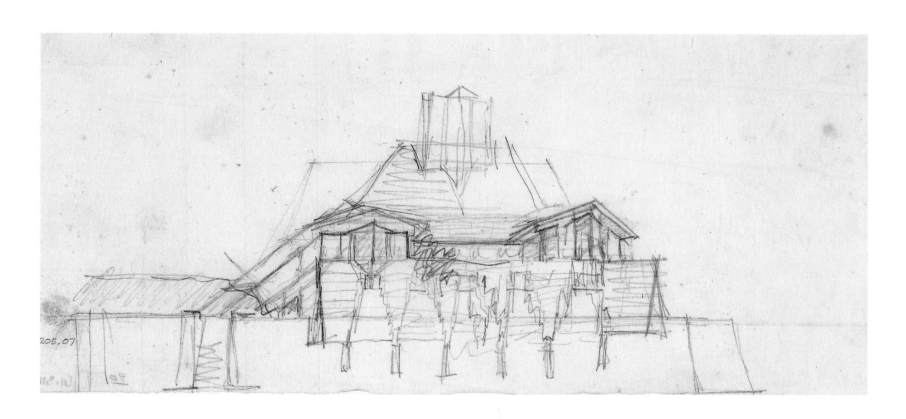

Lake Tahoe Summer Colony (project)
Lake Tahoe, California, 1922-24
Perspective
Graphite pencil on paper
5 x 11 3/4 inches (12.7 x 29.8 cm)
The Frank Lloyd Wright Foundation
FLLW FDN # 2205.007

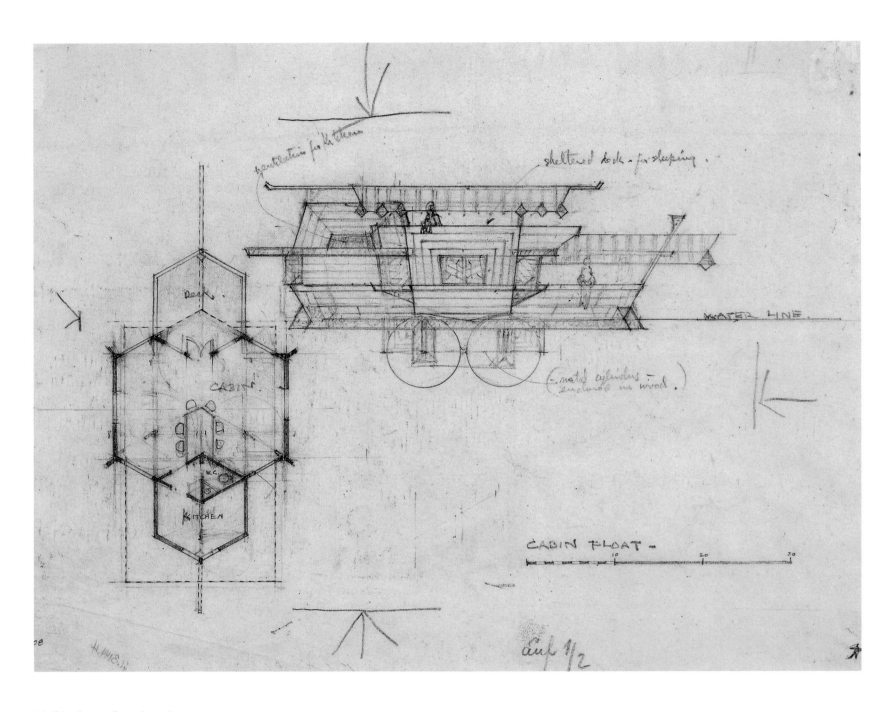

Lake Tahoe Summer Colony (project)
Lake Tahoe, California, 1922–24
Plan and Elevation
Graphite pencil on paper
9 1/4 x 11 3/4 inches (23.5 x 29.8 cm)
The Frank Lloyd Wright Foundation
FLLW FDN # 2205.008

Lake Tahoe Summer Colony (project)
Lake Tahoe, California, 1923
Historic photograph of site
The Frank Lloyd Wright Foundation
FLLW FDN # 2205.0005

Samuel Freeman House
Los Angeles, California, 1923-24
Perspective
Graphite pencil and color pencil on paper
9 1/4 x 15 3/4 inches (23.5 x 40 cm)
The Frank Lloyd Wright Foundation
FLLW FDN # 2402.002

GORDON STRONG AUTOMOBILE OBJECTIVE
AND PLANETARIUM (PROJECT)

Gordon Strong Automobile Objective and Planetarium (project)
Sugarloaf Mountain, Maryland, 1924
Perspective
Color pencil on tracing paper
20 x 31 inches (50.8 x 78.7 cm)
The Frank Lloyd Wright Foundation
FLLW FDN # 2505.039

WRIGHT'S FIRST SPIRAL RAMP

This project, designed as a tourist attraction meant for the top of Sugarloaf Mountain, Maryland, was to be approached by tourists driving their cars. Visitors would park on the main level and enter the building directly, or, rather, as was certainly the intent of the design, they would drive up a spiral ramp and circumnavigate the exterior of the structure until they reached the top. Here attendants would take their cars down another spiral ramp to a parking lot on the ground level. The tourists could then descend the building on yet another pedestrian ramp, and view spread out 360 degrees before them the surrounding landscape, a world of forests, rock formations, water features, and fields. Once having arrived at the ground level, they would then enter the main building and make their way to the planetarium. Here a panorama of galaxies, stars, suns, and planets would unfold on the domed ceiling above. Visitors would find an aquarium surrounding the northeast side of the planetarium. Thus in and on one structure people would experience a space both purely enjoyable as well as educational, bringing together the surrounding landscape, the starry heavens, and the

oceans below. Attached to the main level was a triangular, one-story building providing dressing rooms, checkrooms, and rooms for steam baths, with a garden in the center. Attached at another point of the plan was a tower that enclosed stairs and elevators accessible to all parts of the outer pedestrian ramp as well as the seven levels and top level of the building itself.

As Wright developed his plan, the final set of drawings was labeled: Level "O" is the ground level, with entrance to the planetarium, aquarium, and steam baths. Level "1" provides a wide esplanade circumventing the planetarium, a space reserved for both restaurant and amusements. Level "2" contains storage areas. Level "3" contains a restaurant with views over the ramp to the northeast. At one place in the restaurant a door gives access to a bridge over the outside ramps and on to a triangular terrace garden. A bridge at one edge spans over a waterfall, while steps at the other edge descend to the ground level below. Here the project encourages people to venture more closely into the surrounding landscape, albeit a rocky and precipitous environment. Level "4" provides yet another restaurant, this time facing in a direction opposite to the one

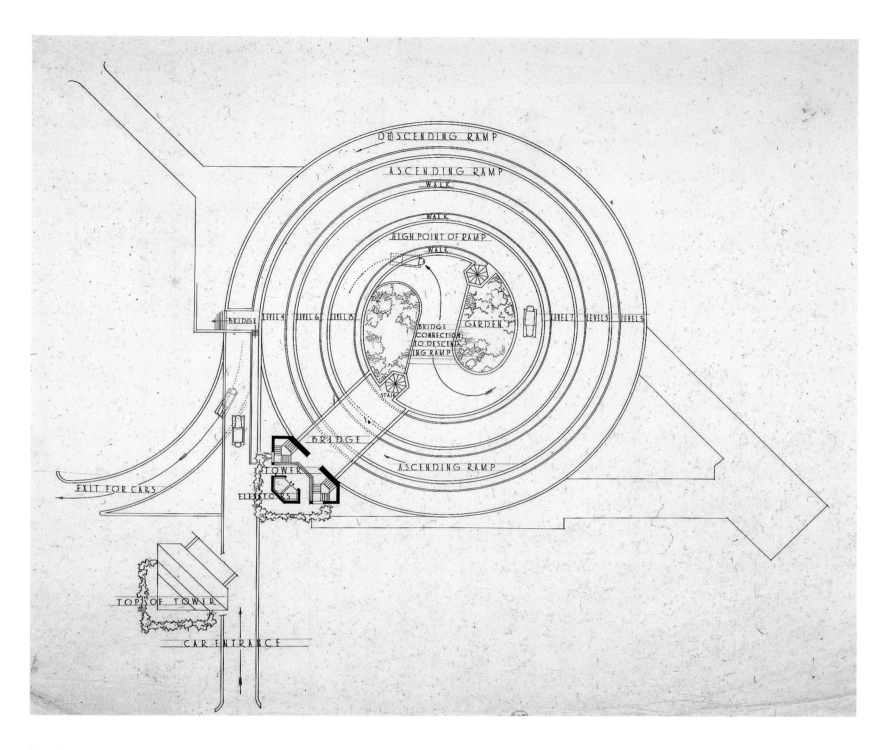

Gordon Strong Automobile Objective and Planetarium (project)
Sugarloaf Mountain, Maryland, 1924
Plan
Ink on paper
24 ½ x 35 ⅞ inches (62.2 x 91.1 cm)
The Frank Lloyd Wright Foundation
FLLW FDN # 2505.066

located on Level "3." Level "5" consists of a lounge and bedrooms for the employees, with more on Level "6." On Level "7" there is a garden, in the center, over the top of the dome below, and the "Top" level is the crossover where cars are met and the descending ramps begin, one for the cars, the other for the pedestrians.

The plans of these levels, along with the elevations and sections, represent the final version of this project, after a great deal of preliminary work. In the Frank Lloyd Wright Archives there are some seventy-four drawings, while others exist in the Gordon Strong Archives, "Stronghold, Inc.," while even more are at the Library of Congress, in Washington, D.C.

This was not an easy commission for Wright. As it progressed, differences in the general concept of the plan eventually grew between architect and client. Gordon Strong was a wealthy and successful Chicago businessman who had acquired a great deal of property on and around the summit of Sugarloaf Mountain, in Frederick County, Maryland. He was eager to construct a tourist facility there that would attract motorists from nearby Washington, D.C., and Baltimore, Maryland. In a long letter to Wright, at the beginning of negotiations concerning the commission, Strong outlined, in great detail, what he wanted in the way of a tourist attraction on Sugarloaf Mountain. The letter was most specific re-

GORDON STRONG AUTOMOBILE OBJECTIVE
AND PLANETARIUM (PROJECT)

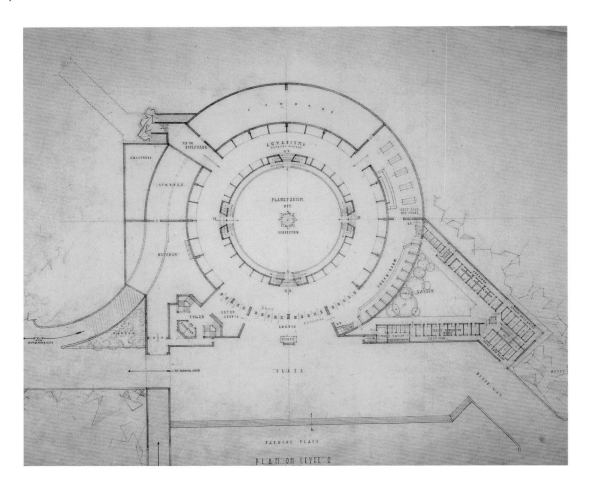

Gordon Strong Automobile Objective and Planetarium (project)
Sugarloaf Mountain, Maryland, 1924
Plan of Level "0"
Graphite pencil on paper
24 3/4 x 31 7/8 inches (62.9 x 81 cm)
The Frank Lloyd Wright Foundation
FLLW FDN # 2505.041

Gordon Strong Automobile Objective and Planetarium (project)
Sugarloaf Mountain, Maryland, 1924
Aerial perspective
Graphite pencil on paper
10 3/4 x 8 3/8 inches (27.3 x 21.3 cm)
The Frank Lloyd Wright Foundation
FLLW FDN # 2505.023

garding parking, structures for viewing, dining, dancing, with open terraces for fair weather and covered galleries for hot weather, both open to the views; as well as inside rooms for wet or cold weather, with windows to, again, optimize views. In summing up his desire for the type of building he envisioned, Strong wrote:

> To provide every sort of arrangement for capitalizing the view. Such capitalizing to include the element of thrill, as well as the element of beauty. To include a summit to the entire structure (and therefore the highest point on the mountain) for a complete panoramic view (360 degrees).
> To be striking, impressive, so that everyone hearing of the place will want to come once.
> To be beautiful, satisfying, so that those coming will want to come again, periodically, indefinitely.[1]

The letter concluded with a fee structure and contained the signatures of both Wright and Strong.

Even from the very beginning of the commission, Wright was exploring the idea of a spiral ramp for a roadway mounting the building. One of the earliest sketches, a perspective drawing accompanied by a plan, represents four turns of the exterior ramp reaching the top, with a crossover for cars to turn around and descend. As preliminaries progressed, the interior of the structure underwent several changes. Gradually it evolved from a dance hall at the center, to a stage, and eventually to a domed planetarium. Originally the support for the structure was planned as a series of posts throughout. However, as the scheme was further explored, a section drawing reveals that Wright was proposing that the very dome of the planetarium itself become the support for all the design's elements surrounding it, which include the restaurants, galleries, rooms, storerooms, and so forth. Springing from these areas around the dome would be the ramps themselves. No detail drawings reveal if, indeed, this was Wright's intended method for supporting the structure.

This project was Wright's first use of circular geometry. It was also his first use of ramps, as well as the large dome inside the building. As noted by scholar David De Long, concerning the design, "[Wright] was pushing the technology of his times to its very limits and

5.23

Small Scale Study
(Birds eye.)

GORDON STRONG AUTOMOBILE OBJECTIVE
AND PLANETARIUM (PROJECT)

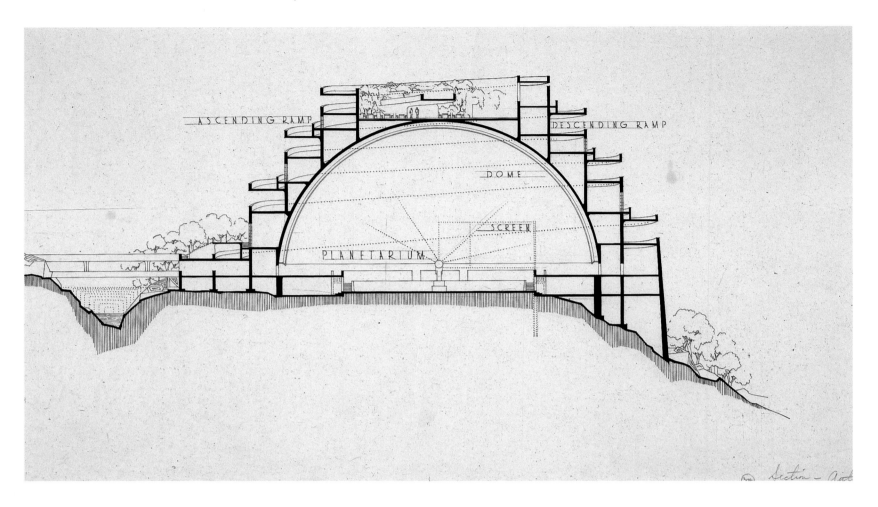

Gordon Strong Automobile Objective and Planetarium (project)
Sugarloaf Mountain, Maryland, 1924
Section
Ink on paper
17 x 35 ⅞ inches (43.2 x 91.1 cm)
The Frank Lloyd Wright Foundation
FLLW FDN # 2505.067

perhaps beyond. Whether it could have been built as designed, and what its costs might have been, were not, however, to be determined."[2]

As the project went along, after seeing preliminary studies, Strong grew dissatisfied with what Wright had proposed. He accused the architect of creating a Tower of Babel; Strong believed this was, finally, not the proper solution for a tourist attraction on the summit of Sugarloaf Mountain. To this accusation Wright replied:

> I have found it hard to look a snail in the face since I stole the idea of his house— from his back. The spiral is so natural and organic a form for whatever would ascend that I did not see why it should not be played upon and made equally available for descent at one and the same time. . . . I am sorry that you fail to see how the natural snail—crown of the great couchant lion—is grown up from his mountain head, the very quality of its movement, rising and adapting itself to the uninterrupted movement of

people sitting comfortably in their own cars in a novel circumstance with the whole landscape revolving about them, as exposed to view as though they were in an aeroplane.[3]

With this letter, the project obviously was drawn to a close. Wright was no doubt disappointed that the Gordon Strong Automobile Objective and Planetarium, upon which he had toiled for more than one year, was finally abandoned.

In retrospect, it is curious to note that the building was designed for the very top of the mountain, even though Wright himself, especially speaking of his home Taliesin that rested on the brow of a hill rather than on its top, had written that no house should be placed on top of the hill, that it would destroy the hill in doing so. Here was a marked contradiction.

According to De Long, "Characteristically, Wright had not shied from a difficult site, but instead placed the structure on the very edge of the summit so that it seemed to complete it. The bridge over the chasm

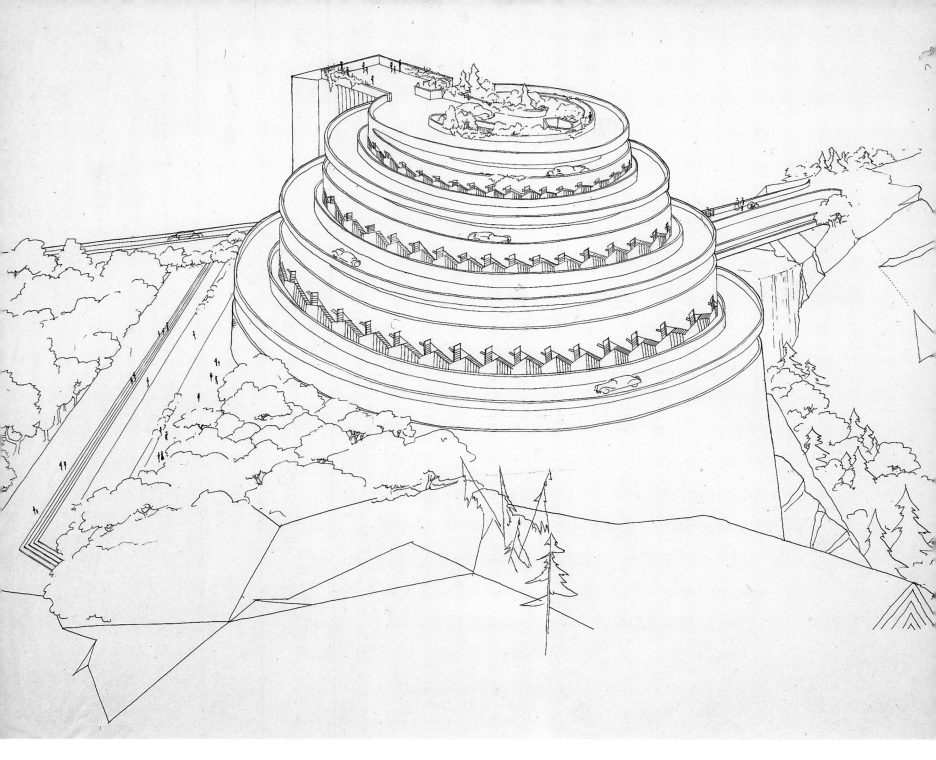

extended this sense of structured land by reconnecting and strengthening elements of the terrain. Never one to be bound by narrow interpretations of his own or anyone else's rule, he had placed the building on the hill, but still made it very much of the hill: indeed he made it the hill itself."[4]

NOTES
1. Gordon Strong to Frank Lloyd Wright, 22 September 1924. Courtesy of Stronghold, Inc., Dickerson, Maryland.
2. David De Long, *Frank Lloyd Wright Designs for an American Landscape 1922-1932* (New York: Harry N. Abrams, 1996), p. 97.
3. Wright to Strong, 20 October 1925. Courtesy of Stronghold, Inc., Dickerson, Maryland.
4. De Long, *Frank Lloyd Wright Designs*, p. 94.

Gordon Strong Automobile Objective and Planetarium (project)
Sugarloaf Mountain, Maryland, 1924
Aerial perspective
Ink on paper
17 x 36 inches (43.2 x 91.4)
The Frank Lloyd Wright Foundation
FLLW FDN # 2505.068

Steel Cathedral (project)
New York, New York, 1926
Elevation
Graphite pencil and color pencil on paper
22 5/8 x 30 inches (57.5 x 78.1 cm)
The Frank Lloyd Wright Foundation
FLLW FDN # 2602.003

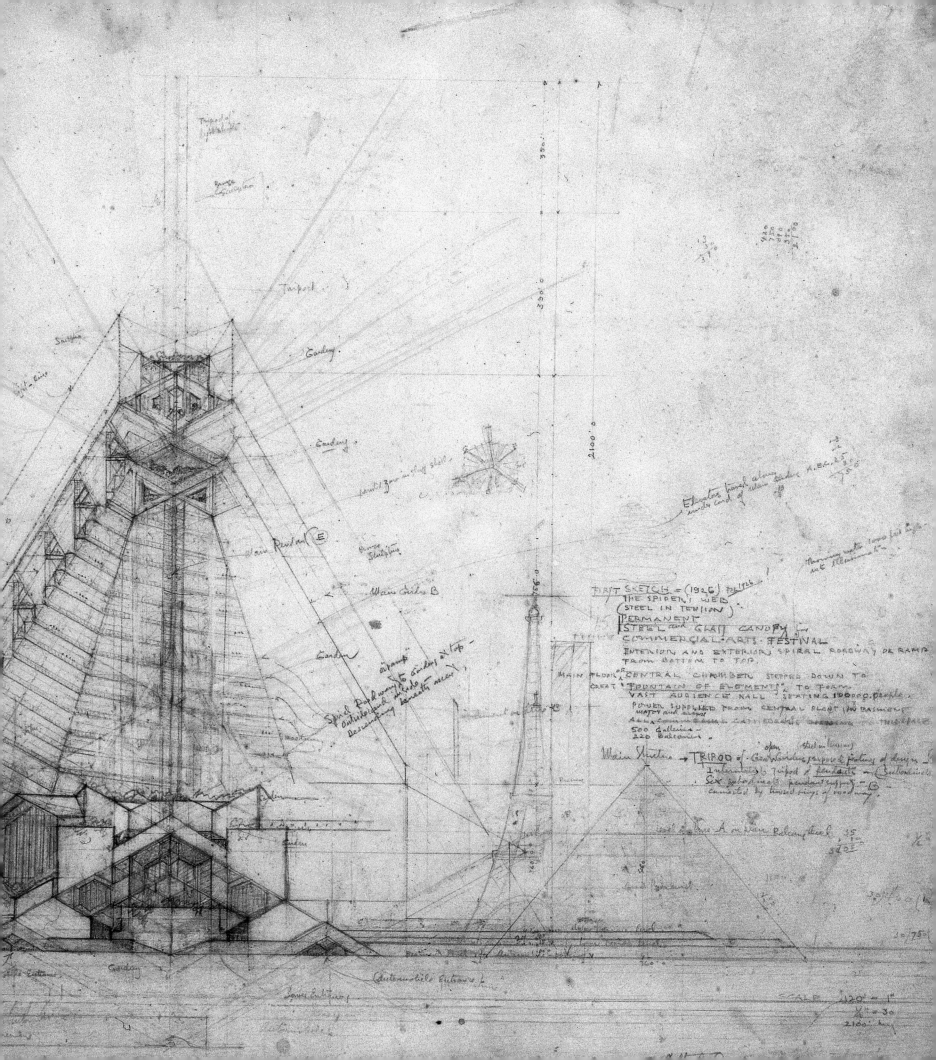

FIRST SKETCH = (1926) for 1926
THE SPIDER'S WEB
(STEEL IN TENSION)
PERMANENT
STEEL and GLASS CANOPY
COMMERCIAL-ARTS-FESTIVAL
INTERIOR AND EXTERIOR SPIRAL ROADWAY OR RAMP
FROM BOTTOM TO TOP.
MAIN FLOOR of CENTRAL CHAMBER STEPPED DOWN TO
CREAT 'FOUNTAIN OF ELEMENTS'. TO FORM
VAST AUDIENCE HALL SEATING 100,000 PEOPLE.
POWER SUPPLIED FROM CENTRAL PLANT IN BASEMENT
500 Galleries
220 Balconies

Main Structure → TRIPOD of

San Marcos-in-the-Desert Resort (project)
Chandler, Arizona, 1928–29
Perspective
Graphite pencil on paper
19 3/4 x 35 inches (50.2 x 99.9 cm)
The Frank Lloyd Wright Foundation
FLLW FDN # 2704.049

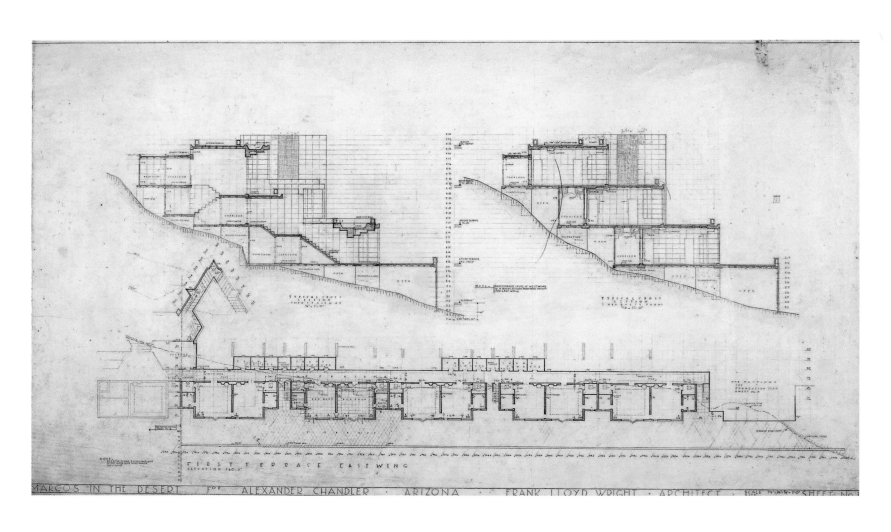

San Marcos-in-the-Desert Resort (project)
Chandler, Arizona, 1928–29
Plan and section
Graphite pencil on paper
30 x 54 inches (75.6 x 138.4 cm)
The Frank Lloyd Wright Foundation
FLLW FDN # 2704.103

Mrs. Owen D. Young House (project)
Chandler, Arizona, 1928–29
Perspective
Graphite pencil and color pencil on paper
16 1/2 x 28 inches (41.9 x 71.1 cm)
The Frank Lloyd Wright Foundation
FLLW FDN # 2707.001

Richard Lloyd Jones House #2
Tulsa, Oklahoma, 1929
Perspective
Graphite pencil and color pencil on paper
9 3/4 x 25 1/4 inches (24.8 x 64.1 cm)
The Frank Lloyd Wright Foundation
FLLW FDN # 2902.004

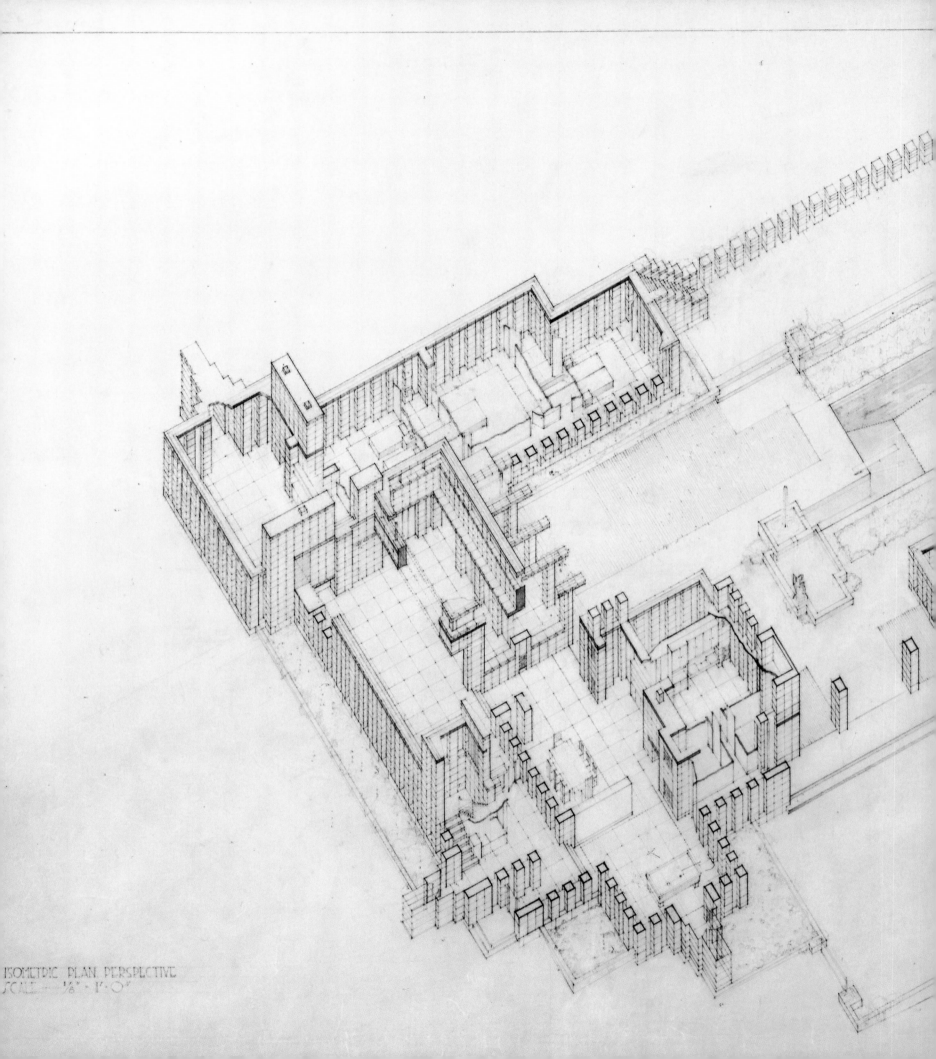

ISOMETRIC PLAN PERSPECTIVE
SCALE — 1/8" = 1'.0"

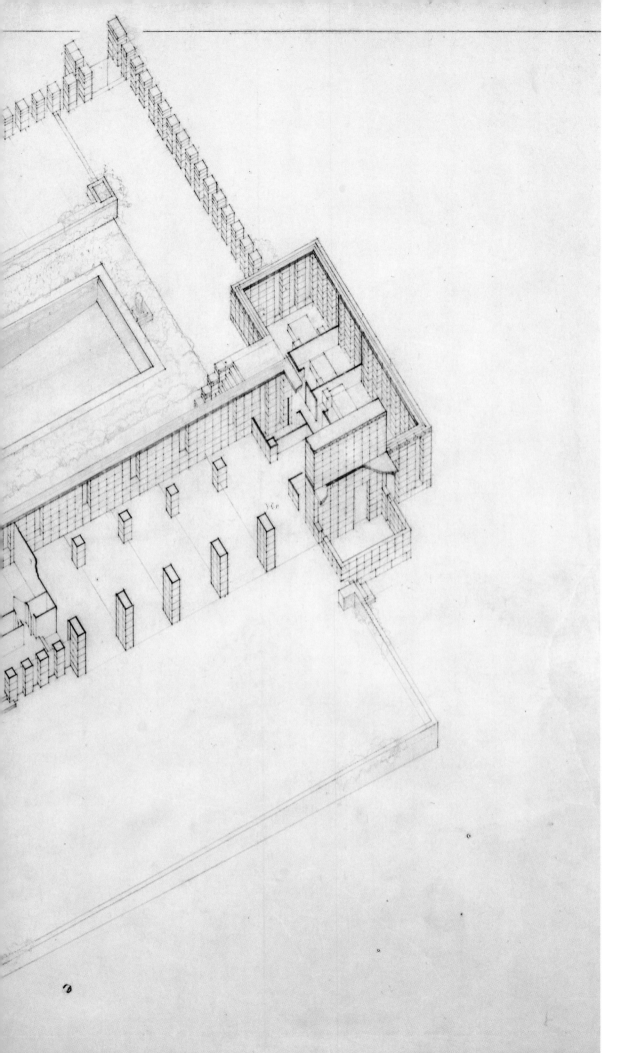

Richard Lloyd Jones House #2
Tulsa, Oklahoma, 1929
Isometric plan
Graphite pencil on paper
27 x 40 1/8 inches (68.6 x 101.9 cm)
The Frank Lloyd Wright Foundation
FLLW FDN # 2902.019

St. Mark's-in-the-Bouwerie Towers (project)
New York, New York, 1927
Perspective
Graphite pencil and ink on paper
39 x 23 ³⁄₄ inches (99.1 x 60.3 cm)
The Frank Lloyd Wright Foundation
FLLW FDN # 2905.002

St. Mark's-in-the-Bouwerie Towers (project)
New York, New York, 1927
Plans, section, and interior perspective
Graphite pencil, ink, and watercolor on window blind fabric
47 x 35 inches (119.4 x 88.9 cm)
The Frank Lloyd Wright Foundation
FLLW FDN # 2905.011

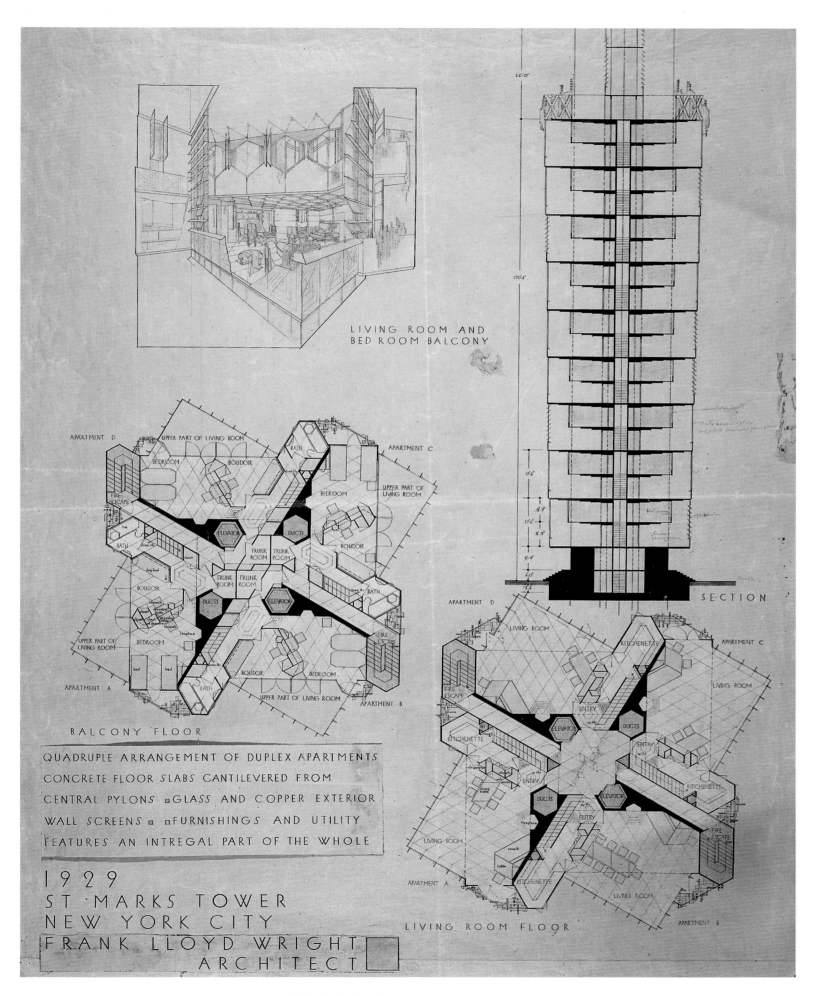

LIVING ROOM AND
BED ROOM BALCONY

SECTION

APARTMENT D   APARTMENT C

APARTMENT A   APARTMENT B

BALCONY FLOOR

LIVING ROOM FLOOR

QUADRUPLE ARRANGEMENT OF DUPLEX APARTMENTS
CONCRETE FLOOR SLABS CANTILEVERED FROM
CENTRAL PYLONS ▫ GLASS AND COPPER EXTERIOR
WALL SCREENS ▫ ▫ FURNISHINGS AND UTILITY
FEATURES AN INTREGAL PART OF THE WHOLE

1929
ST·MARKS TOWER
NEW YORK CITY
FRANK LLOYD WRIGHT
ARCHITECT

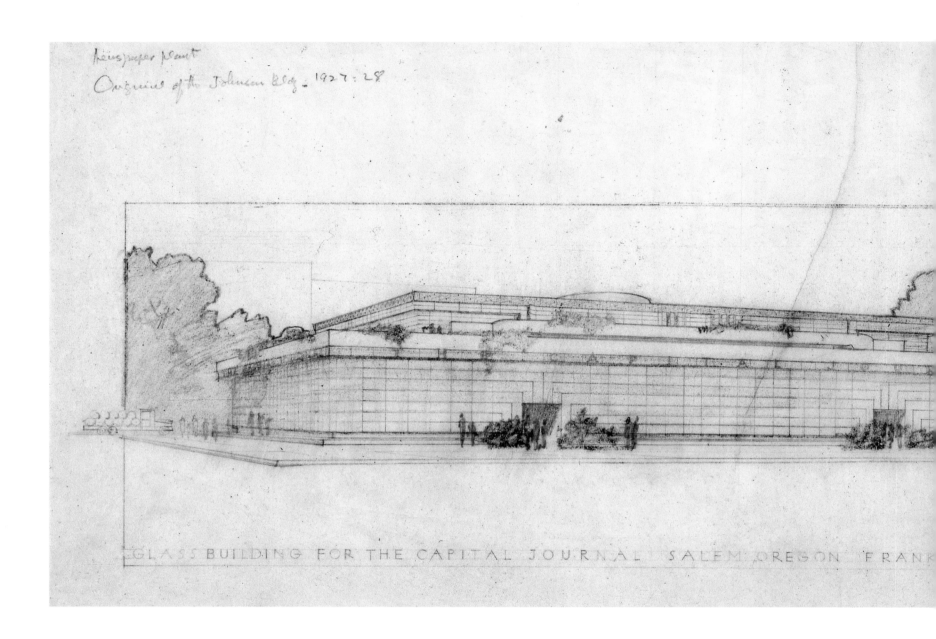

Capital Journal Building (project)
Salem, Oregon, 1931–32
Perspective
Graphite pencil and color pencil on paper
17 x 31 inches (43.2 x 78.7 cm)
The Frank Lloyd Wright Foundation
FLLW FDN # 3101.001

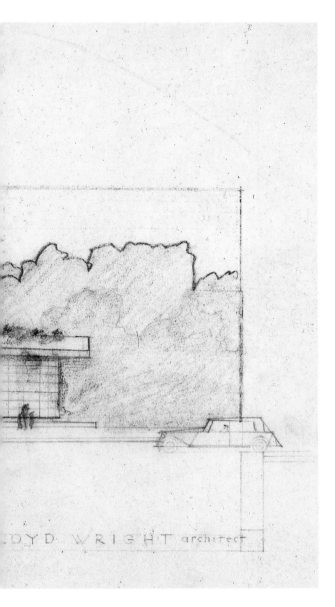

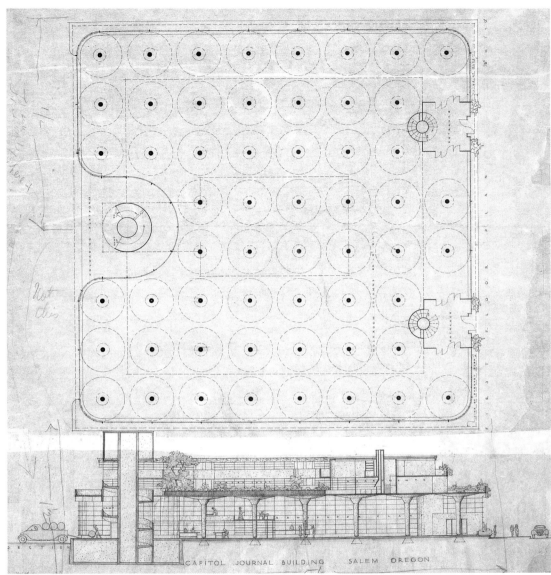

Capital Journal Building (project)
Salem, Oregon, 1931–32
Plan and section
Ink and ink wash on paper
30 1/4 x 28 1/2 inches (87 x 72.4 cm)
The Frank Lloyd Wright Foundation
FLLW FDN # 3101.008

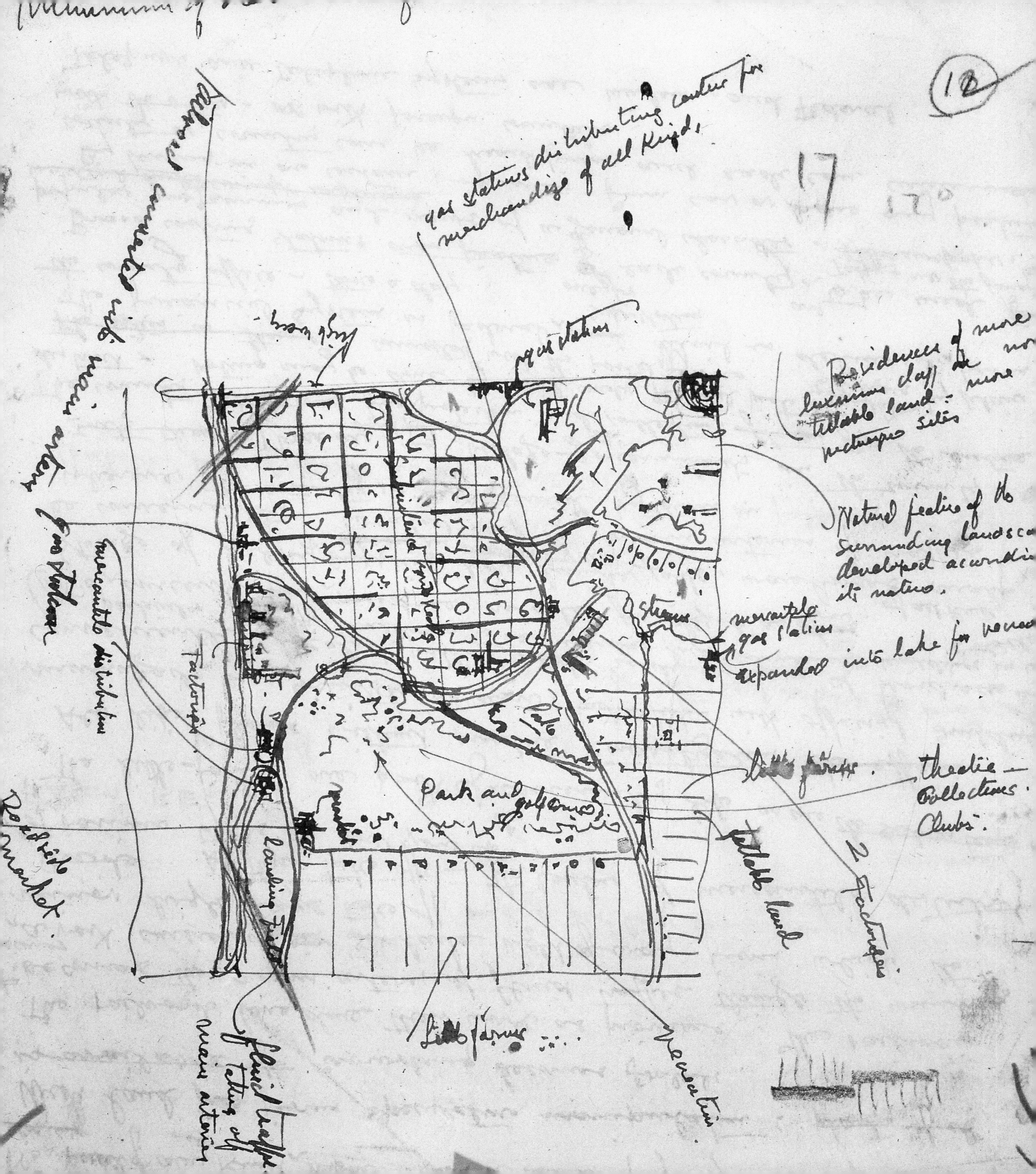

gas stations distributing center for merchandise of all kinds.

17   17°

Residences of more luxurious class on more tillable land = more picturesque sites

Natural features of the surrounding landscape developed according its nature.

mercantile gas stations

expanded into lake for recreation

2 Factories

theatre — collections. clubs.

mercantile distribution

Factories.

traffic

Roadside market.

Loading Field

Park and golf course

little farms

little farms

mercantile

18

Broadacre City Master Plan (project)
1934
Plan and text
Ink on paper
9 3/8 x 8 1/2 (23.8 x 24.1 cm)
The Frank Lloyd Wright Foundation
FLLW FDN # 3402.001

Broadacre City Model
1935
Model from above
Photograph by Skot Weidemann
The Frank Lloyd Wright Foundation
FLLW FDN # 3402.0089

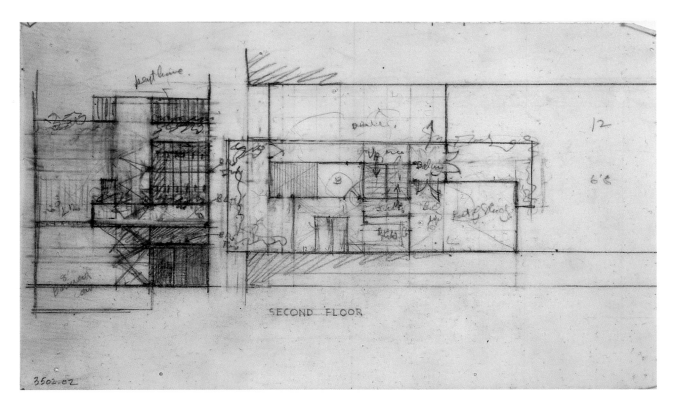

SECOND FLOOR

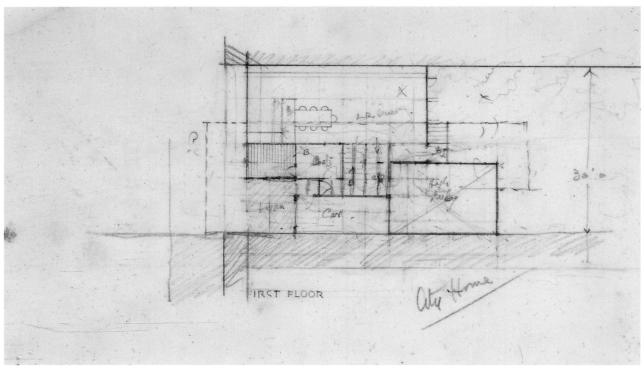

FIRST FLOOR

City Home

The Zoned House (project)
1935
City House elevation and second-floor plan
Pencil on paper
6 ¼ x 10 ½ inches (15.9 x 26.7 cm)
The Frank Lloyd Wright Foundation
FLLW FDN # 3502.001

The Zoned House (project)
1935
City House first-floor plan
Pencil on paper
6 ⅛ x 10 ½ inches (15.6 x 26.7 cm)
The Frank Lloyd Wright Foundation
FLLW FDN # 3502.002

The Zoned House (project)
1935
City House perspective
Graphite pencil on paper
8 x 12 ½ inches (20.3 x 31.8 cm)
The Frank Lloyd Wright Foundation
FLLW FDN # 3502.003

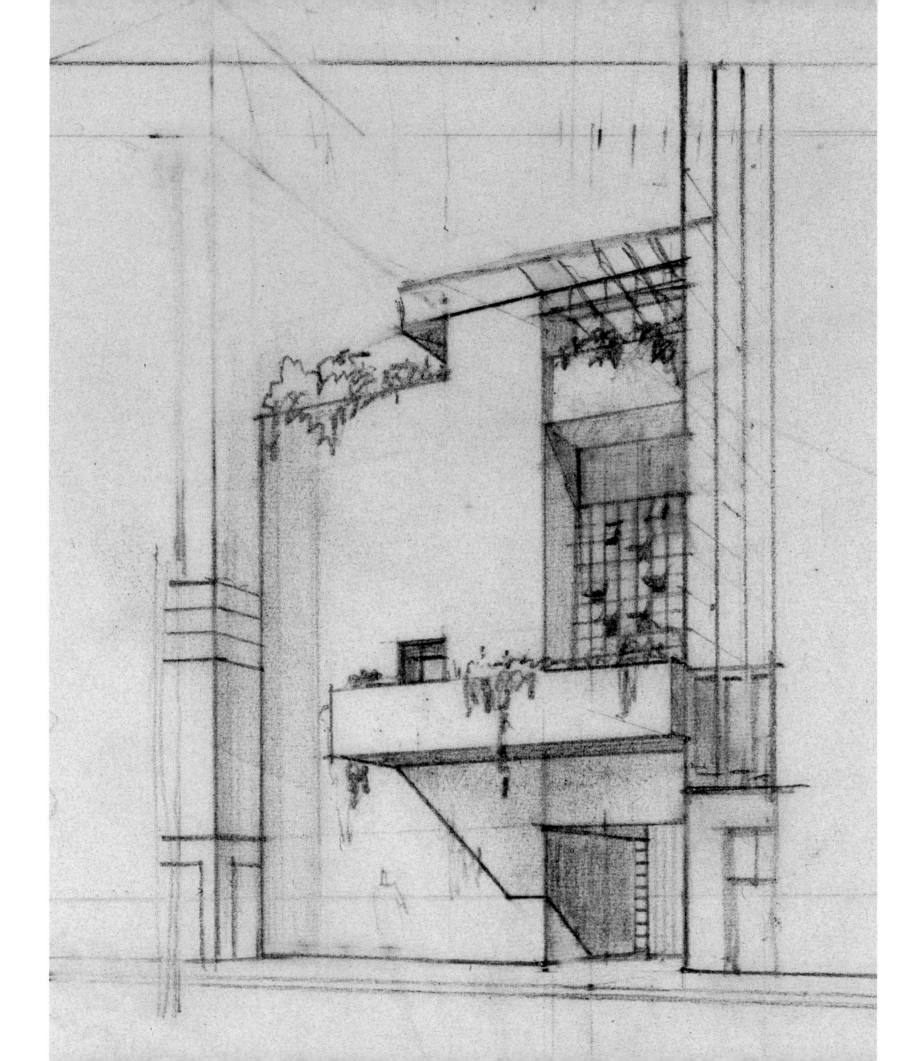

S. C. JOHNSON & SON, INC. ADMINISTRATION
BUILDING AND RESEARCH TOWER

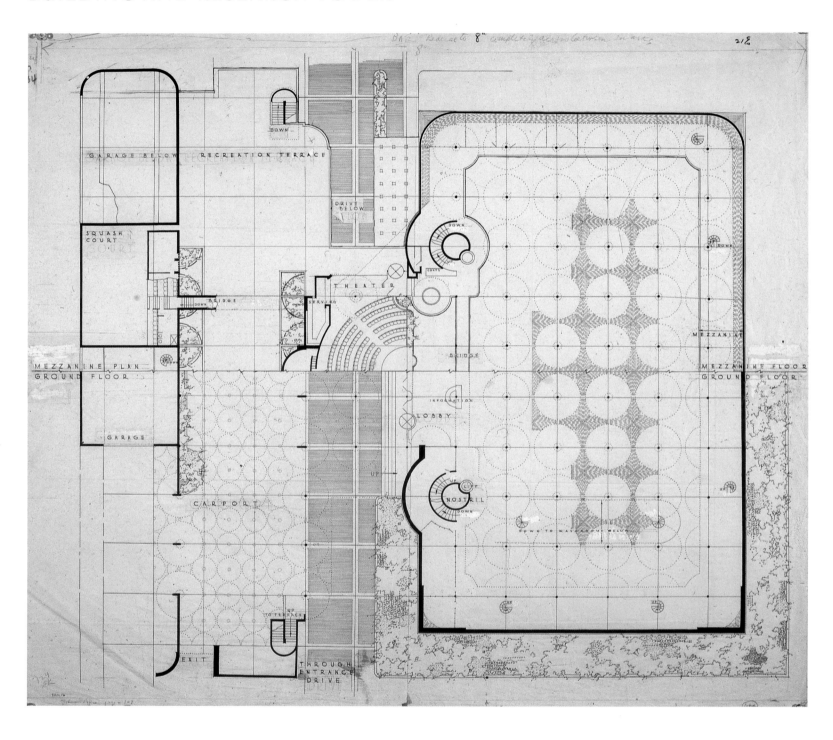

S. C. Johnson & Son, Inc. Administration Building
Racine, Wisconsin, 1936–39
Publication plan
Ink on paper
35 7/10 x 39 1/4 inches (90.8 x 99.7 cm)
The Frank Lloyd Wright Foundation
FLLW FDN # 3601.016

S. C. Johnson & Son, Inc. Administration Building
Racine, Wisconsin, 1936–39
Interior of lobby
The Frank Lloyd Wright Foundation
FLLW FDN # 3601.0044

S. C. JOHNSON & SON, INC. ADMINISTRATION BUILDING AND RESEARCH TOWER

S. C. Johnson & Son, Inc. Administration Building
Racine, Wisconsin. 1936–39
Interior perspective
Graphite pencil and sepia on paper
10 ⅞ x 34 ⅝ inches (27.6 x 87.9 cm)
The Frank Lloyd Wright Foundation
FLLW FDN # 3601.006

A SOCIO-ARCHITECTURAL INTERPRETATION
Frank Lloyd Wright and Herbert F. Johnson first met at
Wright's home Taliesin, in July 1936. Wright was seventy-
two, Johnson thirty-seven. Johnson was president of the
S. C. Johnson & Son, Inc., a manufacturer mainly of
wax products, which was headquartered in Racine,
Wisconsin, not far from Taliesin. At the first meeting, it
seemed that the two men disagreed about almost
everything, except automobiles: Wright owned a
Lincoln-Zephyr, the newly introduced streamlined
luxury car, and so did Johnson. The purpose of
Johnson's trip to Taliesin was to see if Wright would be
the appropriate architect for a new building. By the
time of this meeting of Wright and Johnson in 1936,
the company had grown exceedingly successful, but
at the same time its administration offices had
become outdated and inadequate. Johnson therefore
had employed architect J. Mandor Matson to design

a new building. It was important to Johnson that the
building responded to his father's belief: "My father
had the idea of bringing the employer and worker
together. Call it enlightened selfishness if you like, for
when people get proper wages and proper working
conditions, they don't feel the need to organize to
fight for what they want."[1]

What prompted Johnson to change his mind
about an architect for his building? Two officials of his
company, Jack Ramsey, the general manager, and
William Connolly, the advertising manager, had earlier met with Wright and discussed the possibility of a
new administration building. Johnson and Ramsey
were not satisfied with Matson's building. It did not
seem to address their wish for a structure that was
both new and also respectful of the concept of the
employer and the worker being brought together in
an inspiring space.

After their meeting at Taliesin, both Ramsey and Connolly were convinced that Wright should be their architect. They conveyed this conviction to Johnson, and the result was his trip to meet with Wright. Although they disagreed about many things, one thing in particular—other than automobiles—seemed common to them both: the achievement of a building design that was modern, clean, and comfortable for workers as well as employers, and beautiful. Wright explained what he had done in the office building for the Larkin Company in Buffalo thirty years earlier.

Olgivanna Wright recalled that at one point in the conversation Johnson had stated, "Please don't make the building too unconventional!" Laughing, Wright replied, "Then you came to the wrong man. You'd better find yourself another architect. The Johnson administration building is not going to be what you expect. But I can assure you of one thing—you'll like it when it is put

up." Johnson replied, "It's okay with me then, if you think so. We'll have your kind of building, not the kind of building I had in mind."[2]

Despite the appearance that the two men did not agree at that first meeting on many issues, obviously Johnson quickly surmised that, indeed, Wright was the man who would give him the type of building he wanted, and upon his return to Racine he told Matson that he had decided not to go ahead with his plans. At the same time he wrote to Wright on 23 July, "I am now asking you to proceed with plans and sketches of a $200,000 office building for us in Racine on the basis of 2 ½ % or $5,000 to be paid you when sketches and plans are submitted."[3]

Enclosed in the letter was a check for $1,000 (equivalent to about $15,000 in today's dollars and only about $180 less than what the average full-time employee earned per year in the midst of the Great

S. C. JOHNSON & SON, INC. ADMINISTRATION BUILDING AND RESEARCH TOWER

S. C. Johnson & Son, Inc. Administration Building
Racine, Wisconsin, 1936–39
Interior of Great Workroom
The Frank Lloyd Wright Foundation
FLLW FDN # 3601.0057

Depression) as a retainer for his services. Everyone at Taliesin was excited about this new commission, and when Wright showed his apprentices the letter, and the check, he exclaimed, "It's all right boys, we got the job!"[4]

He continued, "And, the pie thus opened, the birds began to sing again below the house at Taliesin; dry grass on the hillside turned green, and the hollyhocks went gaily into a second blooming. The orchard decided to come in with a heavy crop of big red harvest apples and the whole landscape seemed to have more color....[5]

"What a release of pent-up creative energy—the making of those plans! Ideas came tumbling up and onto paper to be thrown back in heaps—for careful scrutiny and selection. But, at once, I knew the scheme I wanted to try. I had it in mind when I drew the newspaper plant [the Capital Journal Building] in Salem,

Oregon, for Editor George Putnam, which he had been unable to build. A great simplicity."[6]

What Wright had in mind when he referred to the newspaper plant of 1931 was his use of dendriform columns, rising from the base and spreading out in circular pads at the top. In this application they supported the second-floor roof garden and apartments. In the Johnson building they rise to support skylights.

The entrance to the Johnson building is placed under cover, a roofed carport on one side, the approach into the building on the other. Once inside, one is in a tall, three-story lobby lit by slender, three-story-high dendriform columns rising up to skylights above. Here the white columns are more graceful than the Capital Journal scheme. Beyond the entrance lobby is the room for the main clerical workforce, called the Great Workroom, a two-story space 228 by 228

S. C. Johnson & Son, Inc. Administration Building
Racine, Wisconsin, 1936–39
Theater interior
The Frank Lloyd Wright Foundation
FLLW FDN # 3601.0073

feet with a mezzanine running along three sides. These dendriform shafts, as with the lobby, rise to skylights above. Indeed, the very essence of this room is light, a space like a forest of white birch trees with light filtering down from above. The building, as with Larkin, is situated in an industrial neighborhood, and Wright therefore planned it to be sealed and insulated from this environment. Also, where the outer brick walls rise, rather than meeting the ceiling, they are treated as screens, and glass rises above them to meet the skylights. As Wright once explained, where one usually looked up inside the cornice and saw dark, here one sees the sky.

Beneath the Great Workroom is a basement providing restrooms and file storage, easily accessible by iron circular stairs at convenient intervals.

Above the entrance drive, on the mezzanine level, there is a semicircular theater seating 250 for lectures or entertainment. The penthouse level, above the theater, is reserved for the executive offices. From a balcony overlooking the lobby, the Great Workroom can be seen, emphasizing the important connection between the employer and employee. A glass-covered bridge extends from the penthouse to a wood-lined squash court.

All fenestration for the building, both for exterior walls and skylights, as well as several interior partitions,

S. C. JOHNSON & SON, INC. ADMINISTRATION BUILDING AND RESEARCH TOWER

S. C. Johnson & Son, Inc. Administration
Building and Research Tower
Racine, Wisconsin, 1936–50
Exterior
The Frank Lloyd Wright Foundation
FLLW FDN # 3601.0097

is achieved by means of glass tubes set into aluminum frames, caulked on the exterior against rain and snow. The arched ceiling of the glass bridge is likewise composed of glass tubes.

The cost of the construction began with what Wright called "a paltry $250,000. in the 'rock pile.' Before we started, it jumped to $350,000—and as time went on landed in a pile nearer $850,000. But we had more to show for that pile than anybody who ever built a similar industrial administration building of the first rank. The entire thing thoroughly fireproof, air-conditioned, floor heated (gravity heat), and, including appropriate furnishings designed by the architect."[7]

When the completed building opened in the spring of 1939, it instantly generated an enormous amount of publicity in the press, in magazines, on radio, and in motion pictures. (During the 1930s, movie theaters' feature films were accompanied by newsreels, short movies dealing with current events.) *Life* magazine in a feature article, dated 8 May 1939, described the building: "It is like a woman swimming naked in a

stream. Cool, gliding, musical in movement and in manner. The inside of an office building like a woman swimming naked in a stream? Yes, that's right."

William Connolly, advertising executive for the S. C. Johnson & Son Company, claimed that "[t]wo or more millions of dollars could not have bought the front pages in newspapers and top-notch magazines which the building had attracted to itself....[8]

"Meanwhile the stream of visitors came from all over the world and went on and continues to go on to this hour.... Why? Because of something in the universal air, that's why. It was high time to give our hungry American public something truly 'streamlined,' so swift, sure of itself and clean for its purpose, clean as a hound's tooth—that *anybody* could see the virtue of this thing called Modern....[9]

"Organic architecture designed this great building to be as inspiring a place to work in as any cathedral ever was in which to worship. It was meant to be a socio-architectural interpretation of modern business at its top and best."[10]

S. C. Johnson & Son, Inc. Administration Building
Racine, Wisconsin, 1936–39
Glazed bridge
The Frank Lloyd Wright Foundation
FLLW FDN # 3601.0061

S. C. Johnson & Son, Inc. Administration Building
Racine, Wisconsin, 1936–39
Carport entry
The Frank Lloyd Wright Foundation
FLLW FDN # 3601.0078

S. C. JOHNSON & SON, INC. ADMINISTRATION BUILDING AND RESEARCH TOWER

S. C. Johnson & Son, Inc. Administration
Building and Research Tower
Racine, Wisconsin, 1936–50
Perspective
Sepia ink on paper
28 x 54 inches (71.1 x 137.2 cm)
The Frank Lloyd Wright Foundation
FLLW FDN # 4401.002

THE JOHNSON WAX RESEARCH TOWER

By 1943, when the S. C. Johnson & Son Company had expanded its product lines beyond floor wax to include various household and commercial products, it was necessary to expand its research facilities as well. Herbert Johnson explained to Wright that since any new building would be in close relation to the exciting administration building, it seemed only logical that Wright himself be the architect of that new structure. Johnson proposed to Wright, "Why not go up in the air, Frank?"[11]

"So we went up in the air around a giant central stack with floors branching from it having clear light and space all around each floor."[12]

Wright's experience in designing towers began in the early years of his practice when, in 1897, he had

designed the Romeo and Juliet Windmill tower for his aunts Jane and Ellen Lloyd Jones. They had founded the Hillside Home School in 1896, a home school for boys and girls with a curriculum far in advance of its time. Their school was located in the valley to which their father, Richard Lloyd Jones, had migrated from Wales in the mid-nineteenth century. The windmill stood on a high hill, visible from all around. It pumped water up from a deep well into a small reservoir to supply water for the school. In Wright's design, which he called his first "engineering architecture," Romeo, the octagon, carried the iron supports for the tower embedded in the rock and concrete and the base, while Juliet, the lozenge, snuggled beside him.

In 1912 Wright designed another tower, for the

Press Building in San Francisco. This was a reinforced-concrete structure to be built using a slip form, floor by floor, as in grain elevators. It remained a project never built. With the tower for the National Life Insurance Company, Chicago, in 1924, Wright proposed a structure using central pylons supporting cantilevered floors, the exterior walls treated as nonsupporting screens of copper and glass suspended from the floor slabs. It was in the apartment tower St. Mark's in-the-Bouwerie, New York, 1927, that the single tower with central supports and cantilevered floors became sort of a model for what Wright was proposing for the Johnson tower.

The central shaft rising throughout the whole structure as well as supporting all the floors, contains the elevator, stairs, toilets, and all ducts necessary for heating, cooling, and ventilating any chemical fumes in the laboratory spaces. The fourteen floors alternate between square and circular; the exterior nonsupporting walls are of brick and glass tubes. The construction photographs of the tower, before these exterior walls were put in, clearly reveal the cantilevered nature of the building.

An important element in the structure of the tower is its taproot foundation. A deep excavation 45 feet into hard clay was made in order to pour the concrete shaft, or taproot as Wright called it, with the upper petal of the foundation acting as a spread footing. Construction was begun in late 1947; the tower was completed in 1950.

Surrounding the tower on three sides is a large courtyard, the periphery of which provides covered parking. Along with the tower, the commission also

S. C. JOHNSON & SON, INC. ADMINISTRATION
BUILDING AND RESEARCH TOWER

S. C. Johnson & Son, Inc. Research Tower
Racine, Wisconsin, 1943–50
Typical square tower floor
The Frank Lloyd Wright Foundation
FLLW FDN # 4401.0128

S. C. Johnson & Son, Inc. Research Tower
Racine, Wisconsin, 1943–50
Exterior view
The Frank Lloyd Wright Foundation
FLLW FDN # 4401.0125

included the addition of offices, storage spaces, and a deep subterranean testing laboratory, all on the side by the existing carport.

Wright referred to the tower as "Helio-Laboratory" tower, taking the word "helio" from the Greek meaning sun. On all floors there is a continuous source of natural light for those working within the building.

NOTES

1. Jonathan Lipman, *Frank Lloyd Wright and the Johnson Wax Buildings* (New York: Rizzoli, 1986), p. 7.
2. Ibid., p. 13.
3. Ibid., p. 14.
4. Ibid.
5. Frank Lloyd Wright, *An Autobiography* (San Francisco: Pomegranate, 2005), p. 468.
6. Ibid., p. 469.
7. Ibid.
8. Ibid., p. 470.
9. Ibid., p. 471.
10. Ibid., p. 472.
11. Frank Lloyd Wright, *Architectural Forum*, January 1951.
12. Ibid.

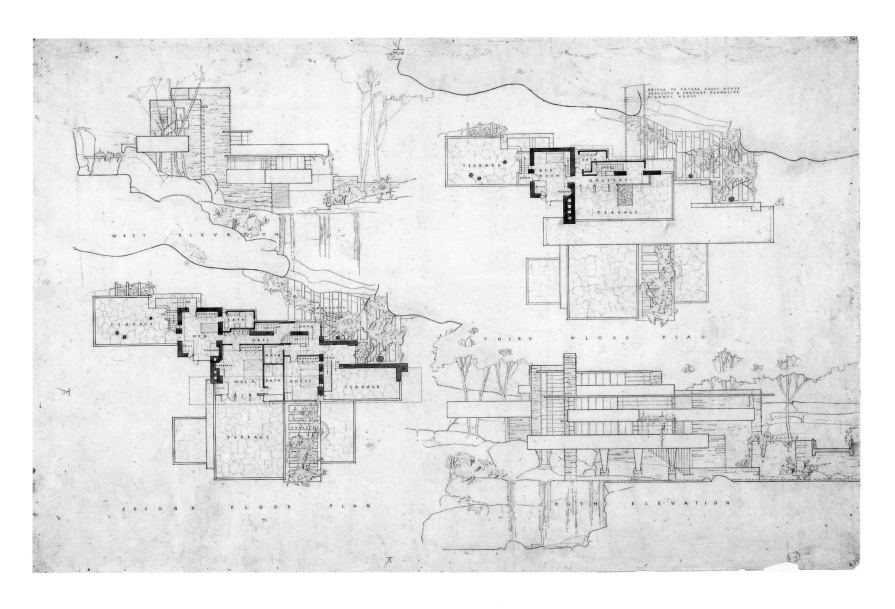

(preceding pages)
Edgar J. Kaufmann House, "Fallingwater"
Mill Run, Pennsylvania, 1934–37
Perspective
Graphite pencil and color pencil on paper
15 3/8 x 27 1/4 inches (39.1 x 69.2 cm)
The Frank Lloyd Wright Foundation
FLLW FDN # 3602.004

Edgar J. Kaufmann House, "Fallingwater "
Mill Run, Pennsylvania, 1934–37
Publication plans
Graphite pencil and ink wash on paper
24 x 36 1/4 inches (61.6 x 92.1 cm)
The Frank Lloyd Wright Foundation
FLLW FDN # 3602.157

Edgar J. Kaufmann House, "Fallingwater"
Mill Run, Pennsylvania, 1934–37
Exterior dusk view
Photo by Paul Rocheleau

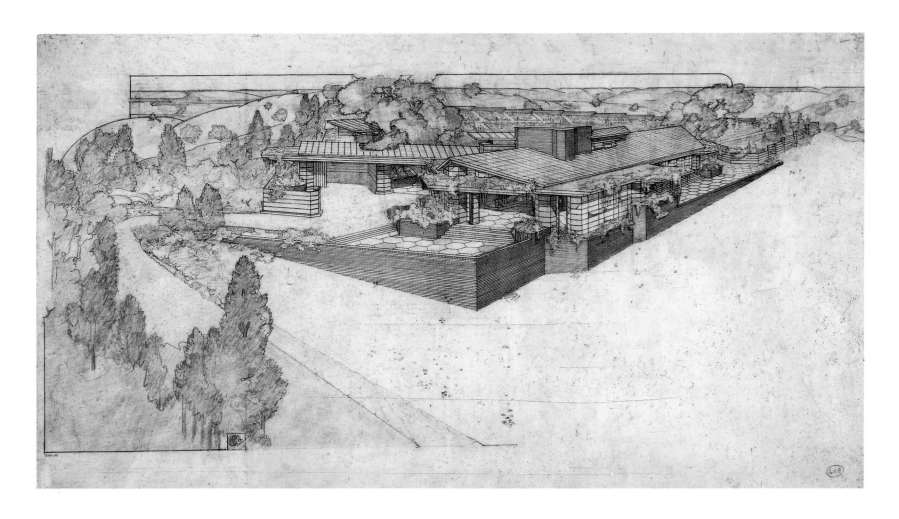

Paul and Jean Hanna House
Stanford, California, 1935
Perspective
Graphite pencil and ink on paper
34 x 39 ³/₈ inches (87 x 100 cm)
The Frank Lloyd Wright Foundation
FLLW FDN # 3701.001

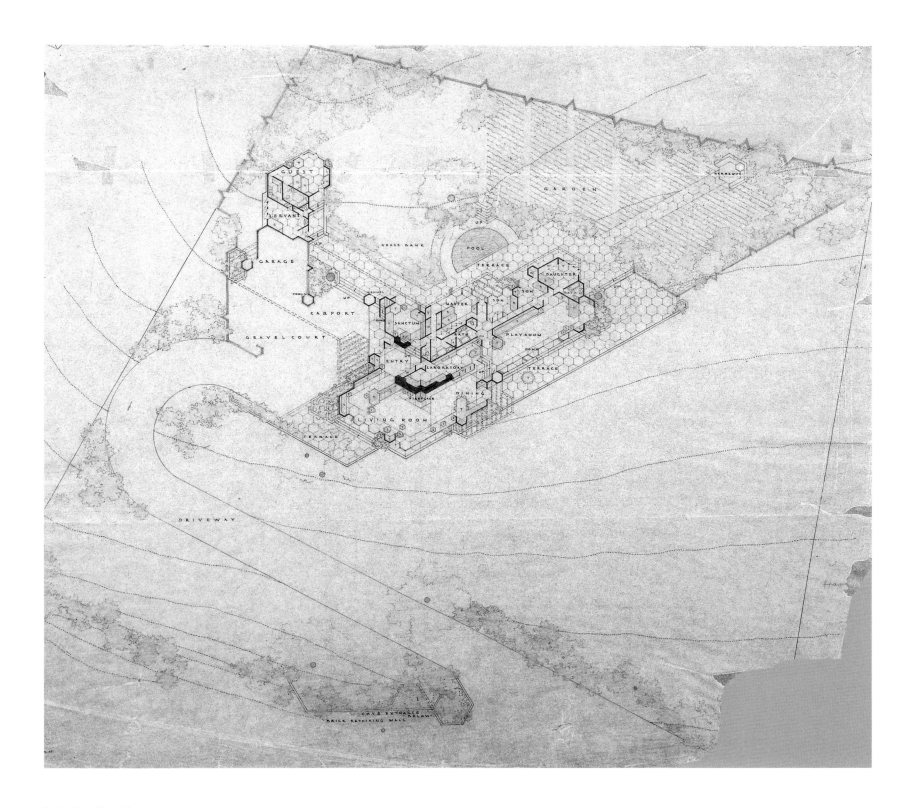

Paul and Jean Hanna House
Stanford, California, 1935
Plan
Graphite pencil and ink on paper
34 x 39 inches (87 x 99.1 cm)
The Frank Lloyd Wright Foundation
FLLW FDN # 3701.005

HERBERT JACOBS HOUSE #1

Herbert Jacobs House #1
Madison, Wisconsin, 1936–37
Perspective
Color pencil and sepia ink on paper
21 x 31 3/4 inches (53.3 x 80.6 cm)
The Frank Lloyd Wright Foundation
FLLW FDN # 3702.002/003

Herbert Jacobs House #1
Madison, Wisconsin, 1936–37
Plan
Graphite pencil and ink on paper
The Frank Lloyd Wright Foundation
FLLW FDN # 3702.005

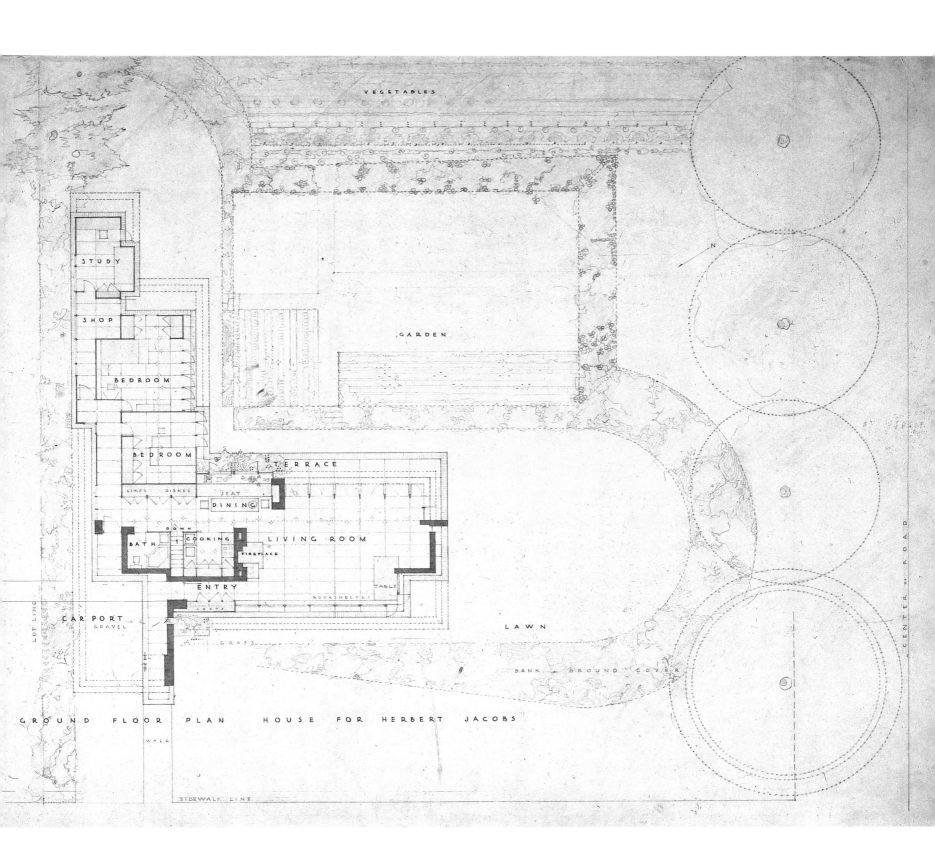

VEGETABLES

STUDY

SHOP

BEDROOM

GARDEN

BEDROOM

TERRACE

N

LINEN DISHES SEAT

DINING

DOWN

BATH COOKING LIVING ROOM

FIREPLACE

ENTRY

TABLE

CARPORT GRAVEL

BOOKSHELVES

LAWN

LOT LINE

GRASS

BANK GROUND COVER

CENTER OF ROAD

GROUND FLOOR PLAN HOUSE FOR HERBERT JACOBS

WALK

SIDEWALK LINE

HERBERT JACOBS HOUSE #1

Herbert Jacobs House #1
Madison, Wisconsin, 1936–37
Exterior view
Photo by David Heald
Courtesy Solomon R. Guggenheim Foundation

THE USONIAN HOUSE IS BORN

In 1938 Wright wrote: "The house of moderate cost is not only America's major architectural problem but the problem most difficult for her major architects. As for me, I would rather solve it with satisfaction to myself and Usonia, than build anything I can think of at the moment."[1]

He further explained that the chief obstacle to any real solution of the moderate-cost house problem is the fact that people do not know how to live, given their idiosyncrasies in matters of "tastes," referring to the current, at that time, ideal of how people should live. He went on to explain: "To be more specific, a small house on the side street might have charm if it didn't ape the big house on the avenue.... I am certain that any approach to the new house needed by indigenous culture—why worry about the house wanted by provincial ignorance—is fundamentally different. That house must be a pattern for more simple, and at the same time, more gracious living: new, but suitable to living conditions as they might so well be in the country we live in today."[2]

"What would really be sensible in this matter? Let's see how far the Herbert Jacobs house at Madison, Wisconsin, is a sensible house. This house for a young journalist, his wife, and small daughter, is now under roof: cost of $5,500 [about $82,000 in today's dollars], including architect's fee of $450."[3]

In order to achieve this ideal of the moderate-cost house that does not ape the mansion, Wright realized that the house had to be constructed using entirely new methods. It meant letting go of past ideas about home building and emphasized the need for the clients themselves to "see life in somewhat simplified terms. It is necessary to get rid of all unnecessary materials in construction. . . . And it would be ideal to complete the building in one operation as it goes along, inside and outside."[4]

Wright had begun work along these lines the year before, when he designed a house for C. R. Hoult in Kansas and then another one for Robert Lusk in South Dakota. Both these houses were based on an L-shaped plan and were to be one-story houses with flat roofs. The walls were to be constructed of boards and battens screwed to a core, most likely plywood, with the same surface inside as well as out. Neither of these homes was constructed, and only preliminary drawings were made.

With the Herbert Jacobs House, in 1936, Wright refined this building system into one that he would successfully employ for a number of other Usonian homes across the United States. According to Wright: "Now to assist in general planning, what must or may we use in our new construction? In this case five materials: wood, brick, cement, paper, glass. To simplify fabrication we must use the horizontal unit system in construction. (See lines crossing plans both ways making rectangles 2 x 4 feet.) We must also use a vertical unit system which will be the board and batten-bands themselves, interlocking with the brick courses."[5]

The wood walls were constructed with a core of plywood, building paper on either side, and then the boards and battens screwed to the core on both sides. In this way, the outer wall and the inner wall were one and the same, a great savings in construction costs. Wright maintained that this type of a wall was high in insulating value and would be vermin-proof and practically fireproof. The walls could be made on the floor and then lifted up into place. In some cases the walls were made in the shop and sent to the building site. The roof framing was designed as a lamination of 2x4s forming three offsets visible to the outside. This way there could be a sufficient pitch to the roof, and the middle offset could provide ventilation for the roof spaces in summer.

Construction of the house began with leveling the site and spreading a course of crushed rock upon which heating coils were laid, then the concrete slab was poured. A small basement was excavated to house the furnace, water heater, and laundry. The system of heating in the Jacobs house was a first of its kind.

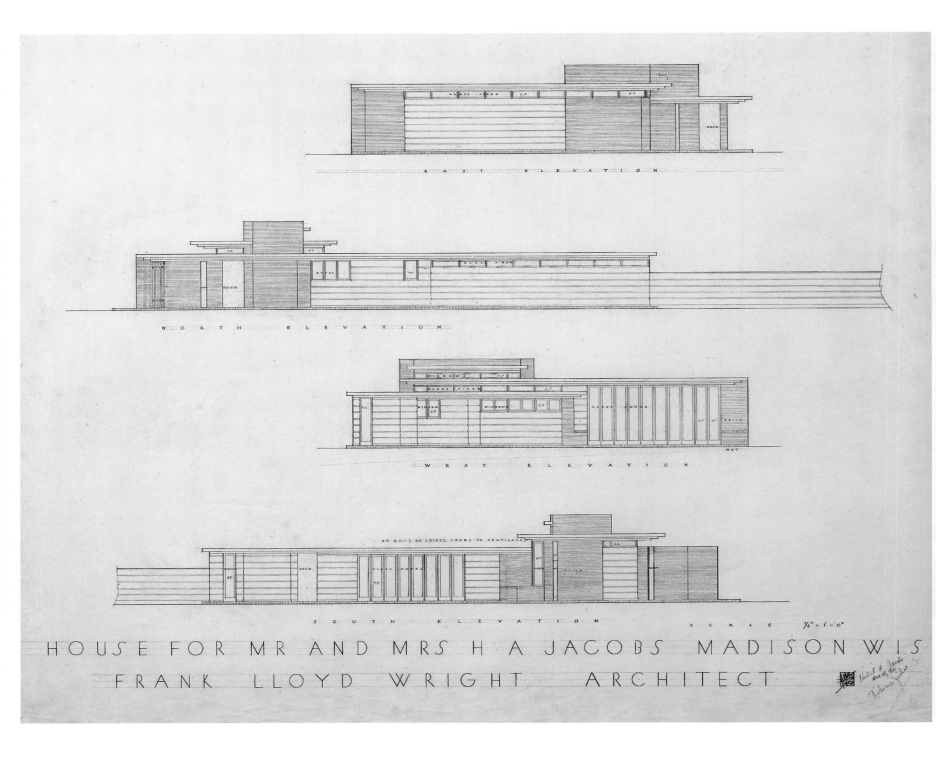

Herbert Jacobs House #1
Madison, Wisconsin, 1936–37
Four elevations
Graphite pencil on paper
24 x 36 inches (61 x 91.4 cm)
The Frank Lloyd Wright Foundation
FLLW FDN # 3702.016

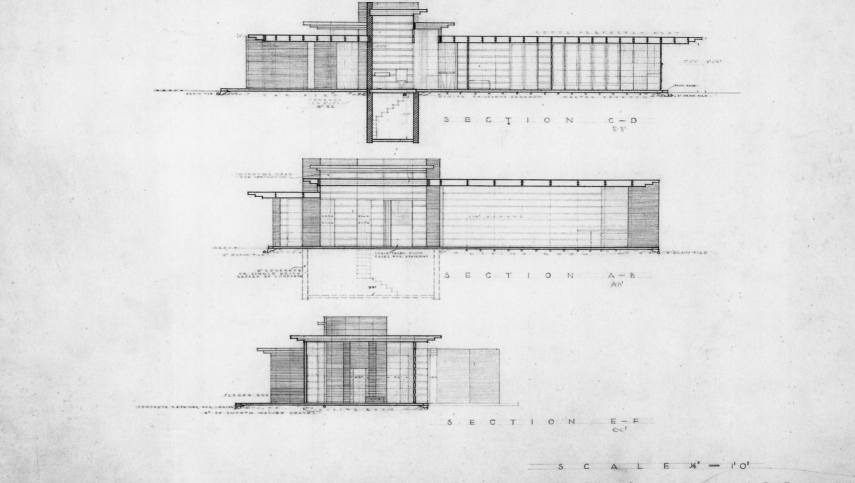

SECTION C-D

SECTION A-B

SECTION E-F

SCALE ¼" = 1'0"

HOUSE FOR MR AND MRS H A JACOBS MADISON WIS
FRANK LLOYD WRIGHT ARCHITECT

Herbert Jacobs House #1
Madison, Wisconsin, 1936–37
Sections
Graphite pencil on paper
24 x 36 inches (61 x 91.4 cm)
The Frank Lloyd Wright Foundation
FLLW FDN # 3702.017

Herbert Jacobs House #1
Madison, Wisconsin, 1936–37
Interior
The Frank Lloyd Wright Foundation
FLLW FDN # 3702.0003

Herbert Jacobs House #1
Madison, Wisconsin, 1936-37
Exterior
Photo by Larry Cuneo
The Frank Lloyd Wright Foundation
FLLW FDN # 3702.0024

While in Tokyo, Wright had experienced, in the home of Baron Okura, a special room, called the Korean Room, which was heated by hollow tiles in the floor, with a fireplace in one corner, the smoke and heat traveling through the tiles and up through a flue in the opposite corner. Most of the time he was in Tokyo, in the winter, he suffered from the damp and cold, but in this room, he suddenly had the sensation not so much of heat but of "climate." He had planned to use hot-water pipes beneath the floor slab in the Nakoma Country Club, Madison, Wisconsin, in 1923-24, but that work was never built. Now with the Jacobs house, he spoke to the clients about this type of heat, telling them that it was new and as yet unproved but that he believed it would work. They agreed, and thus the Jacobs house was the first in Wright's oeuvre to employ this system—what he

called "gravity heating"—by which the cold air falls to the floor, where it is heated and from which it then rises.

In general, the process of construction for the Usonian houses began with the floor slab, and then the brick or stone walls were constructed. Next the roof was propped up in place and the board-and-batten walls set on the slab and joined to the ceiling above. Details of doors, windows (mainly floor-to-ceiling glass doors), and the usual electrical wiring and plumbing were then set into place. The kitchen (called here the "workspace") and the bathroom were adjacent to one another and above the basement below to concentrate piping and plumbing fixtures. Thus all the appurtenance systems—heating, lighting, and sanitation—are simplified and consolidated. All in all, this was a totally new type of design with an equally new method of construction. As Usonian house

Herbert Jacobs House #1
Madison, Wisconsin, 1936-37
Interior view
Photo by Larry Cuneo
The Frank Lloyd Wright Foundation
FLLW FDN # 3702.0027

after Usonian house was designed and built across the nation, Wright found it advantageous to send one of his qualified apprentices to stay with the client, translate the drawings, select various bids for the different aspects of the house, and generally supervise construction. In effect, the apprentice was actually the contractor, assigned to subcontract others as their work required.

The L-shaped plan served especially well in the Herbert Jacobs House, placing the building close to the street on one side and to the neighboring property on the other. The timeworn plan of front yard, backyard, and two side yards is abolished.

"Here is a moderate cost brick and wood house that by new technology of a lifetime has been greatly extended in scale and comfort. . . . There is freedom of movement, and privacy, too, afforded by the general arrangement here, unknown to the current boxment. . . . I think a cultured American housewife will look well in it. Where does the garden leave off and the house begin? Where the garden begins and the house leaves off. Withal, it seems a thing loving the ground with the new sense of space—light— and freedom to which our U.S.A. is entitled."[6]

Herbert Jacobs House #1
Madison, Wisconsin, 1936–37
Exterior
Photo by Larry Cuneo
The Frank Lloyd Wright Foundation
FLLW FDN # 3702.0025

NOTES
1. Frank Lloyd Wright, *Architectural Forum,* January 1938,
   in *The Essential Frank Lloyd Wright,* p. 309.
2. Ibid., pp. 284–85.
3. Ibid., p. 285. This was first written for the January 1938
   Architectural Forum; the house was published in this monograph
   issue, which was devoted to Wright's work at that time.
4. Ibid.
5. Ibid., p. 286.
6. Ibid., p. 287.

Taliesin West
Scottsdale, Arizona, 1937-59
Aerial perspective
Graphite pencil, color pencil, and ink on paper
24 x 106 inches (61 x 269.2 cm)
The Frank Lloyd Wright Foundation
FLLW FDN # 3803.003

Taliesin West
Scottsdale, Arizona, 1937-59
Master plan
Ink on paper
35 5/8 x 85 3/16 inches (90.5 x 216.4 cm)
The Frank Lloyd Wright Foundation
FLLW FDN # 3803.136

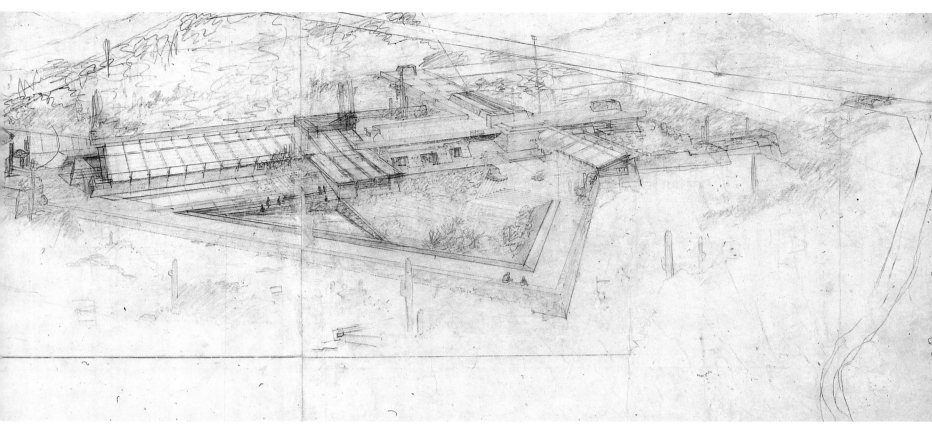

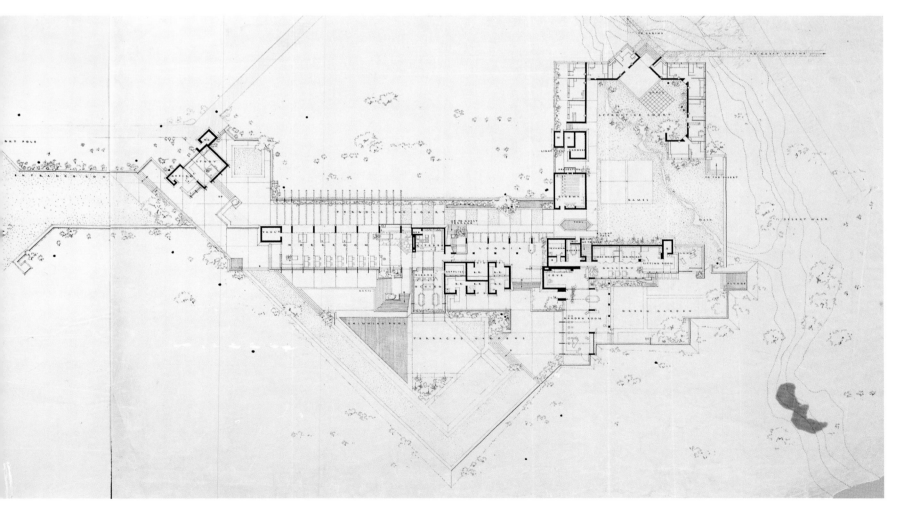

Taliesin West
Scottsdale, Arizona, 1937–59
Pool and dining room
Photo by Maynard Parker
The Frank Lloyd Wright Foundation
FLLW FDN # 3803.0008

Taliesin West
Scottsdale, Arizona, 1937–59
View of sunset terrace
Photo by Maynard Parker
The Frank Lloyd Wright Foundation
FLLW FDN # 3803.0013

Taliesin West
Scottsdale, Arizona, 1937-59
Garden room and section
Photo by Maynard Parker
The Frank Lloyd Wright Foundation
FLLW FDN # 3803.0027

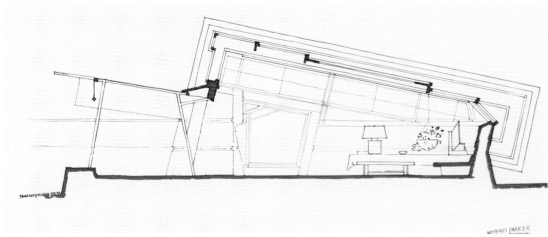

Taliesin West
Scottsdale, Arizona, 1937-59
Garden room interior and detail section
Photo by Maynard Parker
The Frank Lloyd Wright Foundation
FLLW FDN # 3803.0029

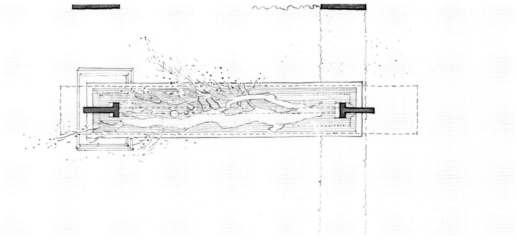

Taliesin West
Scottsdale, Arizona, 1937–59
Dining cove
Photo by Maynard Parker
The Frank Lloyd Wright Foundation
FLLW FDN # 3803.0031

Taliesin West
Scottsdale, Arizona, 1937–59
Sitting room interior and plan
Photo by Maynard Parker
The Frank Lloyd Wright Foundation
FLLW FDN # 3803.0037

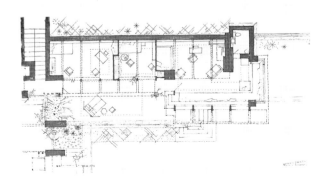

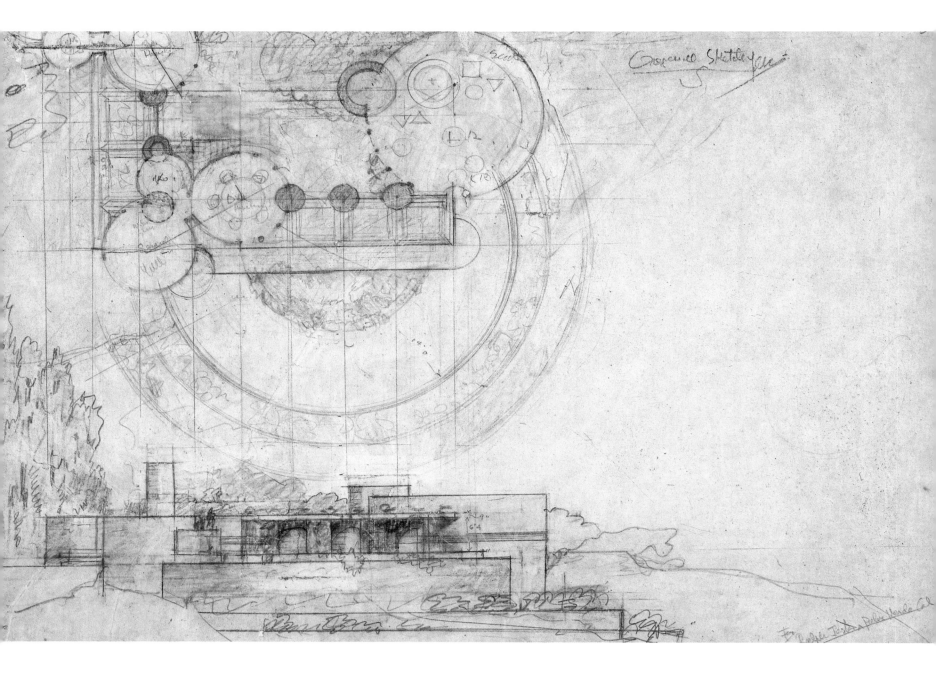

Ralph Jester House (project)
Palos Verdes, California, 1938–39
Plan and elevation
Graphite pencil and color pencil on paper
13 ¾ x 21 inches (34.9 x 53.3 cm)
The Frank Lloyd Wright Foundation
FLLW FDN # 3807.002

Ralph Jester House (project)
Palos Verdes, California, 1938–39
Model
The Frank Lloyd Wright Foundation
FLLW FDN # 3807.0001

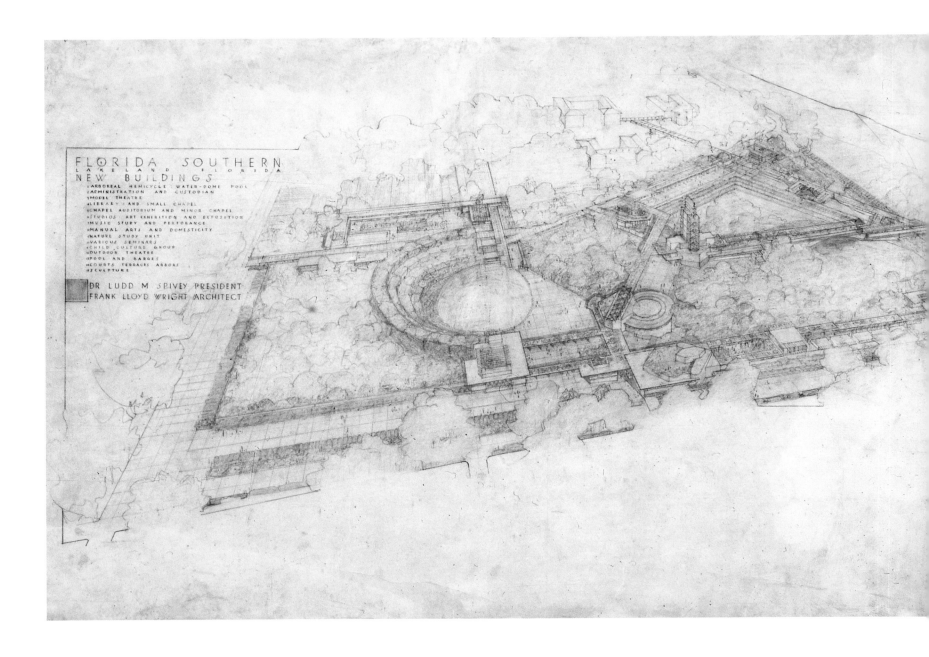

Florida Southern College Master Plan
Lakeland, Florida, 1938
Aerial perspective
Graphite pencil and color pencil on paper
24 x 47 ⅝ inches (61 x 121 cm)
The Frank Lloyd Wright Foundation
FLLW FDN # 3805.002

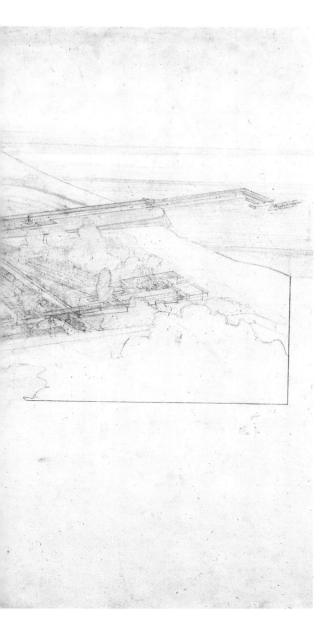

Florida Southern College Master Plan
Lakeland, Florida, 1938
Aerial view
The Frank Lloyd Wright Foundation
FLLW FDN # 3805.0009

Pfeiffer Chapel, Florida Southern College
Lakeland, Florida, 1938–41
Perspective
Graphite pencil and color pencil on paper
19 x 32 5/8 inches (49.5 x 82.9 cm)
The Frank Lloyd Wright Foundation
FLLW FDN # 3816.003

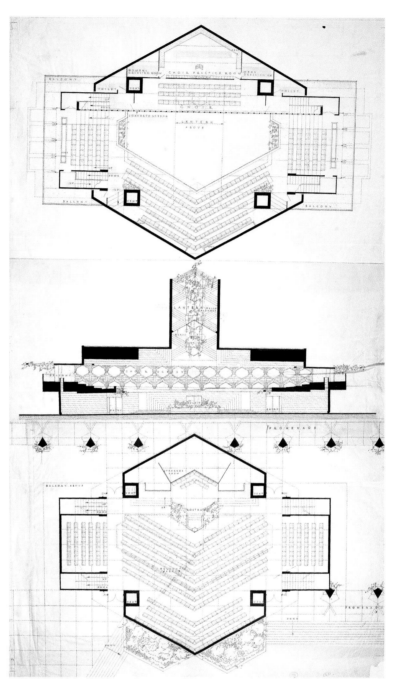

Pfeiffer Chapel, Florida Southern College
Lakeland, Florida, 1938–41
Plan and section
Ink on paper
36 x 60 inches (91.4 x 152.4 cm)
The Frank Lloyd Wright Foundation
FLLW FDN # 3816.097

Pfeiffer Chapel, Florida Southern College
Lakeland, Florida, 1938–41
Exterior
The Frank Lloyd Wright Foundation
FLLW FDN # 3816.0065

Pfeiffer Chapel, Florida Southern College
Lakeland, Florida, 1938–41
Interior
The Frank Lloyd Wright Foundation
FLLW FDN # 3816.0076

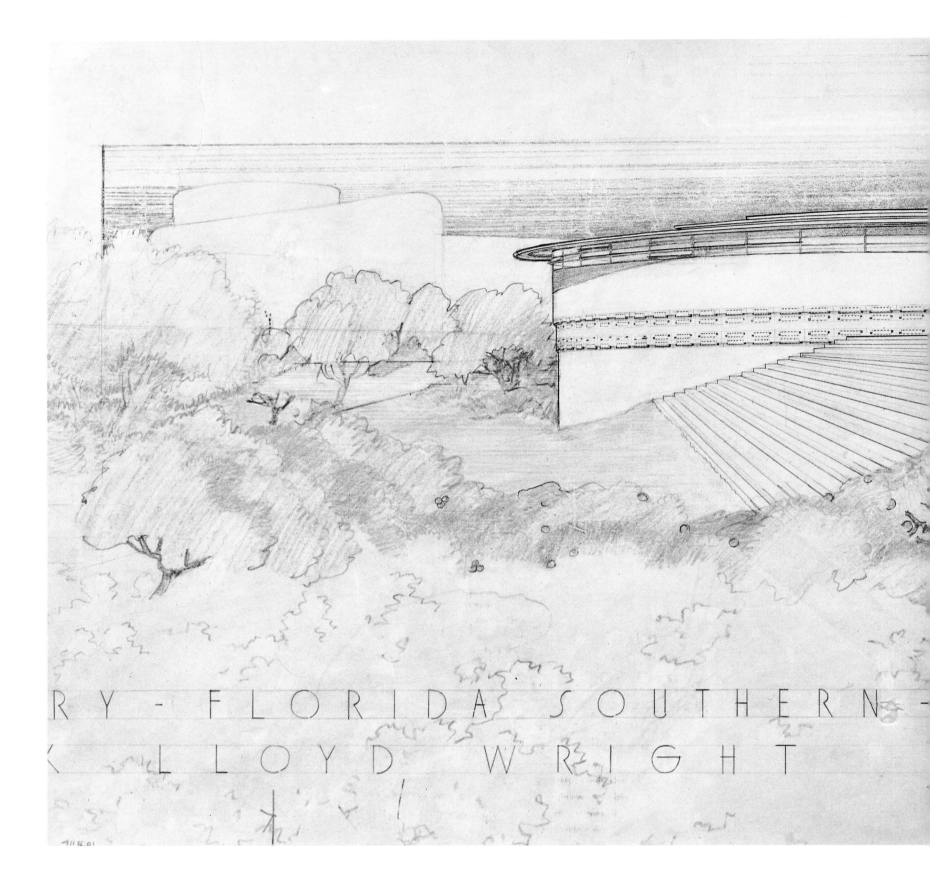

RY · FLORIDA SOUTHERN ·

LLOYD WRIGHT

Roux Library, Florida Southern College
Lakeland, Florida, 1941–42
Perspective
Graphite pencil and color pencil on paper
17 x 37 inches (43.8 x 94 cm)
The Frank Lloyd Wright Foundation
FLLW FDN # 4118.001

LAKELAND FLORIDA
ARCHITECT

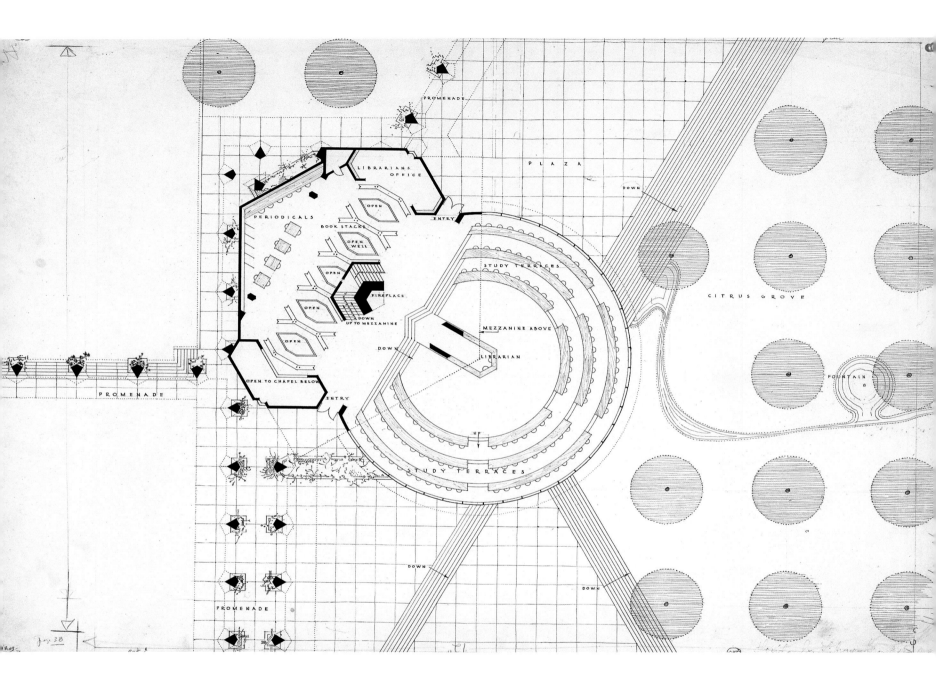

PROMENADE

LIBRARIANS OFFICE

PERIODICALS

OPEN

BOOK STACKS

OPEN WELL

ENTRY

OPEN

OPEN

FIREPLACE

DOWN
UP TO MEZZANINE

OPEN

OPEN TO CHAPEL BELOW

ENTRY

PROMENADE

PLAZA

DOWN

STUDY TERRACES

DOWN

MEZZANINE ABOVE

LIBRARIAN

UP

STUDY TERRACES

DOWN

DOWN

CITRUS GROVE

FOUNTAIN

PROMENADE

Roux Library, Florida Southern College
Lakeland, Florida, 1941–42
Publication plan
Ink on paper
24 x 36 inches (61 x 91.4 cm)
The Frank Lloyd Wright Foundation
FLLW FDN # 4118.003

Roux Library, Florida Southern College
Lakeland, Florida, 1941–42
Exterior
The Frank Lloyd Wright Foundation
FLLW FDN # 4118.0012

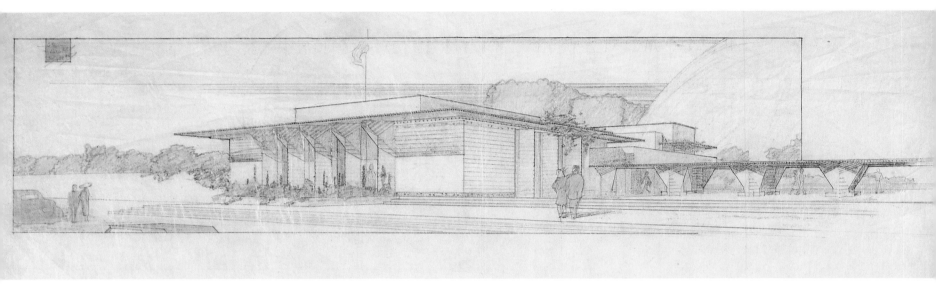

Administration Building, Florida Southern College
Lakeland, Florida, 1945
Perspective
Graphite pencil, color pencil, and sepia ink on paper
13 x 29 inches (34.9 x 74.3 cm)
The Frank Lloyd Wright Foundation
FLLW FDN # 4515.005

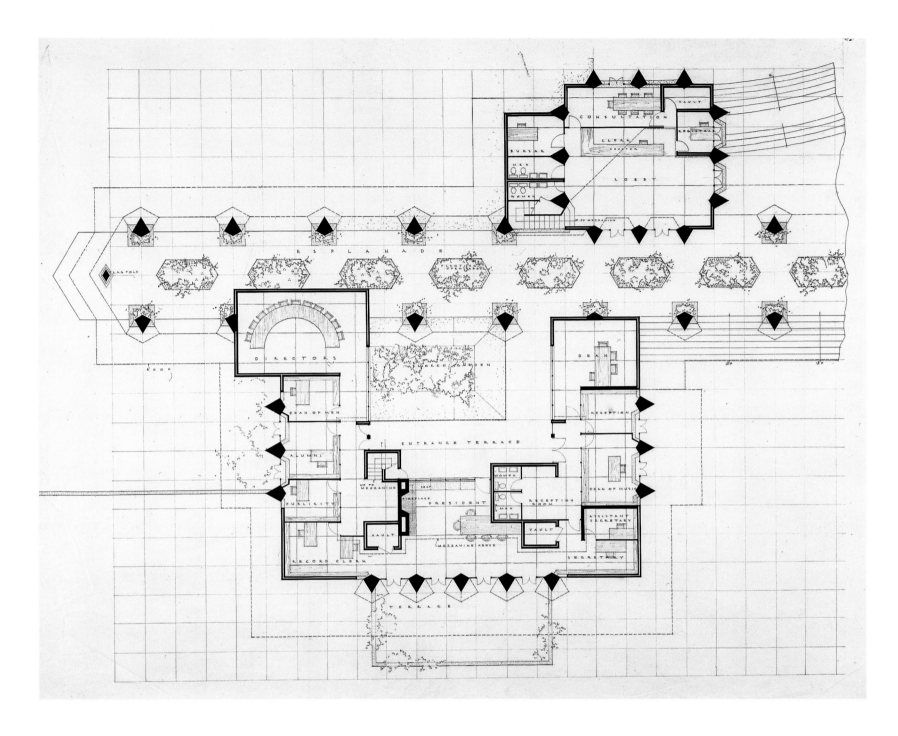

Administration Building, Florida Southern College
Lakeland, Florida, 1945
Publication plan
Ink on paper
36 x 41 ⁵/₈ inches (91.4 x 105.7 cm)
The Frank Lloyd Wright Foundation
FLLW FDN # 4515.007

Administration Building, Florida Southern College
Lakeland, Florida, 1945
Exterior
The Frank Lloyd Wright Foundation
FLLW FDN # 4515.0023

Administration Building, Florida Southern College
Lakeland, Florida, 1945
Interior
The Frank Lloyd Wright Foundation
FLLW FDN # 4515.0024

CRYSTAL CITY (PROJECT)

Crystal City (project)
Washington, D.C., 1940
Aerial perspective
Sepia ink and wash on paper
31 3/8 x 34 3/16 inches (79.7 x 87.6 cm)
The Frank Lloyd Wright Foundation
FLLW FDN # 4016.001

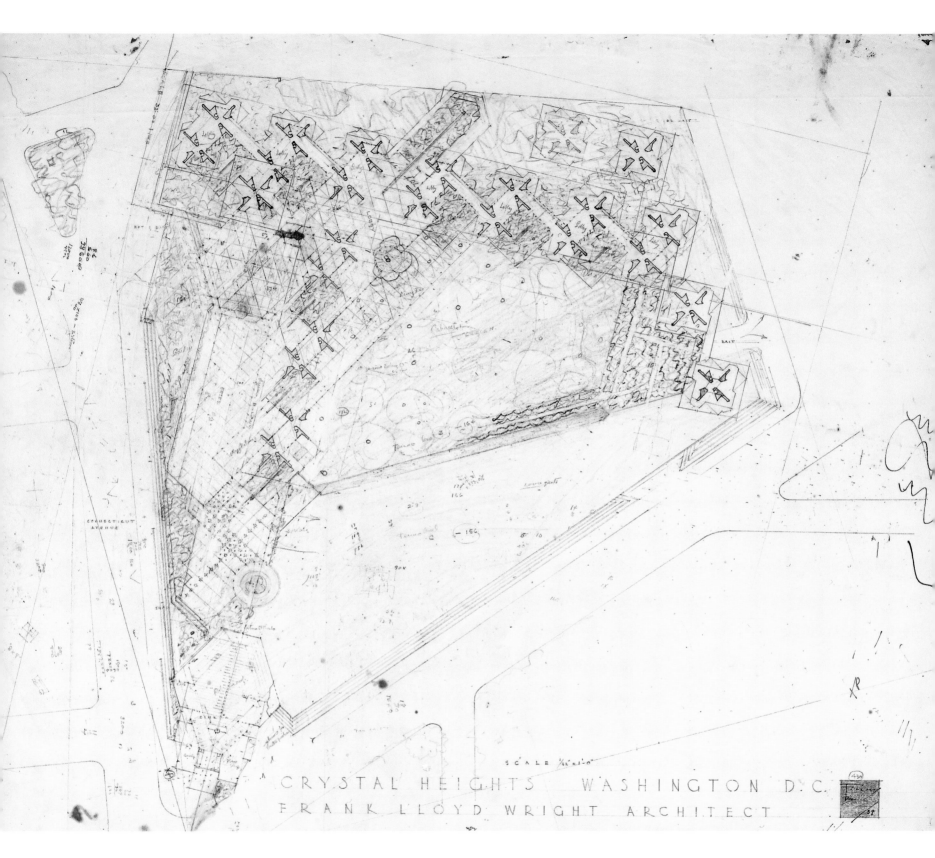

Crystal City (project)
Washington, D.C., 1940
Site plan
Graphite pencil and color pencil on tracing paper
30 x 36 inches (76.2 x 91.4 cm)
The Frank Lloyd Wright Foundation
FLLW FDN # 4016.005

CRYSTAL CITY (PROJECT)

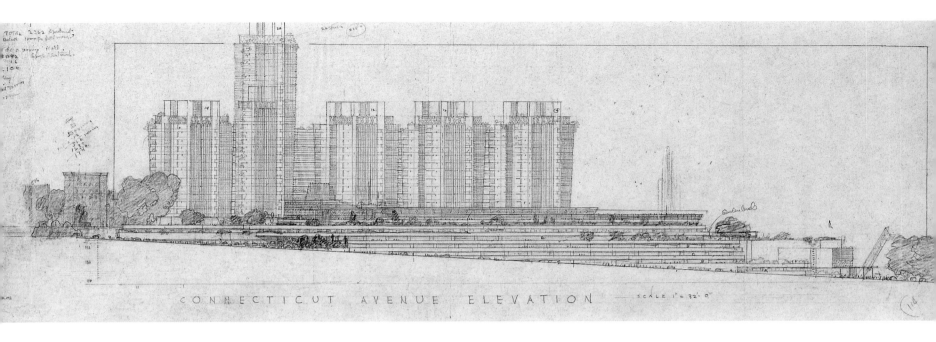

CONNECTICUT AVENUE ELEVATION — SCALE 1"=32'-0"

Crystal City (project)
Washington, D.C., 1940
Elevation
Graphite pencil and color pencil on paper
10 3/8 x 34 3/16 inches (26.4 x 87.6 cm)
The Frank Lloyd Wright Foundation
FLLW FDN # 4016.002

ORGANIC ARCHITECTURE COMES TO THE NATION'S CAPITAL

On 8 August 1940, Roy S. Thurman, a young developer in Washington, D.C., sent a telegram to Frank Lloyd Wright: "I expect to be in Milwaukee within next few days and would appreciate hearing whether it would be convenient to visit you for purpose of discussing most unusual large scale development project approximately heart of Washington DC. Kindly wire me collect Gladstone Hotel." Wright's reply was simply "Will be here and glad to see you."[1]

Upon their meeting it was proposed that Wright design a large and extensive work to include hotel, apartment towers, shops with adequate parking, and cinema on a site vaguely triangular in shape, where Connecticut and Florida avenues slope down from the Oak Tree Garden to meet at the apex below.

On 14 August, a letter from Thurman to Wright, and countersigned by Wright, confirmed the beginning of discussions for a new project to be located at a property known as the "Dean Estate" and sometimes called "Temple Heights." By 21 August, Wright had sent a proposal of a project according to Thurman's requirements.

A few days later Wright made some initial drawings and forwarded them to Thurman with the explanation:

> Herewith a pan-out of the buildings I've planned for you at Washington. I think it will astonish you. . . . The whole thing should be worked out in white marble, verdigris-bronze and crystal . . . and this is to suggest that you change Temple Heights to Crystal Heights because of the crystalline character of the whole edifice. It will be an iridescent fabric with every surface showing of the finest quality. . . . Crystal is the word when you see the buildings. The floor surfaces which are extensive inside and outside will receive great attention—be of white marble with bronze shallow bas-relief inlays—at appropriate places emphasizing the great spaciousness in bright light of the whole structure. The gardens and terraces all contribute to the effect too. I've managed to save the better part of the oaks. The Dining Room, Banquet Hall, and all Private Supper Rooms are all sunlit overlooking garden terraces—gleaming crystal palaces, Versailles is no more. I have assumed that you wanted the last word which is also the first word in all this and we have it—the apotheosis of GLASS. . . . I have assumed that you wanted to make a clean sweep of the success of Crystal Heights—and I am proceeding accordingly with a thorough-bred.[2]

On the upper level of the site, eleven towers, based on the plan for apartment towers for St. Mark's-in-the-Bouwerie, are connected together, as the Grouped Towers project. Three other towers are freestanding. Five of the double towers and one triple tower form the hotel portion of the scheme, in an L-shaped plan. The central tower is twenty-four stories high; the others are fourteen. The hotel provides 1,230 regular guest rooms, 410 large rooms with fireplaces and windows on two sides, and 830 medium-size rooms. The separate apartment towers are also fourteen stories high. Projecting out from the hotel towers along the Connecticut Avenue side is a long galley labeled "Fetes," which was most likely intended as a convention room or for special occasions. At the end of this, where Connecticut and Florida avenues meet, at the lowest point on the property, is a theater seating 1,100. The slope of the property accounts for the five terraces, each one for shops, with parking located behind, accessed where each level is tangent to Connecticut Avenue. For the hotel guests there is further parking on the terrace adjacent to the Oak Tree Garden, which is reached from the entrance of the hotel at ground level below via a long tunnel leading behind the shops and up on to this terrace.

Thurman tried, over and over again, to secure zoning for the property but was continually defeated on the grounds that it was commercial and therefore not appropriate for the area, which was mainly residential. There was also the problem with the height of the hotel tower, exceeding a fixed limit for towers in Washington, D.C., at that time. Wright was amenable to reducing the height but was still faced with the zoning problem. On into October, while this battle for zoning was carried on, Wright, ever the optimist, was conferring with engineers, "working on steel and concrete generalities."[3] Nevertheless, facing defeat at every turn, Thurman wrote, "I have run into something of the nature of a stone wall in the matter of re-zoning the heights to permit the construction of 'Crystal City.' . . . I have been putting up the best kind of fight I know and have not at all taken this thing lying down."[4] It appears at this point in the struggle to get the rezoning for the project, the name was changed to "Crystal City."

Three days later Thurman wrote to Wright, "The enclosed newspaper clippings tell the story, impossible as it may seem. Don't be misguided by the note of willingness on the part of the authorities to make concessions that would make the 'City' possible. Their idea of concessions is complete emasculation, no shops, no theater, in fact nothing on Connecticut Avenue, and the building heights not to exceed 110 feet, which of course makes the idea of 'Crystal City' impossible.

"Excepting that you have been through the same kind of thing often before, and perhaps are a little case-hardened and impervious to the mosquito stings of small men, I think it would be impossible for you to understand the soul-trying aspects of this fight and my utter disgust and dismay at its outcome. My only consolation, and it is a great one, is that I have been honored with your affectionate and wholesome relationship. It may be in the tea-leaves that we shall yet have an opportunity comparable to 'Crystal City.'

"Under separate cover I am sending to you the leather-bound prospectus—if it is any solace—on which I had successfully secured financial commitments to make 'Crystal City' a reality."[5]

At the bottom of this letter, Wright had inscribed, "Dear Roy—Don't give up the ship. All right to get mad and hang up. But listen in and take the receiver down again at the right time. You are a good fighter. FLLW."[6]

Wright once claimed that the reason for the failure of the authorities to accept the project was because "it was neither colonial nor classical, and therefore unfit for the nation's capital." But in reality the reason for the defeat was simply a matter of zoning.

Despite all the struggles, all the hope, and all the frustration, it seemed that the fight was, indeed, over. Washington, D.C., was not ready to subscribe to organic architecture, and the shimmering project of Crystal City was abandoned.

NOTES
1. Roy S. Thurman to Frank Lloyd Wright, 8 August 1940.
2. Wright to Thurman, 17 August 1940.
3. Wright to Thurman, 21 October 1940.
4. Thurman to Wright, 15 January 1941.
5. Thurman to Wright, 18 January 1941.
6. Wright to Thurman, 22 January 1941.

CRYSTAL HEIGHTS WASHINGTON DC FRANK
FOR ROY S THURMAN

Crystal City (project)
Washington, D.C., 1940
Perspective
Sepia ink and wash on paper
20 1/16 x 34 inches (51.4 x 86.4 cm)
The Frank Lloyd Wright Foundation
FLLW FDN # 4016.004

Cooperative Homesteads (project)
Detroit, Michigan, 1942
Perspective
Graphite pencil, color pencil, and sepia ink on paper
19 ³/₈ x 34 ¼ inches (49.2 x 87 cm)
The Frank Lloyd Wright Foundation
FLLW FDN # 4201.009

255 PLATES, 1942

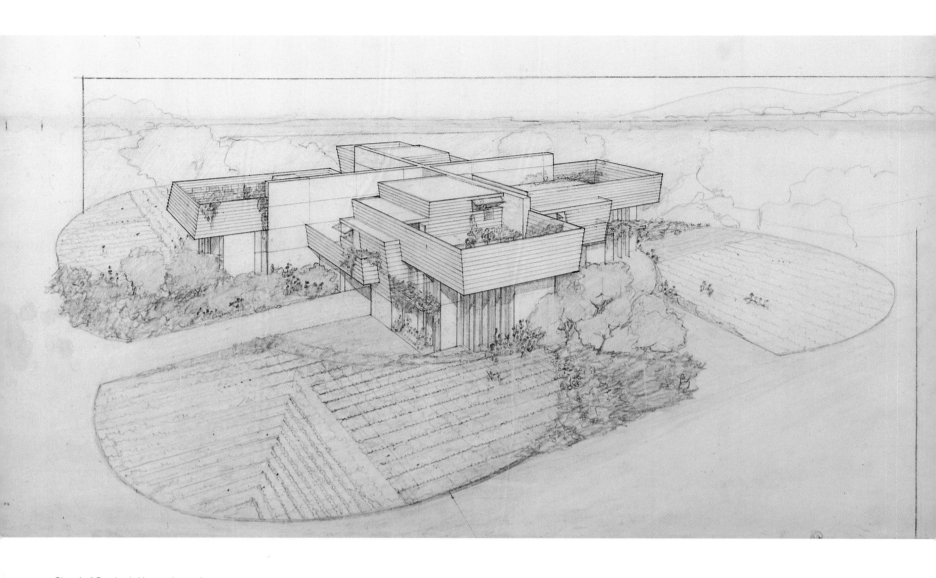

Cloverleaf Quadruple Housing (project)
Pittsfield, Massachusetts, 1942
Aerial perspective
Color pencil and ink on paper
26 x 36 inches (57 x 91 cm)
The Frank Lloyd Wright Foundation
FLLW FDN # 4203.002

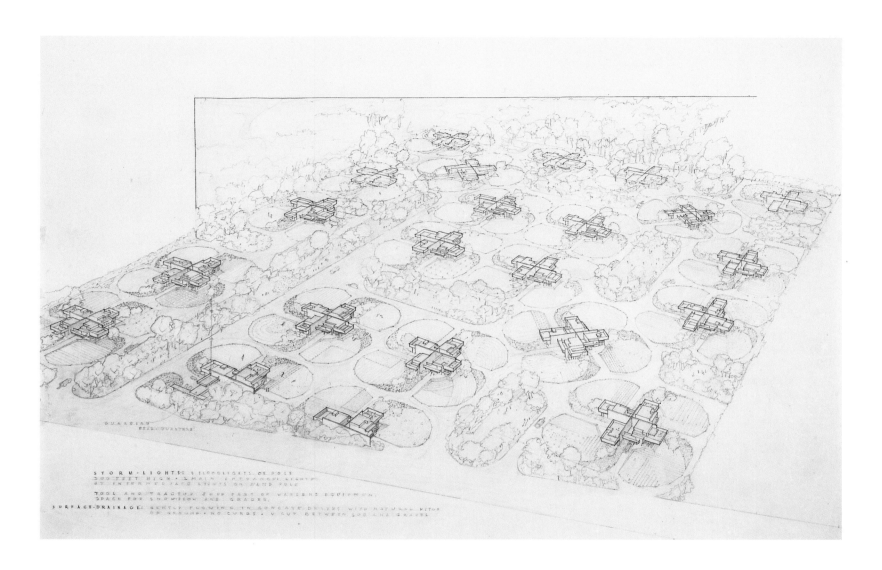

Cloverleaf Quadruple Housing (project)
Pittsfield, Massachusetts, 1942
Aerial perspective
Graphite pencil, color pencil, and ink on paper
29 7/8 x 36 inches (75.6 x 91.4 cm)
The Frank Lloyd Wright Foundation
FLLW FDN # 4203.007

Cloverleaf Quadruple Housing (project)
Pittsfield, Massachusetts, 1942
Interior perspective
Pencil, color pencil, and ink on paper
28 1/8 x 34 3/4 inches (71.4 x 88.3 cm)
The Frank Lloyd Wright Foundation
FLLW FDN # 4203.008

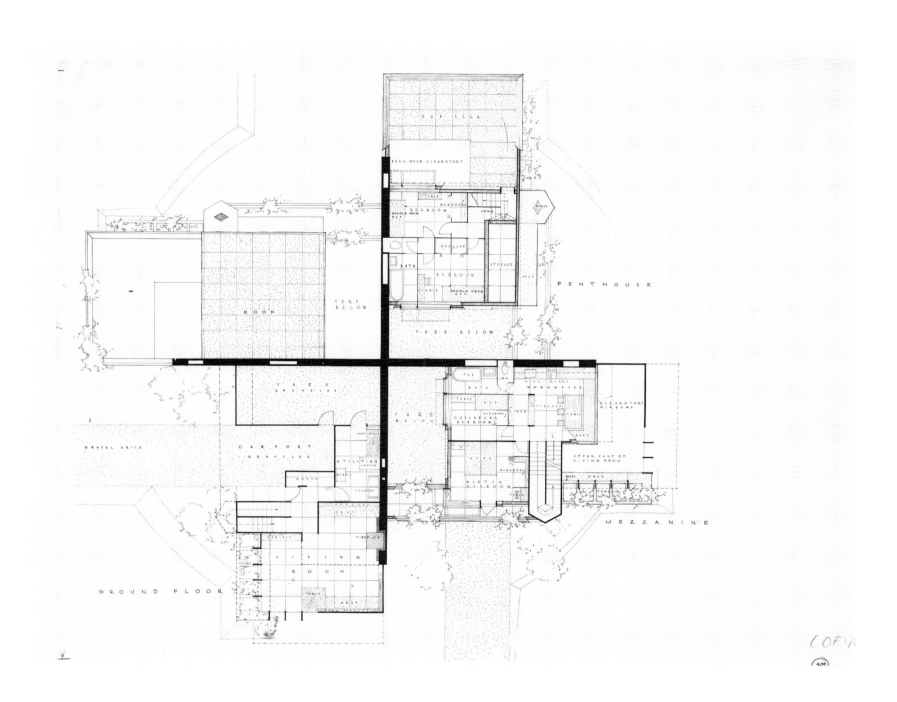

Cloverleaf Quadruple Housing (project)
Pittsfield, Massachusetts, 1942
Publication plan
Ink on paper
29 x 26 inches (73.7 x 66 cm)
The Frank Lloyd Wright Foundation
FLLW FDN # 4203.047

SOLOMON R. GUGGENHEIM MUSEUM

Solomon R. Guggenheim Museum
New York, New York, 1943–59
Perspective
Watercolor and tempera on paper
20 x 24 ⅜ inches (50.8 x 61.9 cm)
The Frank Lloyd Wright Foundation
FLLW FDN # 4305.008

Solomon R. Guggenheim Museum
New York, New York, 1943–59
Interior view of ramps
Photo by Louis Reens

A SAGA OF CHANGES

From the time that the first set of working drawings, what today are referred to as "construction documents," were approved and signed by Solomon R. Guggenheim and Frank Lloyd Wright in 1945, and the final set of working drawings were approved and signed by the architect in 1956, the design for the Solomon R. Guggenheim Museum underwent significant and radical changes. Consistent through all of these changes, however, was the concept of a spiral ramp growing larger as it rose. That was, indeed, the raison d'être for the idea of how to exhibit works of art in a new and exciting manner. It is generally believed that it was Irene, Guggenheim's wife, who strongly urged her husband to select Frank Lloyd Wright as the architect for a building to contain the Solomon R. Guggenheim Foundation's collection of paintings. She,

along with the foundation's curator, Hilla Rebay, accompanied Guggenheim on their trips abroad in search of paintings to acquire from artists living at that time. Paramount in this endeavor was to collect the paintings of Vasily Kandinsky. His work, nonobjective painting, as it was defined, became a deep interest to the three of them, and for Rebay, it was truly a passion. An artist in her own right, she envisioned a building that would be, in her words, "a temple of spirit, a monument."[1] It was her first letter to Wright in 1943 that opened the commission, and Guggenheim assigned her role in the design of the building as somewhat in the nature of the client, with his reserving the final decision in all matters.

In Guggenheim's original contract of 29 June 1943 he specified a figure of $750,000 for the cost of construction, not including the cost of acquiring a site for the building. This issue of the site was of great concern

SOLOMON R. GUGGENHEIM MUSEUM

(top)
Solomon R. Guggenheim Museum
New York, New York, 1943–59
Perspective
Ink and watercolor on art paper
20 ⅛ x 24 ⅛ inches (51.1 x 61.3 cm)
The Frank Lloyd Wright Foundation
FLLW FDN # 4305.745

(bottom)
Solomon R. Guggenheim Museum
New York, New York, 1943–59
Perspective
Ink and watercolor on art paper
20 x 24 ¼ inches (50.8 x 61.6 cm)
The Frank Lloyd Wright Foundation
FLLW FDN # 4305.746

(opposite top)
Solomon R. Guggenheim Museum
New York, New York, 1943–59
Perspective
Ink and watercolor on art paper
20 x 24 inches (51 x 61 cm)
Private collection
FLLW FDN # 4305.747

(opposite bottom)
Solomon R. Guggenheim Museum
New York, New York, 1943–59
Perspective
Ink and watercolor on art paper
20 x 24 inches (51 x 61 cm)
Private collection
FLLW FDN # 4305.748

to Wright. When he received the commission in 1943, there was no site at hand. There was consideration of a site possibly up in Riverdale, but Wright had a "hunch" that Guggenheim, who loved Manhattan, would eventually settle on a city block. Convinced that the museum would go vertical, rather than horizontal, he made several preliminary studies showing the building on an entire block, with the rotunda, or ramp, on the right side, an apartment wing for Rebay on the left, with offices and museum work facilities connecting the two. Guggenheim was intensely pleased with these preliminaries and instantly recognized the novel and innovative way of showing paintings on a spiral ramp.

At last, in March 1944, a site was finally selected on Fifth Avenue, between Eighty-eighth and Eighty-ninth streets. A tall, narrow apartment building was on the Eighty-eighth Street side, and Wright was able to adapt his preliminary studies to take this into account. The spiral ramp was moved to the left, along the Eighty-ninth Street side, and the apartment section for Rebay bordered against the existing building on Eighty-eighth Street. Guggenheim notified Wright, "Your preliminary sketches are entirely satisfactory, and we are now authorizing you to proceed to make detailed plans, described as Second Part of your Contract, which will enable us to build the building."[2]

The next year the first set of working drawings, along with specifications, were prepared.

In the 1945 drawings, there are elements that strongly indicate Rebay's role in the design. In the place where the current theater is, there is a large theater as well, but in this case the spectators recline and look up to the ceiling, a half dome, upon which are projected slides of nonobjective paintings, to the accompaniment of Mozart trios and quartets, as specified by Rebay. One can assume that the architect would also desire to include the late quartets of his great hero, Beethoven. Not content with this one theater, there was also another, called an Ocular Chamber, located in the wing of the building that also housed a rather luxurious apartment for Rebay. Here the same viewers were

seen, reclining to see images on the ceiling above. There also was an observatory, placed above the elevator shaft on the ninth floor, where the starry heavens could be magnified and studied above the skies of Manhattan at night. These elements, surprising to see in any standard museum, reflected Rebay's concern not only for the exhibition of paintings but for the education of the public as to the meaning and significance of nonobjective paintings. It was, for her, truly a religion, and she endeavored to pass on that message to others as well.

Connecting the wing that housed Rebay's apartment was a series of levels containing a restaurant, a banquet hall, offices, shops, storage areas, and other spaces required for the work and mounting of exhibitions. All of this formed a rather complex and somewhat complicated design.

In 1946, soon after the end of World War II and thus the lifting of the government's restriction on building materials not connected with the war effort, Wright urged Guggenheim to go forward with construction. Guggenheim on the other hand, believed that the cost of building materials and construction would go down. Unfortunately, the costs of both materials and labor rose considerably. Guggenheim decided to wait.

In 1949, the benefactor died, never seeing his gift go into construction. Construction began in August 1956, and between the first working drawings, 1945, and the final ones, 1956, four other complete sets, including all engineering drawings and specifications, were produced. These represented the changes to the program of the building and to the designs that reflected and responded to those changes. After the retirement of Rebay in 1952, the role of the museum changed from that of a "Modern Gallery" housing and exhibiting its own collections to that of a typical museum that would produce exhibitions, receive exhibitions, and function as other museums do worldwide.

At this time, the narrow apartment building on Eighty-eighth Street was purchased, and Wright then revised his drawings to place the ramp, as it was in the

THE MODERN GALLERY
MUSEUM FOR THE SOLOMON R GUGGENHEIM FOUNDATION
FRANK LLOYD WRIGHT ARCHITECT
HOLDEN AND McLAUGHLIN ASSOCIATES

Solomon R. Guggenheim Museum
New York, New York, 1943–59
Perspective
Graphite pencil, color pencil, and sepia ink on paper
26 x 39 ½ inches (66 x 100.3 cm)
The Frank Lloyd Wright Foundation
FLLW FDN # 4305.017

Solomon R. Guggenheim Museum
New York, New York, 1943–59
Interior perspective, "The Masterpiece."
Graphite pencil and color pencil on paper
35 x 40 ⅜ inches (88.9 x 102.6 cm)
The Frank Lloyd Wright Foundation
FLLW FDN # 4305.010

THE MASTERPIECE

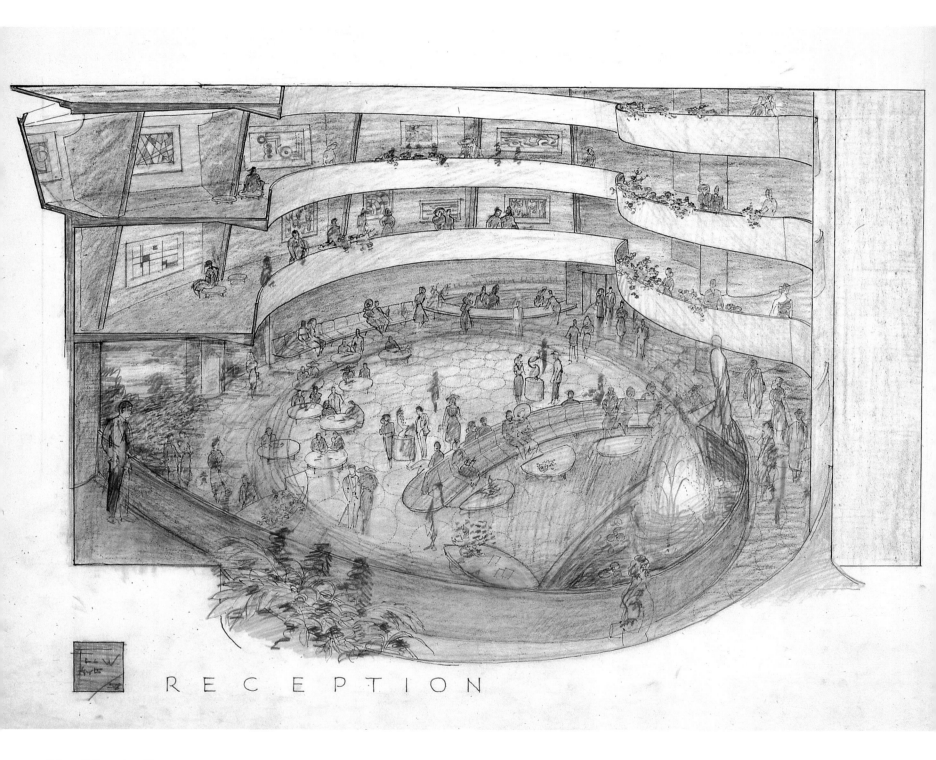

Solomon R. Guggenheim Museum
New York, New York, 1943–59
Perspective, "Reception"
Graphite pencil and color pencil on paper
29 ⅛ x 38 ¾ inches (74 x 98.4 cm)
The Frank Lloyd Wright Foundation
FLLW FDN # 4305.092

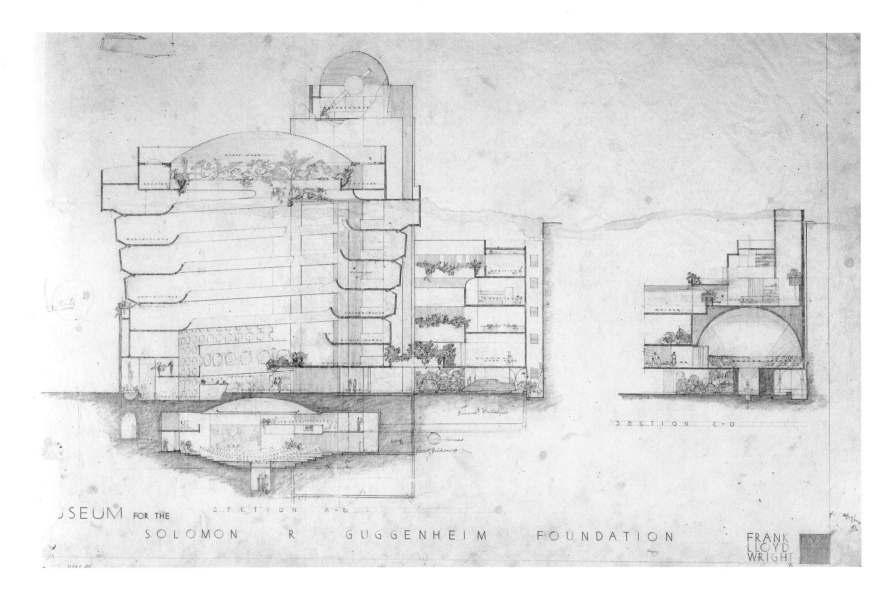

Solomon R. Guggenheim Museum
New York, New York, 1943-59
Cross sections
Graphite pencil and color pencil on paper
26 x 34 ⅞ inches (66 x 88.6 cm)
The Frank Lloyd Wright Foundation
FLLW FDN # 4305.035

early preliminaries, on the right, at Eighty-eighth Street, and the office facilities on the left.

In the mid- to late nineteenth century, it was discovered that the coefficient of thermal expansion—that is, the degree to which a material expands or contracts in relation to the temperature—of concrete and steel was the same. The result? Reinforced concrete, the massive material reinforced by stands of steel, be they mesh, rods, or beams. Wright declared that reinforced concrete was the "body of the modern world." It surpassed the post-and-beam construction and ushered in a revolution in architecture and engineering such as was never imagined in the world before.

The Solomon R. Guggenheim Museum is a building of all reinforced concrete; from the very beginning of his work on the project in 1943, Wright realized that only by means of reinforced concrete could this structure be realized. It is most dramatically apparent in the ramp where floor, balcony edge, and outer wall are all woven together by steel and concrete. A further element to the significance of the ramp is that at any one place on it one is able to see where one was and, at the same time, where one is going. In this sense, the ramp provides a sort of time-space continuum, a sort of "when past is future." The very nature of the ramp itself suggests change and motion.

The general design of the museum underwent changes between the scheme of 1945 and the final one of 1956. Many of these changes were in response to costs of construction. Others were the result of a different program that the museum was engaged in following the retirement of Rebay. The result is that a much simpler, stronger, and in a sense more sculptural, building emerged. At one point, in 1952, Wright proposed a tall apartment structure at the back of the building, to act as a screen to cover the ugly barren wall of an apartment building directly behind the museum. This new structure would serve, Wright reasoned, as rental studio apartments, to help produce further revenue for the museum and provide, on the lower floors, more space for bookstore, gift shop, and historic galleries. This, of course, would have added considerably to the cost of the construction, and the project was ultimately abandoned.

SOLOMON R. GUGGENHEIM MUSEUM

Solomon R. Guggenheim Museum
New York, New York, 1943–59
Perspective
Ink and watercolor on art paper
20 x 24 inches (51 x 61 cm)
Private collection
FLLW FDN # 4305.749

Solomon R. Guggenheim Museum
New York, New York, 1943–59
Exterior
Photo by William Short
Courtesy Solomon R. Guggenheim Foundation

The present tower, designed by Gwathmey Siegel and Associates Architects as part of its 1992 renovation of and addition to the museum, although not placed exactly where Wright had specified for his tower design, nevertheless fulfills his wish to provide a backdrop screen to the main structure.

Wright's participation in the design of the Solomon R. Guggenheim Museum consumed his interest, struggle, persistence, and often exasperation, for sixteen years. Even while in construction, the museum's committee joined with several prominent artists to make clear their contention that a spiral ramp, growing wider as it rose, with sloped walls, was totally inappropriate for the exhibition of paintings.

Up to the very end of his life, Wright carried on a struggle, almost in the nature of a crusade, to see his building built the way he and Solomon R. Guggenheim had envisioned it. Harry F. Guggenheim, Solomon's nephew, took over when his uncle died. Wright then appealed to his good senses, and the memory of his uncle, to preserve the integrity of the design. With the building approaching completion, Wright implored Harry Guggenheim: "Lieber Harry! I suppose I should have given up long before this my struggle to preserve the integrity of the building and the painting. . . . Yes, it is hard for you and the museum director and the members of the Committee to understand a struggle for harmony and unity between the painting and the building. No, it is not to subjugate the paintings to the building that I conceived this plan. On the contrary, it was to make the building and the painting a beautiful symphony such as never existed in the world of Art before."[3]

The year 2009 marks the fiftieth anniversary of the completion and opening of the Solomon R. Guggenheim Museum. It also marks the fiftieth year after the death of Frank Lloyd Wright. The museum's opening ceremonies took place on 21 October 1959. Wright had died six months earlier, on 9 April, without having seen his building completed.

NOTES
1. Hilla Rebay to Frank Lloyd Wright, 1 June 1943.
2. Solomon R. Guggenheim to Frank Lloyd Wright, 27 July 1944.
3. Frank Lloyd Wright to Harry Guggenheim, 15 July 1958.

SOLOMON R. GUGGENHEIM MUSEUM

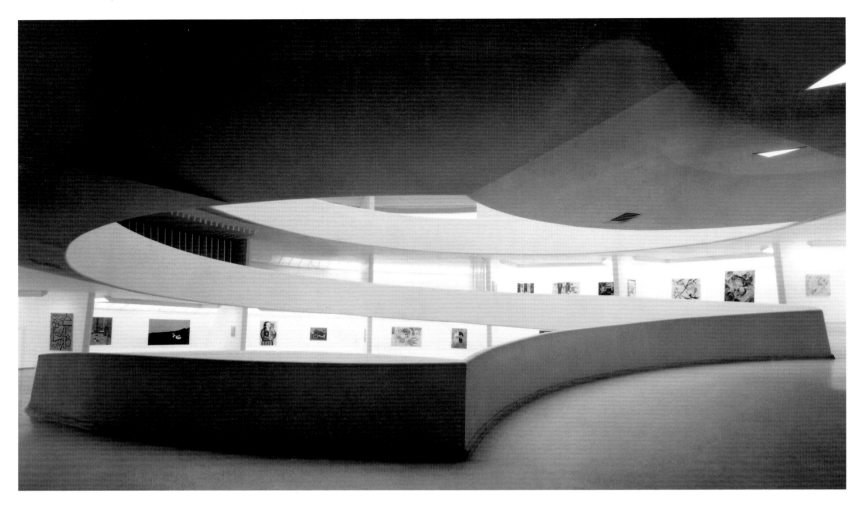

Solomon R. Guggenheim Museum
New York, New York, 1943-59
Interior view of ramps
Photo by Louis Reens

Solomon R. Guggenheim Museum
New York, New York, 1943-59
Interior view of dome skylight
Photo by Louis Reens

Solomon R. Guggenheim Museum
New York, New York, 1943-59
Frank Lloyd Wright on the museum ramp
The Frank Lloyd Wright Foundation
FLLW FDN # 4305.0387

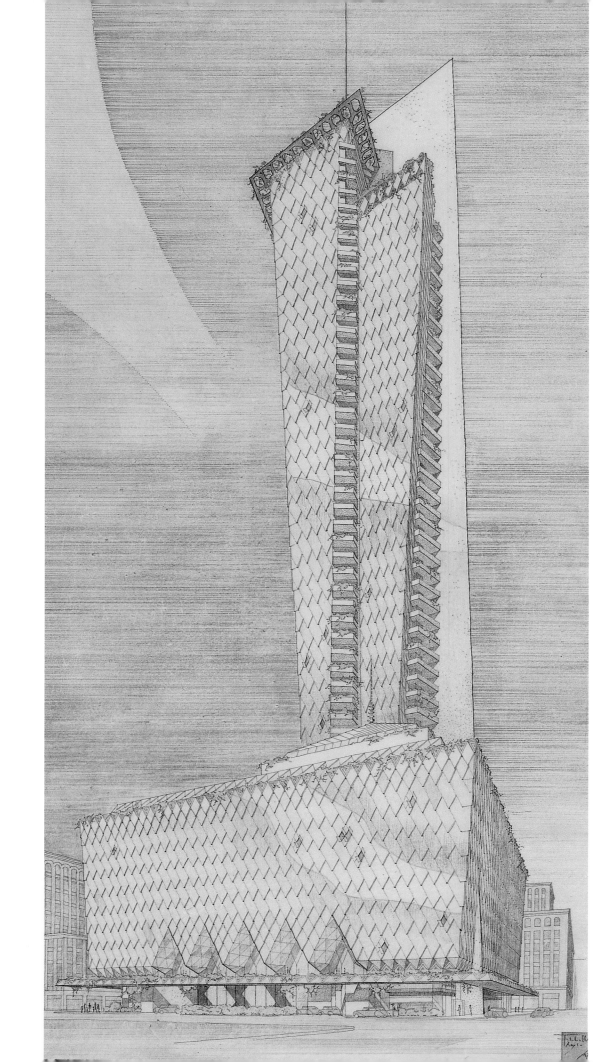

Rogers Lacy Hotel (project)
Dallas, Texas, 1946
Perspective
Color pencil and ink on Japanese paper
52 x 23 7/8 inches (134 x 60.6 cm)
The Frank Lloyd Wright Foundation
FLLW FDN # 4606.001

Rogers Lacy Hotel (project)
Dallas, Texas, 1946
Section
Color pencil and ink on Japanese paper
65 x 36 ¼ inches (167 x 92.1 cm)
The Frank Lloyd Wright Foundation
FLLW FDN # 4606.002

SECTION THROUGH ELEVATOR LOBBIES & DINING ROOM
PRELIMINARY PLANS FOR THE ROGERS LACY
FRANK LLOYD WRIGHT FOR ROGERS LACY   DALLAS TEXAS

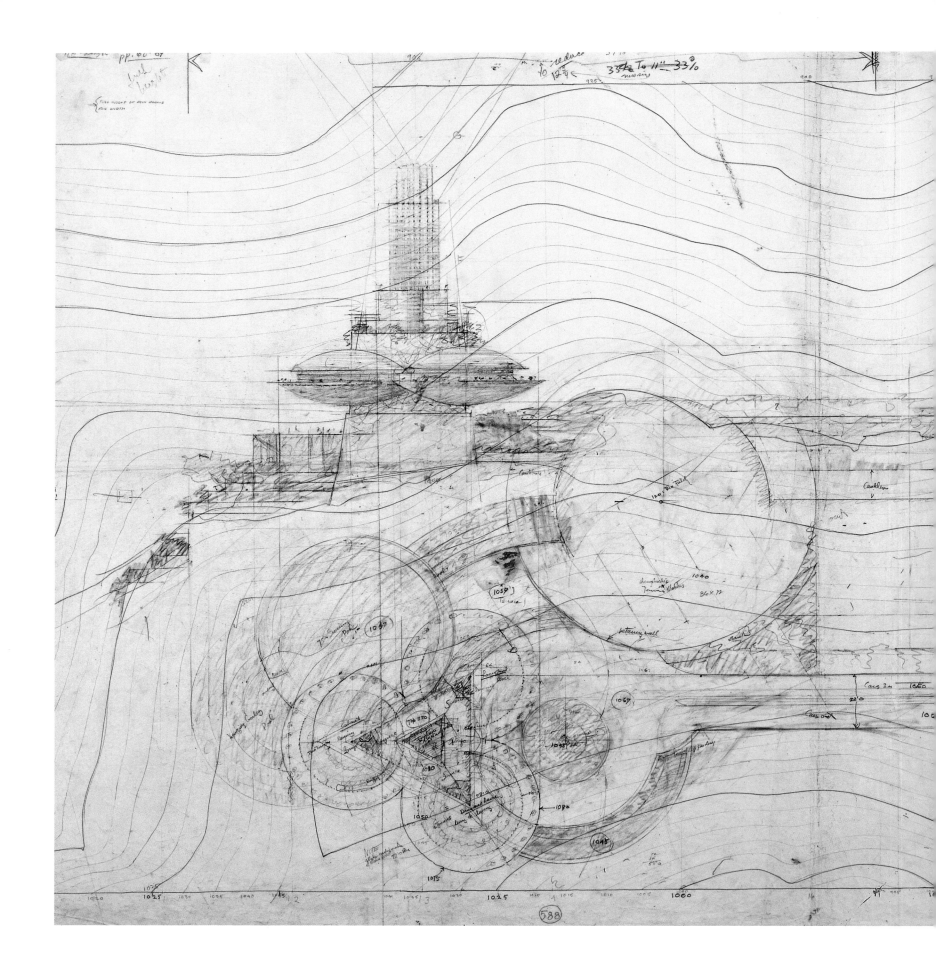

Huntington Hartford Sports Club / Play Resort (project)
Hollywood, California, 1947
Plan and elevation
Graphite pencil, color pencil, and ink on paper
45 5/8 x 74 inches (115.9 x 188 cm)
The Frank Lloyd Wright Foundation
FLLW FDN # 4731.001

COUNTRY CLUB FOR HUNTINGTON HARTFORD HOLLYWOOD
FRANK LLOYD WRIGHT ARCHITECT

Huntington Hartford Sports Club / Play Resort (project)
Hollywood, California, 1947
Perspective
Graphite pencil, color pencil, and ink on paper
35 x 52 inches (90.2 x 132.1 cm)
The Frank Lloyd Wright Foundation
FLLW FDN # 4731.020

Huntington Hartford Sports Club / Play Resort (project)
Hollywood, California, 1947
Section
Ink, gouache, and color pencil on paper
23 x 38 ⁵/₈ inches (60.3 x 98.1 cm)
The Frank Lloyd Wright Foundation
FLLW FDN # 4731.022

Huntington Hartford Cottage Group Center #2 (project)
Hollywood, California, 1946
Perspective
Graphite pencil, color pencil, and ink on paper
18 x 36 inches (47.6 x 91.4 cm)
The Frank Lloyd Wright Foundation
FLLW FDN # 4837.046

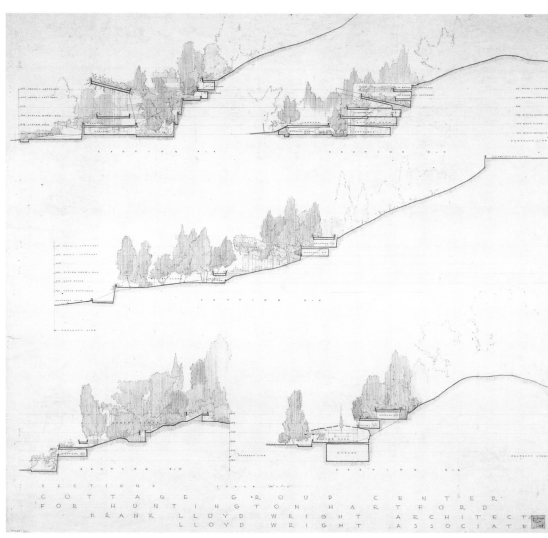

Huntington Hartford Cottage Group Center #2 (project)
Hollywood, California, 1946
Sections
Graphite pencil, color pencil, and ink on paper
35 7/8 x 36 inches (91.1 x 92.7 cm)
The Frank Lloyd Wright Foundation
FLLW FDN # 4837.041

Huntington Hartford Cottage Group Center #2 (project)
Hollywood, California, 1946
Perspective
Graphite pencil, color pencil, and ink on paper
31 x 63 inches (79 x 160 cm)
The Frank Lloyd Wright Foundation
FLLW FDN # 4837.047

Herbert Jacobs House #2, "Solar Hemicycle"
Middleton, Wisconsin, 1943
Aerial perspective
Graphite pencil and color pencil on paper
24 x 31 inches (61 x 79 cm)
The Frank Lloyd Wright Foundation
FLLW FDN # 4812.002

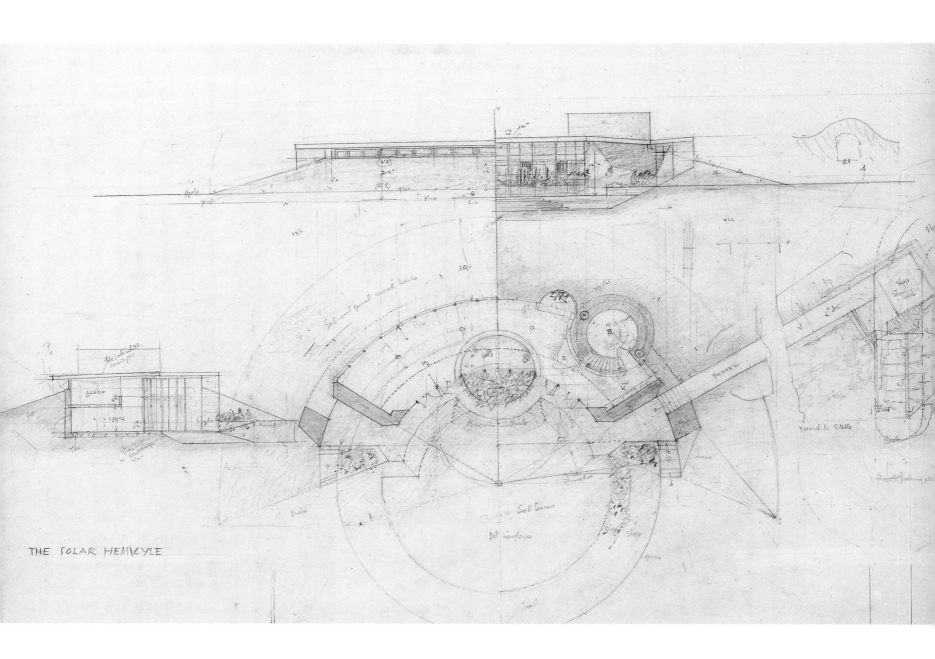

THE SOLAR HEMICYLE

Herbert Jacobs House #2, "Solar Hemicycle"
Middleton, Wisconsin, 1943
Plan, elevation, and section
Graphite pencil and color pencil on paper
19 7/8 x 34 inches (50.5 x 87 cm)
The Frank Lloyd Wright Foundation
FLLW FDN # 4812.001

Herbert Jacobs House #2, "Solar Hemicycle"
Middleton, Wisconsin, 1943
Photo by Ezra Stoller © ESTO

PITTSBURGH POINT PARK CIVIC CENTER #1 (PROJECT)

Pittsburgh Point Park Civic Center #1 (project)
Pittsburgh, Pennsylvania, 1947
Aerial perspective
Graphite pencil, color pencil, and ink on paper
33 x 74 inches (85.1 x 189.9 cm)
The Frank Lloyd Wright Foundation
FLLW FDN # 4821.003

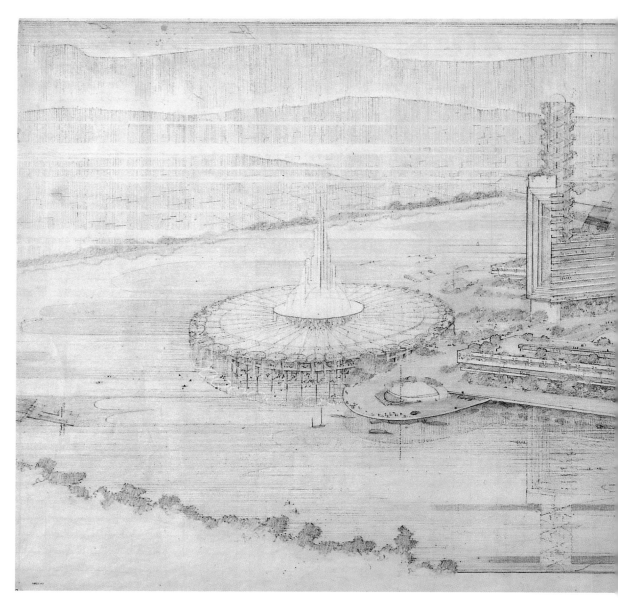

Pittsburgh Point Park Civic Center #1 (project)
Pittsburgh, Pennsylvania, 1947
Longitudinal section
Graphite pencil, color pencil, and ink on paper
30 x 81 ⅜ inches (76.2 x 206.7 cm)
The Frank Lloyd Wright Foundation
FLLW FDN # 4821.005

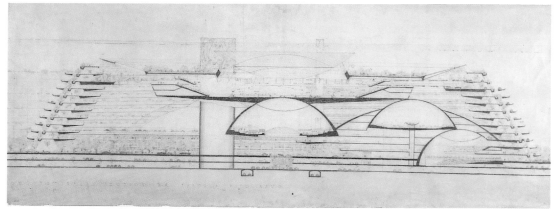

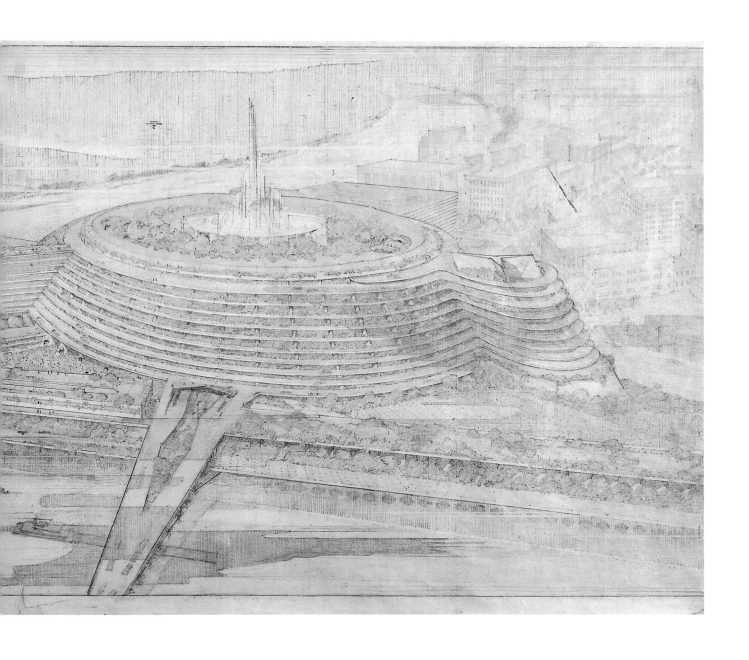

PITTSBURGH POINT PARK CIVIC CENTER #1
(PROJECT)

Pittsburgh Point Park Civic Center #1 (project)
Pittsburgh, Pennsylvania, 1947
Traffic distribution plan
Graphite pencil, color pencil, and ink on paper
18 x 21 ⅜ inches (45.7 x 54.3 cm)
The Frank Lloyd Wright Foundation
FLLW FDN # 4821.040

A MEGASTRUCTURE FOR SOCIAL, COMMERCIAL, AND CULTURAL LIFE

The site for a proposed civic center for Pittsburgh was at Point Park, a tract of land at the tip of the peninsula where the Allegheny and Monongahela rivers merge to form the Ohio River. For all of the components that such a center required, Wright realized that there was not space enough to spread out, and instead one large structure would be needed to house them all. When he began his design in 1947, it was as though, looking at the Gordon Strong project of 1924, he simply expanded the ramp outward so as to contain several features, rather than the one planetarium that was housed in the Strong opus.

The client for this project was a group of concerned Pittsburgh citizens called the Allegheny Conference on Community Development. One of its members was Edgar Kaufmann, Wright's former client for Fallingwater, the Kaufmann weekend home in Mill Run, Pennsylvania. Kaufmann was instrumental in the conference's selecting Wright as its architect. What Wright proposed, in response to Kaufmann's requirements, ranks as certainly Wright's most spectacular and expansive as well as largest single building he ever designed.

In the Strong project the exterior ramp was simply a means to go up and down the outside of the building. In the Pittsburgh project, along the outer rim of the circular megastructure 4 ½ miles of auto ramps rise 175 feet above street level. Here the ramp becomes a great commodity belt: "Upon the inside of the continuous four and one half miles of Grand Ramp direct access is had from the ramps [where there] are several hundred concessions such as hamburger stands, candy, soft drinks to flowers, books, curios, infinite gadgetry and personal services. . . . The Grand Ramp within would resemble a county fair."[1] Tangent to the Grand Ramp are two quick-access ramps that provide easy access up or down without traveling on the main ramp.

On the top level is the 9-acre Sky Park planted with indigenous trees, shrubs, and flowers. The Sky Park also provides landing space for helicopters and for large and small balloons. Directly beneath the Sky Park is a glass-covered playing field with 20,000 seats for summer or winter use. On the large cross section of the project, Wright's apprentices have drawn a hockey game in progress. The sports arena is lit by natural light from a great glass inverted dome on the Sky Park, with water and fountains. Throughout the interior there are a grand opera seating 10,000 to 20,000 people and three cinemas seating 1,500 each, with parking facilities for both opera and cinemas beneath at ground level. There are provisions for a convention hall, seating 12,500, with ample parking provided likewise. The various halls and spaces within the building are constructed out of lens-shaped structures anchored to gigantic pylons. The materials are prestressed steel or cold-drawn mesh (as in the dendriform columns of the S. C. Johnson & Son, Inc. Administration Building) cast in high-pressure concrete with vertical and horizontal glass enclosures. Outside the gigantic circular structure on the main street level on one side is a concert garden seating 15,000 to 20,000 people.

"On and below this same street level opposite there is a novel zoo wherein extraordinary animal life would be sheltered in characteristic fashion natural to the animal. . . .[2]

Overhanging the river at the apex of Point Park is a great glass pavilion containing restaurant above, seating 1000 people at tables, 500 at counter. This restaurant surrounds a novel, extensive under-water aquarium for sea monsters seen from below. A great overhead insectorium or aviary. Below, near the river level, extensive swimming pools. Appropriate greenery and fountain-effects thrown up from the rivers are features throughout. A special play-park and pool for small children with suitable crèche, toilets, etc., is on the street level nearby.

A large planetarium or, instead, several large, specially adapted, exhibition galleries for art and crafts exhibitions.

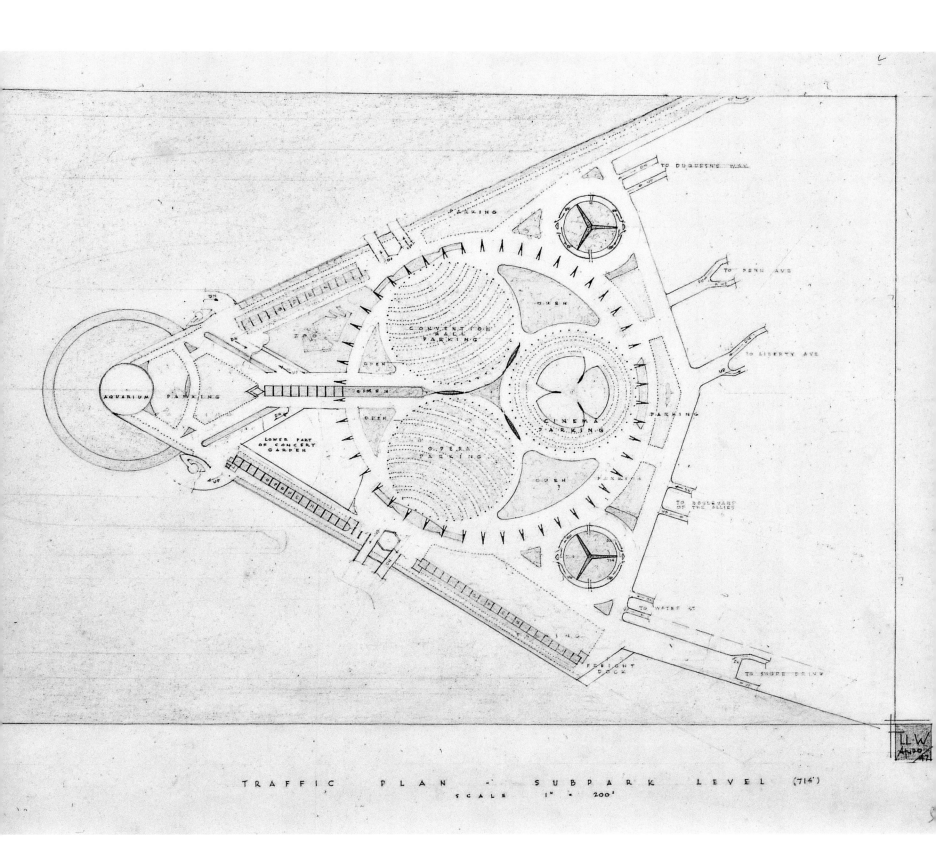

TRAFFIC PLAN - SUBPARK LEVEL (714')

SCALE 1" = 200'

PITTSBURGH POINT PARK CIVIC CENTER #1
(PROJECT)

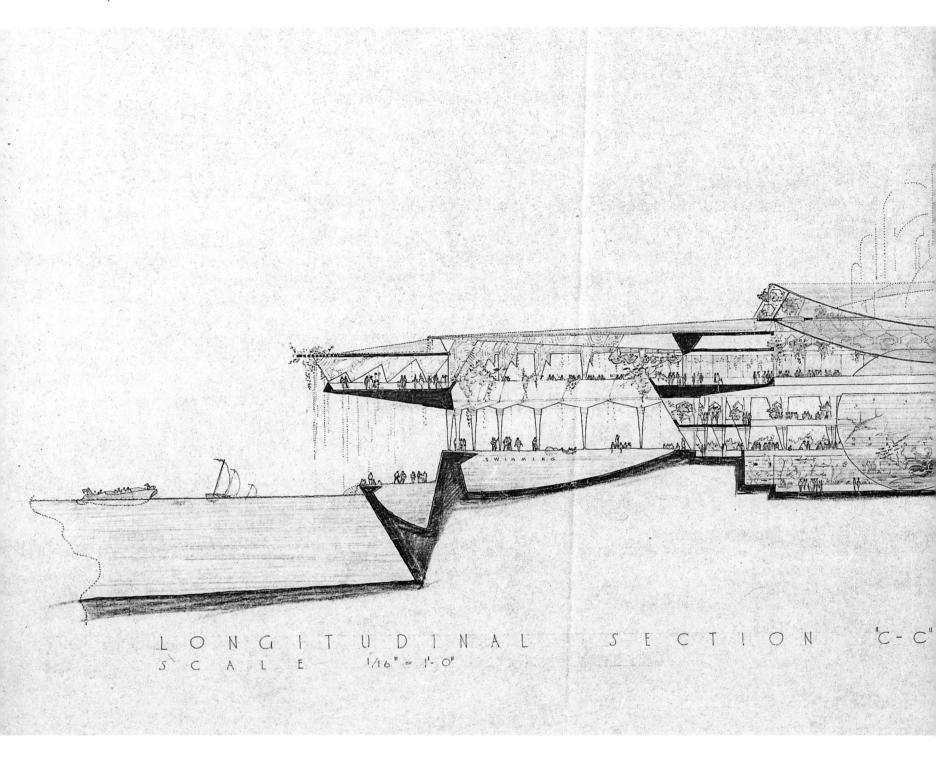

LONGITUDINAL SECTION "C-C"
SCALE 1/16" = 1'-0"

Pittsburgh Point Park Civic Center #1 (project)
Pittsburgh, Pennsylvania, 1947
Section through aquarium
Graphite pencil, color pencil, and ink on paper
39 x 56 inches (101 x 142.9 cm)
The Frank Lloyd Wright Foundation
FLLW FDN # 4821.027

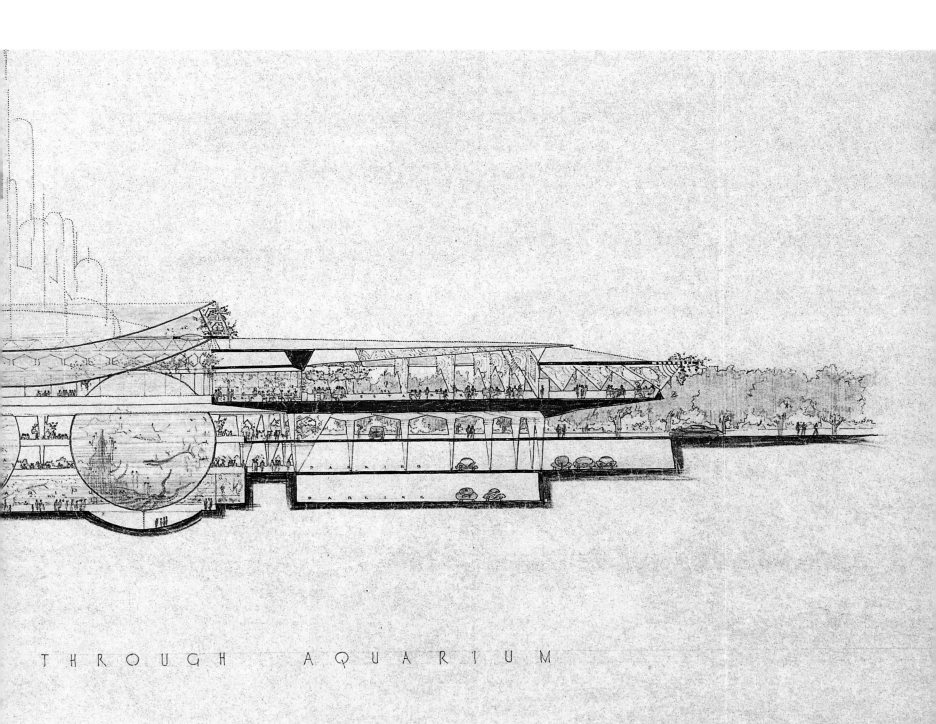

THROUGH AQUARIUM

PITTSBURGH POINT PARK CIVIC CENTER #2
(PROJECT)

Pittsburgh Point Park Civic Center #2, Twin Bridges (project)
Pittsburgh, Pennsylvania, 1947
West elevation
Graphite pencil, color pencil, and ink on paper
31 x 58 inches (79 x 147 cm)
Carnegie Museum of Art
FLLW FDN # 4836.003

All of these structural features are easy of access and provided with generous foyer, toilet and promenade features for enjoyable relaxation. Adequate parking is sustained everywhere.

Adequate office buildings for the State: 150,000 sq.ft. For the county: 150,000 sq.ft. For the City: 150,000 sq.ft.

Beautifully situated adequate offices for civic clubs, culture clubs and various charitable activities of Pittsburgh citizens.

There is also direct automobile access to two flexible suspended docks at pool level for embarking and debarking from river traffic— freight or excursion boats, racing shells, etc.

Elevator service is provided at points directly convenient in handling the various popular concentrations.

The entire scheme is arranged with adequate trees, shrubs, grass and gardening, all of which taken in connection with the broad expanse of the flowing river-surface render the whole architectural mass gentle and humane.[3]

At no time in Wright's career of fifty-four years up to 1947 had he ever submitted to the clients such a long and detailed list of specifications as he did for the Pittsburgh Point Park Civic Center. Certainly in terms of engineering and building construction he was pushing the envelope to its extremes. Yet he had done that eleven years earlier with the S. C. Johnson & Son, Inc. Administration Building, and for the same client, four years earlier with the Research Tower, and again, at the same time, with the Solomon R. Guggenheim Museum. In those three instances, the results, although shadowed with public doubts from the beginning, ended with resounding success. But this project went much further that those. Its scope is nothing less than breathtaking. Could it have been built? Cost not a consideration? It is doubtful that he would ever design a building that could not have been constructed, with possibly the exception of the Mile High Skyscraper. Here, in Pittsburgh, he had a concerned client. The Mile High was a different case altogether.

There was never a scheme so ambitious in his career. The Allegheny Conference on Community Development, however, responded with wonderment and shock at such a proposal. It was obviously far more than the conference had considered. Added to its negative response to the project was the fact that the Pennsylvania state legislature planned to build a

Pittsburgh Point Park Civic Center #2, Twin Bridges (project)
Pittsburgh, Pennsylvania, 1947
View
Ink, gold ink, and color pencil on tracing paper
29 x 44 inches (73.7 x 111.8 cm)
The Frank Lloyd Wright Foundation
FLLW FDN # 4836.004

reconstruction of the historic Fort Duquesne on the same site. Accordingly the conference rejected this project and asked that the Wright design a second scheme, more confined in scope and with a greatly reduced program. This second proposal, the Twin Cantilevered Bridges, featured two bridges springing across the rivers, supported by a huge concrete bastion. "The decision to convert the bridges from cantilevers to stayed-cable structures apparently inspired the transformation of the building into a slender tower and broadcast antenna attached to a colossal cable-mooring. . . . Scheme 2 was spectacular, and Allen Davison's rendering of the Point at night (4836.009) greatly impressed the delegation from Pittsburgh, but the drawings did not win them over."[4]

NOTES
1. Frank Lloyd Wright, *For the Allegheny Conference, May 5, 1947,* Frank Lloyd Wright Archives AV#2401.534, pp. 7–8.
2. Ibid., p. 8.
3. Ibid., pp. 6–10.
4. Richard Cleary, *Merchant Prince and Master Builder* (Pittsburgh: Heinz Architectural Center, Carnegie Museum of Art, 1999), p. 59.

PITTSBURGH POINT PARK CIVIC CENTER #2
(PROJECT)

Pittsburgh Point Park Civic Center #2, Twin Bridges (project)
Pittsburgh, Pennsylvania, 1947
Perspective
Tempera on black illustration board
25 x 38 inches (64 x 97 cm)
The Frank Lloyd Wright Foundation
FLLW FDN # 4836.009

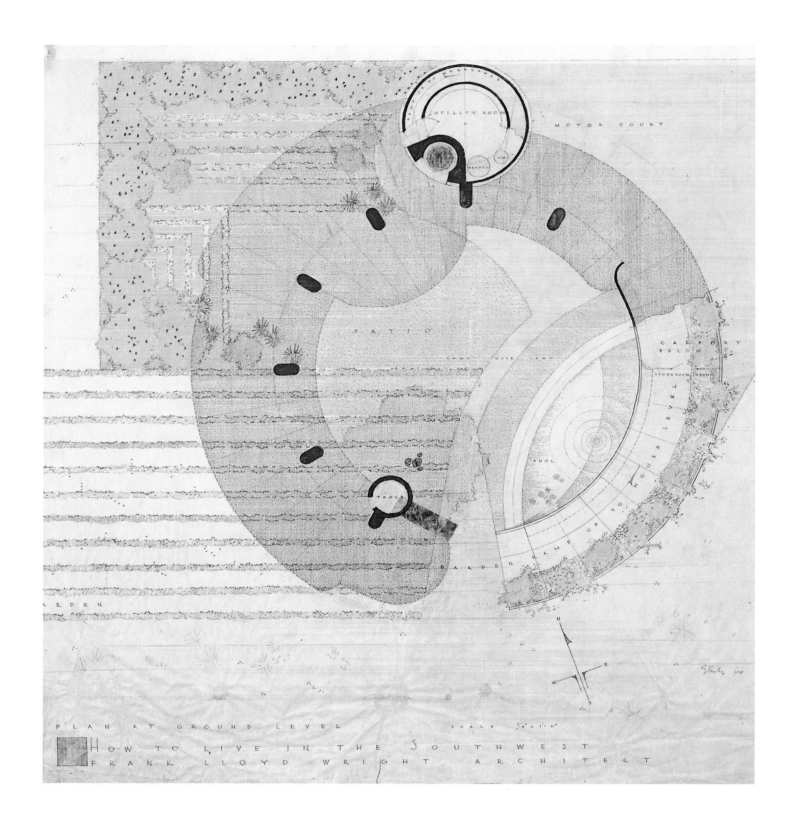

"How to Live in the Southwest"
Phoenix, Arizona, 1950
Ground floor plan
Graphite pencil, color pencil, and ink on paper
31 x 36 inches (79 x 91.4 cm)
The Frank Lloyd Wright Foundation
FLLW FDN # 5011.004

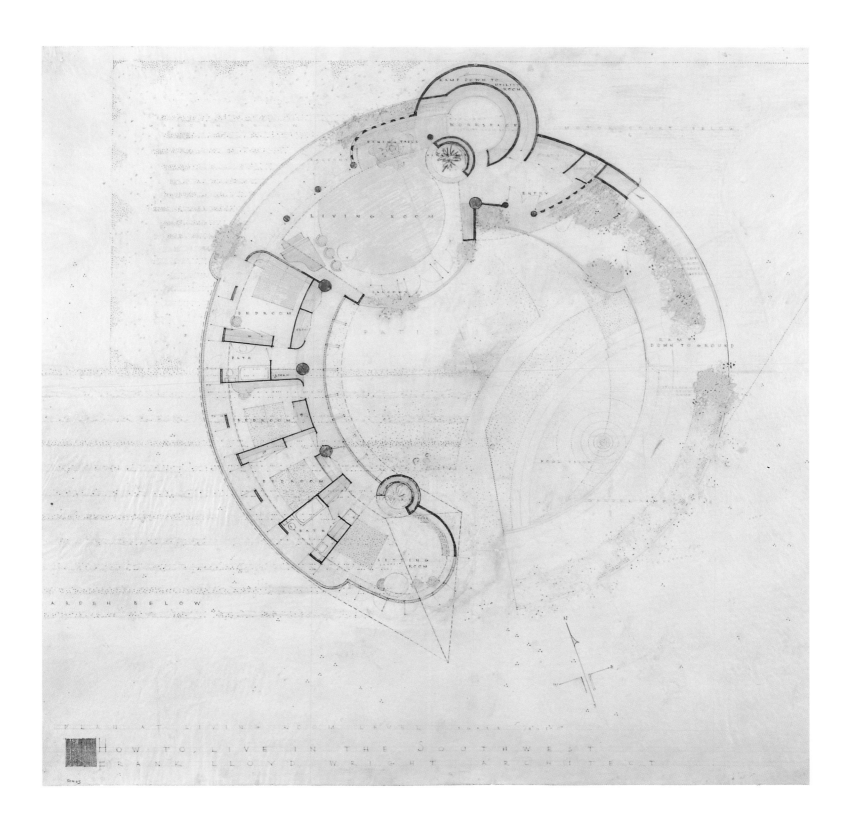

"How to Live in the Southwest"
Phoenix, Arizona, 1950
Upper level plan
Graphite pencil, color pencil, and ink on paper
30 x 36 inches (76 x 91 cm)
The Frank Lloyd Wright Foundation
FLLW FDN # 5011.005

(preceding pages)
David Wright House
Phoenix, Arizona, 1950
Perspective
Graphite pencil on paper
13 x 36 inches (78.7 x 91.4 cm)
The Frank Lloyd Wright Foundation
FLLW FDN # 5030.005

Unitarian Meeting House
Shorewood Hills, Wisconsin, 1945–51
Plan and elevation
Graphite pencil on paper
33 x 43 inches (83.8 x 109.2 cm)
The Frank Lloyd Wright Foundation
FLLW FDN # 5031.002

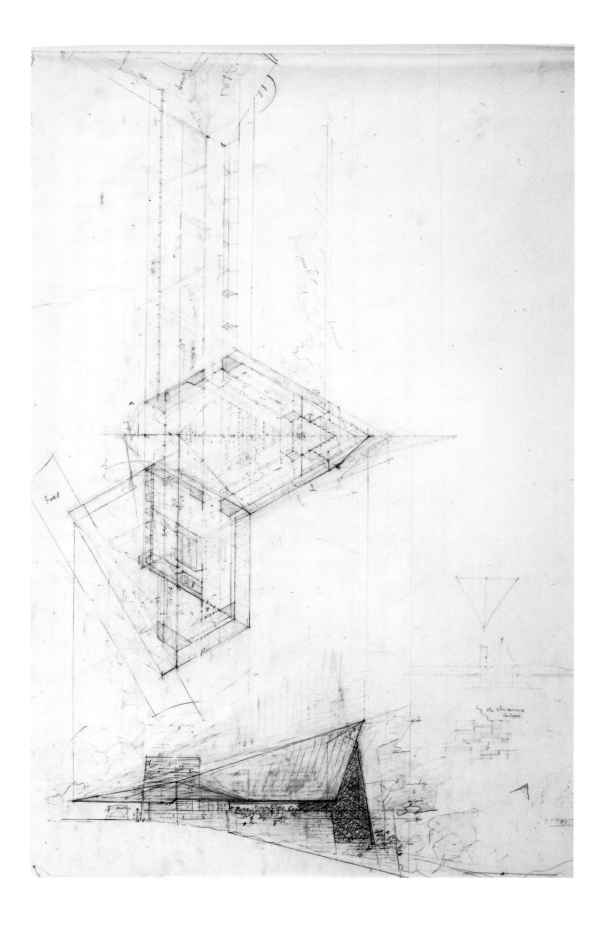

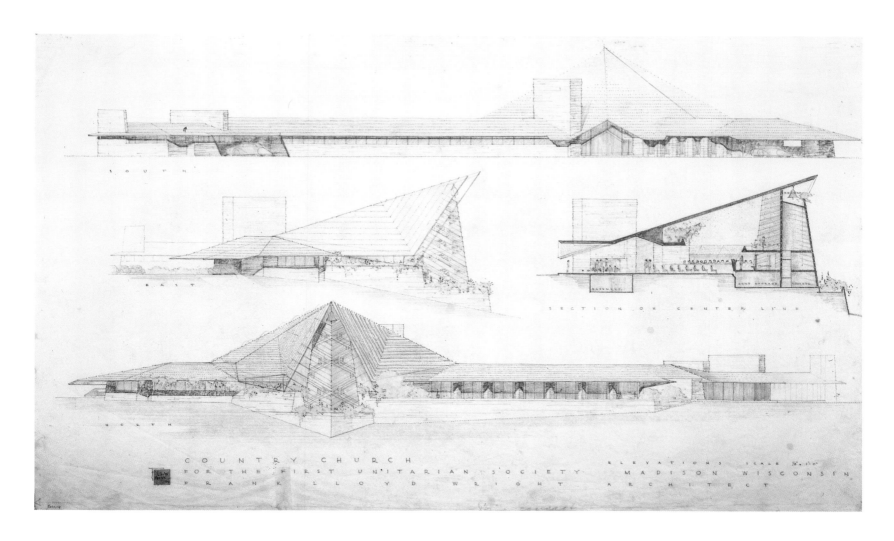

Unitarian Meeting House
Shorewood Hills, Wisconsin, 1945–51
Elevations and section
Graphite pencil, color pencil, and sepia on paper
24 x 40 inches (61 x 102 cm)
The Frank Lloyd Wright Foundation
FLLW FDN # 5031.014

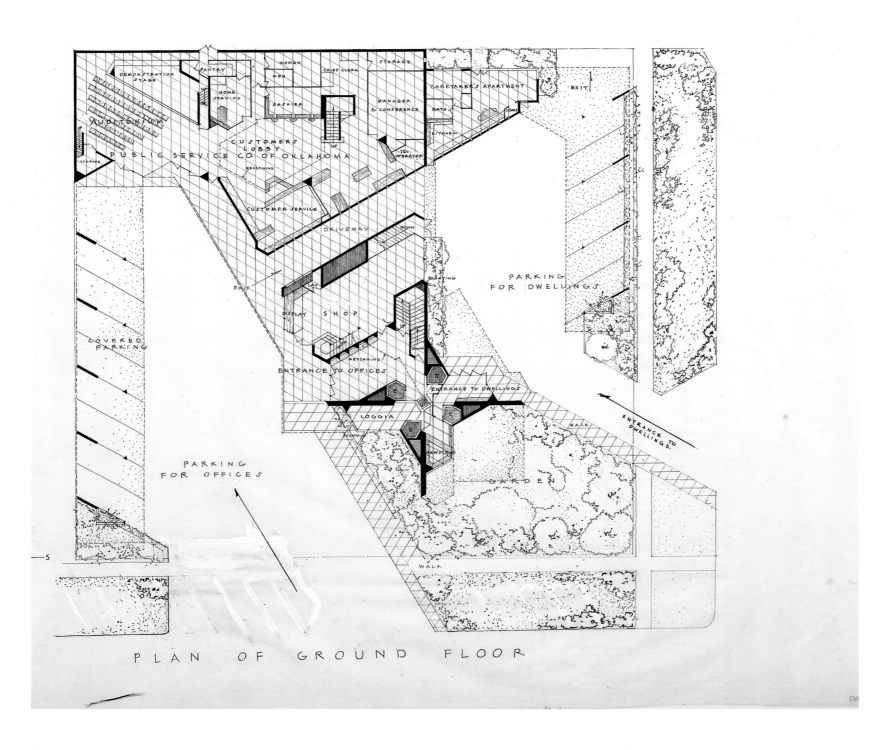

PLAN OF GROUND FLOOR

Harold C. Price Company Office Tower
Bartlesville, Oklahoma, 1952–56
Ground floor plan
Ink on paper
28 x 36 inches (71 x 91 cm)
The Frank Lloyd Wright Foundation
FLLW FDN # 5215.014

Harold C. Price Company Office Tower
Bartlesville, Oklahoma, 1952–56
Perspective
Graphite pencil, color pencil, and ink on paper
43 x 34 inches (109.2 x 86.4 cm)
The Frank Lloyd Wright Foundation
FLLW FDN # 5215.004

VIEW FROM THE SOUTH
BUILDING FOR THE H·C·PRICE CO·
BARTLESVILLE, OKLAHOMA
FRANK LLOYD WRIGHT·ARCHITECT

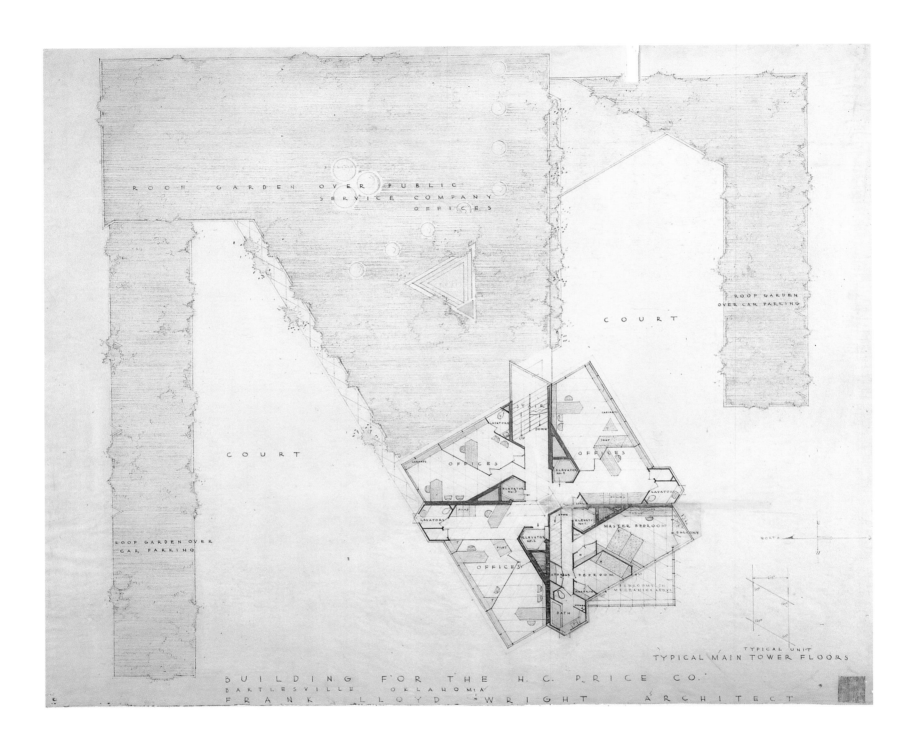

ROOF GARDEN OVER PUBLIC
SERVICE COMPANY
OFFICES

ROOF GARDEN
OVER CAR PARKING

COURT

COURT

ROOF GARDEN OVER
CAR PARKING

STAIR

OFFICES

OFFICES

MASTER BEDROOM

OFFICES

BATH

BEDROOM

NORTH

TYPICAL UNIT

TYPICAL MAIN TOWER FLOORS

BUILDING FOR THE H. C. PRICE CO.
BARTLESVILLE OKLAHOMA
FRANK LLOYD WRIGHT ARCHITECT

Harold C. Price Company Office Tower
Bartlesville, Oklahoma, 1952–56
Plan
Ink and color pencil on paper
36 x 44 ¾ inches (91.4 x 113.7 cm)
The Frank Lloyd Wright Foundation
FLLW FDN # 5215.005

Harold C. Price Company Office Tower
Bartlesville, Oklahoma, 1952–56
Exterior
The Frank Lloyd Wright Foundation
FLLW FDN # 5215.0005

Point View Residences #2 (project)
Pittsburgh, Pennsylvania, 1952
Perspective
Color pencil and ink on paper
34 1/4 x 29 inches (87 x 73.7 cm)
The Frank Lloyd Wright Foundation
FLLW FDN # 5310.001

Masieri Memorial, Student Library, and Dwelling (project)
Venice, Italy, 1953
Perspective
Graphite pencil and color pencil on paper
25 x 19 3/8 inches (63.5 x 48.9 cm)
The Frank Lloyd Wright Foundation
FLLW FDN # 5306.002

MASIERI MEMORIAL   CANAL GRANDE   VENICE
STUDENTS' LIBRARY AND DWELLING
FRANK LLOYD WRIGHT ARCHITECT

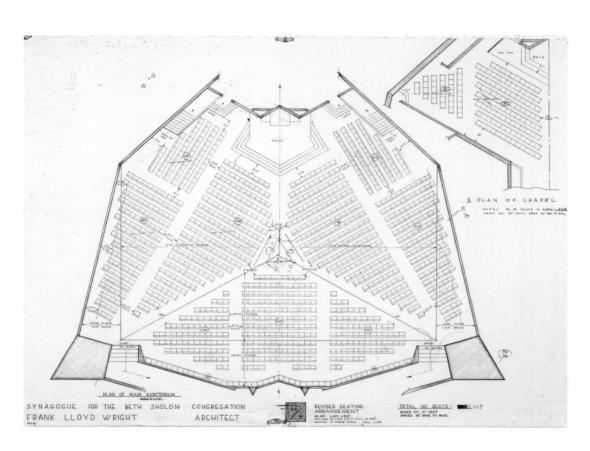

Beth Sholom Synagogue
Elkins Park, Pennsylvania, 1953–59
Main floor seating
Graphite pencil and ink on paper
31 x 43 inches (79.4 x 109.2 cm)
The Frank Lloyd Wright Foundation
FLLW FDN # 5313.049

Beth Sholom Synagogue
Elkins Park, Pennsylvania, 1953–59
Perspective
Graphite pencil and color pencil on paper
18 x 28 7/8 inches (45.7 x 73.3 cm)
The Frank Lloyd Wright Foundation
FLLW FDN # 5313.001

Scheme B American Synagogue for Beth Sholom Friends Cohen
Way be increased up 10000 seats
or Diminished to 500.
Various forms by Modification of planes — infinite.

Beth Sholom Synagogue
Elkins Park, Pennsylvania, 1953–59
General sections
Graphite pencil on paper
36 x 48 inches (91.4 x 121.8 cm)
The Frank Lloyd Wright Foundation
FLLW FDN # 5313.062

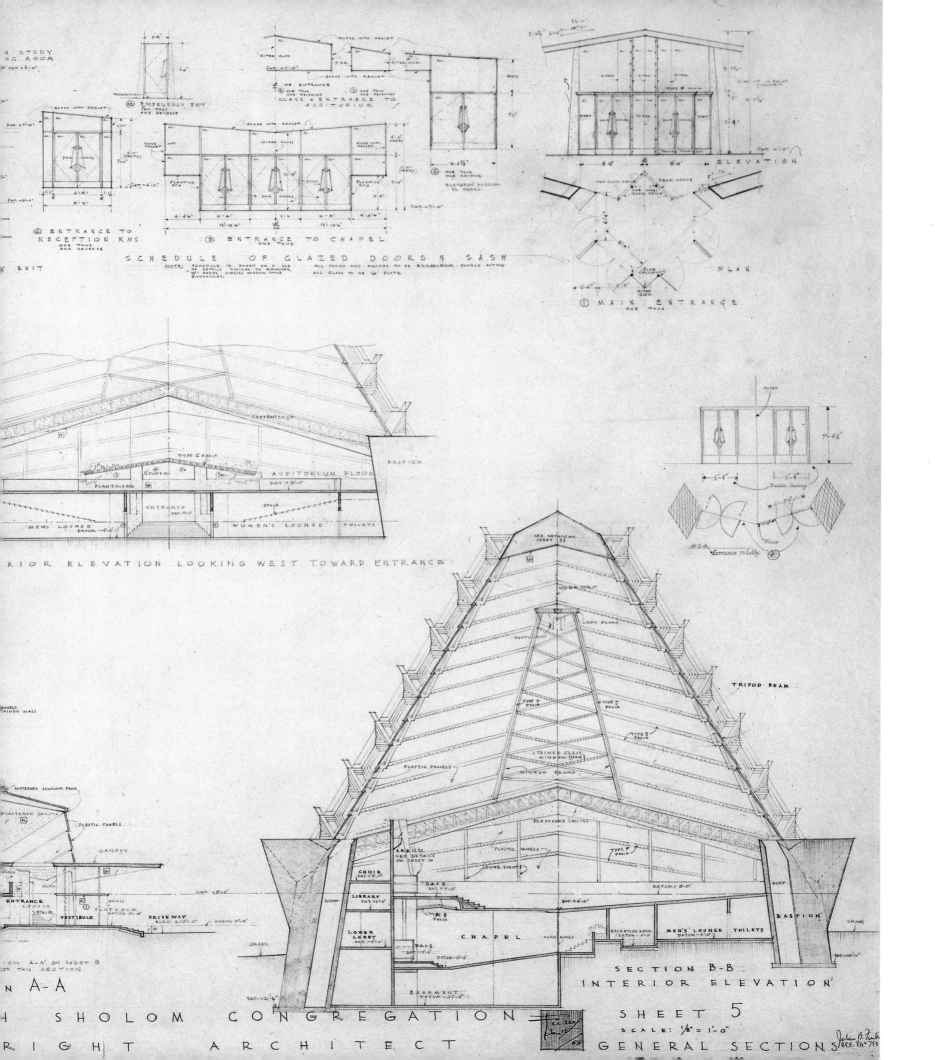

SCHEDULE OF GLAZED DOORS & SASH

⑥ ENTRANCE TO RECEPTION RMS

⑤ ENTRANCE TO CHAPEL

① MAIN ENTRANCE

...RIOR ELEVATION LOOKING WEST TOWARD ENTRANCE

SECTION B-B
INTERIOR ELEVATION

...N A-A

H SHOLOM CONGREGATION

RIGHT ARCHITECT

SHEET 5
SCALE: 1/8" = 1'-0"
GENERAL SECTIONS

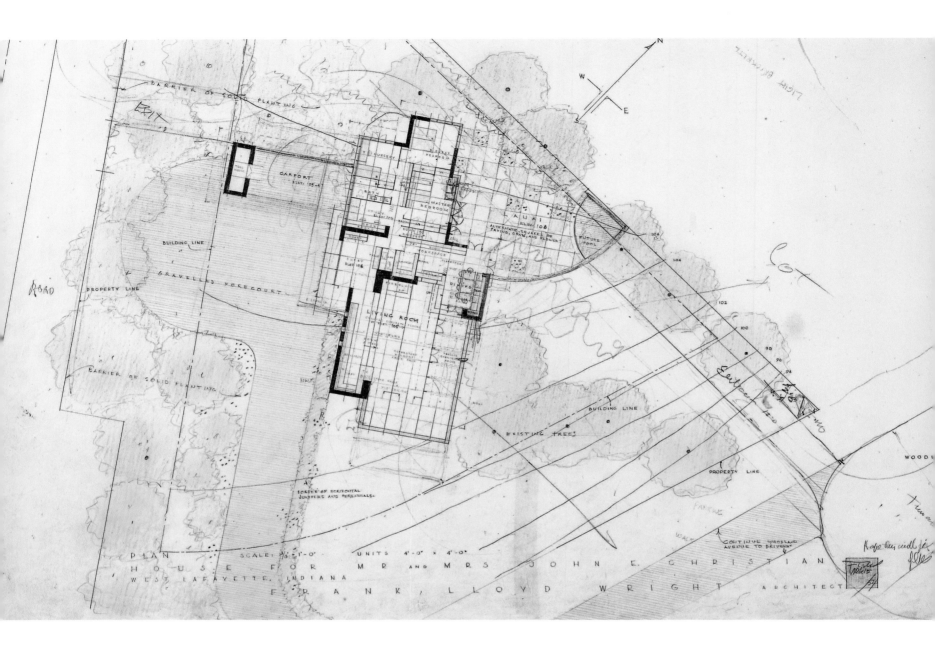

John E. Christian House, "Samara"
West Lafayette, Indiana, 1954
Site and house plan
Graphite pencil and color pencil on paper
20 x 36 inches (51 x 91 cm)
The Frank Lloyd Wright Foundation
FLLW FDN # 5405.002

VIEW FROM SOUTHEAST
HOUSE FOR MR. AND MRS. JOHN E. CHRISTIAN
WEST LAFAYETTE, INDIANA
FRANK LLOYD WRIGHT ARCHITECT

John E. Christian House, "Samara"
West Lafayette, Indiana, 1954
Perspective
Graphite pencil and color pencil on paper
25 x 36 inches (64 x 91 cm)
The Frank Lloyd Wright Foundation
FLLW FDN # 5405.003

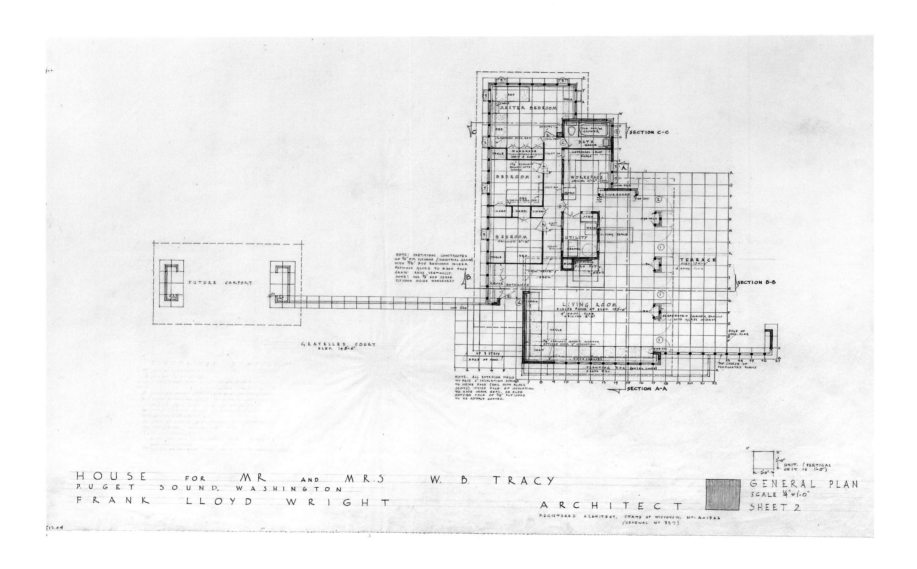

William Tracy House
Normandy Park, Washington, 1954
Plan
Ink and color pencil on paper
25 x 36 inches (63.5 x 91.4 cm)
The Frank Lloyd Wright Foundation
FLLW FDN # 5512.004

William Tracy House
Normandy Park, Washington, 1954
Perspective
Graphite pencil and color pencil on paper
19 ½ x 35 ¼ inches (49.5 x 89.5 cm)
The Frank Lloyd Wright Foundation
FLLW FDN # 5512.001

Dallas Theater Center
Dallas, Texas, 1955
Perspective
Graphite pencil on paper
29 x 47 inches (73 x 118 cm)
The Frank Lloyd Wright Foundation
FLLW FDN # 5514.001

THE NEW THEATER
DALLAS THEATER
FRANK LLOYD

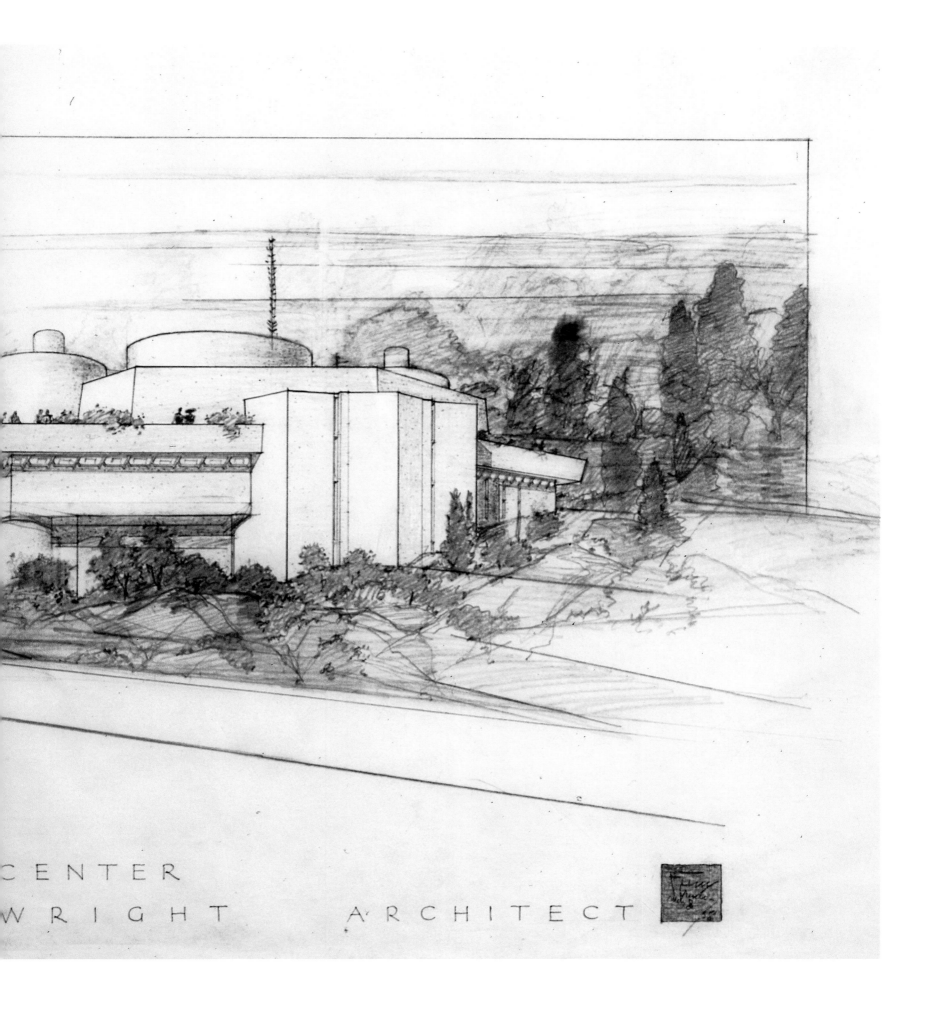

CENTER

WRIGHT   ARCHITECT

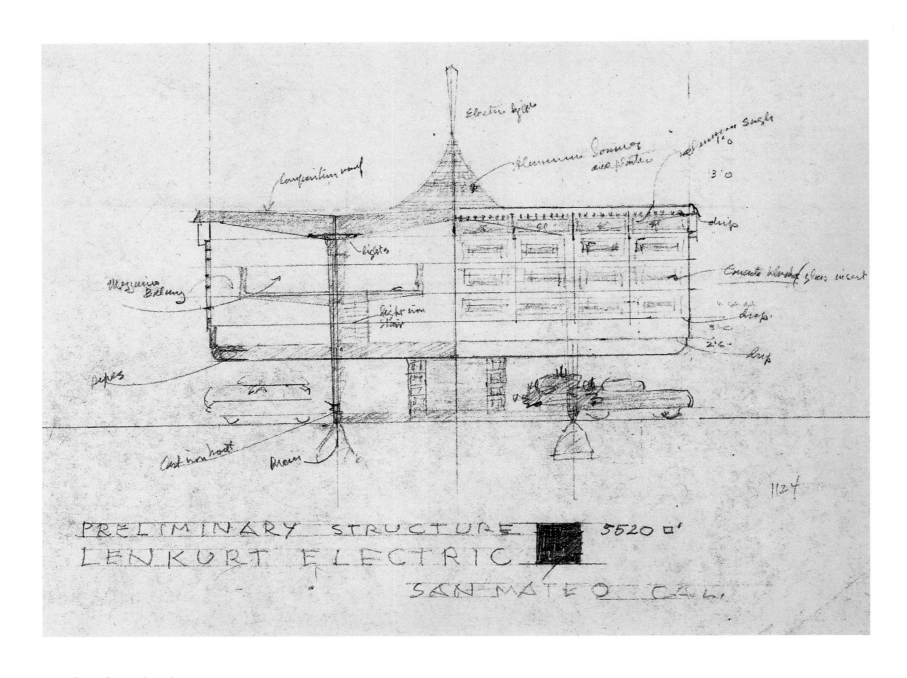

Lenkurt Electric Company (project)
San Carlos, California, 1955
Sectional elevation
Print
15 x 16 inches (37.8 x 40 cm)
The Frank Lloyd Wright Foundation
FLLW FDN # 5520.017

Lenkurt Electric Company (project)
San Carlos, California, 1955
Interior perspective
Color pencil and ink on paper
36 1/4 x 63 7/8
The Frank Lloyd Wright Foundation
FLLW FDN # 5520.004

THE LENKURT ELECTRIC
FRANK LLOYD WRIGHT

ARCHITECT

CHURCH FOR THE MILWAUKEE HELLENIC
MILWAUKEE , WISCONSIN
FRANK LLOYD WRIGHT , ARCHITECT

(preceding pages)
Lenkurt Electric Company (project)
San Carlos, California, 1955
Perspective
Tempera on black illustration board mounted on plywood
31 x 65 ¼ inches (78.7 x 165.7 cm)
The Frank Lloyd Wright Foundation
FLLW FDN # 5520.015

Annunciation Greek Orthodox Church
Wauwatosa, Wisconsin, 1956–61
Perspective
Graphite pencil, color pencil, and ink on paper
19 ¾ x 52 inches (50.2 x 132.1 cm)
The Frank Lloyd Wright Foundation
FLLW FDN # 5611.002

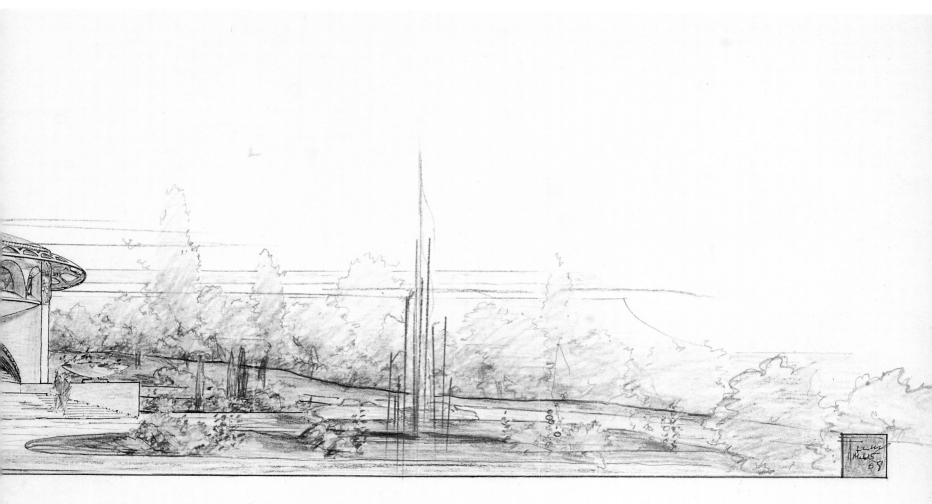

COMMUNITY

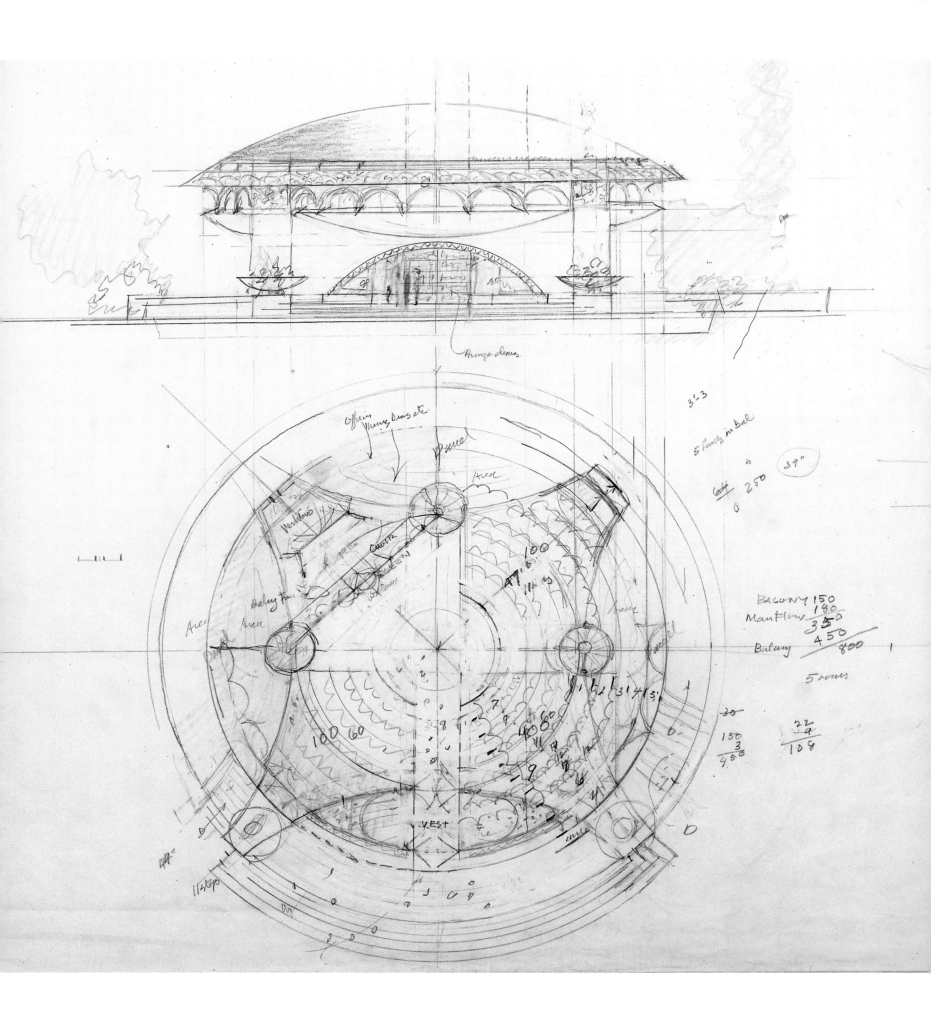

Annunciation Greek Orthodox Church
Wauwatosa, Wisconsin, 1956–61
Plan and elevation
Graphite pencil and color pencil on paper
29 3/4 x 36 inches (75.6 x 91.4 cm)
The Frank Lloyd Wright Foundation
FLLW FDN # 5611.001

Annunciation Greek Orthodox Church
Wauwatosa, Wisconsin, 1956–61
Exterior
The Frank Lloyd Wright Foundation
FLLW FDN # 5611.0044

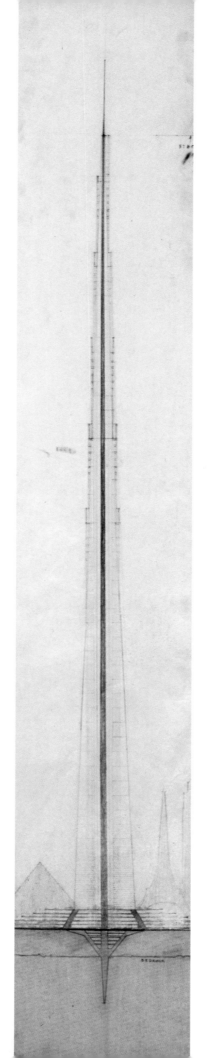

Mile High Office Tower, "The Illinois" (project)
Chicago, Illinois, 1956
Section
Color pencil and ink on paper
94 1/4 x 11 5/8 inches (239.4 x 29.5 cm)
The Frank Lloyd Wright Foundation
FLLW FDN # 5617.001

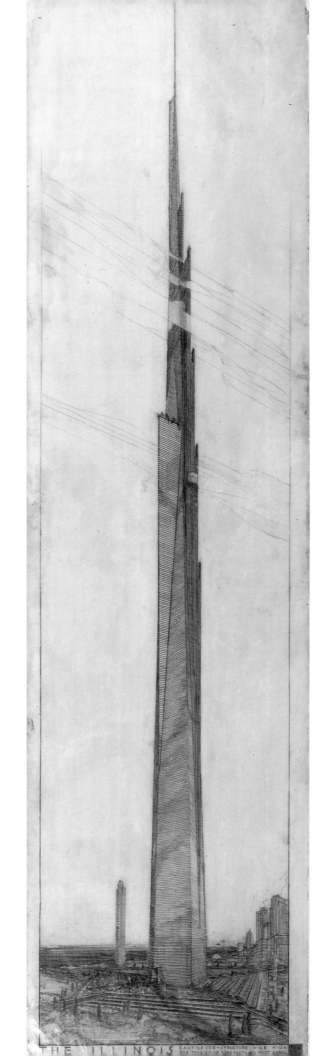

Mile High Office Tower, "The Illinois" (project)
Chicago, Illinois, 1956
Perspective
Color pencil, ink, gold ink, and tempera on paper
95 ¾ 23 ⅜ inches (243.2 x 59.4 cm)
The Frank Lloyd Wright Foundation
FLLW FDN # 5617.002

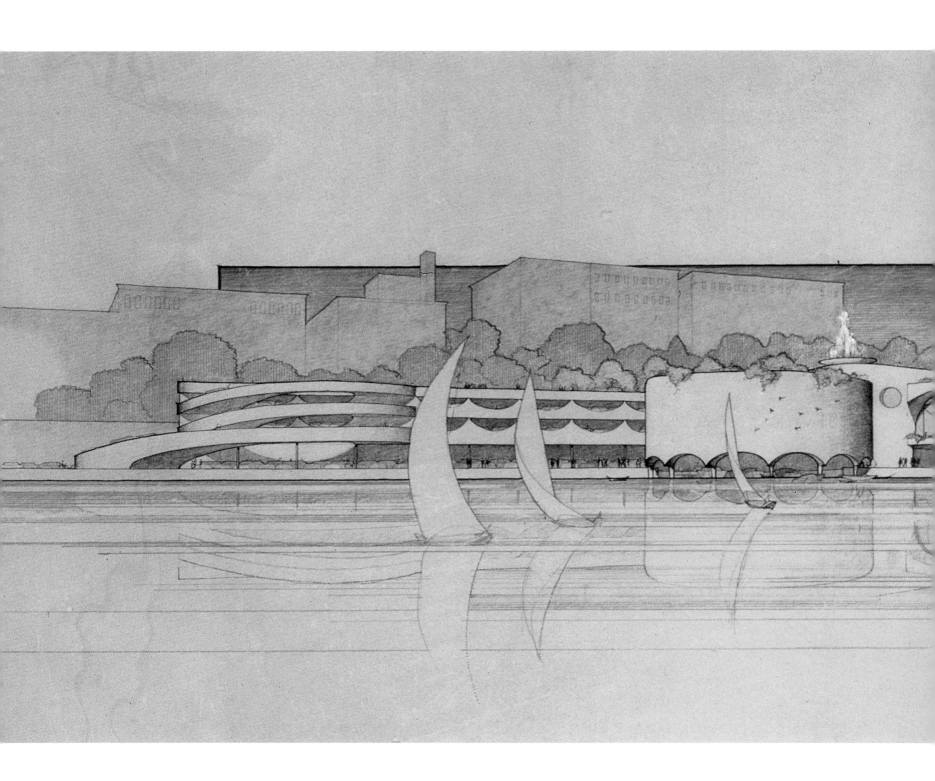

Monona Terrace Civic Center #2 (project)
Madison, Wisconsin, 1959
Perspective
Graphite pencil, color pencil, and ink on art paper
29 x 72 inches (74 x 183 cm)
The Frank Lloyd Wright Foundation
FLLW FDN # 5632.010

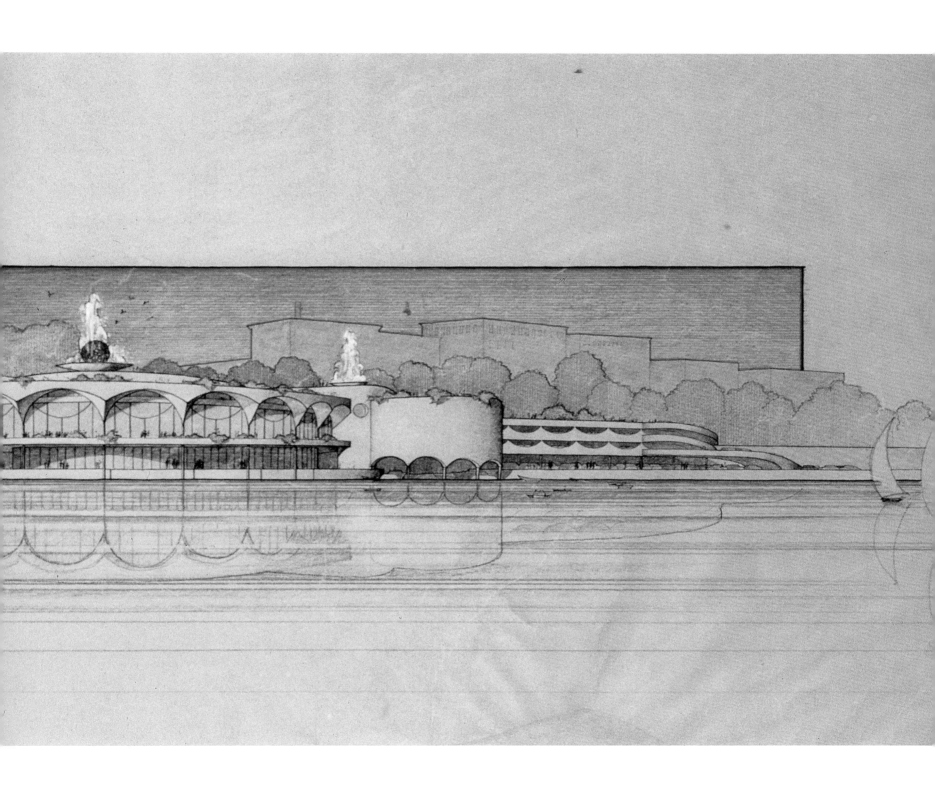

PRO BONO PUBLICO · ARIZONA

FRANK LLOYD WRIGHT ARCHITECT
FEBRUARY 17, 1957

Arizona State Capital, "Oasis" (project)
Phoenix, Arizona, 1957
Aerial perspective
Color pencil and sepia ink on paper
35 1/8 x 45 inches (89.2 x 115.6 cm)
The Frank Lloyd Wright Foundation
FLLW FDN # 5732.001

Arizona State Capital, "Oasis" (project)
Phoenix, Arizona, 1957
Perspective
Color pencil and sepia ink on paper
35 1/4 x 45 5/8 inches (89.5 x 115.9 cm)
The Frank Lloyd Wright Foundation
FLLW FDN # 5732.002

BAGHDAD (PROJECT)

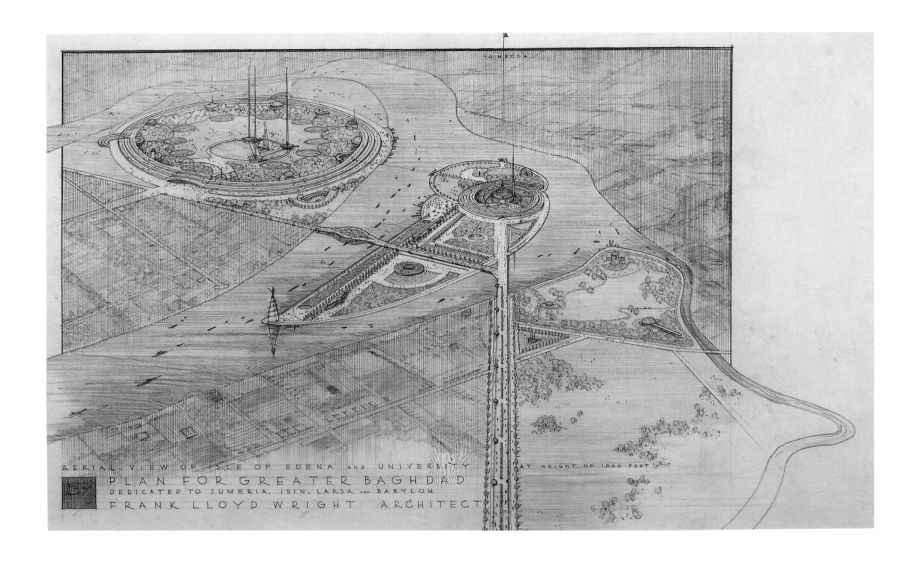

Opera House, Plan for Greater Baghdad (project)
Baghdad, Iraq, 1957
Aerial view of Isle of Edena and University at height of 1,000 feet
Graphite pencil, color pencil, and ink on vellum paper
35 x 52 inches (89 x 132 cm)
The Frank Lloyd Wright Foundation
FLLW FDN # 5733.008

Opera House, Isle of Edena, and University campus,
Plan for Greater Baghdad (project)
Baghdad, Iraq, 1957
Sketch of the master plan for Baghdad on city map
Graphite and color pencil on printed paper
33 ⅝ x 38 inches (85.5 x 96 cm)
The Frank Lloyd Wright Foundation
FLLW FDN # 5733.002

FRANK LLOYD WRIGHT'S OWN AMAZEMENT
The final major urban project of Frank Lloyd Wright's career encapsulates more than half a century of engagement with both urban design and non-Western building traditions. Selected from more than ninety drawings Wright prepared for Baghdad, the seventeen included here convey the general flavor of the thoughtful perspectives he brought to bear on the challenges of urban architecture in the mid-twentieth century.

He worked in a highly political atmosphere. With oil as the central fact of the region and Cold War powers consolidating spheres of influence, Iraq's leaders positioned their newly independent nation firmly in the orbit of the United States. U.S. technical aid and cultural exchange programs flourished. Further, many members of the political elite who served on Iraq's Development Board, educated in the West, were committed to a modern identity recognizable in terms of economic advancement, infrastructural development, and cultural revision. The capital city, of course, was the main stage for the symbolization of modernity. The Development Board's Baghdad commissions resonated with symbolic import—a university by Walter Gropius, a sports complex by Le Corbusier, a museum by Alvar Aalto, an opera house by Frank Lloyd Wright, and a Development Board headquarters building by Gio Ponti.

Every project and every name, save Wright's, signaled that architectural modernism in the International Style was to be the intersection of East and West, the place where difference ceased to be visible, where perceptions of a mysterious, timeless culture fell before the functional forms of modern institutions. Wright alone departed from modernist architectural conventions by attempting mutuality rather than erasure, connecting the cultural imaginations of East and West, suggestions of past, present, and future, and the natural and built environments. While his general sense of the contemporaneous political symbolism of a rebuilt Baghdad was keen, he was tone-deaf to the immediate politics of client aspirations and expectations. There was simply no chance that Wright's cross-cultural symbolisms, echoes of pasts projected into futures, would comport with the modernist values of those guiding the emerging nation-state.

If Wright's Baghdad designs were not to be taken seriously in 1957, why take them seriously today? In the largest sense, because, like all captivating creations, we do not easily get to the end of them. The designs in themselves are provoking and thought-provoking. In addition, these images that half a century ago offered an alternative vision of mutuality between East and West might today evoke some disallowed possibilities buried

BAGHDAD (PROJECT)

within a drastically transformed political context. The Baghdad oeuvre generously repays attention to its technical innovations, broadly conceived sociality, and dialogic relations with Wright's earlier urban work and with architectural modernism itself.

For instance, the apparent antimodernism of Wright's designs can easily obscure how brilliantly he blended technical and imaginative virtuosity. He used aerial photos and planimetric techniques to develop the cultural center plan along the city's greatest asset, the historic Tigris. His technically sophisticated, ziggurat-based structures for shoring up the island in the river

simultaneously protected it from flooding, elegantly accommodated parking (as it did on the university campus), and introduced a terraced profile reminiscent of Babylonian hanging gardens. The gardens and cascading pools on the island, on the campus, and within the Post and Telegraph Building are a thread of allusions to oasis environments, regional histories and narratives, and images of paradise. These oasis themes also extend through Wright's work: the Lake Tahoe resort (unbuilt, 1922–24) and urban projects such as Chicago's Wolf Lake Amusement Park (unbuilt, 1895) and Midway Gardens (1913), Crystal City (unbuilt, 1940)

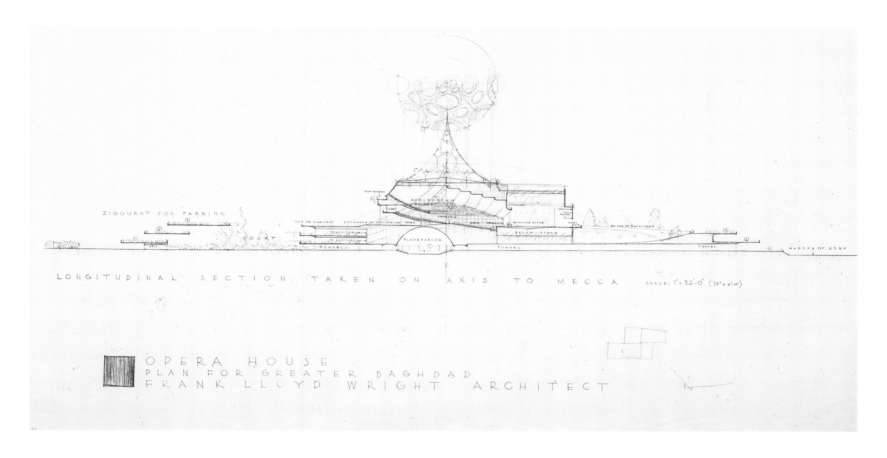

ZIGGURAT FOR PARKING

LONGITUDINAL   SECTION   TAKEN   ON   AXIS   TO   MECCA   SCALE: 1"=32'-0" (⅜"=40'-0")

OPERA HOUSE
PLAN FOR GREATER BAGHDAD
FRANK LLOYD WRIGHT ARCHITECT

Opera House, Plan for Greater Baghdad (project)
Baghdad, Iraq, 1957
Perspective
Graphite pencil, color pencil, and ink on vellum paper
43 x 66¼ inches (109 x 168 cm)
The Frank Lloyd Wright Foundation
FLLW FDN # 5733.023

Opera House, Plan for Greater Baghdad (project)
Baghdad, Iraq, 1957
Longitudinal section taken on axis to Mecca
Graphite pencil and color pencil on blueprint paper
24½ x 45½ inches (62 x 115.5 cm)
The Frank Lloyd Wright Foundation
FLLW FDN # 5733.025

in Washington, D.C., and Pittsburgh Point Park Civic Center (unbuilt, 1947).

If, as this exhibition proposes, a social sensibility infused much of Wright's work, the Baghdad designs are social in the widest sense—in dialogue with natural, historical, and human environments. As Wright expressed it generally, "Ideal architecture is organic expression of organic social life,"[1] which he saw as entwined with land and history. Although the island plan, evoking the oasis, is very much in touch with all these environments, the Central Post and Telegraph Building he designed for the city center most remarkably embodies their mutuality. Forty years ahead of time, it demonstrates green principles while honoring practical, regional building traditions. Here we see passive solar ideas, from evaporative cooling by sunken courtyards with fountains to active cultivation of a green roof and an exterior trellis wall of living plants creating a second skin against extreme heat and a covered arcade over the sidewalk. The internal court and roof garden have much in common with the courtyard houses Wright had seen in Baghdad and Cairo. Aware of local wind towers, Wright consciously designed the green roof-courtyard-fountain scheme as an "organic air conditioning system."[2] Thus Wright improbably made a compact office building an

oasis on a busy urban street, an eloquent, organic dialogue among people, conditions, times, and traditions.

Insofar as Wright prefaced and presented his Baghdad work with a good deal of bombast against modernism, it is easy to see him as an aging dean resisting and designing against change. At first blush, some of the Baghdad plans look like leaps into ungrounded fantasy. But the understated Central Post and Telegraph Building most clearly signals that Wright was imagining Baghdad in many dimensions, intimately related, as culmination of sixty years of thought about sustainable urban life on a human scale and about creating architecture as "a living . . . spirit of time and place."[3]

Yet these remarkable drawings are not a final punctuation mark. They are a hopeful glimpse at something that imagined *beyond* their modern moment. They do not map an urban doctrine or lay out a set of inflexible principles as much as they make material a thought of something beyond or other than capitulation to pro forma, monological modernism then or insistence upon the cultural/national politics of difference now. Wright often wrote and talked as if he had all the answers. But he designed with an openness maintained by creating confluences, unexpected fusions, imperfect repetitions, and delicately suggested family resemblances.

BAGHDAD (PROJECT)

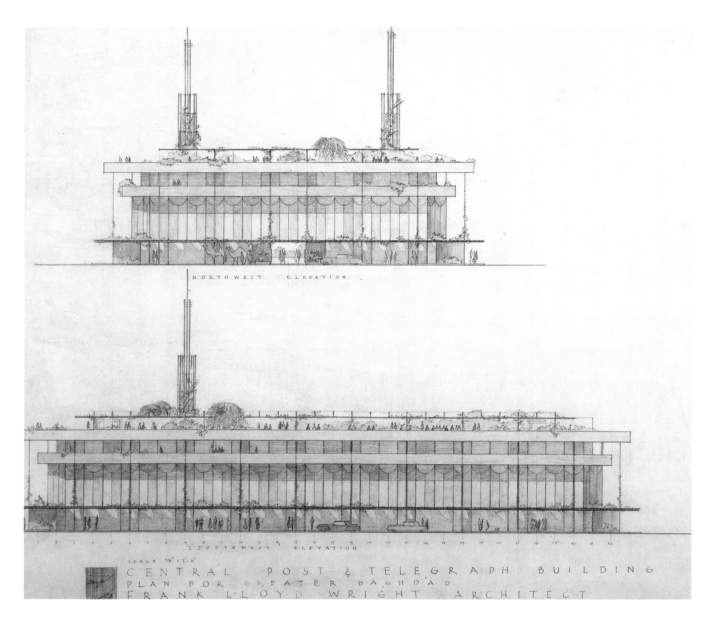

Central Post and Telegraph Building (project)
Baghdad, Iraq, 1957
Elevations
Graphite pencil and color pencil on vellum paper
35 x 44 inches (89 x 112 cm)
The Frank Lloyd Wright Foundation
FLLW FDN # 5734.016

"I am like the lady who played the piano for her own 'amazement,'" the seventy-three-year-old Wright wrote assuredly in 1940 to his client for Crystal City, certain that he had designed something that "would astonish."[4] That childlike joy at the possibilities of building was still exuberantly alive in 1957, as Wright approached Baghdad at age ninety. Fortunately, it yet inhabits the drawings he made for our own amazement.

NOTES
1. Quoted in Bruce Brooks Pfeiffer, ed., *Frank Lloyd Wright Collected Writings, Vol. 4* (Rizzoli: New York, 1994), p. 71.
2. Transcript of video interview with William Wesley Peters by Indira Berndtson and Greg Williams, 14 February 1991, Taliesin West, p. 3.
3. Frank Lloyd Wright, "Frank Lloyd Wright Designs for Baghdad," *Architectural Forum*, 1958: p. 102.
4. Frank Lloyd Wright, letter to Roy Thurman, 27 August 1940. Library of Congress, Prints and Photographs Division; also published (without date) in Bruce Brooks Pfeiffer, *Treasures of Taliesin: Seventy-Seven Unbuilt Designs* (Chicago: Southern Illinois University Press, 1985), pp. 23–24.

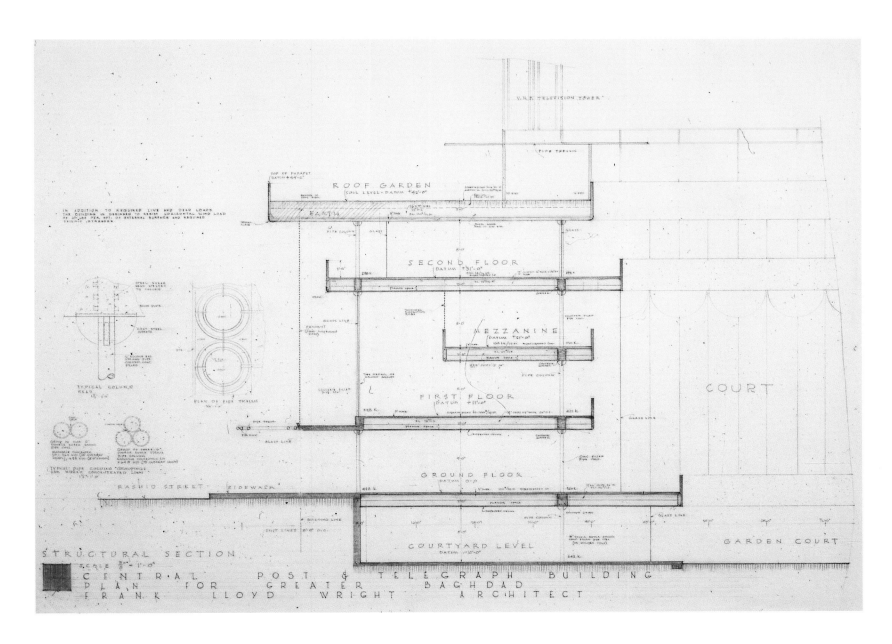

Central Post and Telegraph Building (project)
Baghdad, Iraq, 1957
Structural section
Graphite pencil and color pencil on vellum paper
35 1/4 x 44 1/2 inches (89 x 112 cm)
The Frank Lloyd Wright Foundation
FLLW FDN # 5734.017

BAGHDAD (PROJECT)

Baghdad Art Gallery with sketches of Opera,
Bazaar, and Monument to Haroun Al-Rashid,
Plan for Greater Baghdad (project)
Baghdad, Iraq, 1957
Plan, elevation, section, and sketches
Graphite pencil on vellum paper
36 x 55 inches (91 x 140 cm)
The Frank Lloyd Wright Foundation
FLLW FDN # 5749.003

(following pages)
Baghdad University, Plan for Greater Baghdad (project)
Baghdad, Iraq, 1957
Aerial view
Graphite pencil and color pencil on paper (detail)
31 x 65 inches (78.7 x 165.1 cm)
The Frank Lloyd Wright Foundation
FLLW FDN # 5749.006

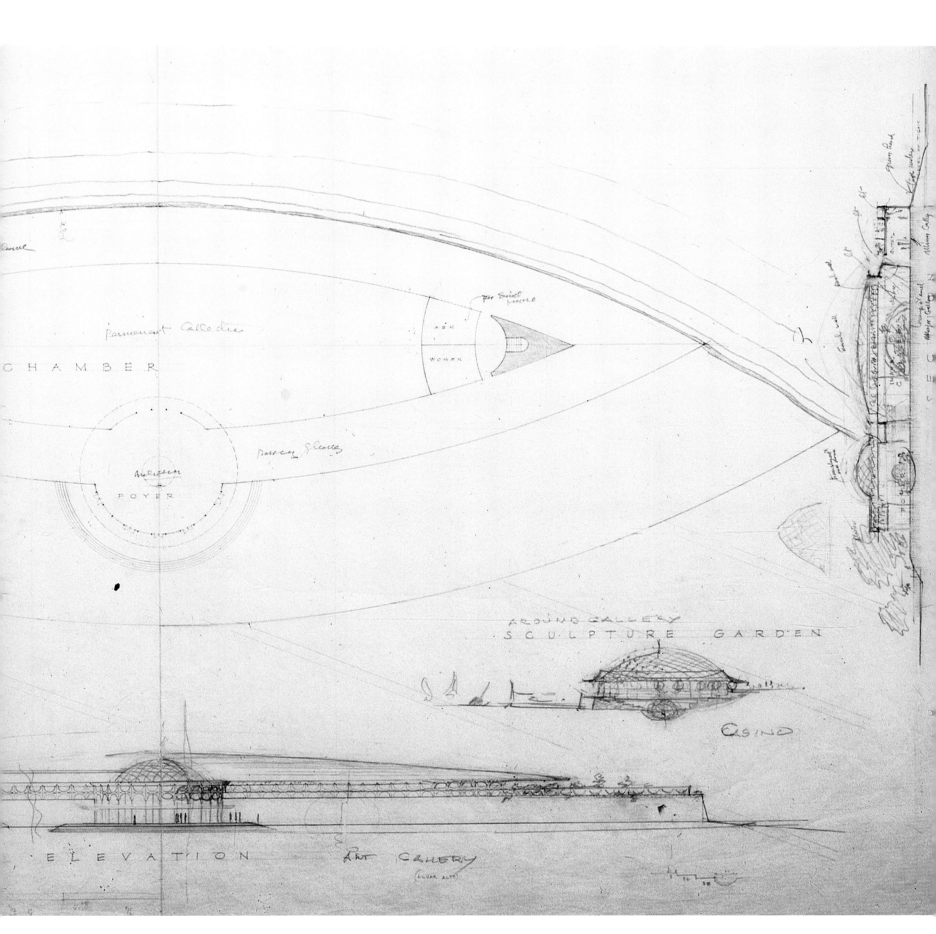

CHAMBER

Permanent Collection

FOYER

AROUND GALLERY
SCULPTURE GARDEN

CASINO

ELEVATION   ART GALLERY
(ALVAR ALTO)

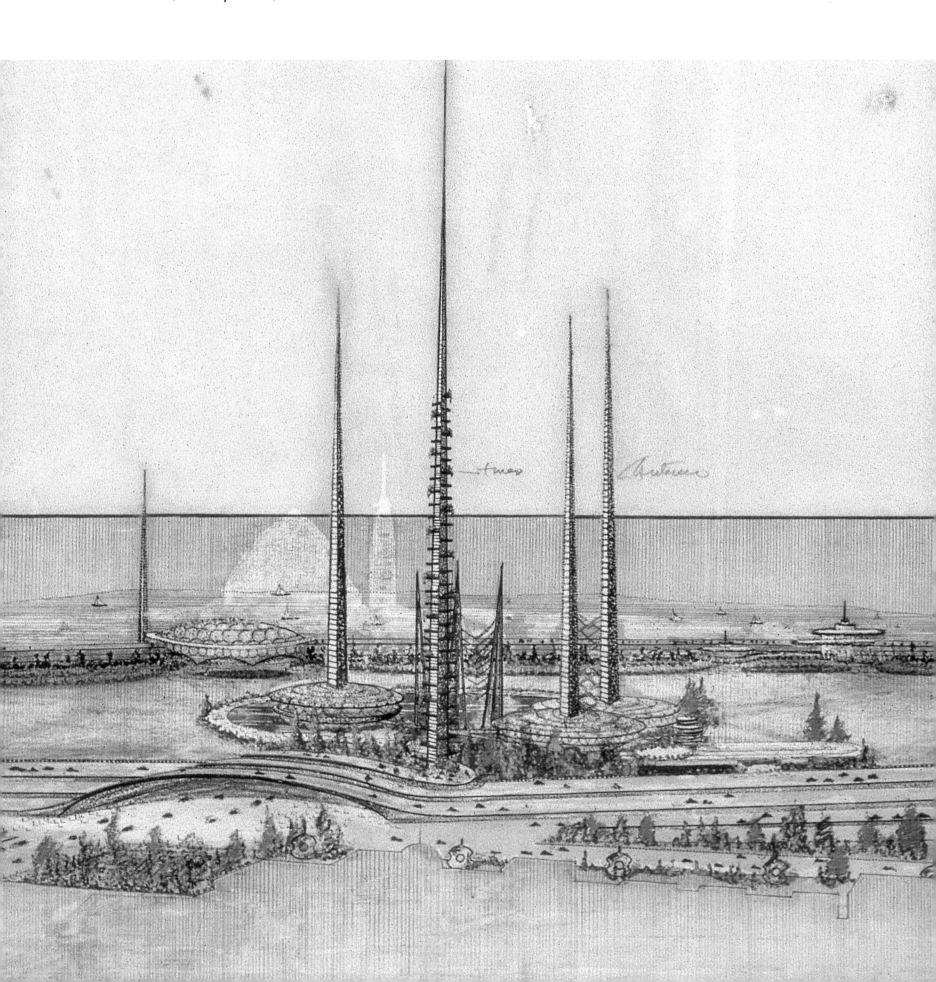

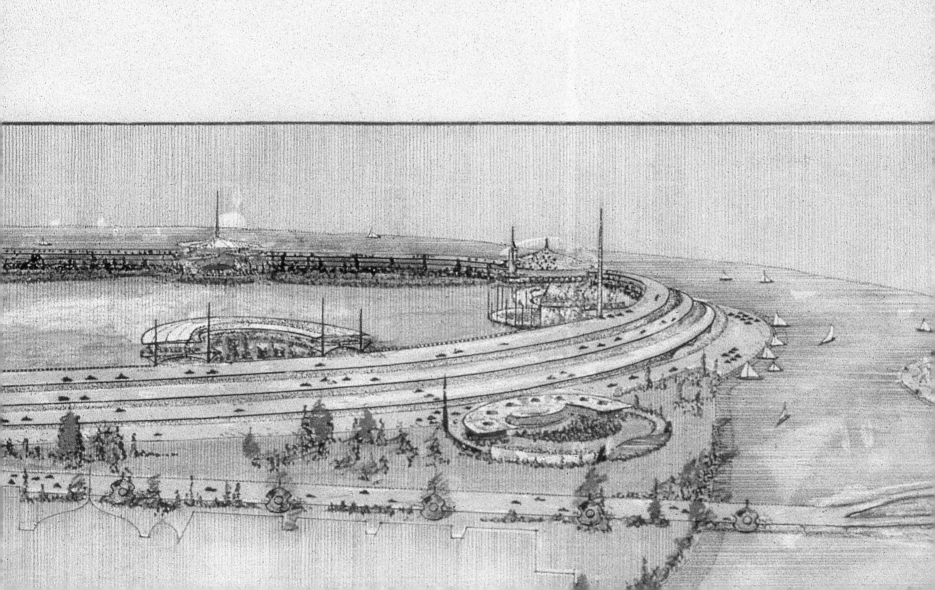

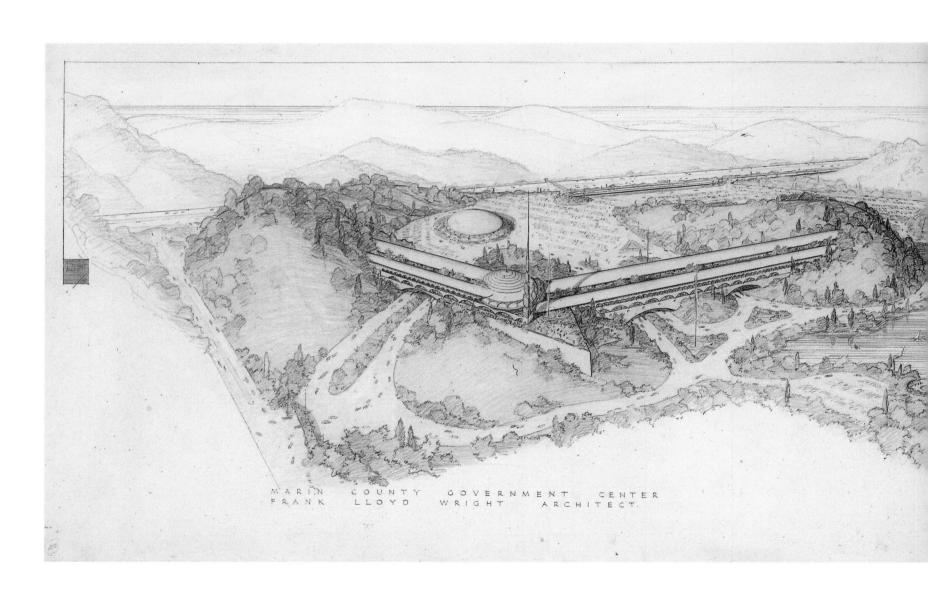

Marin County Civic Center
San Rafael, California, 1957–62
Ink and color pencil on paper
34 1/2 x 74 3/8 inches
The Frank Lloyd Wright Foundation
FLLW FDN # 5746.001

Marin County Civic Center
San Rafael, California, 1957–62
Exterior view
The Frank Lloyd Wright Foundation
FLLW FDN # 5746.0144

Fair Pavilion for the Marin County Civic Center (project)
San Rafael, California, 1957
Perspective
Color pencil and ink on paper
36 x 53 ³⁄₈ inches (91.4 x 135.6 cm)
The Frank Lloyd Wright Foundation
FLLW FDN # 5754.004

The Living City (project)
U.S.A., 1958
Aerial perspective
Graphite pencil on paper
30 1/2 x 40 1/2 inches (77.5 x 102.2 cm)
The Frank Lloyd Wright Foundation
FLLW FDN # 5825.004

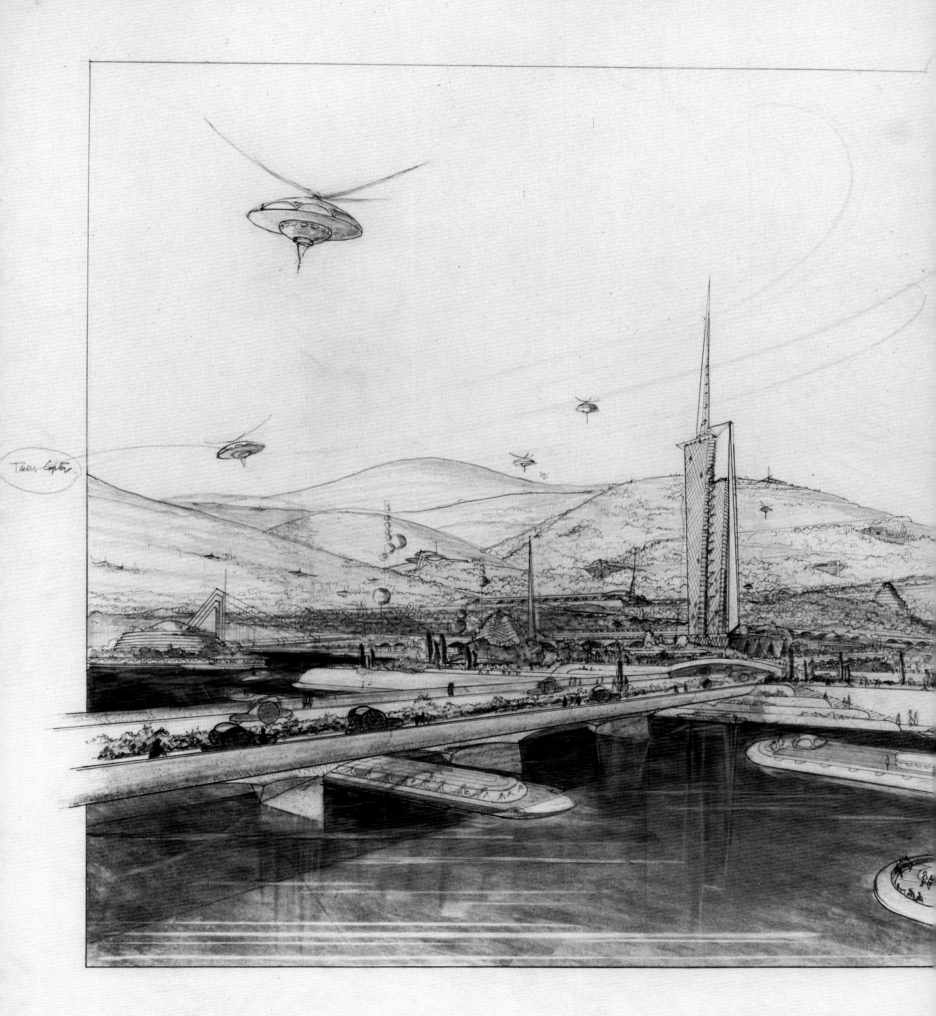

Teen Copter

The Living City (project)
U.S.A., 1958
Perspective
Graphite pencil on paper
30 1/2 x 40 1/2 inches (77.5 x 102.2 cm)
The Frank Lloyd Wright Foundation
FLLW FDN # 5825.006

Helen Donahoe House (project)
Paradise Valley, Arizona, 1959
Perspective
Graphite pencil and color pencil on paper
35 x 56 inches (88.9 x 141.6 cm)
The Frank Lloyd Wright Foundation
FLLW FDN # 5901.021

"THE DONAHOE

FOR MRS.
PHOENIX, ARIZO
FRANK L

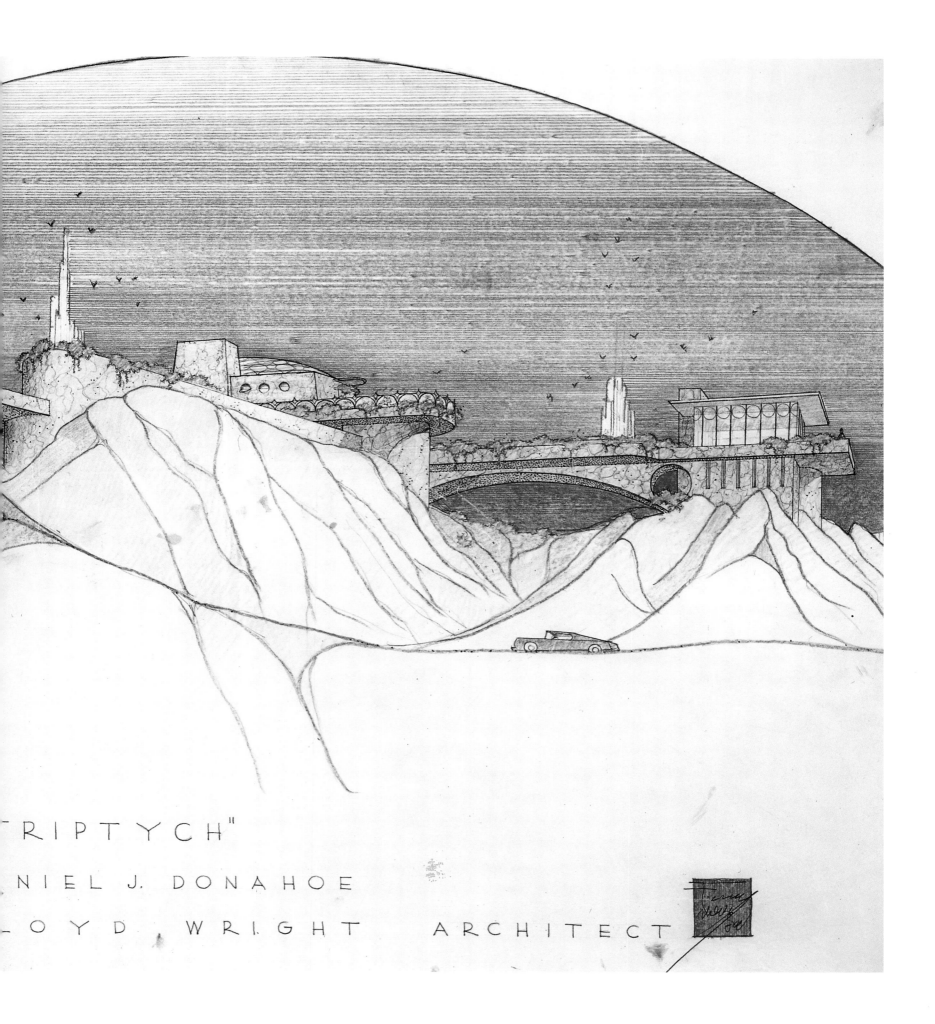

"RIPTYCH"

NIEL J. DONAHOE

LOYD WRIGHT ARCHITECT

SELECTED BIBLIOGRAPHY

PUBLICATIONS WRITTEN BY FRANK LLOYD WRIGHT

"The Art and Craft of the Machine." Chicago: Chicago Architectural Club, 1901. Reprinted in *The Essential Frank Lloyd Wright: Critical Writings on Architecture.* Edited by Bruce Brooks Pfeiffer. Princeton and Oxford: Princeton University Press, 2008.

Ausgeführte Bauten und Entwürfe von Frank Lloyd Wright [Studies and Executed Buildings of Frank Lloyd Wright]. Berlin: Ernst Wasmuth, 1910. Introduction reprinted in *The Essential Frank Lloyd Wright: Critical Writings on Architecture.*

The Japanese Print: An Interpretation. Chicago: Ralph Fletcher Seymour Co., 1912. Reprinted in *The Essential Frank Lloyd Wright: Critical Writings on Architecture.*

The Life Work of the American Architect Frank Lloyd Wright. Edited by H. Th. Wijdeveld. Santpoort, The Netherlands: C. A. Mees, 1925. (Seven articles from *Wendingen.*)

"Two Lectures on Architecture." Delivered at the Art Institute of Chicago, October 1930. *Bulletin of the Art Institute of Chicago*, 1931. Reprinted in *The Essential Frank Lloyd Wright: Critical Writings on Architecture.*

"Modern Architecture: Being the Kahn Lectures for 1930." Princeton: Princeton University Press, 1931. Reprinted in facsimile in *Modern Architecture: Being the Kahn Lectures for 1930.* Princeton: Princeton University Press, 2008.

The Disappearing City. New York: William Farquhar Payson, 1932. Reprinted in *The Essential Frank Lloyd Wright: Critical Writings on Architecture.*

An Autobiography. New York: Longmans, Green and Company, 1932.

Frank Lloyd Wright and Baker Brownell. *Architecture and Modern Life*. New York and London: Harper & Brothers, 1937. Partially reprinted ("Some Aspects of the Past and Present of Architecture") in *The Essential Frank Lloyd Wright: Critical Writings on Architecture.*

An Organic Architecture: The Architecture of Democracy. London: Lund Humphries and Company, 1939.

An Autobiography. Revised and expanded. New York: Duell, Sloan and Pearce, 1943. Reprinted in facsimile in *An Autobiography*. San Francisco: Pomegranate, 2005.

When Democracy Builds. Chicago: University of Chicago Press, 1945.

Genius and the Mobocracy. New York: Duell, Sloan and Pearce, 1949.

The Future of Architecture. New York: Horizon Press, 1953.

The Natural House. New York: Horizon Press, 1954. Reprinted in *The Essential Frank Lloyd Wright: Critical Writings on Architecture.*

An American Architecture. New York: Horizon Press, 1955. Reprinted in facsimile by Pomegranate, 2006.

The Story of the Tower. New York: Horizon Press, 1956.

A Testament. New York: Horizon Press, 1957. Reprinted in *The Essential Frank Lloyd Wright: Critical Writings on Architecture.*

The Living City. New York: Horizon Press, 1958.

CONTRIBUTOR BIOS

Richard Cleary is Professor and Page Southerland
Page Fellow at the School of Architecture of the
University of Texas at Austin.

Neil Levine is the Emmet Blakeney Gleason
Professor of History of Art and Architecture at
Harvard University.

Mina Marefat is a practicing architect in Washington,
D.C., and former senior architectural historian at the
Smithsonian Institution.

Bruce Brooks Pfeiffer is Director of Archives at the
Frank Lloyd Wright Foundation, Scottsdale, Arizona,
and Spring Green, Wisconsin.

Joseph M. Siry is Professor of Art History
and American Studies at Wesleyan University,
Middletown, Connecticut.

Margo Stipe is Curator and Registrar of Collections
at the Frank Lloyd Wright Foundation, Scottsdale,
Arizona, and Spring Green, Wisconsin.

ILLUSTRATION CREDITS

FRANK LLOYD WRIGHT FOUNDATION CREDITS

Drawings that appear on the following pages are copyright © 2009 The Frank Lloyd Wright Foundation, Scottsdale, Arizona: 32–33 (center, rendered by Burch Burdette Long), 34 (right), 39 (upper right & lower right), 40 (right), 49 (left), 51, 52 (left), 58, 60 (bottom), 63 (right), 64 (left & right), 66 (bottom), 68 (left & right), 69 (top left & bottom), 70 (left & right), 71, 74, 76, 77 (top & bottom), 78 (top & bottom), 79, 80, 81, 83, 84, 85, 86, 87, 88, 92, 94–5, 96–7, 98–9, 100, 101, 103, 104, 105, 107, 108–9, 110, 111, 114–15, 116–17, 118–19, 120–21, 122, 126–27, 128, 134, 140–41, 143, 145, 146, 147, 148–49, 151, 154–55, 158–59, 160, 162–63, 164–65, 166, 167, 168, 170–71, 172, 173, 174, 175, 176, 177, 178–79, 180–81, 182, 183, 184–85, 186–87, 188, 189, 190, 191 (right), 192, 194 (top & bottom), 195, 196, 198–99, 204–05, 208–09, 210, 212, 213, 214, 215, 218, 219, 224 (top & bottom), 225 (top & bottom), 228 (bottom), 229 (bottom), 231 (bottom), 232, 234, 236, 237 (right), 240–41, 242, 244, 245, 248, 249, 250, 252–53, 254–55, 256, 257, 258, 259, 260, 262 (top & bottom), 263 (top & bottom), 265 (top & bottom), 266, 267, 268, 272, 273, 274–75, 276, 277, 278, 279 (right), 280–81, 282–83, 284, 286–87 (top & bottom), 289, 290–91, 292 (Courtesy of the Carnegie Museum of Art), 293, 294–95, 296, 297, 298–99, 300, 301, 302, 303, 304, 306, 307, 308, 309, 310–11, 312, 313, 314, 315, 316–17, 318, 319, 320–21, 322–23, 324, 326, 327, 328–29, 330, 332, 334, 335, 336, 337, 338, 339, 340–41, 342–43, 344, 346–47, 348, 350, 352, 353

Photographs that appear on the following pages are copyright © 2009 The Frank Lloyd Wright Foundation, Scottsdale, Arizona: 34 (left), 35 (top, bottom left & bottom right), 43, 49 (left & right), 52 (right), 102, 106, 112, 113, 124 (top & bottom left, center & right), 125, 129, 130 (top & bottom), 131, 132, 133, 135, 138–39 (photo by Allen Lape Davison), 139, 142, 144, 152, 153, 156, 169, 197, 200, 201, 202, 203 (top & bottom), 193 (photo by Skot Weidemann), 206, 207, 220, 221 (photo by Larry Cuneo), 222 (photo by Larry Cuneo), 223 (photo by Larry Cuneo), 235 (right), 238, 239, 243, 246, 247, 261, 270 (top & bottom) 271, 305, 325, 345 (right)

Models that appear on the following pages are copyright © 2009 The Frank Lloyd Wright Foundation, Scottsdale, Arizona: 161, 233

SOLOMON R. GUGGENHEIM FOUNDATION CREDITS

Photographs that appear on the following pages are copyright © 2009 Solomon R. Guggenheim Foundation: 8–9 (photo by David Heald), 12 (photo by David Heald), 20 (photo by David Heald), 22 (photo by David Heald), 33 (right, photo by David Heald), 42 (photo by David Heald), 137 (photo by David Heald), 217 (photo by David Heald), 269 (photo by William Short)

OTHER CREDITS

Drawing courtesy Carnegie Museum of Art: 292
Photo by Kathleen Chesley: endpapers (Hillside Theater #2 curtains)
Photos by Richard Cleary: 48 (center & right)
Drawing by Rabbi Mortimer Cohen: 40 (left), courtesy of the Beth Sholom Archives
Photo by Sam Falk: front endpaper (Frank Lloyd Wright in Solomon R. Guggenheim Museum under construction, ca. 1957), courtesy The Frank Lloyd Wright Foundation
Photo by Michael Freeman: 157
Photo by Henry Fuermann: 60 (top), private collection
Photo by Lois Davidson Gottlieb: 53
Photos © 2009 Pedro E. Guerrero: 46, 54 (left)
Drawings by Reverend William Norman Guthrie: 39 (top left & bottom left), from the William Norman Guthrie papers, courtesy of the Andover-Harvard Theological Library, Harvard Divinity School, Harvard University
Photos by I. N. Hagan: 54 (right), 55
Photo by Hedrich-Blessing: 56, courtesy Chicago History Museum
Photos © Balthazar Korab: 30, 36 (right), 37, 41
Photos by Maynard Parker: 226, 227, 228 (top), 229 (top), 230, 231 (top), courtesy The Frank Lloyd Wright Foundation
Photos by Louis Reens: 261, 270 (top & bottom), courtesy The Frank Lloyd Wright Foundation
Photo © Cervin Robinson: 32 (left)
Photo by Paul Rocheleau: 211
Photo by William Short: 269
Photo by Joseph M. Siry: 38
Photo by Ezra Stoller © ESTO: 285
Photo © Robert D. Stout: 36 (left)

Every effort has been made by Skira Rizzoli Publications to identify and contact the copyright holder for all images in this book. Despite thorough research it has not been possible to establish all copyright ownership. Any inaccuracies brought to our attention will be corrected for future editions.

INDEX

Note: Page numbers in italics indicate illustrations or caption texts.